Study Commentary on Great Chapters of the Bible

Spurgeon's Commentary on Great Chapters of the Bible

Compiled by
Tom Carter

kregel
PUBLICATIONS

Grand Rapids, MI 49501

Spurgeon's Commentary on Great Chapters of the Bible

Copyright © 1998 by Tom Carter

Published by Kregel Publications, a division of Kregel, Inc., P.O. Box 2607, Grand Rapids, MI 49501. Kregel Publications provides trusted, biblical publications for Christian growth and service. Your comments and suggestions are valued.

For more information about Kregel Publications, visit our web site at www.kregel.com.

Cover and book design: Nicholas G. Richardson

Library of Congress Cataloging-in-Publication Data
Spurgeon, C. H. (Charles Haddon), 1834–1892
    Spurgeon's commentary on great chapters of the Bible/ Tom Carter, compiler.
        p.   cm.
    1. Bible—Commentaries. I. Carter, Tom, 1950–.
II. Title.
BS491.2.S69   1998   220.7'7—dc21   97-30361
                                                                    CIP

ISBN 0-8254-2353-8

Printed in the United States of America
1 2 3 / 04 03 02 01 00 99 98

Contents

Introduction

CHARLES HADDON SPURGEON is acclaimed all over the world as "the Prince of Preachers" with good reason. His 3,561 published sermons fill sixty-three yearly volumes totaling thirty-eight thousand pages of small print. These sermons are the most widely read and respected in church history.

Spurgeon was born in 1854. By age twenty-seven he was preaching to crowds of six thousand people in London's Metropolitan Tabernacle, which his congregation had to build to accommodate the multitudes that flocked to hear him. American newspapers printed his sermons in their entirety each week.

But the volume you have in your hands is not a book of sermons. It is a verse-by-verse devotional commentary on great chapters of the Bible.

WHAT MAKES THIS COMMENTARY UNIQUE?

With countless Bible commentaries already on the market, why should this one be added? What makes it different? I can think of four things.

First, the emphasis in this commentary lies not on an exegesis of the text but on its application to our lives. Spurgeon spends his time explaining not so much what the passage means as what it means to us.

Second, this commentary is no ivory-tower treatise on Scripture; it is a down-to-earth unfolding of it. Spurgeon originally gave these expositions orally to his congregation in London. As you read, you will feel as if he were standing in front of you with an open Bible, teaching through the text. Better still, you will hear the voice of the living God speaking through his living Word.

Third, in commentaries the all-important thing is usually the biblical text, but for Spurgeon the goal was always to show Jesus Christ and his saving work at Calvary. Someone once said of him, "Whatever passage of Scripture he chose as his text, he always made a beeline for the cross." Every chapter in this book serves as an example of that.

Fourth, this is not a theological commentary but a devotional one. Spurgeon was far more than an interpreter of the Bible. His fervent appeals to trust Christ, love Christ, and serve Christ will pierce your heart.

Many times Spurgeon allows a verse to move him to prayer, which he inserts into his discussion in much the same way as the apostle Paul often did in his New Testament letters. I invite you to stop each time you read these prayers and echo them up to the throne of God. In this way your study of these great chapters of the Bible will be a worshipful experience.

WHERE DID THESE EXPOSITIONS COME FROM?

In preparation for compiling 2,200 *Quotations from the Writings of Charles H. Spurgeon* (Baker, 1988), I read all of Spurgeon's published sermons. Almost all of them are based on a verse or two of Scripture. But I noticed that scattered throughout volumes 38-63 were this man's verse-by-verse expositions of hundreds of biblical passages, some of them covering an entire chapter. Spurgeon taught through Psalm 51 thirteen times, Isaiah 55 twelve times, John 14 eleven times, and Romans 8 nineteen times.

After making a list of all the extended passages he taught, I singled out what I considered the great chapters of the Bible. I then combined Spurgeon's many expositions of each chapter into one. Much of the material was repetitious, but there were also many jewels to be found and set in place.

Next, I read Spurgeon's sermons—sometimes more than a dozen—on each of the great chapters of the Bible I had chosen for inclusion in this book. I took his striking statements, vivid word pictures, exciting stories, and personal applications from these sermons and placed them where they belonged in the exposition of that Bible chapter. After thirty-one such ecstatic spiritual exercises, the result is this book.

Here for the first time is a synthesis of Spurgeon's many expositions on these great chapters of the Bible.

Some "great" chapters of the Bible are missing. For example, 1 Corinthians 13. Sadly, Spurgeon gave only one brief exposition of that chapter. There simply wasn't enough meaty material on 1 Corinthians 13 to warrant an entry in this commentary.

USES OF THIS BOOK

The thirty-one great chapters of the Bible included in this book are ones that preachers love to teach and Christians love to study. Perhaps the readers most interested in this commentary will be pastors and Bible teachers looking for a practical reference tool filled with striking applications to people's lives. Here is the grist for many a sermon mill.

Individuals and Bible study groups desiring to grow in their relationship to God and their understanding of his Word will also find this commentary helpful. Spurgeon's keen biblical insights will feed the mind, and his Christ-centered teaching will stir the heart of anyone whose life is dedicated to God's glory.

Some have said that Spurgeon is out of date and therefore out of touch with modern Christians, but history has proven that he speaks the wisdom of the ages, unlike the many pop theologians of our day.

EDITORIAL REVISIONS

Some changes were made to bring Spurgeon's original material into the twenty-first century with us. First, the verse-by-verse quotations are cited not from the King James Version that Spurgeon used but from the New International Version.

Second, Spurgeon's Victorian English has been revised. A handful of words that the great preacher often used are now obsolete. Sometimes he addressed his listeners as "thee" or "thou." Though divine truth does not change, human language does. Rest assured that on these pages the utmost care has been taken to allow you to hear Spurgeon's voice, not mine.

I also took the liberty to give each chapter a title. Some come from statements Spurgeon made in his expositions; others are of my own making.

If you find as much spiritual benefit from reading these studies as I did from compiling them, I know you will be richly blessed.

TOM CARTER

Creation—the Old and the New

In the beginning God created the heavens and the earth. Now the earth was formless and empty, darkness was over the surface of the deep, and the Spirit of God was hovering over the waters. (1–2)

We cannot tell when that "beginning" was. It may have been long ages before God made this world as the home of human beings, but it was not self-existent. It was created by God. It sprang from the will and the word of the all-wise Creator.

When God began to arrange this world in order, it was shrouded in darkness, and it had been reduced to emptiness. This is the condition of all people when God begins to deal with them in grace. They are formless and empty of all good things. They have no trace of faith, love, hope, or obedience. They are a spiritually confused mass of sinfulness in which everything is misplaced. The best of people in their natural condition are utterly "formless and empty." As we read in Romans 3:10–12: "There is no one righteous, not even one; there is no one who understands, no one who seeks God. All have turned away."

The Spirit of God hovering over the waters was the first act of God in preparing this planet to be the home of human beings. Likewise, the first act of grace in the soul is for the Spirit of God to move within it. We don't know how that Spirit of God comes there. We cannot tell how he acts, even as we cannot tell how the wind blows where it wants (John 3:8). But until the Spirit of God hovers over the soul, nothing is done toward its new creation in Christ Jesus.

A person may hear a thousand sermons, but no effectual work takes place in the soul until the Spirit of God comes there. The best person mere morality ever produced is still "formless and empty" if the Spirit of God has not come upon him or upon her. "Darkness

10

was over the surface of the deep," but the Holy Spirit could work in the dark. In the same way, the dark depravity of human nature does not prevent the Spirit of God from making us brand new in Christ.

And God said, "Let there be light," and there was light. God saw that the light was good, and he separated the light from the darkness. God called the light "day" and the darkness he called "night." And there was evening, and there was morning—the first day. (3–5)

God had only to speak the word, and the great wonder was accomplished. How there was light before a sun—for the sun was not created until the fourth day of the week—is not for us to say. But God is not dependent upon his own creation. He can make light without a sun. He can spread the gospel without the aid of ministers. He can convert souls with no human or angelic agency, for he does as he wishes in heaven and on earth. How God removes darkness from our understanding and how he illuminates our minds are secrets reserved for himself.

The giving of light is a divine work. As God brought light into the world by his word, so he brought light into our hearts. "For God, who said, 'Let light shine out of darkness,' made his light shine in our hearts to give us the light of the knowledge of the glory of God in the face of Christ" (2 Cor. 4:6). No voice out of that thick darkness cried, "O God, enlighten us!" There was no prayer, no plea that God would send light. The desire began with God and not with the darkness. In the same way, the first work of grace in our hearts begins not with our desire but with God's desire.

Why was the light good? Because it revealed God's power and goodness. And so God loves the spiritual light of grace in our hearts because it makes many of his glorious attributes known. Light is good also because it is like God. "In him there is no darkness at all" (1 John 1:5). Light is good also in its result. It helps us see our danger, it startles us, and it makes us repent of sin. Light is good in its warfare. It battles with darkness, and it is good for darkness to be conquered. When grace comes into you, it will fight with your sin— and it ought to be fought with and overcome.

As far as this world was concerned, light was new. Spiritual light may be new in you also. You were recently converted, and you have had no time to develop your graces. Yet the Lord delights in your new life! Some older believers are suspicious of new converts, but in this they do not have the mind of God.

As soon as the Lord gives light to a believer, he or she begins to withdraw from spiritual darkness. The moment you become a Christian, you will begin to fight the darkness. What God has divided, let us never unite.

It is good to have the right names for things. An error is often half killed when you know the real name of it. Its power lies in its being indescribable, but as soon as you can call it "darkness," you know how to act toward it.

It is also good to know the names of truths. God is very particular in the Scripture about giving people their right names. The Holy Spirit says, "Judas, not Iscariot" (John 14:22), so that there should be no mistake about the person intended. Let us also always call persons and things by their right names: "God called the light 'day,' and the darkness he called 'night.'"

Darkness came first, and then light. It is so with us spiritually. First darkness, then light. I suppose that until we get to heaven, there will be both darkness and light in us, and as to God's providential dealings, we must expect darkness as well as light. They will make up our first day and our last day, until we get where there are no days but the Ancient of Days.

And God said, "Let there be an expanse between the waters to separate water from water." So God made the expanse and separated the water under the expanse from the water above it. And it was so. God called the expanse "sky." And there was evening, and there was morning—the second day. (6–8)

The expanse was a portion of air in which the waters floated, then later condensed and fell on the earth in refreshing showers. These waters above were divided from the waters below. Perhaps they were all one steamy mixture before, but here they were separated.

Note the end of verse 7: "And it was so." You will find these words six times in Genesis 1. Everything God ordains will happen. This is true of all his promises. Whatever he has said shall be fulfilled to you, and you shall one day say of it, "And it was so."

It is equally true of all God's threats—what he has spoken shall surely be fulfilled. Then the ungodly will have to say, "And it was so." These words convey to us the great lesson that the word of God is sure to be followed by the deed of God. He speaks, and it is done.

You were promised salvation, peace, and pardon, "and it was so." Your needs have come. Have the supplies also come? I am sure you will say, "It was so." It is often strangely so, but it is always so. Martyrs have gone to the stake with the promise, "I am with you always, to the very end" (Matt. 28:20), and it was so. Jesus keeps his word to the letter.

And God said, "Let the water under the sky be gathered to one place, and let dry ground appear." And it was so. God called the dry ground "land," and the gathered waters he called "seas." And God saw that it was good.

Then God said, "Let the land produce vegetation: seed-bearing plants and trees on the land that bear fruit with seed in it, according to their various kinds." And it was so. The land produced vegetation: plants bearing seed according to their kinds and trees bearing fruit with seed in it according to their kinds. And God saw that it was good. And there was evening, and there was morning—the third day. (9–13)

No sooner had God made the dry land appear than it seemed as if he could not bear the sight of it in its nakedness. How strange this world must have looked, with its plains and hills and rocks and vales without one single blade of grass or a tree or a shrub. So at once, before that day was over, God threw the mantle of growth over the earth and clad its mountains and valleys with forests and plants and flowers, as if to show us that fruitless things are unattractive in God's sight.

In the same way, the person who bears no fruit for God is displeasing to him. There would be no beauty whatever in a Christian without any good works or graces. As soon as the earth appeared, the herb and tree and grass came. In like manner, let us bring forth fruit to God, and bring it forth abundantly. In this is our heavenly Father glorified, that we bear much fruit (John 15:8).

And God said, "Let there be lights in the expanse of the sky to separate the day from the night, and let them serve as signs to mark seasons and days and years, and let them be lights in the expanse of the sky to give light on the earth." And it was so. God made two great lights—the greater light to govern the day and the lesser light to govern the night. He also made the stars. God set them in the expanse of the sky to give light on the earth, to govern the day and the night, and to separate light from darkness. And God saw that it was good. And there was evening, and there was morning—the fourth day. (14–19)

Are the sun and the moon here said to be absolutely created? Or were they created only so far as our planet was concerned by the dense vapors being cleared away so that the sun and moon and stars could be seen? It makes no difference at all to us.

Let us rather learn a lesson from them. These lights are to rule, but they are to rule by giving light. And this is true in the church of God. He who gives most light is the truest ruler. The leader in the church is the person who aspires to be the servant of others by laying self out for the good of others. Our Savior taught this to his disciples when he said, "Whoever wants to be first must be slave of all" (Mark 10:44). The sun and moon are the servants of all humanity, and therefore they rule by day and by night. Stoop, then, if you wish to lead others. The way up is down. To be great, you must be little. The greatest people are nothing at all to themselves but everything for others.

And God said, "Let the water teem with living creatures, and let birds fly above the earth across the expanse of the sky." So God created the great creatures of the sea and every living and moving thing with which the water teems, according to their kinds, and every winged bird according to its kind. And God saw that it was good. God blessed them and said, "Be fruitful and increase in number and fill the water in the seas, and let the birds increase on the earth." And there was evening, and there was morning—the fifth day. (20–23)

There was no life in the sea or on the land until all was ready for it. God would not make a creature to be unhappy. There had to be suitable food to feed upon and the sun and moon to cheer and comfort before a single bird would chirp in the thicket or a single trout leap in the stream.

So, after God has given us light and blessed us in various ways, our spiritual lives begin to develop to the glory of God. We have the thoughts that soar like birds in the open expanse of heaven and other thoughts that dive into the mysteries of God, as the fish in the sea. These result from that same power that at the first said, "Let there be light."

And God said, "Let the land produce living creatures according to their kinds: livestock, creatures that move along the ground, and wild animals, each according to its kind." And it was so. God made the wild animals according to their kinds, the livestock according to their kinds, and all the creatures that move along the ground according to their kinds. And God saw that it was good.

Then God said, "Let us make man in our image, in our likeness, and let them rule over the fish of the sea and the birds of the air, over the livestock, over all the earth, and over all the creatures that move along the ground." (24–26)

There is as much wisdom and care displayed in the creation of the tiniest insect as in the creation of the elephant. Those who use the microscope are as much amazed at God's greatness and goodness as those who use the telescope. He is as awesome in the little things as he is in the big.

After each day's work, God looked upon it. And it is good for us every night to review the day's work. Some people's work will not bear looking at, and tomorrow becomes all the worse for them because they neither reflected on today nor repented of its sin. But if the errors of today are marked by us, a repetition of them may be avoided tomorrow. It is only God who can look upon any one day's work and say, "It is good." As for us, our best works need sprinkling with the blood of Christ. We need it not only on the doorsteps of our homes but even on the altar from which we worship God.

So God created man in his own image, in the image of God he created him; male and female he created them.

God blessed them and said to them, "Be fruitful and increase in number; fill the earth and subdue it. Rule over the fish of the sea and the birds of the air and over every living creature that moves on the ground.

Then God said, "I give you every seed-bearing plant on the face of the whole earth and every tree that has fruit with seed in it. They will be yours for food. And to all the beasts of the earth and all the birds of the air and all the creatures that move on the ground—everything that has the breath of life in it—I give every green plant for food." And it was so.

God saw all that he had made, and it was very good. And there was evening, and there was morning—the sixth day. (27–31)

God meant the two sexes—male and female—to complete the man. Humanity is unfulfilled without them both. The earth was completed when people began to live on it, and people are completed when the image of God is in them—or better still, when Christ is formed in them as "the hope of glory" (Col. 1:27). When we rule over ourselves and all earthly things through the power of God, we become what he intended us to be.

You can see God's provision for food. He did not make all these creatures to starve them. Instead, he supplied them with great variety and abundance of food that their needs may be satisfied. Does God care for the cattle, and will he not feed his own children? Does he provide for ravens and sparrows, and will he let you lack anything, O you of little faith? Note that God did not create people until he had provided for them. Neither will he ever put one work of his providence or his grace out of its proper place, but what goes first shall prepare for what follows.

Taken in its completeness, and all put together, God saw that his creation was very good. We must never judge anything before it is complete.

The Devastating Consequences of Sin

*Now the serpent was more crafty than any of the wild animals the
LORD God had made. He said to the woman, "Did God really say,
'You must not eat from any tree in the garden'?" (1).*

The serpent was so crafty that he later entangled Solomon, who
"was wiser than any other man" (1 Kings 4:31). Satan is stronger
than the strongest person, for he overthrew Samson. Even David, a
man after God's own heart (1 Sam. 13:14), was led into adultery
and murder by Satan's seductions.

The serpent began by asking Eve a question. Much evil begins
with questions. The serpent did not dare to state a lie, but he suggested one: "Did God deny you all the fruit of these many trees in
the garden?"

*The woman said to the serpent, "We may eat fruit from the trees in
the garden, but God did say, 'You must not eat fruit from the tree
that is in the middle of the garden, and you must not touch it, or you
will die.'" (2–3)*

Eve had begun to feel the fascination of the Evil One, for she
softened the word of God. The Lord had said concerning the tree
of the knowledge of good and evil, "When you eat of it you will
surely die" (Gen. 2:17). A little doubt had crept into Eve's mind, so
she quoted God as saying, "When you eat of it or touch it you will
surely die."

*"You will not surely die," the serpent said to the woman. "For God
knows that when you eat of it your eyes will be opened, and you will be
like God, knowing good and evil." (4–5)*

17

The serpent insinuated that God had selfishly kept them back from the tree so they would not grow too wise and become like God himself. The Evil One suggested ambition to the woman's mind and imputed wicked designs to the holy God. He said nothing more. The Devil is too wise to use many words. I fear that the servants of God sometimes weaken the force of the truth by their wordiness, but the serpent did not do so when he craftily suggested lies to Eve. He said enough to accomplish his evil purpose, then no more.

When the woman saw that the fruit of the tree was good for food and pleasing to the eye, and also desirable for gaining wisdom, she took some and ate it. She also gave some to her husband, who was with her, and he ate it. Then the eyes of both of them were opened, and they realized they were naked; so they sewed fig leaves together and made coverings for themselves. (6–7)

Sin entered the human race by the eye, and that is the way Christ comes in—by the spiritual eye of faith. "Look unto me, and be ye saved" (Isa. 45:22 KJV) is the counterpart of and antidote to "when the woman saw. . . ."

Both Adam and Eve rebelled against God. It may have seemed a small thing, but it meant a great deal. They had cast off their allegiance to God. They had set up their own account. They thought they knew better than God. They imagined they were going to be gods themselves.

The only thing Adam and Eve gained by their sin was a discovery of their nakedness. How the serpent laughed as his words were fulfilled, "Your eyes will be opened" (v. 5). They were opened indeed, and Adam and Eve knew good and evil. Little could they have dreamed in what a terrible sense the serpent's words would come true.

Then the man and his wife heard the sound of the LORD God as he was walking in the garden in the cool of the day, and they hid from the LORD God among the trees of the garden. But the LORD God called to the man, "Where are you?" (8–9)

When they had heard the Lord's voice before, they ran to meet him as children do a father when he comes home. But now how different their action! What fools they were to think they could hide from God! The fig leaves were to hide their nakedness, and now the trees were to hide them from God.

God came to judge his fallen creature, but he dealt kindly with him. In tones of mingled pity and rebuke he asked, "Where are you?" He then wanted to hear from Adam's own lips that he had sinned. He summoned no other witness.

He answered, "I heard you in the garden, and I was afraid because I was naked; so I hid."

And he said, "Who told you that you were naked? Have you eaten from the tree that I commanded you not to eat from?" (10–11)

Adam should have sought God. He should have gone through the garden crying out, "My God, my God, where are you?" But sin had caused an alienation from God in Adam's heart—just as it does in our hearts.

Adam had to answer the Lord's question. In our courts of law we do not require defendants to answer questions that would incriminate them. But God does, and on the Judgment Day the ungodly will be condemned by their own confessions of guilt.

The man said, "The woman you put here with me—she gave me some fruit from the tree, and I ate it." (12)

Here is the clear proof of Adam's guilt. First, he threw the blame on Eve, whom he was obligated to love and shield. Second, he threw the blame on God himself, because he had given him the woman to be with him. While trying to avoid confessing his sin, Adam became guilty of unkindness to his wife and blasphemy against his Maker. It is a bad sign when we cannot be brought frankly to confess sin.

Adam had been an unfallen man a few hours before, but now he had broken the commandment of the Lord, and you see how completely death came into his moral nature. If this had not been so, he would have said, "My God, I have sinned. Can you and will you forgive me?"

Then the Lord God said to the woman, "What is this you have done?"
The woman said, "The serpent deceived me, and I ate." (13)

How far-reaching the Lord's question was! By Adam and Eve's action, the floodgates had been pulled up, and the floods of sin had been let loose on the world. They had struck a match and set the world on fire with sin. Every one of our sins is essentially just like that. It has in it the same harm. It is good when God asks us, after we have sinned, "What is this you have done?"

What Eve said was true, but it was no excuse for her sin. She should not have been deceived by the serpent. How often we, like Eve, blame the Devil for our sin. He has enough to bear without the added guilt of our iniquity. The Lord did not go on to ask the serpent anything, for he knew he was a liar. At once he pronounced sentence upon the serpent.

So the LORD God said to the serpent, "Because you have done this, 'Cursed are you above all the livestock and all the wild animals! You will crawl on your belly and you will eat dust all the days of your life. And I will put enmity between you and the woman, and between your offspring and hers; he will crush your head, and you will strike his heel.'" (14–15)

There is no creature so degraded as that once-bright angel, who is now the Devil. He is always going out with serpentine wriggling, seeking to do more damage. He moves on his belly as a fallen creature and so delights in what is foul, material, and carnal.

If Satan knows any pleasure, it is the foulest and most unsatisfactory kind, for dust is his food. There is nothing satisfying in the pleasures of rebellion.

"He will crush your head" is the Bible's first proclamation of the gospel. Isn't it remarkable that this gospel promise was given so soon after Adam and Eve's sin? No sentence had yet been pronounced against them, but the promise was given in the form of a sentence against the serpent.

Strange to say, while God was pronouncing a curse upon the enemy of humanity, he was uttering a blessing on everyone who would belong to Christ, for Christ is Eve's "offspring" whom God promised here. Our Lord is the head of one offspring, and Satan is the head of the other. Our opponents are the demonic descendants of the serpent—crafty, cunning, full of deceit—and there is enmity between these two offspring.

No human being is our enemy. We fight for nonbelievers, not against them. "For our struggle is not against flesh and blood, but . . . against the powers of this dark world and against the spiritual forces of evil in the heavenly realms" (Eph. 6:12).

The "heel" of Christ was his human nature. All his life it suffered. Jesus was betrayed, bound, accused, struck, scourged, and spit on. He carried our sicknesses and sorrows. But the striking came mainly when his enemies pierced his hands and feet and he endured the shame and pain of death by crucifixion. The Devil had let loose Herod, Pilate, Caiaphas, the Jews, and the Romans against Jesus. But that was all. It was not his head, just his heel, that was struck, for the champion rose from the grave!

By the heel that was struck Jesus crushed the head that devised the striking. By his sufferings Christ overthrew Satan. When the Lord Jesus died, he put away sin, slew death, and defeated hell. The old serpent's head is crushed, while the wounded heel of our Savior is the joy and delight of our hearts!

The serpent's head is broken even in our lives, in that we are no longer under the dominion of sin. His head is broken also in that our guilt is gone. The great power of Satan lies in unforgiven sin. He cries, "Through sin I have brought you under the curse!"

But we say, "No, I am delivered from the curse and blessed, for it is written, 'Blessed is he whose transgressions are forgiven'" (Ps. 32:1).

Let us resist the Devil always with the belief that his head has been broken. His power is gone. He is fighting a lost battle. He is contending against God's omnipotence. So be strong in faith and give glory to God.

To the woman he said, "I will greatly increase your pains in child-bearing; with pain you will give birth to children. Your desire will be for your husband, and he will rule over you."

To Adam he said, "Because you listened to your wife and ate from the tree about which I commanded you, 'You must not eat of it,' cursed is the ground because of you; through painful toil you will eat of it all the days of your life." (16–17)

How obliquely the curse fell on Adam. God did not say to him, "You are cursed," as he had said to the serpent, but "the ground is cursed because of you."

"It will produce thorns and thistles for you, and you will eat the plants of the field." (18)

Adam had been used to eating the fruit of the many trees of Paradise. Now he had to come down and eat "the plants of the field." He was lowered from royal dainties to common food.

Notice how sweetness can be extracted from something sour. If the ground was to "produce thorns and thistles" for Adam, it meant he would continue to live to till that ground. Had the sentence been carried out in full, a yawning grave would have opened at his feet, and there would have been no more Adam. When thorns and thistles spring up on your path, perhaps even a thorn in your flesh (2 Cor. 12:7), do not murmur. Thank God that you are still alive and out of hell.

If you think that because you are a Christian, everything will go smoothly with you and you will have no more troubles, you will be bitterly disappointed when the thorns and thistles spring up. Expect them. Look forward to them. Then, when they come, half of their sting will be gone.

The only crown Jesus ever wore on earth was a crown of thorns (John 19:2). This curse of the earth was on his head and wounded him mortally. If Jesus was crowned with thorns, how can you wonder why they grow up around your feet? Instead, bless him that he has consecrated the thorns by wearing them for his diadem. Be willing to wear the thorn-crown too.

"By the sweat of your brow you will eat your food until you return to the ground, since from it you were taken; for dust you are and to dust you will return." (19)

God was saying, "You shall get your life out of the ground until you yourself shall go into it."

Adam named his wife Eve, because she would become the mother of all the living.

The LORD God made garments of skin for Adam and his wife and clothed them. And the LORD God said, "The man has now become like one of us, knowing good and evil. He must not be allowed to reach out his hand and take also from the tree of life and eat, and live forever." So the LORD God banished him from the Garden of Eden to work the ground from which he had been taken. After he drove the man out, he placed on the east side of the Garden of Eden cherubim and a flaming sword flashing back and forth to guard the way to the tree of life. (20–24)

This was a very significant gospel action. The Lord took away from Adam and Eve the withered fig leaves and put on them the skins of animals. This shows, in symbol, that we are covered with the sacrifice of Christ. The giving up of the animal's life brought a better covering than the growth of nature. So today the death of Christ brings us a better covering than we could find in anything that grows from fallen human nature. Because the Lamb of God has made us a garment that covers our nakedness, we are unafraid to stand even before the judgment seat of God. Thanks be to God for thus thinking of us when he provided clothes for our first parents!

It would have been horrible for Adam and Eve to be unable to die and so to continue forever in a sinful world. It is by passing through death that we come out into the realm of perfection.

What a fall this was! At that time you and I and everyone else fell down. Yet even the fall by Adam's sin was not without the promise of a gracious recovery through the "last Adam" (1 Cor. 15:45), the Lord from heaven. Well did Isaac Watts set forth the contrast between the fall of the angels and the fall of humanity:

> Down headlong from their native skies
>> The rebel angels fell,
> And thunderbolts of flaming wrath
>> Pursued them deep to hell.
> Down from the top of earthly bliss
>> Rebellious man was hurled;
> And Jesus stooped beneath the grave
>> To reach a sinking world.

Jesus took on him not the nature of angels but human nature. Then he died in our place to save us from the devastating consequences of sin. May we trust in him for so great a salvation!

Abraham's Greatest Test—and His Greatest Blessing

Some time later God tested Abraham. He said to him, "Abraham!"
"Here I am," he replied. (1)

Abraham seemed to say, "Here I am, Lord, at your service. I
don't know what the orders are, but speak, Lord, for your servant
is listening." Are you always in that condition, ready to be taught by
God and to obey him? Is his Word precious to you?

Then God said, "Take your son, your only son Isaac, whom you love,
and go to the region of Moriah. Sacrifice him there as a burnt offer-
ing on one of the mountains I will tell you about." (2)

Abraham had two sons, Ishmael and Isaac. Both Ishmael and
Isaac were his only sons, each of them the only son of his mother.
See how specifically God pointed out to Abraham the son who
would be the means of the great test of his faith. Was there nothing
in Abraham's tent that God would have but his son? He would have
cheerfully given him flocks of sheep. He would have eagerly poured
out from his bag all the silver and gold he possessed. If a human
being must be offered, why not Abraham's servant Eliezer? Must it
be his son? How this tugs at the father's heartstrings!

God even reminded Abraham that Isaac was the one "whom you
love." Must he be reminded of his love for his son at the very time he
is to lose him? It seemed to be a stern command with no compassion.

It was God's usual custom with Abraham to make him sail under
sealed orders. When Abraham was first commanded to leave his
country and family, he had to go to an unknown land God would
show him (Gen. 12:1). "By faith Abraham . . . obeyed and went,
even though he did not know where he was going" (Heb. 11:8).

Now the Lord was giving him an even greater test. They have true faith who can go forward at God's command without knowing where they are going.

Not only was this tender father to lose his beloved son, but he was to lose him in the most bitter way. He must be sacrificed by Abraham himself. If the Lord had said, "Tell Eliezer to sacrifice your son," it would have softened the trial for Abraham. But no, Abraham had to be the priest. Everything was designed to make this trial severe.

Abraham might have said, "This act violates every instinct in my nature. I must offer up my child? Horrible! Murderous! It will rob me of all my comfort. People will hate me for it. How will I explain this to Isaac's mother, Sarah? How can God ask me to do what tears up by the roots every affection that he himself planted in me?" But in the end none of these things mattered to Abraham. Let others count him a devil, but God's will must be done!

The Word of God may call us to acts of obedience that may seem to us to violate all our natural affections. But our love for Christ must be unrivaled by our love for father, mother, husband, wife, or children (Matt. 10:37).

Early the next morning Abraham got up and saddled his donkey. He took with him two of his servants and his son Isaac. When he had cut enough wood for the burnt offering, he set out for the place God had told him about. On the third day Abraham looked up and saw the place in the distance. He said to his servants, "Stay here with the donkey while I and the boy go over there. We will worship and then we will come back to you." (3–5)

Obedience should be prompt. Abraham showed his obedience to the Lord's command by refusing to delay. Abraham could have replied to the Lord, "Do you really mean it? Can a human sacrifice be acceptable to you? I know it can't! How can you, a God of love and kindness, delight in the blood of my son?" But there was not a word of argument or even prayer. "God is God," he seemed to say. "It is not for me to ask him why. He has given me a command, and I will do it."

The lesson is this: When you know your duty under God, never pray to be excused. Go and do it in the name of Christ and the power of faith.

All the details are mentioned, for true obedience is careful about each detail. If we would serve God at all, we must serve him faithfully in little things as well as great ones. Abraham had to saddle his donkey, call two servants as well as Isaac, and split the wood for the burnt offering. We must do everything included in the bounds of God's commands to us and do it with meticulous care. Indifferent obedience to God's commands is for all practical purposes disobedience. Careless obedience is dead obedience, for there is no heart in it. Let us learn from Abraham how to obey.

Abraham could bear suspense. For three days he pondered the matter of sacrificing his son while he set his face like a flint to follow his Lord. It was a bitter pill to swallow, but he was determined to obey God.

Abraham told the servants to stay where they were because he did not want them to see everything he was about to do before the Lord. He feared perhaps that they would be moved by pity to prevent the sacrifice. Often our highest obedience must be a private one. Friends cannot help us in such emergencies, and it is better for them and us that they should not be with us.

He did not deceive the servants when he said that he and Isaac would return to them. He believed that he and Isaac would come back to them. He had faith that though he would be compelled to slay his son, God could not lie, his word could not fail, and therefore God would raise Isaac from the dead. He seemed to say, "Even if my son's body is consumed to ashes, the Lord can still restore him to life." The Book of Hebrews comments on this when it says, "And figuratively speaking, he did receive Isaac back from death" (Heb. 11:19).

Abraham took the wood for the burnt offering and placed it on his son Isaac, and he himself carried the fire and the knife. As the two of them went on together, Isaac spoke up and said to his father Abraham, "Father?"

"Yes, my son?" Abraham replied.

"The fire and wood are here," Isaac said, "but where is the lamb for the burnt offering?" (6–7)

When Abraham placed the wood on Isaac, what a burden he placed on his own heart! The knife had been cutting into Abraham's heart all this time, yet he took it. Unbelief would have left the knife at home, but genuine faith carried it.

Abraham answered, "God himself will provide the lamb for the burnt offering, my son." And the two of them went on together. (8)

Abraham here spoke like a prophet. In fact, throughout this

whole incident he never opened his mouth without making a prophetic utterance. I believe that when people walk with God and live near him, they will, often without being aware of it, speak very important words that will be more significant than they realize.

So it was with Abraham. He spoke like God's prophet when he spoke to his son in the anguish of his spirit, and in his prophetic utterance we find the sum and substance of the gospel: "God himself will provide the lamb for the burnt offering." The Lord is the great provider. He provides the offering not just for us but for himself, because the sacrifice is as necessary for God's glory as it is for our salvation.

Whatever you need, God will provide it. Do you cry, "Lord, I must have a broken heart"? He will provide it for you. Do you cry, "I cannot master sin or the power of my own passions"? He will provide strength for you. Do you mourn, "Lord, I will never hold out to the end"? Then he will provide perseverance for you. "He who did not spare his own Son, but gave him up for us all—how will he not also, along with him, graciously give us all things?" (Rom. 8:32).

This ends with a picture of the heavenly Father going with his Son Jesus and of Jesus going with his Father up to the great sacrifice at Calvary. It was not Christ alone who willingly died or the Father alone who gave his Son. "The two of them went on together," even as Abraham and Isaac did here.

When they reached the place God had told him about, Abraham built an altar there and arranged the wood on it. He bound his son Isaac and laid him on the altar, on top of the wood. Then he reached out his hand and took the knife to slay his son. But the angel of the Lord called out to him from heaven, "Abraham! Abraham!"

"Here I am," he replied. (9–11)

Imagine Abraham pulling out the large, rough stones lying around the area and then piling them into an altar.

Because Abraham fully intended to slay his son, he had now consummated the sacrifice. Therefore we read in Hebrews 11:17, "By faith Abraham, when God tested him, offered Isaac as a sacrifice. He who had received the promises was about to sacrifice his one and only son." In God's eyes he had as good as done it, though no trace of a wound would be found on Isaac.

Often God looks at his people and accepts their will for their deed. When he finds us willing to make the sacrifice he demands, he often does not require it at our hands. If you are willing to suffer for Christ's sake, you may not be called on to suffer. If you are willing to be a martyr for the truth, you may be permitted to wear the martyr's crown, even though you are never called to be burned at the stake or to have your head sliced off at the block.

Abraham gave the same answer to the Lord's call as we heard in verse 1: "Here I am." I think it was his habit to respond to the Lord this way. Instead of trying to hide when God called him to do something, Abraham would say, "Here I am."

"Do not lay a hand on the boy," he said. "Do not do anything to him. Now I know that you fear God, because you have not withheld from me your son, your only son." (12)

The necessary test had been applied, and Abraham's faith had passed the test with flying colors. God knows everything by his divine omniscience, but now he knew by this severe test he had given Abraham that the patriarch truly loved him best of all.

God also knew that Abraham feared him. I do not think that the gracious use of godly fear has ever been sufficiently estimated by most of us. Here the stress is laid not on Abraham's faith but on his reverential fear. This holy awe of God is the essence of our wisdom and fellowship with God. "The fear of the LORD is the beginning of wisdom" (Prov. 9:10). "The LORD delights in those who fear him" (Ps. 147:11). This is very different from the fear of a slave. It is a right kind of fear, not the kind that love drives out, as in 1 John 4:18. Instead, love lives in happy fellowship with this godly fear.

Abraham teaches us that the nearest way to get to the end of a trial is to resign yourself to it.

Abraham looked up and there in a thicket he saw a ram caught by its horns. He went over and took the ram and sacrificed it as a burnt offering instead of his son. So Abraham called that place "The LORD will provide." And to this day it is said, "On the mountain of the LORD it will be provided." (13–14)

Here is another type of our Savior's great sacrifice on Calvary. The ram was offered in the place of Isaac. How often do you and I have our great substitute very near us, yet we do not see him because we do not lift up our eyes to look. If you look up to the right place, you will see the great sacrifice close to you, held fast for you, even as this ram was caught to die instead of Isaac. Oh, that you may have grace to turn your head in the right direction and look to Christ and live! "Look unto me, and be ye saved . . . for I am God, and there is none else" (Isa. 45:22 KJV) is the text that brought me to the Savior.

The word *provide* comes from two Latin roots that mean "to see beforehand." God will have everything ready for the time it will be needed. He who provided the ram for a burnt offering in the place of Isaac will provide everything else we need. Depend on this: Since God, in the greatest emergency ever, provided his only Son to die as the substitute for sinners, he will foresee every other emergency that can occur, and he will provide everything necessary to meet it. Blessed be our Lord who provides for us!

God will provide for us in our extremity. In Abraham's case, God came through when the death of Isaac was imminent and when Abraham's anguish had reached a fever pitch.

Again, God will provide for us graciously. Abraham did not seek the ram. He did not fall down and pray, "O Lord, in your mercy provide another victim instead of my son!" It probably never entered his mind. But God in his free grace put the ram where Abraham found it. You and I did not pray for Christ to die. It is not in human nature to seek a Savior, but it is in God's nature to give a Savior. Our pleasure is to sin, and God's pleasure is to save.

The angel of the LORD called to Abraham from heaven a second time and said, "I swear by myself, declares the LORD, that because you have done this and have not withheld your son, your only son, I will surely bless you and make your descendants as numerous as the stars in the sky and as the sand on the seashore. Your descendants will take possession of the cities of their enemies, and through your offspring all nations on earth will be blessed, because you have obeyed me." (15–18)

The King James Version reads, "In blessing I will bless thee." As if God had said, "Whenever I bless, I will bless you, Abraham. I will not pronounce a blessing that you will not share." Abraham endured the greatest trial, but God gave him the greatest blessing.

The first blessing Abraham received was that he avoided evil. This trial prevented him from loving Isaac more than God and so having an idol in his life.

The second blessing of this trial was that it revealed Christ to Abraham. Our Savior said, "Abraham rejoiced at the thought of seeing my day; he saw it and was glad" (John 8:56). On the top of Mount Moriah, when his own son was on the wood and his own hand was lifted up to slay him, Abraham saw the Son of God and the uplifted hand of the heavenly Father offering the great sacrifice. When he took the ram from the thicket and so saved the life of his son, how clearly he must have understood that blessed doctrine of substitution. This is the very heart of the gospel.

Third, Abraham was blessed by this test in that he entered more deeply into the heart of God. I do not wonder that we read of being in "Abraham's bosom" (Luke 16:22 KJV). I long to get as near as I can to Abraham, that I may have sympathy and fellowship with my heavenly Father.

This section speaks of "descendants" in the plural, but the Hebrew word is singular, and the highest fulfillment of this prophecy is found in Abraham's greatest descendant, Jesus Christ. As Paul wrote to the Galatians, "The promises were spoken to Abraham and to his seed. The Scripture does not say 'and to seeds,' meaning many people, but 'and to your seed,' meaning one person, who is Christ" (Gal. 3:16).

Only in Christ will all the nations of the earth be blessed. If there is a nation that has not yet heard the gospel, it must hear it, for so the promise stands, "Through your offspring all nations on earth will be blessed." We may look for a glorious future from the preaching of Christ throughout every land, for so the covenant was made with Abraham because he had obeyed God's voice. God had been good to Abraham before then, for he was his beloved friend. But now he lifted him up to a higher platform altogether and made him a greater blessing than ever.

See the result of one person's grand act of obedience, and note how God can make that person a channel of blessing to future generations. Oh, that you and I might possess the Abrahamic faith that thus obeys the Lord in practical ways and thus brings a blessing to all the nations of the earth!

Then Abraham returned to his servants, and they set off together for Beersheba. And Abraham stayed in Beersheba. (19)

Remember that Abraham promised he would return to his servants in verse 5.

So the Lord carried his servant Abraham through this great trial and blessed him more than he had ever blessed him before. God may be about to test you as he did Abraham, and for the same purpose—so that he may later make you a greater and more useful servant than you ever were before.

Here in Genesis 22, faith and obedience made Abraham willing to sacrifice his son for God. But in the New Testament, love moved God literally to sacrifice his Son for sinners. In return, let us love this great God for his indescribable gift!

The Day Job Lost His Ten Children and His Wealth

In the land of Uz there lived a man whose name was Job. This man was blameless and upright; he feared God and shunned evil. He had seven sons and three daughters, and he owned seven thousand sheep, three thousand camels, five hundred yoke of oxen and five hundred donkeys, and had a large number of servants. He was the greatest man among all the people of the East (1–3).

Job was a true man of God. This was his character before the trial that made him famous. If it had not been for his trial, perhaps we would never have heard of him. Now, as the apostle James wrote, "You have heard of Job's perseverance" (James 5:11). By great afflictions God gave his servant Job the usefulness for which he had probably prayed—without knowing how his prayer would be answered.

A long life of prosperity may not so truly glorify God as a life checkered by adversity, and God, who intended to put honor on his servant, did as kings do when they confer the honor of knighthood. They strike with the back or flat of the sword. So God smote the patriarch Job that he might raise him above his contemporaries. The Lord intended to make him famous for persevering faith, but as a means to that end he first had to make him famous for suffering.

I do not know if I would bless God more for my sorrows or my joys. The best piece of furniture I have ever had in my house is the cross of affliction. Adversity is the richest field in all the farm of life.

Job was blameless and upright, yet he was not perfect. There were imperfections deep down in his character that his trials developed and the grace of God no doubt later removed. Still, Scripture says Job was a "blameless" man. He was sincere, true in heart, and consecrated. As an "upright" man, he leaned neither to the left nor right in his faithfulness to God. He had no twist in him, no selfish ends to serve. Job had both sides of a godly character: a loving respect for God and a holy hatred of sin.

It was a great privilege to have such a large family, but it brought Job great responsibilities and many anxieties. A man may be both good and rich, but it is not usually the case. I am afraid that what John Bunyan said very often is true:

> God and the gospel seldom agree;
> Religion sides with poverty.

Yet it doesn't have to be this way, for God can give people grace enough to use all their wealth to the Lord's glory. I wish it were oftener the case that we could see a holy Job as well as a godly Lazarus (Luke 16:19-31). May God raise up a company of people who will prove their consecration to him by never allowing their wealth to become their master, by being master of all their substance, and by realizing constantly that it all belongs to the Lord. Job in adversity could possess his soul in perseverance because in his prosperity he had not let his riches possess him, but he had possessed them. He was both a rich man and a man of God—one of those "camels" that manage to go through "the eye of a needle" (Mark 10:25).

His sons used to take turns holding feasts in their homes, and they would invite their three sisters to eat and drink with them. When a period of feasting had run its course, Job would send and have them purified. Early in the morning he would sacrifice a burnt offering for each of them, thinking, "Perhaps my children have sinned and cursed God in their hearts." This was Job's regular custom. (4-5)

Job did not go to his children's feast. Perhaps he felt too old, or his character was too staid. Job had higher joys nearer his heart than any feast could give him.

This feast was not a drunken orgy, or Job's sons would not have wanted their sisters there. Yet we are all mortal and fallible, and feasting times are dangerous times. The Puritans used to call fasting "soul-fattening fasting," but they called feasting "soul-weakening feasting." Solomon truly said, "It is better to go to a house of mourning than to go to a house of feasting" (Eccl. 7:2). There is always a risk in feasting, and Job was therefore a little afraid that his sons might have misbehaved.

Job's sons might have spoken rashly or even taken God's name in vain. There might have been something about their conduct that was improper, so their father desired to put the sin of it away by burnt offerings. He lived before the Jewish law was given, yet he felt the instinct concerning the need of a sacrifice that every believing heart feels when it approaches the holy God. It "was Job's regular custom" to sacrifice a burnt offering for each of his children. He tried to keep his household right before the Lord.

Never give up the idea of coming to God by means of a sacrifice, for there is no other way of access. Nothing else will quiet the conscience and bring us near God except the divinely appointed sacrifice. Job knew this. He did not think that his sons could be cleansed by his prayers alone. He had to offer burnt sacrifices for each son, so that each of them might have a share in the blessings that those sacrifices typified.

One day the angels came to present themselves before the LORD, and Satan also came with them. The LORD said to Satan, "Where have you come from?"

Satan answered the LORD, "From roaming through the earth and going back and forth in it." (6–7)

Angels and all kinds of intelligent spirits had a general assembly. Perhaps on some remote star far away in the universe a high festival of honor to God was celebrated that day. But since sin has come into the world, since even among the twelve apostles there was a Judas, so in this assembly of angels there was sure to be a devil. If he is not anywhere else, he is sure to be where "the sons of God" (KJV) are gathered together. Yet what impudence he has to dare to come into the assembly of saints! And what hardness of heart he must have, for he comes in as a devil and goes out as a devil! The sons of God offer their spiritual prayers inspired by the Holy Spirit, but the Devil offers diabolical petitions.

God is Satan's master, so he asked him where he had been. If the Lord should ask you, "Where have you come from?" would you give a satisfactory answer?

Satan is always busy, restless, and never quiet. He cannot sit still. He "prowls around like a roaring lion looking for someone to devour" (1 Peter 5:8). We do not know how near Satan is to us now. Even in our hours of prayer, when we are nearest God, he may come and assail us.

Then the LORD said to Satan, "Have you considered my servant Job? There is no one on earth like him; he is blameless and upright, a man who fears God and shuns evil." (8)

In what sense does Satan consider believers? He considers the difference between us and himself and is amazed. He also wonders at our happiness. He feels within himself a seething sea of misery. Again, he considers us to detect our flaws and faults. He looks up and down, as a horse dealer does with a horse, and soon finds out where our weaknesses lie. He also considers us the great barriers to the progress of his kingdom. Finally, he considers us with the goal of harming us. He seeks to make us unhappy and to spoil our usefulness as servants of Christ.

Little did Satan know that God was also considering Job. He was considering how much he would let Job be tempted. He was considering how he would sustain his servant under the trial. He was considering how to sanctify Job by his trial. Job's afflictions have been a lasting blessing to the church, and they have inflicted incredible disgrace on Satan. If you want to make the Devil angry, throw the story of Job in his teeth.

"Does Job fear God for nothing?" Satan replied. "Have you not put a hedge around him and his household and everything he has? You have blessed the work of his hands, so that his flocks and herds are spread throughout the land. But stretch out your hand and strike everything he has, and he will surely curse you to your face." (9–11)

Even the Devil could not bring a charge against Job's conduct. All he could do was insinuate that his motives were impure. If there had been anything bad in Job, rest assured Satan would have discovered it and used it against him. However godly a person is, though there are none like him or like her on the earth, you can find fault with that person if you want to. Satan found fault with Job because he had prospered, and his friends found fault with him later because he did not prosper. So you can make anything into a blot on the character of a person if you want to.

The black dog of hell had been prowling around to see where he could get in, so he knew there was a hedge all around Job, his house, and all he had. The Devil insinuated that Job feared God for what he could get out of him. He was saying, "Job finds that it pays and fulfills his purpose to be spiritual."

Even the Devil did not dare deny that Job was a working man. Nor did he accuse Job of getting rich by theft. He admitted that God had "blessed the work of his hands." There are still some who say, "Yes, it is easy for Christians to be good when they are rich and all goes smoothly for them. But would those who are now such devout servants of God be like that if they were in poverty or cruelly slandered or treated with contempt? Would the grace of God carry them over those rough bridges? Their Christianity is a fine thing, but when they are tried and tested, we learn what they are really made of."

The Lord delights in proving the graces of his people, for it brings great glory to his name when tests are made on them to let even their greatest adversary know how true they are and what a genuine work of God has been done in them.

The LORD said to Satan, "Very well, then, everything he has is in your hands, but on the man himself do not lay a finger."
Then Satan went out from the presence of the LORD. (12)

Satan could go only so far, but no farther. There is a condition in the permission granted him: "But on the man himself do not lay a finger." Satan imagines great harm against righteous people. But though he is mighty, he is not almighty. He is malicious, but there is One far wiser and stronger than he, who can always overpower him.

The Lord was present not as a mere spectator but as master of the situation. He had not handed over the reins to Satan. In our lives, the dog of hell is allowed to snap and snarl, but his chain is not removed, and the collar of omnipotent restraint is on him. You who are in trouble, remember that God is in your sorrow, ruling it to his desired goal.

One day when Job's sons and daughters were feasting and drinking wine at the oldest brother's house, a messenger came to Job and said, "The oxen were plowing and the donkeys were grazing nearby, and the Sabeans attacked and carried them off. They put the servants to the sword, and I am the only one who has escaped to tell you!" (13–15)

Satan selected that day because it was full of joy, so it would make the trials of Job all the more startling. If Job could have had his choice, he would have preferred that his trouble come when his sons and daughters were praying rather than when they were feasting and drinking wine.

Job had not wronged these Sabeans. They were plunderers on the lookout for spoil, and when Satan moved them, they came and stole Job's oxen and donkeys and slew his servants.

The bad news came to Job suddenly, when he was thinking of something different. There was only one servant left to tell the news. He was spared that Job might know it was true. The Devil knows how and where to strike. Yet this was only the first blow for poor Job. There were heavier ones to follow.

While he was still speaking, another messenger came and said, "The fire of God fell from the sky and burned up the sheep and the servants, and I am the only one who has escaped to tell you!" (16)

Job had no time to rally his faith and encourage his heart. While the first messenger was still speaking, another came with more bad news of lightning burning up the sheep and the servants. This calamity must have distressed Job all the more because the lightning burned up the sheep that he normally offered to God in sacrifice.

If that lightning had fallen on the Sabeans while they were robbing and plundering, we might have thought nothing of it. But for it to fall on the sheep and servants of a man of God who had clothed the naked with the fleece of his sheep—that did seem strange. This trial appeared more severe than the former one because it seemed to come distinctly from God: "The fire of God fell from the sky and burned up the sheep and the servants."

Poor Job had no time to recover from this shock before the next blow fell on him.

While he was still speaking, another messenger came and said, "The Chaldeans formed three raiding parties and swept down on your camels and carried them off. They put the servants to the sword, and I am the only one who has escaped to tell you!" (17)

Three such heavy blows were surely enough to test Job, but a fourth messenger came with the worst news of all.

While he was still speaking, yet another messenger came and said, "Your sons and daughters were feasting and drinking wine at the oldest brother's house, when suddenly a mighty wind swept in from the desert and struck the four corners of the house. It collapsed on them and they are dead, and I am the only one who has escaped to tell you!" (18-19)

Did any other person ever have to endure such troubles and agonies piled one on another with no relief? Job must have felt stunned and choked by these consecutive griefs. Satan had arranged to bring on Job's troubles so quickly one after another that he would feel utterly overwhelmed. At least the Devil hoped that would happen. But by the grace of God it did not!

Job had lost not just one child out of a numerous family nor a few thousand dollars out of a vast fortune. All ten of his children were killed at the same time. He had been reduced to abject poverty and a terrible torment of mind. But despite it all, as the New Testament remarks, "You have heard of Job's perseverance" (James 5:11). What a mercy to know that someone just like us passed through the fiery furnace heated sevenfold and yet was not consumed!

If Job persevered in faith under trial and affliction, why shouldn't I persevere too? He was just human. What God accomplished in one he may accomplish in another. Though Job's tribulation looked bad, untold blessings were coming to him as he seemed to be losing everything. It was not simply that after Job's trial was over the Lord "gave him twice as much as he had before" (Job 42:10), but all along, every part of the testing process worked for his highest good. God tested Job with one hand but supported him with the other.

We would never have heard of Job's perseverance if he had continued in his prosperity. That first part of his life would have made a very poor history compared to what we now find in the pages of Scripture. Camels, sheep, servants, and children make up a picture of wealth, but we can see that any day. The rare sight is perseverance in faith through the worst of trials. This is what raised Job to his true glory.

If God had doubled the number of Job's camels and sheep at the beginning of this story, it would only have enlarged Job's anxiety, since he already had enough. But to give him twice as much spiritual help, twice the experience, twice the knowledge of God was an enrichment that only the Lord in his wisdom could have provided. Thus Job received not only double grace but also double honor from God.

All the ages have Job for their teacher. He makes a glorious comforter and example of perseverance, but no one turns to his friends Bildad, Zophar, or Eliphaz—those miserable comforters—because they never went through the fire.

Because "you have heard of Job's perseverance," imitate it.

At this, Job got up and tore his robe and shaved his head. Then he fell to the ground in worship and said: "Naked I came from my mother's womb, and naked I will depart. The LORD gave and the LORD has taken away; may the name of the LORD be praised." (20–21)

With all his burden on him, "Job got up"! He did not pull his hair out as a pagan or maniac would have. He deliberately "tore his robe and shaved his head" and worshiped the Lord.

Job said, "The LORD gave." Then we must worship the giver and not his gifts. We degrade ourselves when we worship the things God gives us.

Job also said, "And the LORD has taken away." You say the fever took your child's life. Perhaps that was the immediate cause of death, but if you can realize the fever was only the instrument in God's hand to transfer the little one from your care to his, surely you will dry your tears. Also, once we know that God has done something, we will not complain. It must be right because the Lord did it. We may not know why, but he knows, and that is enough for us. God deserves our praise as much when he takes away as when he gives, for there is as much love in his taking as in his giving.

These words of Job are the noblest in the whole record of human speech. Considering his circumstances, his ability to speak like this was a miracle of grace.

In all this, Job did not sin by charging God with wrongdoing. (22)

In all our affairs, the main thing is not to sin. If the grace of God prevents affliction from driving us into sin, Satan is defeated. Satan did not care what Job suffered as long as he could hope to make him sin, and he was foiled when Job did not sin. He must have regretted that he had tried Job when he found that he could not make him sin.

God is glorified not so much by preserving us from trouble as by upholding us in trouble. In our trials we are tempted to grow impatient for God's deliverance, to doubt his wisdom, and to despair of being happy again.

As I read this twenty-second verse, I wetted it with a tear. In all Job's trials he did not sin by blaming God, yet I, who have suffered so little, have often sinned and blamed God. Haven't you? If so, let your tear follow mine. But the tear will not wash out the sin. Fly to the fountain filled with blood, and with it wash away your sins of impatience, bitterness, rebellion, and unbelief.

Again from James 5:11, we have not only heard of Job's perseverance, we have also "seen what the Lord finally brought about." The Lord brought about several lessons from Job's experience. First, we learn that correction is the reason God sends us affliction. Sanctified sorrow is a sharp frost that kills the germs of spiritual disease.

Second, our trials are an education for the future. I don't think Job was ready for more wealth until his heart had been enlarged by trouble. Only then could he bear twice as much as he had before. God's children are unprepared to enjoy success until they have tasted defeat.

Third, affliction is sent for the display of grace. You cannot see the stars while the sun shines. Wait until dark, and then you will see them. And many a Christian grace is quite imperceptible until the time of trial, but then it shines out with great luster. Oh, the triumphs of almighty grace! May it grant us Job's perseverance in all our trials!

The Lord Jesus Christ Is My Shepherd

The LORD is my shepherd, I shall lack nothing. (1)

It is right to call the Lord a shepherd. The "Shepherd of Israel" (Ps. 80:1) is a very blessed title for him, but "my shepherd" is best of all. Can you say that? The words in themselves are noble, but the personal experience of them is the real honey of life. If you can use these words and lay the emphasis on the word "my," you are one of the happiest people out of heaven.

If the Lord is our shepherd, we are his sheep. Are we like sheep? They are gentle creatures. A person who cannot bear an insult but seeks revenge is surely not a Christian.

Sheep also depend completely on their shepherd. All by themselves they are easy prey for the wolves. Do we sense our dependence on God? We sometimes assume we can do a little for ourselves, but only pride makes us think that. When we sincerely pray, "Give us today our daily bread" (Matt. 6:11), we have learned that the Lord is our shepherd.

Again, sheep love to be in flocks. And "we know that we have passed from death to life, because we love our brothers" (1 John 3:14). It is very hard work to love some of my fellow Christians. I know some with whom I would rather live in heaven forever than on earth for half an hour, yet I must love them for Christ's sake. If I do not, I must question whether I really am one of his sheep.

Sheep also know their shepherd's voice. Jesus said, "My sheep listen to my voice" (John 10:27). Did Christ ever speak to you so that you recognized his voice? When your pastor preaches, do you listen to his voice alone or the voice of Christ through him? Judge the genuineness of your conversion by that.

Jesus also said of his sheep, "They follow me" (John 10:27). He

40

has called us his friends (John 15:14). If we are friends, we should show ourselves friendly. We are more than Jesus' friends, we are his sisters and brothers (Heb. 2:11). And where is happiness to be found but in walking near Christ, our brother? Our daily needs demand that we live near him. When we are out of fellowship with him, our dangers are infinite. When we are unfaithful to his love, we are easily seduced by every temptation.

Finally, we know that Jesus is our shepherd when we confess that he has brought us back from our wanderings, supplied all our needs, and fed us each day in good pasture.

How can a sheep lack anything when it has a good and wise shepherd able and willing to provide for it? And how can we believers lack anything when we have God himself, the gracious and omnipotent Lord of all, to prevent us from ever being in need?

Since I am Christ's property, he will preserve me, protect me, provide for me, guide me, and be everything to my weakness, folly, and need that a shepherd is to a sheep. I cannot provide for myself, but I shall not lack anything. Christ not only provides for me, but also he himself is my provision. Famines may come, and others who have no God to go to may pine and perish, but I shall not have a need as long as Christ my shepherd lives. Though I am only one out of his countless flock, he cares for me.

He makes me lie down in green pastures, he leads me beside quiet waters, he restores my soul. He guides me in paths of righteousness for his name's sake. (2–3)

Here are four blessed things the Lord does for a believer. First, "He makes me lie down." I am so weak that I need God's help even to lie down. Rest for the soul is so hard to attain that no one ever reaches it except by God's power. He who made the heavens must make us lie down if we are truly to rest.

In making me lie down, Christ gives me perfect rest and so much spiritual provision that I am unable to take it all in. So I lie down and rest in it as a sheep does in the deep pastures where it seems lost in the fodder. There are such deep doctrines, such glorious privileges, such wondrous revelations of the heart of God in this blessed Bible that you and I cannot comprehend it all. But we can lie down in it. Take a good stretch as you lie down in Scripture. Don't be afraid to lie down and rest in the green pastures of the Word.

"He makes me" do this, and God would not make us do what was not good for us. A sheep needs to lie down sometimes. It needs to digest its food as much as eat it. May the Lord graciously give you the sweet rest of meditation that faith receives when it grows into firm confidence.

The second blessing is found in this sweet promise: "He leads me beside quiet waters." Our spiritual lives are not to be spent always lying down. There must come a time for going forward. David did not say, "He drives me," or "He drags me," but "He leads me." He goes first to show the way. Joseph H. Gilmore's hymn makes these words ring out over and over again in a charming way:

> He leadeth me, O blessed thought!
> O words with heavenly comfort fraught!
> Whate'er I do, where'er I be,
> Still 'tis God's hand that leadeth me.
> He leadeth me, he leadeth me!
> By his own hand he leadeth me!
> His faithful follower I would be,
> For by his hand he leadeth me.

You and I sometimes wander beside the noisy brooks that ripple over the stones and make great noise because they are so shallow, but when our Lord guides us, it is beside the deep, quiet waters.

The third blessing is this: "He restores my soul." When my soul gets empty, he fills it up again. When I get spiritually sick, he gives me a sweet medicine that renews my health.

Fourth, "He guides me in paths of righteousness." Nothing is more pleasant for a believer than to walk in "paths of righteousness." God has built into us a harmony between our righteousness and peace. If we get out of the right way, we get out of the way of peace. But as long as he guides us in paths of righteousness, we enjoy perfect peace.

The Lord guides us in paths of righteousness "for his name's sake." That is, not because of any goodness in us, but because of the goodness in him, and for the glory of his holy name.

Even though I walk through the valley of the shadow of death, I will fear no evil, for you are with me; your rod and your staff, they comfort me. (4)

Some think God's people will have no distress or trouble, but it is not so. Even they "walk through the valley of the shadow of death." But they are secure even there, for David said he would "walk through" it. As the train of our lives enters the dark tunnel of tribulation, by faith we can say, "I will come out on the other side."

It is an easy thing to walk through a "shadow," so it need not frighten us. Trials and troubles, if we see them with the eye of faith, are mere shadows that cannot hinder us on the road to heaven. Sometimes God even overrules our afflictions so that they help us on to glory. Therefore, let us keep on walking and never be afraid.

Who shall hinder us when God is with us? Was there ever a better reason for being fearless than this: "for you are with me"? A girl is confident because her mother is with her. Much more should we have peace in our hearts, because the all-powerful, ever-faithful Lord is with us. He is on our side. He has promised to help us. He has never failed us. He must cease to be God before he can reject one person who trusts him. How then can we be terrified?

When a shadow is cast across the road, you pass through it, hardly realizing it is there. You have your eyes fixed on the light up ahead. Believers are so comforted by the presence of Christ that they do not notice they are in the shadow of death. When they pass from one world to another, it is like going from England to Scotland. It is all one kingdom, and one sun shines in both lands.

Christ can sympathize with his people, because he also walked through the valley of the shadow of death when he died on the cross. It is a great comfort to the sheep to know their shepherd has walked the gloomy way before them.

Christ uses his rod to discipline us. We receive comfort from that, for "the Lord disciplines those he loves" (Heb. 12:6). We also derive comfort from knowing this: "No discipline seems pleasant at the time, but painful. Later on, however, it produces a harvest of righteousness and peace for those who have been trained by it" (Heb. 12:11).

The staff of Christ urges us forward. Have you ever felt the divine arousals? Perhaps under a sermon you have felt a sharp thrust. It is a bad sign when a person can be comfortable doing nothing, but it comforts believers to understand that the staff is prodding them onward.

You prepare a table before me in the presence of my enemies. You anoint my head with oil; my cup overflows. (5)

What courage David here displayed! When a warrior is in the presence of his enemies, he usually snatches a hurried mouthful or two while getting ready for the fight. But though David's enemies were all around him, he sat down at a table prepared for him, as if it had been a holiday instead of the day of battle. This shows how much confidence David had in the Lord.

Our enemies may watch us if they like. They may wish they could devour us, but they cannot prevent us from sitting down to the Lord's table and feasting. Our table is being prepared for us while Satan, armed to the teeth, seeks to slay us. He may grin and howl, but we believers take no notice of him.

This is our anointing with the Holy Spirit for new service, just as "God anointed Jesus of Nazareth with the Holy Spirit and power" (Acts 10:38). This anointing proves we will have delicacies as well as staple food. We will have joy as well as safety. We will be prepared for service as well as preserved from destruction.

What is this cup? Elsewhere the psalmist called it "the cup of salvation" (Ps. 116:13). Such a heavenly cup belongs to every believer, but some only hope they are saved. Others believe they are saved now but not for eternity. Their cups fail to overflow.

Jeremiah speaks of "the cup of consolation" (Jer. 16:7 KJV). That cup is yours, believer. You have your trials, but what a comfort to know that all your trials work for your good (Rom. 8:28)! And what a consolation it is to know your trials are just "for a little while" (1 Peter 1:6).

We read also in 1 Corinthians 10:16 of "the cup of thanksgiving." I feel like that good old saint who said that if she got to heaven, Jesus Christ would never hear the end of it. Truly he never shall, for my cup overflows with thanksgiving for who Christ is and what he has done.

Some people's cups never overflow. Many even fail to be filled because they are taken to the wrong source. Such are the cups held beneath the drippings of the world's leaky cistern. People try to find fulfillment in wealth, but they never do.

As Christians, our cups overflow when we receive a great deal more than we prayed for. Hasn't that happened to you? If your cup overflows, think of the fullness that is in Christ, from whom the blessing comes. Then think of the happiness in store for you when your cup will run over in heaven forever!

Once more, if your cup overflows, be sure to call in your neighbors to catch the mercy that runs over. If you have more blessing than you can hold, ask some other Christian to share it with you. Remember what Peter and the other fishermen did when, at Christ's command, they let down the net and caught more fish than their net could hold without breaking: "They signaled their partners in the other boat to come and help them" (Luke 5:7). Help them fish? No. They wanted their partners to help them eat the fish.

Many people invite you to a meeting because they want to get something out of you. But it is better to be invited because there is something to be given away, and those who have an overflowing cup want you to share the blessing with them.

Now for a question. How full would your cup be if God had filled it in proportion to your faith?

Surely goodness and love will follow me all the days of my life, and I will dwell in the house of the LORD forever. (6)

I will never be able to outrun the goodness and love of my God. These two holy angels will watch over my footsteps and track me wherever I go. The Lord's goodness will supply my needs, and his love will forgive my sins.

Goodness and love will follow me not merely now and then but every day of my life. These heavenly messengers will never forsake me in all my dark days as well as the bright ones.

Our lives in God's house begin here, for this earth is the lower part of God's house for every Christian. When the time comes for us to leave this earth, we who are the Lord's children will go only upstairs to higher rooms.

This Twenty-third Psalm is true of God's children, but there are some to whom David's language seems strange. They cannot sing this sweet psalm, for they are not sheep but goats. Their lives are as restless as the waves of the sea. No quiet pastoral poem could set forth their joy, for the sound of war is heard in the streets of their souls.

This psalm is very good to read but far better to write out from your own experience. May it be not merely a song in the Bible but a song in your heart!

David's Confession of Sin: The Music of Tears

DAVID WROTE THIS PSALM after Nathan confronted him with his great sin of adultery with Bathsheba (2 Sam. 11–12). If David had not been in a sad state of heart, he would not have fallen into the sin. His spiritual indifference left him so hardened that he needed Nathan pointedly to say to him, "You are the man!" (2 Sam. 12:7). After that, David wrote and prayed this truly penitent psalm.

Though much was lost to the cause of righteousness through David's sins of adultery and murder, the church is enriched for all time by the possession of this psalm. It is a marvelous recompense. Surely this psalm proves that the Lord reigns, for he brings good out of evil and blesses generations through what in itself was an act of defiance against God.

These words were directed to the chief musician, so it is meant to be sung. Yet it is not a joyous piece of music that can be sung with the harp and the violin. We must have the liquid melody of sighs, groans, and tears. The proud and self-righteous will say, "That is a melancholy dirge," and turn away from it in disgust. But to someone under the burden of sin, there is no music like the Fifty-first Psalm.

If you would get to the heart and soul of David's language here, you must have the picture before your mind's eye of him weeping. The only thing on David's heart was the consciousness of his great sin. That seemed to swallow up everything else. He felt that he could not rest until he knew his sin was pardoned.

May God give you and me the grace that will enable us to enter into the repentant spirit so remarkable in this psalm! The person who has never prayed through this psalm needs to do so at once. Those who have never repented will have to repent to enter eternal life. Let us therefore come with David's language on our lips and in our hearts.

Have mercy on me, O God, according to your unfailing love; according to your great compassion blot out my transgressions.(1)

David used to talk about being God's servant, but he said nothing about that here. He used to speak of God's great love for him, but he couldn't realize that now. After trying to hide his sin, David finally broke the silence, and the first thing he spoke of was God's mercy. God's justice frowned on him, and the Lord's anger frightened him. Nothing but God's mercy would do for him.

No eye is quicker to see the mercy of God than the eye washed with the tears of repentance. When the burning justice of God seems as if it would strike us with blindness, we can turn to that glorious rainbow of mercy around the throne.

David talked as if the Lord had said to him, "What is the measure of mercy you want?" He knew of nothing by which he could measure it except the "unfailing love" and "great compassion" of his Lord. It was as if he had said, "O Lord, let your mercy be the only judge of the mercy I need."

Sinners under the sense of sin have keen eyes for the mercy of God, for they know it is their only hope of forgiveness. So they look for it as a sailor at sea looks for a star. There was no more powerful plea David could urge than that God would act according to his unfailing love and great compassion.

Wash away all my iniquity and cleanse me from my sin. (2)

It was not enough that God would blot David's sin out of his book. He also wanted it blotted out of his nature. Forgiveness of sin was not enough. David wanted the defilement of his sin also removed. David loathed his sin. It was disgusting in his sight. His whole spirit seemed sickened at the very reminder of it. He wanted to be washed not merely from sin but also from his "iniquity" or inequity—the wrongdoing of it.

As if David's request that God would "wash away" his iniquity were not enough, he added, "and cleanse me from my sin." He thought washing with water might not be enough. He may have needed to be cleansed by fire. "Lord, cleanse me any way you can. Just make sure you rid me of my sin!"

Hypocrites are satisfied with the cleansing of their clothes, but David cried, "Cleanse me from my sin." Sin was the only thing he could truly call his own.

For I know my transgressions, and my sin is always before me. (3)

David had tried to forget his sins of adultery and murder, but he couldn't. They haunted him wherever he went. It seemed as if they were painted on his eyeballs, and he could not see anything without seeing through his sin. He had put his sin behind his back, but now it was in front of his face. This is how God makes people repent. He makes sin like a gall and wormwood to them.

There is no hope of pardon unless we keep our sins before us. Our sins must be a ghost that haunts us, a black cloud that hangs over us. Only when we put our sins before our faces will God put them behind his back. Confessed sin has the teeth extracted from it, but when sin is neither felt nor known, it breeds the canker of pride and is deadly to the heart.

Against you, you only, have I sinned and done what is evil in your sight, so that you are proved right when you speak and justified when you judge. (4)

David had sinned against his people by setting a bad example for them. He had sinned against Bathsheba when he called her to his bedroom. He had sinned against Uriah when he set him up to die on the battlefield. But the virus, the venom of the sting seemed to David to lie in this, that he had sinned against God.

Nonbelievers overlook that. They care nothing about sinning against God. Offending people and harming others may cause them trouble, but as for offending God, they snap their fingers at that and count it to be something not worth even thinking about. But when a person is awakened by divine grace, he or she sees that sin is an attack against God, an offense against his very nature, and this becomes the heaviest burden to bear. Do you know what this experience feels like?

Even when we have not left our rooms or done an act or said a word, still our proud hearts that rebelled against God and our murmuring spirits that refused to tolerate his will are enough to lay us in the dust, for they are sins against God.

Other judges have to decide by the evidence brought before them, but this Judge has seen the evil for himself. It was done before his very eyes, and therefore he is "proved right" and "justified" when he judges. Whatever God may say to us, however sharp, and whatever he may do to us, however terrible, we deserve. We may plead no extenuating circumstances for our sins. We always think this way when we are in a repentant frame of mind.

Surely I was sinful at birth, sinful from the time my mother conceived me. (5)

David said this not as an excuse for his sin but to increase his guilt. David went beyond seeing sin on him. He saw it in him. He saw his very nature steeped and dyed in sin. David's mother was no doubt godly, but he still had the tendency to sin because he descended from fallen parents.

A greater evil than our acts of sin is that we are sinners by nature. Sin would never come out of us if it were not in us. It does not happen as an accident but flows from within us as naturally as foul water runs from a polluted spring. What a bottomless depth of sin there is in human nature! No wonder it bursts forth as it does. As the volcano is the index of a mighty seething ocean of devouring flame deep in the earth, so any one sin is only a token of far greater sinfulness that seethes and boils within the cauldrons of our natures. We do wrong because we are wrong.

David did not say, "Lord, I was acting contrary to my nature when I committed this sin. You know it was not like me to do that." Instead, he said, "Lord, you know I was acting in accordance with my nature. It was just like me to fall into these terrible sins. I acted wickedly because I am wicked at the core. The streams have betrayed the fountain."

Some people are surprised to find themselves guilty of certain sins. Don't you be surprised. Rather, be surprised to find yourself kept from guilt. Be amazed when you are preserved from sin, for the whole tendency of human nature is toward iniquity.

Surely you desire truth in the inner parts; you teach me wisdom in the inmost place. (6)

Then outward morality is not enough for me. I confess, Lord, that truth isn't in my heart, where you want it. I have looked there but have seen only sin. It is not truth, but the reverse of truth that I find in my inward parts. Lord, you will never have what you desire to see in me unless you bring it about in me.

The outward part of our lives is important, but the inward part is much more so, because the outward springs from the inward. We would not be outwardly guilty if we were not first inwardly sinful. We might be able to rectify the external wrong and to reform our outward actions, but who can make his or her heart clean? We can prune the tree and cut it to any shape we like, but we cannot change the sap.

Yes, God can teach us! Even those hidden parts that no human teaching can reach, God can touch, and there he can teach us wisdom.

Cleanse me with hyssop, and I will be clean; wash me, and I will be whiter than snow. (7)

Hyssop dipped in sacrificial blood was used for cleansing lepers. David took the place of a leper when he asked God to cleanse him "with hyssop." David did not hope to cleanse himself. He did not trust in outward ceremonies, so he asked God to cleanse him.

Snow is not like a white wall—white on the surface only. Snow is white even on the inside. Yet when God washes a believer, she or he becomes "whiter than snow," for snow soon becomes tainted. But we never will if God washes us.

This is a wonderful expression of faith. I do not know of any Scripture that seems more full of holy confidence than this. David had such a deep sense of his sinfulness that it was amazing that he should have, side by side with it, such a perfect confidence in the power of God to cleanse him. It is easy to say, "Other sinners will be whiter than snow." We can easily say, "I will be whiter than snow" when we do not realize what scarlet sinners we are. But when the crimson is before us and we are startled by it, it requires a real and living faith to be able to say to God, "Wash me, and I will be whiter than snow." No faith brings God greater glory than the faith of the consciously guilty when they dare to believe that God can forgive them.

Our own washings make us no cleaner but only fouler than we were before. If we washed ourselves in the sea, we would turn every wave crimson with our iniquities sooner than one single stain of our guilt would be washed away. But if God washes us with the sacrificial blood of Christ, we will be "whiter than snow."

Let me hear joy and gladness; let the bones you have crushed rejoice. (8)

David had heard nothing but groans and sighs. Now he wanted to hear joy and gladness. David wrote seven verses before he dared to pray for joy and gladness. Those seven verses are either all confessions of sin or petitions for deliverance from it. My sinful friend, you must not first seek to get rid of your sorrow. Rather, be thankful for your sorrow for sin, and pray that you may never lose that sorrow until you lose the sin that caused it.

We cannot sin with impunity. Worldly people may do so as far as this life is concerned, but a child of God will find that discipline follows closely on the heels of sin. If we fall into sin, God does not wink at it but disciplines us so severely that it feels like broken bones. I suppose that no pain can be much worse than that of a broken bone, but God can make the pain of sin in the conscience as intense as that of broken bones. And then he knows how to heal the bones he has broken and to make each one "rejoice." Whereas they groaned before, God can make those same bones a mouth out of which praise to him will flow.

Hide your face from my sins and blot out all my iniquity. (9)

Lord, no longer look at them. Hide your face not from me but from my sins. David did not say, "Don't let the news of my sin leak out to others." Nor did he pray, "Help me to forget my sins." Instead, he asked, "Hide your face from my sins."

We cannot blot out our sins with our own blood, much less with our tears. But the Savior can blot them out with his blood. Obliterate them, Lord, as if they had been written in books of wax and you put the whole record of them away with a hot iron. Don't let my sins stand against me in the book of your remembrance! And when you have blotted out my sins from your book of remembrance, blot them out from my memory, too.

Create in me a pure heart, O God, and renew a steadfast spirit within me. (10)

It was not freedom from punishment that David asked for but freedom from the power of sin. A thief dreads the gallows, but this sinner wanted a new heart. He wanted to have removed from him the defiling power of sin over his affections. He felt that he needed his Creator to perform again his great work of creation. David knew better than to ask the Lord to make his old heart clean. "Flesh gives birth to flesh" (John 3:6), so David's cry to God was, "Create in me a pure heart, O God." Let it be a new creation; give me a new, pure heart.

Here David blended justification with sanctification. His prayer for pardon was accompanied by a prayer for purity. He did not want to have his sin blotted out so he could continue in sin. He wanted forgiveness, then a new heart so the trend of his life would become holiness.

There was a time when people had steadfast spirits in them. But through sin the human spirit has lost its beauty, its tenderness, and its holiness. So each one of us needs to pray, "Renew a steadfast spirit within me."

In this tenth verse David asked not only for a new creation but also for a daily renewal. Without the daily renewal, God's creation of us would soon be marred, as his first natural creation was. All created things need renewal. Nothing God made is self-existent. Self-existence belongs exclusively to the One whose name is "I AM WHO I AM" (Ex. 3:14).

Do not cast me from your presence or take your Holy Spirit from me. (11)

David had been filled with an unholy spirit, so he feared that God would take his Holy Spirit from him. If God takes his Holy Spirit from us, we are without hope. We will go from bad to worse. We will never repent or believe. When David sinned, he acted as if God had not been present. But now he pleaded that God would not cast him from his presence. David compared the withdrawal of the Holy Spirit to being thrown into a dungeon in solitary confinement, far from God's presence. He dreaded the removal of the Holy Spirit more than anything else.

When God flogs his children, they still cling to him and cry to him. They do not wish to run away and hide from him. Their only comfort is to weep on their Father's heart and to wait for the kiss of forgiveness.

Restore to me the joy of your salvation and grant me a willing spirit, to sustain me. (12)

David had been happy once, and now he asked the Lord to "restore . . . the joy of . . . salvation." He could not live on old mercy. The remembrance of his spiritual joy could not satisfy him. It only made him hunger for fresh joy.

Lord, I will slip again unless you hold me up. Since you cannot trust your little child by himself, come and teach me how to walk.

Then I will teach transgressors your ways, and sinners will turn back to you. (13)

David could teach "transgressors" God's "ways" of discipline—he would use the rod on those who wander—and of mercy—he would forgive and restore those who repent. No one teaches the mercy of God as well as the person who has tasted it. Pardoned sinners make great preachers. The person who has never felt the burden of sin is unfit to preach to burdened souls. But when that burden is lifted off our backs and our hearts, we are ready to leap for joy!

David was saying, "Lord, if you will only teach and save and cleanse me, I will tell others what great things you have done for me. I will tell the story of your love that others may also know its power firsthand." David would turn preacher if only God would bless him. He felt sure that if he once told his tale of love, others would be melted and would turn to God. No doubt it was the case.

This verse implies that we must be in a right state of heart if we are to serve God well. We can't teach sinners God's ways and expect them to come to him unless we ourselves possess the joy of salvation and are upheld by his good Spirit. If we try to do God's work out of order, we will make a mess of it and accomplish nothing fruitful.

Our goal is the conversion of sinners, not their reformation. And they must be converted to God. "Sinners shall be converted unto thee" (KJV). I am glad to convert people to the scriptural view of baptism and other doctrines. It is always desirable to see them learn the truth. But what good will it do if a person is not first converted to God? If anything can be the means of converting sinners, it is the loving and faithful testimony of one who has tasted that the Lord is gracious. If God has been merciful to you, do not be silent about it. Let the world know what a gracious God he is!

Save me from bloodguilt, O God, the God who saves me, and my tongue will sing of your righteousness. (14)

This was an amazing prayer, but it was not amazing that David would get relief when he called his sin by its right name. He did not mince matters. He did not call his sin manslaughter or an unfortunate accident. When Uriah first died, David excused himself by saying, "I did not kill Uriah. Granted, I had him put where he was likely to be slain, but you never know who is going to die in battle" (see 2 Sam. 11:25). But now that his conscience had been aroused, he confessed that he was a murderer who needed to be saved "from bloodguilt." David called a spade a spade.

Be honest with God. Do not give fair names to foul sins. Call them what you will, they will smell no sweeter. As long as you call your sins by petty names, they will not be forgiven. God can see through you, so what's the use of trying to hide anything from him? Come out with your sin, that God may get it out of you too. Confess it by name, that God's pardon covering your confession may cover all your sin.

"But surely," you may say, "I do not need to ask God to forgive me of murder, as David did."

Note

Really? If anything in your example should lead others to sin or if your neglect of an opportunity should lead others to continue in their sin until they perish, will not the blood of sinners be on your hands?

It is remarkable that when David confessed his sin in the strongest language he could use, at the same time he laid hold of God with the boldest faith he could exercise, for he called him "the God who saves me." The deeper our sense of sin becomes, the stronger God's grace can make our faith!

David said he would be a teacher; here he promised to be a singer. God's people feel they cannot do too much once they get a sense of pardoned sin. The tongues that confess sin are the best ones to sing with.

Shouldn't David have said, "My tongue will sing of your mercy"? That would have been correct, yet David knew that God had a way of showing his mercy in complete consistency with his "righteousness." Since this is the unusual part of divine forgiveness, David highlighted it.

O Lord, open my lips, and my mouth will declare your praise. (15)

David was afraid to open his lips himself, lest he should say something wrong. He had already learned he was not to be trusted to open his own eyes, for they had led him into the sin of adultery. Pardoned sinners are always afraid that they will sin again. In the eighth verse David prayed, "Let me hear." Now he prayed, in effect, "Let me speak." Sin puts all the organs of the body out of order, and grace is needed to put them all right again.

The unclean leper covered his lips in confession that he was unfit to speak. So here the unclean David, with the covering over his lips, would not speak until the Lord had taken his sin away and opened his mouth for him.

You do not delight in sacrifice, or I would bring it; you do not take pleasure in burnt offerings. (16)

Under the law there was no sacrifice for the pardon of adultery. Some sins were left out of the catalog, and this was one of them. A true sense of sin always puts people on the track of teaching about Christ. David could see that sin was too grievous a thing for the blood of sheep and bulls to wash away. Though he did not despise the ritual that God had ordained, he looked beyond it to something greater and better of which it was only the type.

The sacrifices of God are a broken spirit; a broken and contrite heart,
O God, you will not despise. (17)

When Augustine lay dying, he had this verse written on his wall,
so that whenever he awoke, he might read it. Some spices are never
perfect in fragrance until they are pounded with the pestle in the
mortar. And so is a broken heart. A whole heart is a scentless thing,
but when it is broken and bruised, it is like the precious spice
burned as holy incense in the ancient tabernacle. A broken heart is
a sweet fragrance to the Lord, because it means his child hates sin.

Even for the person who has committed the most atrocious
crimes, there is still acceptance if he or she brings God the sacrifice
of a broken spirit. This is all the sacrifices put into one. The person
who brings a bleeding heart to God is accepted when the one who
brings a bleeding bull is rejected. Bring God the sacrifices of your
broken spirit, your troubled conscience, and your bleeding heart.
Bring all your fear because of your sin. Best of all, bring to God's
altar the sacrifice of the bleeding Savior.

A broken heart is similar to a broken bottle. People throw it away,
because it no longer holds its contents. David said God would not
despise the broken heart, because he was sure that everyone else
would. And what is a broken heart? It is one in which all feelings of
self-importance have spilled out.

In your good pleasure make Zion prosper; build up the walls of
Jerusalem. (18)

This was a blessed goal of David's mournful psalm. He felt that
his sin had injured the church of God, that he had in fact pulled
down the towers of Zion by his iniquity. So he prayed, "Lord, undo
the spiritual damage I have done. Build up the walls of Jerusalem."

Then there will be righteous sacrifices, whole burnt offerings to delight
you; then bulls will be offered on your altar. (19)

Once David came to God and was forgiven, ordinances took their
proper place. You can't teach someone how to live until he or she is
born, and you can't teach spiritual life until a person is born again.
All religious rites and ceremonies that precede the new birth go for
nothing. First there must be the inward life and the broken heart;
then everything else will drop into its proper place.

Never do people give so freely to the cause of God as when they
are rejoicing over pardoned sin. Keep a sense of your indebtedness

to God alive in your soul, and you will feel that you can never do enough for him who has forgiven you so much. You are sure to bring God the best you have when you get your sins forgiven. After you have looked to Christ, the one great sacrifice for sin, you will bring God all you can to show how grateful you are for his pardoning mercy.

Highest Praise

THIS PSALM IS a song of exuberant thanksgiving, overflowing joy, and highest praise. There is not a single request in it. In this it is like heaven, where they cease to pray but never cease to praise.

Praise the LORD, O my soul; all my inmost being, praise his holy name.
(1)

David was talking to himself. He was a soul talking to his soul with all his soul. Every person should learn to "soliloquize." Self is the first congregation anyone should preach to.

We are to praise the Lord not with our mouths only, nor with a musical instrument, but with our souls. Soul music is the soul of music. Let us wake up our souls to do this great work of praising our Lord. It is work that angels do forever before God's throne in heaven. God has always been blessing us. Now let us begin to praise him. His blessings have been real; let our praises be just as real.

We must praise God with everything inside us, because divided powers lead to failure. The person who is a jack of all trades is a master of none. Either praise God with all your might, or do not pretend to praise him at all. Let every string in your heart be touched by the fingers of the Holy Spirit. Let no power or faculty exempt itself from this blessed service. Your memory, your will, your judgment, your intellect, your heart—all your "inmost being" is to be stirred up to praise God's holy name. Even your anger can praise the Lord—if you are angry at sin.

It must be not your lips alone but your inmost being that praises God. If things around us are not joyous, let everything inside us wake up to praise our God. He will hear us even if we don't speak. If we keep the praise within ourselves, he will hear the music of our souls.

Once we were terrified that God had a "holy name," for we were unholy. But he has cleansed and washed us, and now we can rejoice in his holiness.

Praise the LORD, O my soul, and forget not all his benefits. (2)

This is the third command to praise the Lord. He is a triune God; let us give him triune praise. Doesn't he multiply his blessings to you? Then bless him repeatedly. Never weary of the work. Practice giving God grateful praise.

God's benefits are quite memorable. To forget them is a base form of ingratitude, yet we do have a bad memory for good things. Our poor memories have often been the graves of God's mercy, but now let us call for a resurrection. Let his mercies rise before our eyes, and let our praises rise with them.

The rest of the psalm names these benefits. Don't pass over them as if they made up a dry and uninteresting list, as in an auctioneer's catalog. Instead, bedew every one of these benefits with a tear of heartfelt thanks.

[He] forgives all your sins and heals all your diseases. (3)

Note the present tense. It is not "He will forgive all your sins on your deathbed." Nor is it "He forgave all your sins years ago, but now he condemns you." No! God forgives our sins daily! This is the sweetest note in our song of praise. David was sure God had forgiven him, for no one sings over an uncertain pardon. Since forgiveness is a present blessing, seek it now through faith in the crucified Christ! If we are pardoned through the death of Christ, let us love him, commit ourselves to him, and praise him forever.

Just one of your sins, like a millstone around your neck, would be sufficient to sink you into hell, but God forgives them "all." From your childhood until now you have been full of sin, and the Lord has been equally full of forgiveness. The blessed scapegoat has carried the whole mass of your sins into the wilderness, where they will never be found again. "All your sins" were very many, but they have gone from you once and for all! How can you not sing about that? If you do not leap for joy at the thought of your forgiveness, you have never felt the weight of your sin on your heart.

David wrote that God "forgives all your sins" before he said, "and heals all your diseases." Forgiveness comes first, because it is the foremost blessing. Would a person on death row rejoice to be healed of a disease? Neither can unforgiven sinners fully enjoy any physical blessing from God.

Only God, who created us, can heal "all" our diseases. Our Lord has begun to heal the sinful nature—healing us of pride, sloth, and unbelief. Will we not praise him for this? The present tense "heals" means that God continues to heal all our spiritual diseases. Let's not forget that David was still speaking to his "soul" (vv. 1–2). The diseases of our souls are the worst diseases of all, for they would drag us down to hell if they remained unhealed.

Just think. Every day God is healing us of the mortal disease of sin! Even our trials are often the lancet and the scalpel with which he removes from us the foul taint of evil.

[He] redeems your life from the pit and crowns you with love and compassion. (4)

God has redeemed us with the precious blood of his Son Jesus (1 Peter 1:18–19). He has caused his own life to indwell us, and it is a redeemed life! How can we be silent in view of the precious blood that purchased us? Isn't this the sweetest theme we could sing about? If we do not sing about this, the very stones in the street will cry out against us.

What a crown! What gems are in it! No gold or silver can equal love and compassion. There is around your head even now a halo of love and compassion. It is invisible to all but the eyes of grace and gratitude. According to the old saying, "Uneasy lies the head that wears the crown." But happy are you if the Lord crowns you with love and compassion. No emperor ever wore a crown with gems this precious. God treats us like kings. Shall the head crowned refuse to praise him who crowned it? No! "Praise the Lord, O my soul" (v. 1).

[He] satisfies your desires with good things, so that your youth is renewed like the eagle's. (5)

People's desires are very hard to fill, for in their greed they are always hungry for more. The richest person in the world has not found satisfaction in wealth, but God has satisfied our desires "with good things"—the best of which is his Son. God might have left us to pine in spiritual hunger. Instead he has fed us by making us know, love, feed on, and rejoice in what is good. This is heavenly feasting on heavenly food. We receive divine satisfaction from the finished work of Christ. We are satisfied not with ourselves but with God. Will we not praise him for this?

In Christ we grow young again! Our faith is revived. Our hope is brightened. The smoldering flame of our love has been stirred up.

How can we not bless God who restores us in these ways? Can we, with renewed strength, be silent? No! We must use all the strength God has given back to us to praise and glorify him. If your youth is renewed, renew your praise to the One who has renewed you.

The Lord works righteousness and justice for all the oppressed. (6)

God is the supreme governor of this world. He will rectify all wrongs in his own time and way. Let those who have been despised and trampled on exult in God, who "opposes the proud but gives grace to the humble" (James 4:6). He is both the executor of the needy and the executioner of those who oppress them.

He made known his ways to Moses, his deeds to the people of Israel. (7)

An unknown God is an unpraised God, but when he reveals himself to his people, they cannot refrain from blessing his holy name. Our God makes himself known! He might have hidden himself behind his works but instead gave a revelation of his ways to Moses, and it made David sing. But you and I have a deeper revelation, one made not to Moses but to us through Jesus Christ.

Revelation is a constant source of thanksgiving to those who understand it through the illumination of the Spirit who inspired it. Shall we not praise him for making known his ways and acts to us in Christ? Read the Scriptures, then let them lead you to praise the Lord of whom they speak.

The Lord is compassionate and gracious, slow to anger, abounding in love. (8)

Shouldn't this make us overflow in our songs of praise? He is such a good God to such great sinners! He is full of compassion and grace, slow to anger and quick to love. Let us be slow to murmur and quick to praise!

He will not always accuse, nor will he harbor his anger forever. (9)

Sometimes God does accuse us of sin. He would not be a kind Father if he did not. When Eli failed to restrain his rebellious sons, God judged him (1 Sam. 3:11–14). When we feel God's accusations, we ought to bless him, because they last such a little while. Our faults are so many that if God were always accusing us, we could not blame him. But he will not always accuse. He does not hold a grudge against us! He makes us know the foolishness of our hearts when we wander from him, but he will not always accuse.

If we cannot sing because of anything else, let us bless the name of the Lord that he will not be angry with us forever. God's anger toward his people is very short-lived. In fact, it is not the same kind of anger that he lets loose against rebels, for he has promised us, "I have sworn not to be angry with you" (Isa. 54:9).

He does not treat us as our sins deserve or repay us according to our iniquities. (10)

If God had dealt with us as our sins deserve, we would not now be in a spirit of praise. Instead, we would be in the place of punishment. We would be driven from his presence instead of being invited to seek his face. Let us thank God that we are not in hell and that we are on praying ground and pleading terms with him. We can also praise him that we shall never be condemned, for he has saved us with an eternal salvation. If we did not praise God for this, every column that supports the roof over our heads would have the right to burst out in rebuke for our ingratitude.

For as high as the heavens are above the earth, so great is his love for those who fear him. (11)

What music can be as lofty as "the heavens"? Surely the best music our lips can give—and better than that—should be offered to our Lord. Look up into the blue sky. Try to imagine what is beyond the stars, then say to yourself, "So great is his love for those who fear him." Then try to praise the Lord as he deserves. If we have a God like this, we can never overdo his praises. It is impossible to exaggerate our exaltations of him.

As far as the east is from the west, so far has he removed our transgressions from us. (12)

There is an infinite distance between east and west. There is no place on earth where east ends or west ends. And so there is neither latitude nor longitude for praise. Because God's forgiveness has no bounds, let us give him boundless praise!

In the third verse we read that God "forgives all your sins." Now we learn how—by removing our sins from us "as far as the east is from the west." They have been removed an infinite distance from us. They were once ours. We could not deny them. But he has removed them and laid them on our scapegoat, Jesus Christ. That scapegoat has carried them away, and they will never be found. It is impossible that sin will ever be charged against us again.

This figure implies that God has forgotten our sins. Some Christians think you can never be certain you are forgiven while in this world. That is an insult to the God who removed our sins from us as far as the east is from the west.

If David had said our transgressions are removed from God, he would have spoken the truth. But he said something more personal. They are removed "from us." So why do we try to carry a burden of guilt? We can forgive ourselves!

If God removes our sins from us as far as the east is from the west, then surely he will also remove our troubles from us. But even if he does not, we have true cause for joy!

As a father has compassion on his children, so the LORD has compassion on those who fear him. (13)

The best of God's children still need compassion. God looks with a tender heart at all believers. He feels for us and suffers with us. No earthly father or mother is half as compassionate as God is to his children. What great amounts of compassion you and I need!

Think of the compassion Jesus showed to his disciples. They were people of little faith and unspiritual in their judgment. When Jesus was thinking of suffering and death, they were thinking of places of honor in the kingdom (Mark 10:32-45). They argued over which of them was the greatest (Mark 9:33-37). They slept in Gethsemane when Jesus told them to pray (Luke 22:39-46). James and John wanted to call down fire from heaven to destroy the Samaritans (Luke 9:51-56). Peter rebuked Jesus for predicting his death (Matt. 16:21-23). Thomas doubted the Lord's resurrection (John 20:24-25). Yet in all these cases, Jesus showed them compassion, even as a good father does his children! Our Lord's example is a challenge to us to show compassion to others.

For he knows how we are formed, he remembers that we are dust. (14)

Our bodies are just dust. Even our souls are so weak and feeble that they may be compared to dust in God's sight. Some people forget this and treat us as if we were made of iron or steel, but God remembers that we are dust. He knows that sickness is just a preview of the death that will dissolve our mortal frames. Our bodies are held together only by a continual miracle. It is odd that this heap of bodily dust does not dissolve much sooner. It is no wonder that it should return to the dust from which it came. The wonder is that it takes so long to return. Dust must be handled carefully, lest it should separate into particles. Likewise, God handles us delicately.

As for man, his days are like grass, he flourishes like a flower of the field; the wind blows over it and it is gone, and its place remembers it no more. (15–16)

This is all we mortals are. Not mighty cedars. Not solid rocks. Just grass or flowers of the field. We are like a primrose by a riverbank or a daisy in the meadow. As God gives to each blade of grass its own drop of dew, so he gives each one of us a glistening drop of mercy. As the sunlight of his favor sparkles in every drop of that mercy, let us praise his holy name.

Death does not need to come as a sharp sword, for a mere wind is enough to blow us away. The hot winds of the east blow over a meadow, and it is burned up immediately. In the south of France, when the sirocco has blown across from Africa, I have seen the fairest flowers look in a short time as if they had been burned with a hot iron. That is the way we are when pestilence comes. It is but a breath of poisonous wind, and we are soon gone.

Shall we be sorry about this? No, for though this world forgets us, our names are engraved on the palms of God's hands (Isa. 49:16).

But from everlasting to everlasting the LORD's love is with those who fear him, and his righteousness with their children's children—with those who keep his covenant and remember to obey his precepts. (17–18)

"The LORD's love" had no beginning, and it will have no end. Unlike our mortal bodies, it is not a fading flower. It is everlasting for us and for our children. What a blessing to think that our father's friend is our friend and the friend of our children too! As David loved Mephibosheth for Jonathan's sake, so does God look on the children of his children and keep his covenant with them. Grace does not run in the blood, but it often runs side by side with it. It is often God's way to bless a child for a parent's sake. If you are a believer, pray with confidence for your sons and your daughters.

The LORD has established his throne in heaven, and his kingdom rules over all. (19)

Not only does God crown us (v. 4), but now the psalm suggests that he is crowned too. Do not believe the people who attribute sickness and death to the Devil. They try to make it appear that God has left his throne, but he reigns where war rages and where peace rules. If God did not reign everywhere, he would not be God at all, and this would be an intolerable world to live in. Nothing happens without his permission. Even the little things of life are ordered by him. The leaves that fly in the wind are steered as surely as the stars in their courses, for with God nothing is great, and nothing is little.

Praise the LORD, you his angels, you mighty ones who do his bidding, who obey his word. (20)

As if David could not praise God well enough himself, he called in the angels to help him. He wanted them to lend him their harps and tongues.

Praise the LORD, all his heavenly hosts, you his servants who do his will. (21)

Sun, moon, and stars—"all his heavenly hosts"—and all creatures that live on earth, burst into song and extol the Lord. And we people, who should be God's hosts, let us also praise him.

God's servants, whether you be wind, rain, snow, or intelligent agents, as long as you do God's will, praise him while you do it!

Praise the Lord, all his works everywhere in his dominion.
  Praise the LORD, O my soul. (22)

This is the spirit in which we should always sing our hymns of praise to God. Our entire lives should be psalms of joyous thanksgiving and thanks-living. While all the glorious anthems from angels, God's heavenly hosts, his servants, and his works are ascending to heaven, we must not be silent. We must join them in praising the Lord with our entire beings. So we say with David, "Praise the LORD, O my soul." We must not go to heaven grumbling. We have good reason to praise the Lord, for he has dealt bountifully with us. Let us lead the song, and may the whole world join in joyful adoration of the triune Lord: Father, Son, and Holy Spirit!

Praise is the rehearsal of our eternal song. What will you do when you get to heaven if you go grumbling all the way? Begin now to bless the name of the Lord.

The psalm ends as it began: "Praise the LORD, O my soul." Let us learn from this that praise is the alpha and omega of our Christian lives. Praise is the life of our lives in Christ. May our lives from beginning to end praise his holy name!

An Intimate Prayer to a Personal God

O LORD, you have searched me and you know me. (1)

God does not need to search us, for that implies a lack of knowledge. This verse means God knows us as well as if he had explored us, as miners dig in mines and make subterranean excavations. It is true that God knows everything, but that is not what David said here. He did not talk about God's knowledge of other people; he spoke to God about himself. "You have searched me," as if God were looking for contraband goods. God has ransacked us, gone down into our hearts, and spread out every secret part of our lives. He sees the most intricate labyrinths of our spirits. It is not as if he has searched and been unable to discover the secret of my nature. His search has been an efficient one, for he has searched me, and now he knows me. He has read the secrets of our souls and knows us perfectly, far better than we know ourselves.

You know when I sit and when I rise; you perceive my thoughts from afar. (2)

It is a common thing to sit down and to rise up. I myself hardly know why I do one or the other. But God knows and understands it all. God knows when we sit down to do nothing and rise up to do something. He knows our most trivial deeds and important movements.

Our hearts form a thought that never comes to a word or an act, but God understands it. Before we think something, before it becomes a thought and is still unformed and far away, God understands it. He not only knows what it is but also understands the motive from which it springs, the state of mind out of which it arises. God does not need to come near us to know us. His eye is so strong that if he only looks at us from a vast distance as an astronomer looks at a star in the midnight sky, he understands our thoughts. He knows what we think and why we think it. Often we cannot understand our own thoughts, but God always understands them.

You discern my going out and my lying down; you are familiar with all my ways. (3)

God is all around us—behind us, in front of us, above us, and beneath us—as if he were a ring of observers. We lie down to go to sleep, but he never sleeps. We cannot think of God while we sleep, but he thinks of us.

> Awake, asleep, at home, abroad,
> We are surrounded still with God.

God is familiar with our habits and the exceptions to our habits. We cannot tell him anything he does not know, nor can we hide anything from him. God is familiar with everything we have done or are doing or will do.

Before a word is on my tongue you know it completely, O LORD. (4)

God sees the word that lies quietly on the tongue as well as the one that has been spoken. He knows it "completely." God's knowledge is not partial or imperfect. He never misjudges anyone, for he is familiar with every part of every person.

You hem me in—behind and before; you have laid your hand upon me. (5)

Like a person lying in ambush, God hems us in from the back and the front. We are like a person under arrest, on whom the officer lays a hand so that we may have no opportunity to escape. We are in God's grip. He has taken such a firm hold on us that we cannot get away.

We are also like a child enfolded in its mother's arms. God not only knows our thoughts and words but also comes into contact with us. He comes so near us that he touches us, like a physician who both looks at the wound and probes it. God probes our spiritual wounds and sees the depths of our sins.

Such knowledge is too wonderful for me, too lofty for me to attain. Where can I go from your Spirit? Where can I flee from your presence? (6–7)

David's first impulse was to run from a God whose attributes were so lofty. It was a temporary impression. God is everywhere, and his far-seeing eye will watch us in every place. It is vain, therefore, to think that we can ever flee from his presence. Is it not a striking thought that every sin is committed in God's presence? Only very bold rebels would insult their monarch to the face. People are generally on their best behavior when they stand on the palace floor. Yet the whole earth is the dwelling of the great, eternal King. He is immortal and invisible. Every time we sin, we sin in his very presence and with his eye resting on us.

If I go up to the heavens, you are there; if I make my bed in the depths, you are there. If I rise on the wings of the dawn, if I settle on the far side of the sea, even there your hand will guide me, your right hand will hold me fast. (8–10)

There is no hope of escaping from God by any speed to which we may attain, for if we could travel the speed of light—186,000 miles per second—still the Lord would be at our destination ahead of us. His hand would lead us, and his right hand would hold us.

Missionaries in the farthest part of the earth are led by God. When they get lost in the jungle, God leads them. And when missionaries in foreign lands have no friends to encourage them, God's hand brings strength. What a comfort to you if you must travel far from your family! You cannot be alone, for God is there. So go as bravely as if you walked the crowded streets of your hometown.

If I say, "Surely the darkness will hide me and the light become night around me," even the darkness will not be dark to you; the night will shine like the day, for darkness is as light to you. (11–12)

Darkness is light in the eyes of God, for he depends not on the light to see. Light is a most welcome aid to our poor vision, but God sees just as well in the darkness. This is an obvious truth, yet how seldom do people realize it. They still imagine that when the night comes and they are not seen by mortal eyes, they may do what they want. But there is no curtain in the night that can hide a deed of guilt from the eyes of the omniscient Lord.

You have seen bees in a glass hive and watched all their movements. Or you have put an insect under a powerful microscope and examined every part of it. Even so does the omniscient God watch and examine us. There is nothing we do that he does not observe.

> Almighty God, your piercing eye
> Strikes through the shades of night;
> And our most secret actions lie
> All open to your sight.

For you created my inmost being; you knit me together in my mother's womb. I praise you because I am fearfully and wonderfully made; your works are wonderful, I know that full well. (13–14)

God has created our innermost beings for himself. He knows as much about us as people know the rooms in their own house.

Just when the psalmist felt stricken with awe over this august attribute of the omniscience of God, he looked up to his God and said, "I praise you." This is a good resolution for each of us to make. As God sees us, let us praise him. It will please him to hear us praise him.

Galen, the oldest and best known of the ancient surgeons, used to say that an ungodly anatomist had to be insane, for there is a marvelous display of skill and wisdom, delicacy and force, in the making of human beings. Those who study the beautiful arrangement of veins, nerves, sinews, muscles, and bones must say, "I am fearfully and wonderfully made."

So fearfully are we made that human life stands in constant jeopardy. It looks as if every breath might be the last and every pulse might quickly end our lives. You cannot examine a blood vessel, especially some of the very small ones, through a microscope without being utterly astonished. There are many times in an hour, perhaps even in a minute, when a simple thing would put our lives in imminent peril of destruction. Every person is a world of wonders. We need not go abroad to see miracles, for we are a combination of marvels and miracles. Truly we are fearfully and wonderfully made.

> Our life contains a thousand springs,
> And dies if one be gone;
> Strange, that a harp of a thousand strings
> Should keep in tune so long.

How there can be a compound of spirit and matter—how the earth on which we walk should enter into our composition, and yet we should be like angels—how there can be something about us that links us with the dust, yet much about us that joins us to God himself—these are extraordinary things we do not understand. Where is the point in which the spirit touches matter? How is it that the will can move the hand or the finger? How does the spirit act on matter? Those are questions much more easily asked than answered.

My frame was not hidden from you when I was made in the secret place. When I was woven together in the depths of the earth, your eyes saw my unformed body. All the days ordained for me were written in your book before one of them came to be. (15–16)

We are too apt to forget the goodness God showed us in our infancy. We did not come into this world without a Creator, and in that Creator we found the best friend we can have. Oh, for grace never to wish to stray from him in whom "we live and move and have our being" (Acts 17:28).

God not only sees us now (vv. 7–12), but he has always seen us. He saw not only our well-formed frames in our mothers' wombs but also the lives we would have before they came into being. It was as if God embroidered us with a needle. So extraordinary is the human body that it may be compared to the needlework of God.

God's wonderful foreknowledge enabled him to know us even before we knew ourselves or anyone else knew us. In the very making of the body and mind and spirit, God was with us. Just as an architect sketches a plan for a building and specifies so much of this and that, so the psalmist represented God as writing down in a book all the days of our lives. God mapped out what he intended we would be, even before we existed. And from our earliest days he cared for us.

If we look back on our infancy, when we were utterly unable to do anything for ourselves, it ought to check our unbelief, because if God took care of us and protected us and caused us to grow then, we may fairly trust that he will take care of us now. And if we through sickness should ever be reduced to such a helpless state that we can do nothing for ourselves, yet he who cared for us before we saw the light and when we saw it with feeble trembling eyes will still take care of us.

How precious to me are your thoughts, O God! How vast is the sum of them! Were I to count them, they would outnumber the grains of sand. When I awake, I am still with you. (17–18)

We do not say, "How terrible are your thoughts to me, O God!" but "How precious—how consoling, how full of promises of blessing to me." What deep thoughts, what bright thoughts, what faithful thoughts God has for us! The psalmist did not tell exactly how precious God's thoughts to him were because they were beyond value. He simply rejoiced in that truth.

If God's thoughts are precious to us, his words ought to be even more precious to us! In the Bible we have the thoughts of the divine thinker put on paper. Hence we should highly prize every word in this blessed book. Again, if God's thoughts are precious to us, then his acts, which spring from his thoughts, also ought to be precious to us. Are they? Finally, as God's thoughts are precious to us, we should make the best return we can by thinking precious thoughts of him—thoughts of love, trust, and service we can render for him.

Sadly, many never think of God. To them it would be precious if there were no God at all. How often God has thought of us! If you were the only person in all the world, he would think no more of you than he does now, though you are one among the billions. The infinite mind of God is not divided by the multiplicity of objects brought before it. His whole mind goes out to contemplate each person. We cannot count the number of thoughts God has for us, nor can we estimate how precious they are.

Happy believer, who is always with God! It is happy living, and it would be happy dying to feel that if we never wake again on earth, we will wake up with God! How precious it is to think that when Christians fall asleep, they will awake to be with the Lord forever! Your turn and mine will come. Why should we not always be consciously in his presence now? If we can live from day to day without realizing that God is near us, we are falling into a sad and dangerous condition. Before we fall asleep, we put our souls into his hands, and when we awake, we find them there.

Suppose we should count up all God's thoughts to us and then fall asleep. We would then just begin to count again, for the Lord would continue to thrust out mercies from his hand. Our counting will never catch up with God's thoughts of us—much less will our gratitude and the service he deserves.

If only you would slay the wicked, O God! Away from me, you bloodthirsty men! (19)

God must slay the wicked. He cannot let sinners continue to live and provoke him to his face. He must one day take down the sword of justice, unsheathe it, and smite the foes of righteousness. They have committed wickedness in his presence. God has seen all their wicked acts and read their wicked thoughts. He will need no witnesses, no jury. When people offend in the very presence of the judge, it is easy work for him to try them. Isn't he the judge of all the earth, and will he not do right? (Gen. 18:25).

We want them away from us so that when God comes to slay them, we will not have to watch them die.

They speak of you with evil intent; your adversaries misuse your name. Do I not hate those who hate you, O LORD, and abhor those who rise up against you? I have nothing but hatred for them; I count them my enemies. (20–22)

We are to love our own enemies, but we are not to love God's enemies, because they hate him. We love them as our fellow human beings, but we hate them as those who hate God. We are to forgive our personal enemies, but we cannot forgive God's enemies. We are to wish them a gracious conversion that they may receive God's pardon and become his friends and followers and servants. Still, we do not love the truth unless we hate the lie. We do not love the right unless we have anger for wrong.

We are living in an age in which we are practically told that truth and error are the same, that the Devil's lie and the divine revelation may lie down together. If we will not endorse this falsehood, we are called dogmatic bigots. Bless the Lord, we mean to be a great deal more dogmatic than we have been and to stick even closer to the truth of God than we have done before.

Search me, O God, and know my heart; test me and know my anxious thoughts. See if there is any offensive way in me, and lead me in the way everlasting. (23–24)

Is it not beautiful that what the psalmist started with as doctrine here became a prayer? He began this psalm with the declaration, "You have searched me and you know me" (v. 1). Now here he prayed, in effect, "Search me again, and keep on doing it. Never take your great searchlight away from me."

David was saying, "Lord, look for the dross and consume it. Look for the spots and wash them away."

We must all have a way. We must be on a journey, for this world is not our resting place. Therefore, it is of utmost importance that our way be the everlasting one. Whatever way we take, others will be influenced by it. Little ones who gather around their parents' knees will think their "way" is the way for them.

The way of sin is not "the way everlasting." Nor is the way of many religious people "everlasting," for some of them are hypocrites. Do not tell me that if you are sincere, it will not matter which way you take. You know better. The sincere belief of many that they will be saved will not prevent their condemnation if they persist in refusing to trust in Jesus Christ.

David was a spiritual man, yet even he needed to be led in the right way. And so he prayed, "Lead me in the way everlasting."

This entire psalm is a blessed prayer. May God hear it from you and me, for his dear Son's sake!

The Gospel According to Isaiah

THIS CHAPTER LIES at the very heart of the Scriptures. It is the holy of holies in God's Word. Let us, therefore, put off our shoes from our feet, for the place we stand upon is holy ground. This chapter is a Bible in miniature. We may properly call it the gospel according to Isaiah.

I thought that our beloved friend Dwight L. Moody answered with extreme wisdom a question that was put to him when he came to London. A number of ministers had come together to meet Mr. Moody, and they began to discuss various points and ask what the evangelist's views were upon certain doctrines. At last one brother said, "Would you be so kind as to give us your creed? Is it in print?"

In a moment the good man replied, "Certainly my creed is in print. It is the fifty-third chapter of Isaiah."

It was a splendid reply. How could a man come closer to the very essentials of the faith? I trust that you will say not only "This is my creed," but also, "This is the foundation on which I have built all my hopes for time and eternity. This is the source of my sweetest consolation. This is the sun that makes my day and the star that guides my night."

Who has believed our message and to whom has the arm of the LORD been revealed? (1)

This is a cause for sorrow upon sorrow—for the prophets to have God's message to deliver, and yet for people to reject it—for them to have to tell it but tell it in vain. Yet this has been the lot of some of God's most faithful servants in all ages, and we must not complain if it should be ours also. This is the great grief of God's ministers today. So often we have to go back to our homes and cry, "Who has believed our message?" It is neither a doubtful message nor an incredible one. It is a plain, earnest, and noble message, the accuracy of which is guaranteed by the God of truth. Yet who has believed it? We are accepted by God not on the basis of our success but on the basis of our faithfulness.

Still, no true minister of Christ can be content unless people believe his message. It will be a matter for sighing and groaning if unbelief is the only answer to our earnest declarations of Christ.

I should not have voluntarily chosen to be Jeremiah, the weeping prophet. Yet I think not one of God's servants deserves greater honor than he does, for he continued bravely to deliver his Master's message even when everyone rejected his testimony. Isaiah links himself with all the other prophets who had been rejected and says, "Who has believed our message?"

No one believes in Christ unless the arm of the Lord is revealed or stretched out, for faith is the product of omnipotence. This is the work of God's Spirit and grace.

He grew up before him like a tender shoot, and like a root out of dry ground. He had no beauty or majesty to attract us to him, nothing in his appearance that we should desire him. (2)

This is why Christ was not received by his own people (John 1:11) and why the testimony of the prophets concerning Christ was rejected by those to whom it was delivered. He came to them not as a towering palm tree or widely spreading cedar but "like a tender shoot, and like a root out of dry ground." Jesus had no visible majesty to impress those who cherish such things.

A root that springs up in fat and fertile soil is in debt to that soil for its growth. But Jesus grew "out of dry ground." He derived no benefit from his followers. He did not choose eminent scholars as his first converts. Among them were uneducated fishers, a despised tax collector, a political activist, and a traitor.

Nor did Jesus owe anything to his nationality. The nation of Israel had reached its dregs. Its religious leaders were dreaming over letters of Scripture but blind to its spiritual meaning. Its elders were clinging to traditions and so sinking into superstition. It was a "dry ground" out of which Jesus sprang. His ministry did not depend on any external influence.

Carnal minds are unbelieving minds, for the beauties of Christ are spiritual. To carnal eyes there was nothing outwardly attractive about him. He came here in the utmost simplicity. Remember the angel's message to the shepherds: "This will be a sign to you: You will find a baby wrapped in cloths and lying in a manger" (Luke 2:12). There was nothing of pomp or show about him, "no beauty or majesty."

He made no display of scholarship, no pretense of deep philosophy, nothing that the carnal mind cherishes. But the all-glorious deity revealed in human form spoke sublime truth, and therefore people rejected him. They heard him say he had nowhere to lay his head (Matt. 8:20), and they despised such a Messiah. As he spoke in simple parables to the people, they asked, "Where is his wisdom?"

Jesus Christ has no beauty in the eyes of self-righteous, self-sufficient men and women. What do they want with a Savior? What do they care for his atoning sacrifice? They can't admire the love and holiness of Jesus, for they don't know their own unloveliness and unholiness. Alas, that God's own Son, the most beautiful of all beings, should have no beauty or majesty to unspiritual eyes!

But we can't blame them, for not very long ago many of us were just as blind as they are now. Don't you feel that you can smite your breast with deepest regret for the length of time you were blind to the beauties of your Redeemer?

He was despised and rejected by men, a man of sorrows, and familiar with suffering. Like one from whom men hide their faces he was despised, and we esteemed him not. (3)

How sad that the Son of God received such base treatment as this! How equally sad that his glorious gospel should still be the object of contempt to multitudes!

O eyes, shall you ever cease to weep over your former blindness? O heart, shall you ever cease to grieve over your former hardness? He who was heaven's darling "was despised and rejected by men," and we partook in the guilt, for we also despised and rejected him. Though he is now exalted in heaven, he is still despised and rejected by the world.

Some are people of pleasure, others people of wealth, but Jesus was "a man of sorrows." Isaiah might have called him a man of holiness, for there was no sin in him (1 Peter 2:22), a man of obedience, for his food was to do his Father's will (John 4:34), a man of eloquence, for no one spoke as he did (John 7:46), or a man of love, for never did love glow more brightly than in his heart (John 13:1). But the prophet singled out Jesus' sorrows as his prominent feature, for the agonies he endured on the cross paid for our salvation.

What a wonderful expression "familiar with suffering" is! Our blessed Lord knew it, understood it, slept with it, rose up with it, walked with it every day. Hence he knows your sorrows, and he can meet them. He is such a master comforter because he was such a mighty sufferer.

Shame upon us that we who have been redeemed by him, we whom he loved from eternity, we who now delight in him, hid our faces from Christ. We held him in contempt, neglected him, and preferred other methods of salvation to salvation by faith in Christ. We were afraid to speak out for him. Like sheep, we wandered from him. Like prodigals, we refused to believe in him. In many ways we hid our faces from the one we now worship as Lord.

The last section is the universal confession of the human race. Even we to whom Christ is all our salvation and our desire, we to whom he is now most precious, "esteemed him not." We gave no thought to his Word, his people, or Christ himself. Why? Because we esteemed ourselves so highly. Love of self prevents love for the Savior.

Surely he took up our infirmities and carried our sorrows, yet we considered him stricken by God, smitten by him, and afflicted. (4)

This is substitution—Christ suffering instead of us, the innocent dying for the guilty, the Lord of glory bearing the sin of rebels. Why do people argue with this precious truth?

Can you also say, "Surely he took up our infirmities"? If you have truly learned that he took up your infirmities, you may indeed bless his name, for it is the best news that ever reached your ears. Go and tell it to your fellow sufferers: "Surely he took up our infirmities." There is no explanation for the sufferings of the perfect Christ except that he was bearing our infirmities that we ought to have carried for our own sin.

The Jews thought God had stricken Jesus, and so he had. But they wrongly assumed some sin in him had caused God to strike him, when in fact he was holy, harmless, and pure (Heb. 7:26). God punished Jesus only because he was carrying our sorrows and the sins that caused them.

But he was pierced for our transgressions, he was crushed for our iniquities; the punishment that brought us peace was upon him, and by his wounds we are healed. (5)

Ever since the fall of humanity into sin, healing has been our chief need. Sin is the most disgusting disease. You may not feel it, but that just makes it all the worse. What marvelous medicine we have from the wounds of Christ! The physician drinks the bitter cup and so cures the patient! The physician is put to death, and the great sacrifice brings the dead patient to life!

The wounds of Christ heal our unbelief, our stony hearts, our paralysis of doubt, our numbness of soul, the fever of pride, the leprosy of selfishness, the fit of anger, the cancer of covetousness, and the spiritual decay caused by worldliness. Christ's wounds heal us not only by forgiving our sins but also by delivering us from their deadly power. His wounds heal us even from our love for sin.

No sprinkling can wash away sin. No rituals can confer grace. Your hope must be in Jesus. A crucified Savior is the sole hope for a sinful world. Every wound on the back of Christ says to us, "You are not your own; you were bought at a price. Therefore honor God with your body" (1 Cor. 6:19-20). If you profess to be healed, what do you say to this? Will you live for the Savior who died for you?

We all, like sheep, have gone astray, each of us has turned to his own way; and the LORD has laid on him the iniquity of us all. (6)

The verse begins with "We all" and ends with "us all." Here is universal sin: "We all, like sheep, have gone astray." Here also is a personal sin: "Each of us has turned to his own way." Everyone sinning, but each one in her or his own particular way. We have no right to find fault with one another, for "we all, like sheep, have gone astray." But we have good reason to find fault with ourselves, for "each of us has turned to his own way."

We are here compared to sheep, for sin brings out the beast in us. We are compared not to one of the more noble and intelligent animals but to stupid sheep. All sin is foolishness, and all sinners are fools.

Then Christ gathers up the sin—all kinds of sin of all sorts of sinners—and of his whole church it is truly said, "The LORD has laid on him the iniquity of us all." These words have been the means of the conversion of multitudes. You were among the "all" who went astray, but if you are a believer in Christ, you will be found among the "all" whose iniquities were laid on him and carried away by him.

We sometimes sing "I lay my sins on Jesus" from Horatius Bonar's hymn. But according to Isaiah, the real laying of sin on Jesus was done by God himself.

He was oppressed and afflicted, yet he did not open his mouth; he was led like a lamb to the slaughter, and as a sheep before her shearers is silent, so he did not open his mouth. (7)

The sin laid upon him was none of his, so he could have repudiated it. But he did not. When a word could have released him, he would not speak it. He never pled for himself. Omnipotence restrained omnipotence. His was indeed golden silence. Our blessed Master uttered seven cries from the cross but not one word of murmuring, no complaint even against his enemies.

Jesus could have called "more than twelve legions of angels" from heaven for his protection (Matt. 26:53). Or a single word of his could have destroyed his enemies. But "he did not open his mouth." Jesus was more eloquent in his silence before Herod and Pilate than in his ordinary language. "No one ever spoke the way this man does" (John 7:46), yet no one was ever silent as he was for our sakes.

I went to see a friend the other day who has a great number of painful afflictions, yet I found her cheerful and content. When I spoke with her about it, she said, "I have for years enjoyed perfect submission to the divine will, and it was through what I heard you say."

"What did I say?" I asked.

She replied, "You told us that you had seen a sheep in the hands of its shearers, and although all the wool was clipped off its back, the shears never cut into its flesh, because the sheep was lying perfectly still. You said, 'Lie still, and the shears will not cut you, but if you kick and struggle, you will not only be shorn, for God has resolved to do that, but you will be wounded.'"

It is a blessed thing to lie still under the shears—so still as not even to bleat! May the perfect example of the Lamb of God teach us a holy submissiveness to the will of God.

By oppression and judgment, he was taken away. And who can speak of his descendants? For he was cut off from the land of the living; for the transgression of my people he was stricken. He was assigned a grave with the wicked, and with the rich in his death, though he had done no violence, nor was any deceit in his mouth. (8–9)

No more cheering light ever falls on a tearful eye than this: "for the transgression of my people he was stricken." Christ's substitution is the brightest star in the galaxy of revelation.

Dying between two thieves, as though he had been the worst criminal of the three, "he was assigned a grave with the wicked." All his sufferings were not because he was guilty but because he was innocent. The only crime that I have ever heard rightly laid to his charge is what the poet sweetly describes as "found guilty of excess of love." He loved sinners so much that he had to give his life rather than let them perish.

Because "he had done no violence, nor was any deceit found in his mouth," he was qualified to bear our sin. If he had used either violence or deceit, he might have escaped. But because he was harmless and true, he had to die.

Yet it was the LORD's will to crush him and cause him to suffer, and though the LORD makes his life a guilt offering, he will see his offspring and prolong his days, and the will of the LORD will prosper in his hand. (10)

Wicked people slew our Lord, and their crime was the blackest in the world's history. But unconsciously they were fulfilling the Father's will. He was behind it all. Peter agreed when he told the Jews, "You, with the help of wicked men, put him to death by nailing him to the cross," yet he "was handed over to you by God's set purpose and foreknowledge" (Acts 2:23). Not Pilate nor Herod nor Judas nor Jews nor Romans but the heavenly Father crushed Jesus. If ever there was someone whom God should have protected from injustice, it was Jesus. Unless he died as the substitute for sinners, his death was the greatest miscarriage of injustice.

Jesus became a guilt offering because he was carrying our sins, and sin always brings guilt. God calls sin "this detestable thing that I hate!" (Jer. 44:4).

People have offspring by life. Christ has his by his death. People die, leave their children, and do not see their offspring. But in our Lord's case, death extended his life. He died that he might see his offspring. As he told his disciples, "Unless a kernel of wheat falls to the ground and dies, it remains only a single seed. But if it dies, it produces many seeds" (John 12:24). For Christ, the path to prosperity was by way of adversity. And often it shall be with the servant as with the Master.

Up from the grave he arose in newness of life, and back to heaven he returned to immortal life. He thus prolonged his days. Here the strain changes completely. From the depths of woe we see the happy result of all Christ's suffering, sorrow, and shame. Glory be to the name of Christ, he has a mighty right hand, into which God has placed that work which is according to his own good pleasure—the work of saving guilty people. That work, in his prolonged days until the end of time, shall prosper in the hand of Christ.

After the suffering of his soul, he will see the light [of life] and be satisfied; by his knowledge my righteous servant will justify many, and he will bear their iniquities. (11)

We are not to depreciate the bodily sufferings of Jesus, but his deeper agony came from the suffering of his soul. The soul sufferings of Christ were the soul of his sufferings.

Christ's blood could not fall to the ground in vain, as some think. A sure and glorious result must come of the suffering of his soul. Whatever the aim of his cross was, it shall be accomplished. I could imagine failure in creation, if it should please God, but not in redemption. His death pangs were our birth pangs.

By their knowledge of him, by their trusting him, many shall be justified and saved. Will he justify you? Do you know him? If you know him so as to trust him, he has justified you.

How very expressive this passage is. Christ does not merely bear our punishment but our iniquities too! The top and bottom of it all is, "He will bear their iniquities." Here is a literal substitution of Christ in our place. Our sins are given to him, and his righteousness is credited to us. Sin can't be in two places at one time. So when Christ takes our iniquities, they are gone, and we are righteous in God's sight. He takes our burden, and we are unloaded.

Therefore I will give him a portion among the great, and he will divide the spoils with the strong, because he poured out his life unto death, and was numbered with the transgressors. For he bore the sin of many, and made intercession for the transgressors. (12)

"The spoils" that Christ divided are human hearts and the love of those he has redeemed.

Jesus not only died but also poured out his "soul" (KJV) unto death. There is no meaning in this chapter unless it teaches that Christ carried the sin of his people and suffered in their place. There is nothing that can make a heavy heart glad until it sees sin removed by the death of Christ. Thanks be to God for this great sacrifice!

The intercession Christ made from the cross he still makes from heaven today: "Father, forgive them, for they do not know what they are doing" (Luke 23:34). If Jesus pleads for sinners, they can be confident he will not reject them for trusting in him. Christ prays for those who do not pray for themselves. If he made intercession for transgressors, he is even more intent on pleading for believers whom he has cleansed from every transgression.

If Jesus prayed for the people who killed him, we can forgive those who sin against us. They have not nailed us to crosses or pierced our hands and feet. Again, since Jesus prayed for us, let's pray for ourselves. Let us also intercede for transgressors, just as Jesus did. And since Christ appears in heaven for us, let us be glad to appear on earth for him.

Blessed intercessor, let your mighty intercession benefit each one of us, for your own name's sake!

Come to the Waters

*"Come, all you who are thirsty, come to the waters; and you who have
no money, come, buy and eat! Come, buy wine and milk without
money and without cost." (1)*

God would have the attention of sinners, so he calls for it. Aren't
sinners eager for God? No! Their ears are full of the world's com-
motion. It is God who is eager for sinners. Never did a seller plead
with customers more earnestly than God here pleads with sinners,
yet it is not God who is profited by the transaction. He gains nothing but the indulgence of his love. God says, "Come" four times in
this first verse. Do not ask if you may come to Christ for salvation,
for you are here commanded to come. Whoever wants Christ is welcome to have him.

This description of gospel blessings grows sweeter as it advances.
We come to the "waters" of life first, then the "wine" of joy and
the "milk" of satisfaction—and all "without cost." Christ is as free
as the air. As you can take in the air simply by breathing, so you can
receive Christ into your heart. As any dog may lap up the water in
a river and every ox may stand knee-deep in its stream, for there is
no one to keep even the animals away, so it is with Christ. You are
welcome to come to him!

Our first idea of the gospel is very simple. It is water for our
thirst. Soon we find that it is food for our hunger. Now we discover
it to be wine for our delight and milk for our ongoing health. There
is everything in Christ! When God invites us to the waters and then
promises to give us wine, it is like the wedding at Cana in Galilee.
There the servants went to the water jars and found them full of
wine (John 2:1-11).

This invitation is given not to people who are full and can satisfy
their own needs out of the buckets of their own righteousness. No,

the prophet spoke to "you who are thirsty," you who feel an awful necessity that will not let you rest. Hunger may be appeased, but thirst is terrible. No one can bear its pangs long. Whatever your age, sex, rank, character, or position in life, if you just thirst, the gospel invitation is for you! In the Lord Jesus Christ there is all you want—and more than you know you want. Right now you only thirst, but in Christ you have bread for your hunger as well as drink for your thirst.

"Why spend money on what is not bread, and your labor on what does not satisfy? Listen, listen to me, and eat what is good, and your soul will delight in the richest of fare." (2)

Why do you seek rest where it can never be found? Why do you crave temporary delights that can never satisfy your immortal nature? That road takes you nowhere! Your ceremonies, religious rituals, works, and feelings cannot feed your soul. But Christ is "the bread of life" (John 6:35). You will find in him all the largest desires you can long for. You will have not only the necessities, such as bread, but also the delicacies, which God here calls "the richest of fare." They will satisfy you completely. You will not be able to conceive of anything that will be more rich and full than the grace of God in Christ.

The less value there is in a religion, the more people have to pay for it. The pardon that costs a nickel is not worth a penny, but the forgiveness that costs us nothing is worth more than the whole world. I have no lean Christ to preach to you, no half-starved salvation that will drag you into heaven and save you "as one escaping through the flames" (1 Cor. 3:15). In coming to Christ your soul will delight in the richest fare. A Christian cannot be too happy. The joy of the Lord is beyond all description. You must taste it to prove its sweetness. As honey among the sweets, such is the joy of the Lord among joys. As the sun amid the lesser lights in the sky, such is the joy of Christ compared to all the other delights we can know.

"Give ear and come to me; hear me, that your soul may live. I will make an everlasting covenant with you, my faithful love promised to David." (3)

The ear is the gate by which salvation comes into us. We do not live by sight. All the sights of gorgeous processions and external ceremonies will never convert a single person. "Faith comes from hearing the message, and the message is heard through the word of

Christ" (Rom. 10:17). God is saying in this part of the verse, "Bend your ear forward as if you would catch every word. Take out the earplugs of prejudice and be willing to hear what I have to say."

It seems a very small and easy thing to do—simply to hear—yet that is the way of salvation! We must listen to God, because we cannot find happiness apart from our Creator. The sinner will never be complete apart from the Savior. God has so constituted the human heart that it cannot be content without him.

How do nonbelievers come to the Lord? The first step is to think of him. Many are so busy with making money and becoming successful that God is not in their thoughts. No wonder they have not come to him in faith. Second, come to Christ by confessing your sins to him. You have lived all these years without him. Confess that neglect. You have not loved the Lord with all your heart, soul, mind, and strength, as he commands you to do (Mark 12:28-30). You have broken every command. Tell him, "Father, I have sinned." Third, come to Christ by believing prayer. Ask him to save you from your sins, and believe that he will make your life new.

Someone says, "I can understand God making a covenant with David, but will he make a covenant with me?" Yes—and the same kind of covenant. God will promise to bless you, save you, preserve you, and present you in the glory of Christ when he returns. God makes his "everlasting covenant with you"—you who have a desire for it, you who long for a right standing with God. Think of the covenant God makes with needy and thirsty sinners. God strikes hands with guilty men and women in the person of Jesus Christ. It is a sure covenant, not made up of *ifs* and *buts* and *maybes*. This covenant is sealed with blood and signed by him who gives an oath that he will never turn from it. We can count on him who is faithful not to break his covenant.

"See, I have made him a witness to the peoples, a leader and commander of the peoples." (4)

Jesus, our greater David, comes to us to bear "witness" that God's love never changes. I do not know how God could show his love more fully than he does in the life and death of his Son. Will you not clasp hands with God across this great sacrifice of his only Son? God did not give us an angel to bear witness to us; he gave us his Son, who bore witness more with his blood than with his mouth. He was born among us, lived among us, died for us, and now he lives for us in heaven.

You cannot doubt God's readiness to receive guilty people, since

Christ has come in the flesh. You cannot doubt his love to sinners, since his only Son has been made a witness to it. Since Jesus is God's witness, let us believe him.

As our leader Jesus guides us into peace and happiness. As our commander he gives us power with which we fight Satan and his powers of darkness that hold people in bondage. Since Christ leads, let us follow. Since he commands, let us obey. He commands us to believe and be baptized in his name. Let us not disobey any part of his holy will. Happy are the people who accept Jesus as their leader and commander!

David in the cave of Adullam gathered to himself "all those who were in distress or in debt or discontented . . . and he became their leader" (1 Sam. 22:2). Now the great antitype, David's son and Lord (Luke 20:41-44), is willing to gather to himself those who are spiritually bankrupt, discontented with sin, and weary with the world. Then he becomes their leader.

"Surely you will summon nations you know not, and nations that do not know you will hasten to you, because of the Lord your God, the Holy One of Israel, for he has endowed you with splendor." (5)

The "you" in this verse is the "leader and commander" of the previous verse, namely, Christ. What joy this gives to us who love him! God has "endowed . . . with splendor" his Son Jesus and given him the power to call to himself a people that he did not know in a saving sense. He never saw you in his house before. He never knew you to fall on your knees in prayer, but he is calling even you by his grace and gospel! When he calls those nations that did not know him, they "will hasten," or run, to him.

We do not preach the gospel as an experiment. We are sure it will bring results, for Jesus could not have died in vain. He will not be a leader without disciples. He will not be a commander without an army. If we speak of faith in the name of Christ, people must be saved. They must run to Christ. A head without a body would be ghastly. A shepherd without sheep would be one without an occupation. And a Savior with no souls saved by him would be a Savior in name only. There is a divine hand that secretly touches the springs of the human will so that when Christ calls people, they run to him.

Some who often hear the gospel are very slow in coming to Christ, but I pray that others who hear it for the first time may run to him at once and be saved. Love for Christ at first sight is the wisest love of all. Oh, that he would now call those farthest off, that they may run to him, that he may be endowed with splendor!

Here is the test of all our teachings: Do they endow Christ with splendor? We can endow Christ with splendor in our lives by our holy living, our labors for his kingdom, our generosity in giving, and our trust of him for all our needs and concerns.

"Seek the LORD while he may be found; call on him while he is near." *(6)*

The time the Lord may be found is now. These are the happy gospel times when Christ may be found!

Jesus is near now. He is always near when the gospel is preached with a holy anointing, when Christians are praying, when hearts are breaking for the conversion of sinners, and when his Spirit is working in their hearts, helping them to repent of sin.

"Let the wicked forsake his way and the evil man his thoughts. Let him turn to the LORD, and he will have mercy on him, and to our God, for he will freely pardon." *(7)*

It is a bad way, a downward way. It is a way that will end in destruction. Do not follow it any longer. Forsake it now. Do not wait until you have fulfilled this or that goal. Run away from your old master, your old self, and your old way at once! "Christ Jesus came into the world to save sinners" (1 Tim. 1:15) but not to spare their sins.

Someone says, "I won't be hanged for my thoughts!" Maybe not, but you can be condemned for them. No one has really forsaken the way of wickedness until she or he hates the very thought of wickedness. If your thoughts run after evil, your tongues will soon speak evil, and your hands will soon do evil. In the previous clause God deals with the outward condition when he commands us to forsake our ways. Here he deals with the inward spirit when he commands us to forsake our thoughts. Conversion must show itself both in our hearts and in our outward lives.

The nonbeliever has wandered from the heavenly Father's house, so "let him turn to the LORD." Those who live apart from Christ are like the dove that flew away from Noah's ark and "could find no place to set its feet" until "it returned to Noah in the ark" (Gen. 8:9).

The King James Version translates the end of this verse, "for he will 'abundantly' pardon." God's pardon is abundant because it wells up from an infinitely deep fountain. Think of the countless people since Adam and Eve who have been forgiven. It requires abundant pardon to forgive so many sinners and their sins. The sins of our minds alone are as numerous as the gnats that swarm the air at night.

If a king should forgive rebels, it would take great mercy. But to take those rebels and make them his friends requires even greater mercy. Then to adopt them as his children and make them priests in his empire takes nothing less than abundant pardon.

God gives abundant pardon to cover our abundant sin. We provoked him abundantly and rejected his Word abundantly, but now God pardons us abundantly. Our sins may pile as high as the tallest mountains, but Jesus' blood, like Noah's flood, drowns them all. That is abundant pardon. Since God abundantly pardons, we ought to be abundantly grateful. Never think you can do too much for God.

"For my thoughts are not your thoughts, neither are your ways my ways," declares the Lord. *(8)*

God's thoughts are love, compassion, and tenderness. Our thoughts are forgetfulness, ingratitude, and hardheartedness. God considers our interests, but we do not think of his glory. God thinks of us as a shepherd thinks of a lost sheep or a father thinks of his prodigal child, but our thoughts are not the same. In its wandering state the sheep has no thought of returning to the shepherd. The rebellious child has no thought of love for his or her father.

God's thoughts of forgiveness, mentioned at the end of the previous verse, are also different from ours. Our thoughts are narrow. We find it hard to forgive great offenses, to forgive many offenses, to forgive many offenders, and to forgive completely. All this is very hard for us, but it is second nature to God. You may think that God cannot possibly mean that he will blot out your sins, but he does mean it!

God's thoughts will never become like ours, so ours must rise to his. But how? Only by the miracle of grace.

This is why the previous verse commands "the wicked" to "forsake his way." It is different from God's way. What a mercy it is to be led in God's ways! It is the entrance into a new life. No ordinary life can reach this elevation. The mind of God is given only to those who have the Son of God in their hearts.

"As the heavens are higher than the earth, so are my ways higher than your ways and my thoughts than your thoughts." (9)

Think of the biggest thought you ever had concerning God's forgiveness of sin. Try again. Let your thoughts rise higher still. Even then, God's thoughts are higher than yours "as the heavens are higher than the earth."

"As the rain and the snow come down from heaven, and do not return to it without watering the earth and making it bud and flourish, so that it yields seed for the sower and bread for the eater, so is my word that goes out from my mouth: It will not return to me empty, but will accomplish what I desire and achieve the purpose for which I sent it." (10–11)

If you believe this great promise, you will have the full benefit of it. Let the gracious rain of God's Word drop on you, and it will refresh you. Let this blessed snow fall on you, and it will melt into your heart and remain there to bless you forever. It will not return to God with its mission unfulfilled.

As for us who preach the Word or teach it in the Sunday school, we may have a full assurance that we will not labor in vain or spend our strength for nothing. Raindrops do not go on an errand that can fail. The snowflakes that fall to the earth accomplish the purpose for which they were sent. Much more will the purpose of God's Word be accomplished! It drops like gentle rain. The messages of mercy from the lips of the Lord himself fall like snowflakes, and they will not fall in vain. So our sermons ought to be full of Scripture, for it is not our word but God's Word, and it is sure to bring about the salvation of our hearers.

My first student, T. W. Medhurst, went out to preach Sunday after Sunday. He came to me and said, "I have been out preaching now for several months, and I have not seen one person trust in Christ."

I asked him rather sharply, "Do you expect God to bless you with conversions every time you open your mouth to preach?"

"Oh, no, sir!" he was quick to reply.

I answered, "Then that is why you do not get the blessing. God has promised that his Word will not return to him empty but will always fulfill the purpose for which he sent it. So you ought to look for a harvest and expect conversions."

"You will go out in joy and be led forth in peace; the mountains and hills will burst into song before you, and all the trees of the field will clap their hands." (12)

When there is joy in your heart, there will seem to be joy everywhere. When you receive Christ, you have put everything around you in its true position. The whole creation is a vast organ, and we put our tiny fingers on the keys and evoke the thunders of harmony to the praise of God.

The mountains do not look like they are singing, do they? The hills look as if their only music is the howling of the wild winds about their brows or the roaring of the wild beasts along their sides. But for you, thirsty one, "the mountains and hills will burst into song before you."

Trees seem to have little sympathy with weary hearts, but when weary hearts find peace with God in Christ, even the trees of the field seem to be in harmony with them, and they "clap their hands" in jubilant exultation.

"Instead of the thornbush will grow the pine tree, and instead of briers the myrtle will grow. This will be for the LORD's renown, for an everlasting sign, which will not be destroyed." (13)

This speaks of the change God brings about in the conversion of a sinner. The thornbush is everywhere today, pricking our feet and bruising our hands. In Genesis 3:17–18 thorns were part of the curse God put on this earth as a penalty for human sin. Here in Isaiah the thornbush represents the nonbeliever. You cannot enter some people's homes without seeing the marks of the curse. Listen to their speech, and they can hardly get through a sentence without some word that betrays the curse of sin.

The thorn serves no useful purpose. Almost everything has its use, but what is the use of thorns? What have lost people done for God? Thorns are fruitless things, and God gets neither prayer nor praise from ungodly people. They live in neglect of him. Thorns cut and bruise people who walk by, and nonbelievers, when unrestrained by grace, breathe out vengeance against God and his people.

Here we read that in place of the thornbush will grow the pine tree. This teaches that God works moral and spiritual transformations in our lives. What became of the thorns when the beautiful pine tree replaced them? God placed them on the bleeding brow of Christ. He has worn thorns as a crown!

Wherever God's grace begins to work, it cuts up briers and plants in their place the myrtle tree. Here again we see a poetic picture of conversion, and it leads to the Lord's renown. When the briers of sin are replaced by the myrtle of grace, people learn what God is like, the gracious power he has, and the goodness that comes from him.

This everlasting sign will be accepted only by Christians. "A wicked and adulterous generation asks for a miraculous sign" (Matt. 12:39), but the only sign God has given is his converting grace in the church. Better than miracles, we have the work of the Holy Spirit in the hearts of sinners. If any will not believe when the sign is sent to them, neither will they believe if someone rises from the dead (Luke 16:31). God's "everlasting sign . . . will not be destroyed."

King of the Jews and King of My Heart

*After Jesus was born in Bethlehem in Judea, during the time of King
Herod, Magi from the east came to Jerusalem and asked, "Where is
the one who has been born king of the Jews? We saw his star in the east
and have come to worship him." (1–2)*

Because the "king of the Jews" had now been born, he had to be
acknowledged. But at the same time he would be attacked. His birth
was in the days of another king, Herod, an Edomite who usurped
the throne of David. The world's kingdom is opposed to that of our
Lord. Wherever Jesus is born, there is sure to be a Herod in power.

It is amazing that Magi from the east should know that a great king
had been born and should come from so great a distance to worship
him. The world's wise are not often found bowing at the feet of Jesus.
When the wise seek our king, they are truly wise. These were devout
men to whom the stars spoke of God. An unusual star was understood by them to indicate the birth of the coming One for whom
many in all lands were looking. Stars might guide us if we were willing to be led. Lord Jesus, make everything speak to me of you, and
may I be truly led until I find you!

The Magi were not content to say, "We saw his star." They had
to see Christ himself. And when they saw him, they had to worship
him. What better thing can you and I do than worship Christ? The
wise men thought all other pursuits mattered little compared with
this. Lord, make all the wise worship you!

The Magi supposed that the king of the Jews would be born in
a palace in the metropolis of Jerusalem, but it pleased the heavenly
Father that everything about Jesus' birth should have the stamp of
lowliness. The poorest and humblest of people may understand that
Christ took on himself the nature not of the world's great ones but
of our common humanity. Hence Jesus was born of a lowly virgin,

cradled in a manger in Bethlehem, a city whose name means "House of Bread." How appropriate, for Jesus is the Bread of Life to us (John 6:35)!

The Magi supposed that the birth of Christ would be well known among the Jews, and so, when they reached Jerusalem, they inquired, "Where is the one who has been born king of the Jews?" When the heart is awakened to the love of Christ, it often dreams that everyone else feels an equal interest in him, but it is not so. The world is dead and cold to Christ. Some have said that the Magi meant to pay Jesus only the homage of a king. If that were true, why didn't they worship Herod, and why did Herod say that he wanted to worship Jesus (v. 8)? No, the Magi believed that he who was born king of the Jews was more than a human being. They had come to worship Christ as their God.

Whenever people fail to preach the gospel, do not be discouraged, because God can guide people to his Son by a star. When one pastor falls into sexual sin and another fights against the inspired truth of Scripture, remember that their apostasy will be their own loss, not the loss of Christ or of his church. God is not dependent on human lights, for he himself is the Shekinah light of heaven.

When King Herod heard this he was disturbed, and all Jerusalem with him. When he had called together all the people's chief priests and teachers of the law, he asked them where the Christ was to be born. "In Bethlehem in Judea," they replied, "for this is what the prophet has written: 'But you, Bethlehem, in the land of Judah, are by no means least among the rulers of Judah; for out of you will come a ruler who will be the shepherd of my people Israel.'" (3–6)

The Magi brought the best news ever told, yet it disturbed people. Herod is here called "King Herod." In that office he was the enemy of King Jesus. Anyone who is "disturbed" over Jesus is in a sad state. Herod was troubled about the kingship he had no right to possess, for he thought that if the king of the Jews had really come, it would mean the end of his own kingdom. Some, like Herod, are disturbed because they fear they will lose position and honor if Christianity makes progress. Many have an undefined fear that the presence of Jesus will deprive them of pleasure or call them to make unwilling sacrifices. O King of heaven, I am not disturbed by you. I am filled with joy!

See the influence of one person. When Herod was disturbed, all Jerusalem with him was also troubled, for this cruel prince delighted in shedding blood, and the darkness of his brow meant death to many. Unhappy Jerusalem, to be disturbed by the birth of the Savior! Unhappy people, to whom true godliness is weariness!

Does the gospel disturb you? Then I am afraid you must be of Herod's clan. It is a bad sign of your heart if a great blessing disturbs you. Only a bad stomach turns good meat to poison.

Think of this hypocrite studying his Bible. When worldly leaders dabble in theology, it signals no good to the truth. Herod among chief priests and teachers of the law is still Herod. Some people may become well instructed in their Bibles and yet be all the worse for what they have discovered. Like Herod, they make ill use of what they have learned. Or like these religious leaders, they may know much about the Lord Jesus and yet have no love for him.

The religious leaders were well versed in the Scriptures. They counted the very letters of the Word. They could tell which was the middle letter of the Old Testament. They were great at the letter, but they had missed the spirit! Many people know a great deal about the Bible who know nothing of it. The husks of Scripture yield small profit. We need to come to the kernel, the real corn, the spiritual meaning of the inspired Word of God.

The priests and teachers of the law were sharp to declare that Christ would be born in Bethlehem, and Jesus was born there. This fulfilled the prophecy of Micah 5:2, which had been given hundreds of years earlier. Though Bethlehem was a little city, Jesus' birth there made it famous. Jesus dignifies everything he touches. These scribes knew where to find the text about the Savior's birth, and they could put the finger on the spot on the map where he would be born, yet they did not know the King, nor did they care to find him. May it never be our case to master scriptural geography, prophecy, and theology and yet miss the Christ of whom Scripture speaks!

With joy we note that Jesus is here called "a ruler." You are a member of the spiritual Israel if he rules over you. Oh, that the day may soon come when the literal Israel will submit to the rule God has placed on Christ's shoulder!

Then Herod called the Magi secretly and found out from them the exact time the star had appeared. He sent them to Bethlehem and said, "Go and make a careful search for the child. As soon as you find him, report to me, so that I too may go and worship him." (7–8)

Herod half suspected that he would not see the Magi again, so he determined to get all the information he possibly could out of them. It is good to be an anxious inquirer, but Herod was a wicked one. Many people pry into holy things so they can ridicule them. What an evil diligence this is! When very private inquiries are made, we may suspect that something is wrong, and yet it is not always so. In any case, truth does not fear the light. Whether people inquire secretly or openly, we are ready to give them information about our Lord and everything that concerns him.

Murder was in Herod's heart, but pious pretenses were on his tongue. There is no worse sin than the one a person covers with the cloak of religion. How often under the pretense of worshiping Christ has the very truth of Christ been murdered. People invent new sacraments, new doctrines, new forms and ceremonies, all supposedly for the building up of the church and the glory of Jesus, but really they may stab at the heart of God's gospel and put the living truth to death. May neither you nor I be Herod's in hypocrisy! To promise to worship while intending to destroy is an everyday piece of deceit in our time.

The Magi never promised to return to Herod. They probably guessed that all this eager zeal was not quite as pure as it seemed, and their silence did not mean consent. We must not believe everyone who makes loud professions, nor must we do everything they ask us to do, otherwise we may help them in their evil plans.

After they had heard the king, they went on their way, and the star they had seen in the east went ahead of them until it stopped over the place where the child was. When they saw the star, they were overjoyed. On coming to the house, they saw the child with his mother Mary, and they bowed down and worshiped him. Then they opened their treasures and presented him with gifts of gold and of incense and of myrrh. And having been warned in a dream not to go back to Herod, they returned to their country by another route. (9–12)

Neither Herod with his hypocrisy nor Jerusalem with its troubles nor the scribes and priests with their knowledge of Scripture sought Christ. But none of those obstacles hindered the wise men from going to Bethlehem by themselves. When the wise men went on their way, they were wise to get out of Herod's vile company. The star reappeared when the tyrant disappeared. If you are wise, you will say, "I will find Christ alone, even if no one else will join me. If the ministers of the gospel are indifferent to me, I will still seek Jesus."

This star was not a wandering star or a shooting star but a guiding star, the kind the Magi had never seen before. It shined long enough in the western sky to guide them to Judea, then ceased to be visible, then appeared again as they left Jerusalem. We must not always expect to have visible signs to cheer us, but we are very glad when the Lord gives them to us. We seek not the star of inward feelings or outward signs but of Jesus himself. Then we have great joy when heavenly comfort shines into our souls.

Lord, if you show me a sign that promises blessing to me, I will rejoice. But if you show me yourself, I will be "filled with an inexpressible and glorious joy" (1 Peter 1:8).

Mark how the stars above as well as people below paid homage to the newborn King. Let us not be slow to adore the Savior! As the star "stopped over the place where the child was," so may our hearts never rest until they find the Lord Jesus!

The light of the star was taken from the Magi for a while, just as sometimes the delightful presence of God is withdrawn from his people. Then we walk by faith alone and not by sight, just as these men did. But oh, when the light comes back, we can feel what the Magi felt when they saw the star: "They were overjoyed."

The Magi were watchers of the stars, so God used a star to call them to his Son. Some of the disciples were fishers, and by means of an amazing catch of fish the Lord Jesus made them aware of his superior power and called them to be fishers of men (Luke 5:1-11). Are you engaged in business? Then surely you hear a voice saying, "Buy God's truth and do not sell it." Are you a baker? Then haven't you asked yourself, "Has my soul eaten the bread of heaven?" Are you a farmer? If so, hasn't God ever spoken to you and said, "Don't you wish that your heart were plowed and sown, like this field?" God's voice is everywhere! Listen to it!

Those who look for Jesus will see him. Those who truly see him will worship him. Those who worship him will dedicate everything they have to him. The wise men kept their treasure chests closed until they saw Jesus, and then they opened them. Let us keep our love and holy service for our Lord's eye and never wish to expose them to the world's gaze.

If ever there was an opportunity to worship Mary, this was it. But the three gifts of gold and of incense and of myrrh were presented not to Mary but to the child. When Jesus was dependent on his mother, why didn't the Magi say, "Ave Maria"? Because they were wise men.

Providentially the Magi brought the gold that Joseph would use to pay the expenses incurred in traveling to Egypt and supporting his family there until he could return to his home and business. God always takes care of his own children. According to an old saying, "Omnipotence has servants everywhere." Before the child travels to Egypt, oriental sages must pay his way.

It is good for us, like the Magi, to give Christ the best we have. Lord, you will have my worship and my gifts, for you are the only monarch of my soul. I will help your missionary cause, so that when you go to Africa with your gospel, my gifts may go with you.

Wise people are generous. But if you do not have gifts of gold and incense and myrrh, bring to Christ your faith, your repentance, and your love. Fall down before him and give him the reverence of your heart.

The wise men probably had already half suspected Herod, and the Lord in a dream led their thoughts further in the same direction. Wise men and women need to be warned by God, and when they are, they change their minds at once. Though these Magi had planned to return one way, they took another route. May we never be disobedient to a hint from God's throne. Along with the psalmist we can pray, "You guide me with your counsel" (Ps. 73:24).

When they had gone, an angel of the Lord appeared to Joseph in a dream. "Get up," he said, "take the child and his mother and escape to Egypt. Stay there until I tell you, for Herod is going to search for the child to kill him." (13)

Angels were busy in those days, for they had a special duty concerning their royal Master. Joseph's high office as guardian of the young child and his mother involved him in an anxious situation and drove him into exile from his country.

We cannot expect to serve the Lord and have an easy time of it. We must cheerfully journey across a desert if we have a duty to keep for our God. We must wait in banishment, if necessary, and never try to come back until our Lord sends us our passports. Our orders are the same as Joseph's in this verse: "Stay there until I tell you." As the Lord's servants we must wait for his word before we can make a move, whether to go to the foreign mission field or to come home. Waiting is hard work, especially in Egypt, but it is safe to wait until we have our marching orders.

So he got up, took the child and his mother during the night and left for Egypt, where he stayed until the death of Herod. And so was fulfilled what the Lord had said through the prophet: "Out of Egypt I called my son." (14–15)

Night journeys, both literal and spiritual, may fall to the lot of those who carry Jesus with them. Even the Son of God had to leave for Egypt like the rest of his family and stay there until he was called back. Let us not be surprised if we too have to go down to a spiritual Egypt in a hurry, go by night, and stay there for a long time. We also will be called out of there in the Lord's good time. The angel of the Lord who leads us into Egypt will bring us word to come out of it, for our times are in the Lord's hands (Ps. 31:15). Let us never forget that though the chosen must sometimes go into Egypt, they must also be brought out of it.

The end of verse 15, "Out of Egypt I called my son," is a quotation from Hosea 11:1. There it referred to Israel, the nation, as God's son. But here in Matthew 2:15 the saying found its deeper fulfillment in Jesus, the great Son of God. It applies also to all God's sons and daughters. We have to be called out of Egypt. By the blood of "Christ, our Passover lamb" (1 Cor. 5:7) we are saved and brought out of Egypt with a strong arm when God delivers us from our sins.

If Jesus had willed it, even as a child he could have blasted Herod, just as he did another Herod in later years, who "was eaten by worms and died" (Acts 12:23). Jesus could have sent a legion of angels to drive Herod off his throne if it had pleased him, but no violence was used. He chose a gentler course. When Jesus stands up to fight, he wars by nonresistance. He says, "My kingdom is not of this world. If it were, my servants would fight" (John 18:36). Jesus conquers by flight rather than by fight. In later years he taught his followers, "When you are persecuted in one place, flee to another" (Matt. 10:23). A fighting church is the Devil's church, but a suffering and enduring church belongs to Christ.

When Herod realized that he had been outwitted by the Magi, he was furious, and he gave orders to kill all the boys in Bethlehem and its vicinity who were two years old and under, in accordance with the time he had learned from the Magi. Then what was said through the prophet Jeremiah was fulfilled: "A voice is heard in Ramah, weeping and great mourning, Rachel weeping for her children and refusing to be comforted, because they are no more." (16–18)

With all his craftiness, Herod still missed his mark. He realized he had been made a fool of, though the Magi had no such intention. Proud people are quick to imagine insults. Herod was furious. He felt he had to kill this newborn King to save his crown. Therefore, he ordered the death of every boy in Bethlehem two years old and under, taking good measure so that no one might escape through a miscalculation of age. What did Herod care if a few babies were slain? He had to make sure that the little King was destroyed. He thought that a speedy and indiscriminate slaughter of all who had reached their second year would put him beyond all fear of his so-called rival.

Augustus said, "It is better to be Herod's hog than Herod's son." That was true, for Herod would not kill a hog, because he respected the Jewish ceremonies. Though he did not kill swine, he did not mind killing anyone who aroused his passion. Like Herod, people will go to great lengths to rid themselves of Jesus. They do not care how many children, men, or women are destroyed, as long as they can resist submitting to the kingdom of Christ and crush his holy cause in its infancy. Yet their rage cannot fulfill its purpose. The holy child is beyond their jurisdiction and their reach.

Our prince stepped along a pathway paved with prophecies, yet trouble followed him. The prophet Jeremiah foretold the weeping and great mourning over the innocent children slain by Herod. Jesus is the innocent cause of death of many innocent people. People say that Christianity has been the cause of cruelty and bloodshed. Honesty should compel them to admit that the blame rests not with Christianity but with the opposition to it. Would you blame Jesus because Herod tried to murder him and therefore made so many mothers weep over their dead babies?

Our Rachels today still weep, but these holy women who know the Lord Jesus do not say concerning their little ones, "They are no more." Christian women know that their children are, they know where they are, and they expect to meet them again in glory. Surely the mothers in this verse would have been comforted if they had known that though their little ones had been slain, the children's Friend had escaped and still lived to be the Savior of all who die before they are old enough to commit sin.

At the beginning of Jesus' life Herod tried to kill him, and at its end Judas betrayed him. Thus Jesus' life began and ended in sorrow.

After Herod died, an angel of the Lord appeared in a dream to Joseph in Egypt and said, "Get up, take the child and his mother and go to the land of Israel, for those who were trying to take the child's life are dead." (19–20)

An angel of the Lord appeared here again. Angels are still busy around us, God's other children. Joseph here was faithful to protect his honorable responsibility, even as the other Joseph protected Israel in Egypt (Gen. 45:7).

Note the order in which the family was arranged: "the child and his mother." The Lord Jesus was placed first. Roman Catholics, by contrast, say, "the Virgin and child." The angel was unwilling to mention Herod's name in this verse, but simply said, "Those who were trying to take the child's life are dead." Such a wretch did not deserve to be named by a holy angel. Herod had gone to his own place, and now God was bringing back his banished ones to their own place. The tyrant, instead of making Jesus die, himself died. With his sword in hand, he missed the young child, but without a sword the child's heavenly Father struck Herod down.

It is a relief to the world when some people die. It was certainly so in the case of Herod. Those who keep our king away from where God wants him are not likely to live long. Let us ponder the lessons of history concerning the king's enemies.

So he got up, took the child and his mother and went to the land of Israel. But when he heard that Archelaus was reigning in Judea in place of his father Herod, he was afraid to go there. Having been warned in a dream, he withdrew to the district of Galilee, and he went and lived in a town called Nazareth. So was fulfilled what was said through the prophets: "He will be called a Nazarene." (21–23)

Joseph obeyed God with no questions asked. He got up. As soon as he woke up, he began doing what the Lord through his angel had ordered him to do. He immediately made the trip and came into the land of Israel. In the same way, we should be quick to obey God. Joseph had fears about Judea, yet he did not follow his fears but went only as his guide from heaven directed him.

This Joseph was a dreamer, like his namesake (Gen. 37:19). He was also a practical man who turned his dreams into wise obedience. He came into the land of Israel, but he was allowed to go into the part that was under a gentler sway than that of Archelaus, who was no improvement on his father, Herod. He was a chip off the old block, and a chip of very hard wood, too, for he was equally cruel.

Galilee, a despised country where Gentiles mixed with the Jews, where darkness and ignorance reigned, was to be the land of our Lord's early days. He had a bond with the despised people, and he was educated in a rustic region among plain folk who had none of the fine manners of the towns.

Blessed King, the days of your youth were spent not in a palace but among the common multitude, and you still delight to bless them! I ask you to withdraw to the district of Galilee today and live with me!

In a prophecy of the coming Messiah, Isaiah 11:1 said that a "shoot" would come up from the withered stump of Jesse, David's father. The word translated "shoot" is the Hebrew *netser*. When the dynasty of David was like a tree cut down and only the stump of it was left, a *netser* sprang up out of it. So Jesus was found living in a city whose name was built on the same root: "Nazareth." Certainly Jesus has been called a Nazarene both by Jews and violent unbelievers. Many a time his fierce adversary, spitting on the ground in disgust, has hissed out the name "Nazarene" as if it were the climax of contempt. Yet, oh, Nazarene, you have triumphed!

Jesus of Nazareth is the greatest name in the world. Oh, Lord, my King, as you are dishonored by your foes, so will you be adored by your friends with all their hearts and all their souls! While others despise you by calling you the Nazarene, we worship you by calling you Jesus, Yahweh, King of Kings and Lord of Lords!

Jesus' Sermon on the Mount—Part 1

Now when he saw the crowds, he went up on a mountainside and sat down. His disciples came to him, and he began to teach them, saying: (1-2)

It was suitable that such elevated ethics should be taught from a mountainside. Those who desired to follow Jesus as disciples gathered closely around the seated rabbi, who held the throne of instruction in their midst. Then in outer circles the multitudes stood to listen. They were attracted by Christ's love and willingness to bless them.

Even when Jesus' mouth was closed, he taught by his life. Yet he did not withhold the testimony of his lips. When people address others fervently, they neither mumble nor stumble but speak distinctly, opening their mouths. When Jesus opens his mouth, let us open our ears and hearts.

"Blessed are the poor in spirit, for theirs is the kingdom of heaven." (3)

The King's first laws were blessings. He began his teaching with them. The Old Testament ends with a curse (Mal. 4:6); the New Testament opens here with a blessing. Jesus is a cloud full of rain that pours out blessings on those under him. The moment we begin to know Christ, we begin to be blessed. The more we know him, the more blessed we become.

Spiritual poverty is both commanded and commended. It is the basis of Christian experience. No one begins properly who has not felt a poverty of spirit—a lowliness of heart and an absence of selfishness. This is sweet poverty. Even to this first sign of grace is the kingdom given as a present possession: "Theirs is the kingdom of heaven."

The poor in spirit do not vainly think they trust Christ because they repent. Instead, they trust Christ to make them repent. They do not come to Christ because they have broken hearts. They come to him that he may give them broken hearts. They do not come to Christ because they are fit to come. They come because they are unfit. Their unfitness is their fitness. Their qualification is their lack of qualification.

The poor in spirit seem to have nothing, but since "theirs is the kingdom of heaven," they have everything. People who think the least of themselves are those of whom God thinks the most. If you are poor in spirit, you are rich in God's sight.

"Blessed are those who mourn, for they will be comforted." (4)

These seem worse off than the merely poor in spirit, for they mourn. They are a stage higher, though they seem a stage lower. The way to rise in the kingdom is to sink in ourselves.

These people are grieved by sin and tried by the evils of the times, but for them spiritual rest and joy are promised. Those who laugh about sin will lament, but those who sorrow over sin will sing. How great a blessing is sorrow, since it gives room for the Lord to minister his comfort! Our griefs are blessed, for they are our points of contact with the divine Comforter. The beatitude reads like a paradox, but it is true, as some of us know very well. Our times of mourning have brought us more comfort than our days of mirth.

"Blessed are the meek, for they will inherit the earth." (5)

It looks as if the meek will be pushed out of the world, but they will inherit the earth. Wolves devour sheep, yet there are more sheep in the world than wolves, and the sheep continue to multiply and feed in green pastures.

Because the meek are lowly minded, they are ready to give up their part in the earth. Therefore it will come back to them. They neither boast nor argue nor exult over others, yet they are heirs of all the good that God has created on the earth. In their meekness they are like their King, and they will reign with him. The Promised Land is for the tribes of the meek. Before them the Canaanites will be driven out. They have the best of this world who think least of it and least of themselves.

"Blessed are those who hunger and thirst for righteousness, for they will be filled." (6)

Those who hunger and thirst for righteousness are not full of their own righteousness. They pine for the holiness of Christ. They long to serve God. They are anxious to spread the good news of Christ. Such is their longing for goodness that it seems as if both the appetites of hunger and thirst are concentrated in their one passion for righteousness.

The blessing comes when the hunger for righteousness kills worldly hungers. One master passion, like Aaron's staff, swallows up all the rest (Ex. 7:12). These people hunger and thirst for righteousness, and therefore they are done with the craving of lust, the greed of avarice, the passion of hatred, and the pining of ambition.

Where God works such an insatiable desire, we may be sure he will satisfy it and fill it to the brim. When God fills people with his fullness, they are truly full. Nothing in this world can fill an immortal soul, and since it is written, "They will be filled," we look forward with joyful confidence to a heaven of holiness with which we shall be eternally satisfied.

"Blessed are the merciful, for they will be shown mercy." (7)

The merciful forgive and are forgiven. They judge mercifully, and they will not be condemned. They help the needy, and they will be helped in their need. What they are to others, God will be to them. Some have to labor hard with their thrift to be kind, but the blessing lies not only in doing a merciful act but in having a merciful attitude. Followers of Jesus must be people of mercy, for they have found mercy, and mercy has found them. Since we look for mercy from the Lord at the judgment, we must show mercy now.

"Blessed are the pure in heart, for they will see God." (8)

Dirty hearts make our eyes dim to see God. To clear the eye we must cleanse the heart. Only purity has any idea of God or any true vision of him. It is a great reward to be able to see God. There are no pure hearts on earth unless the Lord has made them so, and no one will see God in heaven who has not been purified by grace while here below. "Create in me a pure heart, O God" (Ps. 51:10) so that I may see you both now and forever!

"Blessed are the peacemakers, for they will be called sons of God." (9)

These people are not only passively peaceful, like the meek who keep the peace, but actively peacemakers by endeavoring to end wars and arguments. These not only are the children of the peace-loving God but also come to be "called" so, for people are struck by their likeness to their Father. This is how we prove to ourselves and others that we are God's children. People of peace are the children of the God of peace, and their Father's blessing rests on them.

This seventh beatitude is a very high and glorious one. Let us endeavor to obtain it. May we never be peacebreakers but always peacemakers. Yet we must not cry, "Peace, peace . . . when there is no peace" (Jer. 6:14). The verse before this speaks of purity, and now this one of peace. First pure, then peace-loving. This is God's order (James 3:17), and it should be ours, too.

"Blessed are those who are persecuted because of righteousness, for theirs is the kingdom of heave." (10)

This is the exclusive blessing of God's elect, and it stands up in the list of honor. The only respect that wickedness can pay to righteousness is to persecute it. Those who in the first blessing were poor in spirit are here despised as well as poverty-stricken. In this they get a new royal charter that for the second time ensures to them "the kingdom of heaven."

The Lord's Daniels are hated not because of any personal fault but simply because of their godly characters. But they are blessed by what looks like a curse. Ishmael mocks Isaac, but Isaac still has the inheritance, and Ishmael is cast out (Gal. 4:21–31). It is a gift from God to be allowed to suffer for his name (Phil. 1:29). So may we be helped to rejoice in Christ's cross when we are honored by being reviled for his name's sake.

"Blessed are you when people insult you, persecute you and falsely say all kinds of evil against you because of me. Rejoice and be glad, because great is your reward in heaven, for in the same way they persecuted the prophets who were before you." (11–12)

Persecution of the tongue is more common but no less cruel than that of the hand. Slander is unscrupulous and indulges in accusations of every kind. "All kinds of evil" leaves nothing out. No crime is too base to be laid at the door of the innocent. Nor will the persecutor have any hesitation as to the vileness of the charge. The rule seems to be, "Throw plenty of mud, and some of it will stick."

To be blessed, the slander against us must be false and for Christ's sake. There is no blessing to the cause of Christ if we are truthfully criticized.

Under this grievous trial Christians are to overflow with joy, for thus they are elevated to the rank of the prophets. Upon them the storm of falsehood beat with terrible fury. "They were stoned; they were sawed in two; they were put to death by the sword" (Heb. 11:37). But the honor of suffering with the prophets for the Lord's sake is so great that it may well reconcile us to all it involves.

There is a succession of persecutors and a succession of saints ordained to glorify the Lord in the fires. To this succession it is our high privilege to belong, and we are happy it is so. Our joy and gladness are to exceed all ordinary bounds when we are honored with the decoration of the iron cross. If we are persecuted with the prophets, we will also reign with them.

"You are the salt of the earth. But if the salt loses its saltiness, how can it be made salty again? It is no longer good for anything, except to be thrown out and trampled by men." (13)

Thus Jesus spoke to those whom he enrolled in his kingdom. In their character there is a preserving force to keep the rest of society from utter corruption. If they were not scattered among people, the race would putrefy. But if they are Christians in name only, and the real power is gone, nothing can save them, and they are of no use whatever to those among whom they mingle.

Here is a secret to the believer's power—savor. It is not easy to define, but it is absolutely essential to usefulness. Worldly people may be of some use even if they fail in certain respects, but a counterfeit Christian is "no longer good for anything," utterly useless to anybody and everybody. Complete rejection awaits that person, who will be "thrown out and trampled by men." That person's religion makes a footpath for fashion or for scorn, as this world may happen to take it. In either case it is no preservative, for it does not even preserve itself from contempt.

This teaches the security of the believer, for if the savor of divine grace could be completely gone from a person, it could never be restored. The text is very clear about that. What unscriptural nonsense to talk of a person being born again, losing the divine life, and then getting it again! Regeneration does not fail. If it did, the person must be forever hopeless. One could not be born again and again and again. The case would be beyond the reach of mercy. Still, even we Christians should beware of forgetting our purpose for doing.

The great lesson is that if grace itself fails to save us, nothing else can be done for us. You can salt meat but not salt. If grace fails, everything fails. If we cease to glorify God, we are like a pencil that does not write or a watch that does not tell time. We are good for nothing.

Gracious Master, do not permit me to try any experience as to how far I may lose my savor, but always keep me full of grace and truth.

"You are the light of the world. A city on a hill cannot be hidden. Neither do people light a lamp and put it under a bowl. Instead they put it on its stand, and it gives light to everyone in the house. In the same way, let your light shine before men, that they may see your good deeds and praise your Father in heaven." (14–16)

The Bible is not the light of the world; it is the light of the church. The world does not read the Bible, but it does read Christians.

As light, we are to remove the darkness of ignorance, sin, and sorrow. Christ has lit us that we may enlighten the world. We must not hide our faith. God intends his grace to be as conspicuous as a city built on the top of a mountain. To try to hide his Spirit is as foolish as to put a lamp under a bowl. The lamp should be seen by everyone in the house, and so should the Christian's graces. Household piety is the best piety. If our light is not seen in the house, we have none. Candles are meant for living rooms and bedrooms. Let us not cover up the light of grace.

In fact we cannot be hidden if the Lord has truly built us on the hill of his love. Neither can we live in darkness if God has lit us and made us lamps. Since you will be seen, make sure you are worth seeing.

The light is ours, but the glory is for our Father in heaven. We shine because we have light, and we are seen because we shine. We shine best before others by good works. True shining is silent but also useful. Angels glorify God whom they see, and people are forced to glorify God whom they do not see when they mark the good deeds of his saints. We need not object to be seen, though we are not to wish to be seen. Since people will be sure to see our virtues, if we possess any, let us be sure that all the glory goes to our Lord, to whom it is entirely due. "Not to us, O LORD, not to us but to your name be the glory" (Ps. 115:1).

"Do not think that I have come to abolish the Law or the Prophets; I have not come to abolish them but to fulfill them. I tell you the truth, until heaven and earth disappear, not the smallest letter, not the least

*stroke of a pen, will by any means disappear from the Law until every-
thing is accomplished. Anyone who breaks one of the least of these commandments and teaches others to do the same will be called least in the
kingdom of heaven, but whoever practices and teaches these commands
will be called great in the kingdom of heaven. For I tell you that unless
your righteousness surpasses that of the Pharisees and the teachers of
the law, you will certainly not enter the kingdom of heaven." (17–20)*

Jesus did not come to improve or annul the Old Testament but
to confirm it. He knew nothing of modern criticism. He established
in its deepest sense everything written in holy Scripture. He was
himself the fulfillment and substance of the types, commands, and
prophecies of the Law and the Prophets.

Not a syllable will become broken down. Even to the smallest letters, the dot of every i and the crossing of every t in the Law will
outlast the creation. The Old Testament is as sacredly guarded as the
New. "The word of the Lord stands forever" (1 Peter 1:25).
Modern critics try to deny the inspiration of this sacred book or
some of its verses, but we cannot do that. Those who read the Bible
to find fault with it will soon discover that it finds fault with them.

It is vain to teach God's commandments without first doing
them. If a teacher's example cannot be safely followed, it will be
unsafe to trust her or his words. Jesus' commands are eternal. If anyone should teach that any command of his is no longer in effect,
that person will lose rank. The aristocracy of Christ's kingdom is
ordered according to obedience. Neither birth, knowledge, nor success will make a person great, but only humble and precise obedience both in word and in deed.

The Lord Jesus did not set up a milder law, nor will he allow any
of his servants to presume to do so. Our King fulfills the ancient
law, and his Spirit creates in us a desire to obey the unchangeable
statutes of righteousness.

Lord, make me a loyal subject of your kingdom, and may I both
practice and teach your commandments. Whether I am little or great
on earth, make me great in obedience to you.

The Pharisees and the teachers of the law were supposed to be
righteous beyond everyone else. But Christ said we must surpass
them. Their righteousness was all an outward show. At the heart
level they were corrupt. Believers are not to be worse in conduct but
far better than the most precise legalists. In our hearts and our
behavior we are to be superior to the law-boasters.

The kingdom is not for rebels but for those who show exact obedience. It not only requires in us holiness, reverence, integrity, and

purity but also works all these in our hearts and lives. The gospel does not give us outward liberty to sin because of the superior excellence of a supposed inner sanctity. Rather, it produces outward holiness through working in our inmost souls a glorious freedom in the law of the Lord.

What a king we have in Jesus! What kind of people we ought to be as members of his holy kingdom! How careful we ought to be to obey our Father's revealed will! How determined to allow no trifling with the Law and the Prophets!

"You have heard that it was said to the people long ago, 'Do not murder, and anyone who murders will be subject to judgment.' But I tell you that anyone who is angry with his brother will be subject to judgment. Again, anyone who says to his brother, 'Raca,' is answerable to the Sanhedrin. But anyone who says, 'You fool!' will be in danger of the fire of hell." (21–22)

Antiquity is often pleaded as an authority, but our King made short work of "the people long ago." He began with one of their alterations of his Father's Law. They added to the sacred oracles. The first part of the saying that our Lord quoted was divine, but it was dragged down to a low level by the addition about the human court and the murderer's liability to appear there. It thus became more of a proverb to people than an inspired utterance from the mouth of God.

Its meaning as God spoke it had a far wider range than when the offense was restrained to actual killing, which was the only kind that could be brought before a human court. To make a command narrow is to annul it. We do not have a license to do this even with antiquity. Better the whole truth newly stated than an old falsehood in ancient language.

Murder lies within anger, for we wish harm to the person or even wish he or she did not exist. This is to kill that person in desire. God sees the emotions from which acts of hatred may spring, and he calls us to account as much for the angry feeling as for the murderous act.

Words also come under the same condemnation. We shall be judged for what we say to others. To call a person "Raca," which means "a worthless person," is to kill that person's reputation. And to say, "You fool!" is to kill a person's noble character. In first-century Judaism you could take a person to court for using these words. But even worse, the hatred that spits out such words is still liable to the punishment given by the highest court of the universe: "the fire of hell."

Thus our Lord and King restores the law of God to its true force and warns us that it denounces not only the outward act of killing but every thought, feeling, and word that would tend to injure a brother or sister by contempt.

What a sweeping law this is! My conscience might have been easy as to the command, "Do not murder," but if anger is murder, I can answer it only in the words of Psalm 51:14: "Save me from blood-guilt, O God, the God who saves me."

"Therefore, if you are offering your gift at the altar and there remember that your brother has something against you, leave your gift there in front of the altar. First go and be reconciled to your brother; then come and offer your gift." (23–24)

Hypocrites would excuse their sin on the grounds that they brought sacrifices to make atonement, but our Lord wants us to reconcile with others before we present the offerings. We ought to worship God thoughtfully. If you remember that someone has something against you, stop. It is much easier to go to the person who has wronged you than to the one you have wronged. We easily remember if we have something against someone else, but now the memory is to be turned the other way. Only when we have remembered our wrongdoings and made reconciliation can we hope for acceptance with the Lord. The rule is: first peace with people, then acceptance with God. If you have wronged another, pause from your worship and seek reconciliation.

"Settle matters quickly with your adversary who is taking you to court. Do it while you are still with him on the way, or he may hand you over to the judge, and the judge may hand you over to the officer, and you may be thrown into prison. I tell you the truth, you will not get out until you have paid the last penny." (25–26)

In all disagreements, be eager for peace. Leave strife behind before you begin talking with the other person. In lawsuits seek speedy and peaceful settlements. In our Lord's day this was often the best way, and it is usually so now. Better lose your rights than get into the hands of those who will only fleece you in the name of justice and hold you fast as long as an appearance of a demand can stand against you or another penny can be extracted from you. In a country where justice meant robbery, it was wisdom to be robbed and make no complaint. Even in our own time, a lean settlement is better than a fat lawsuit. Many go to court to get wool who come out closely shorn. Carry on no angry suits in court, but make peace as quickly as you can.

Some debts we cannot repay to "the last penny." And there is a prison that no one will come out of. God grant that we will never know what it is to be shut up in that dreadful dungeon!

"You have heard that it was said, 'Do not commit adultery.' But I tell you that anyone who looks at a woman lustfully has already committed adultery with her in his heart. If your right eye causes you to sin, gouge it out and throw it away. It is better for you to lose one part of your body than for your whole body to be thrown into hell. And if your right hand causes you to sin, cut it off and throw it away. It is better for you to lose one part of your body than for your whole body to go into hell." (27–30)

Here the divine law against adultery is shown to refer not only to the criminal act but even to the desire, imagination, or passion that would suggest such a sin. So it is with every commandment. They are like stars. When seen with the naked eye, they appear to be brilliant points. But if we could draw near to them, we would see that they are vast worlds.

What a King is ours, who stretches his scepter over the realm of our inward lusts! How sovereignly he puts it: "But I tell you. . . ." Who but a divine person has authority to speak like this? His word is law. So it ought to be, since Jesus touches vice at the fountainhead and forbids uncleanness in the heart. If sin were not allowed in the mind, it would never reveal itself in the body. This, therefore, is an excellent way of dealing with the evil. But how searching! How condemning! Irregular looks, unchaste desires, and strong passions are of the very essence of adultery.

Who can claim a lifelong freedom from them? Yet these are the things that defile a person. Lord, purge them out of my nature, and make me pure from the inside out.

We are to avoid not just sin but anything that leads to it. If adultery is forbidden, so is the glance with which adultery starts. The cause of sin is to be given up as well as the sin itself. It is not sinful to have an eye, but if the eye of knowledge leads us to sin, it becomes the cause of evil, and it must be put to death. I am to get rid of anything, however harmless, that leads me to do or think or feel wrongly, as if it were in itself an evil thing.

Though this involves deprivation, yet I must dispense with it, since even a serious loss in one direction is far better than losing the whole person. Better a blind saint than a clear-seeing sinner. To be thrown into hell is too great a risk to run just to indulge the evil eye of lust or curiosity.

Many Christians, if the right hand causes them to sin, in effect tie it up in a sling. But that is not obeying the command of Christ. We are to make a clean sweep of anything that leads us to do wrong. The cause of sin may be more active than mental, as the hand is more active than the eye, but we are better off hindered in our work than enticed by temptation. The most dexterous hand must not be spared if it encourages us to do evil. Just because a certain thing may make us clever and successful does not mean we should allow it. If it proves to be the frequent cause of our falling into sin, we must be done with it and place ourselves at a disadvantage in our careers rather than ruin our lives by sin.

Holiness is to be our first goal. Everything else must take a secondary place. The right eye and the right hand are no longer right if they lead us to do wrong. Even hands and eyes must go that we may not offend our God with them. Still, we must not read this literally and mutilate our bodies, as some foolish fanatics have done. The real meaning is clear enough.

Lord, I love you better than my eyes and hands. Let me never hesitate for a moment to give up everything for you!

"It has been said, 'Anyone who divorces his wife must give her a certificate of divorce.' But I tell you that anyone who divorces his wife, except for marital unfaithfulness, causes her to become an adulteress, and anyone who marries the divorced woman commits adultery" *(31–32).*

This time our King quotes and condemns a permissive law of the Jews. Men thought that if they told their wives the marriage was over, the divorce was final. But Moses insisted on "a certificate of divorce" so that angry passions might have time to cool and that the divorce, if it must come, might be performed with caution and legal formality. Divorce was tolerated because the Jews' "hearts were hard" (Matt. 19:8). It was never God's perfect will.

Therefore, our Lord forbade divorce "except for marital unfaithfulness" or adultery. The state should recognize that the adulterer severs the one-flesh bond between a husband and wife. Our Lord would never have tolerated the laws that grant divorce on the grounds of irreconcilable differences. A person who divorces for any cause other than adultery and remarries commits adultery before God, despite what any human law may say. Thus Jesus gave a sanctity to marriage, and human laws ought not to violate it.

Let us not be among those who seek to deform the marriage laws under the pretense of reforming them. Our Lord knows better than our modern social reformers. We do well to leave God's laws alone, for we will never discover any better laws.

"Again, you have heard that it was said to the people long ago, 'Do not break your oath, but keep the oaths you have made to the Lord.' But I tell you, Do not swear at all: either by heaven, for it is God's throne; or by the earth, for it is his footstool; or by Jerusalem, for it is the city of the Great King. And do not swear by your head, for you cannot make even one hair white or black. Simply let your 'Yes' be 'Yes,' and your 'No,' 'No'; anything beyond this comes from the evil one." (33–37)

False oaths were outlawed by the Jews, but now every kind of oath has been forbidden by our Lord Jesus. He told his followers simply to say yes or no. There is no evading the plain sense of this passage. Every oath, however solemn or true, is forbidden to a follower of Jesus. Whether in court or out of it, the rule is, "Do not swear at all." Yet in this Christian country we make oaths everywhere, and especially among lawmakers. Our legislators begin their office by taking an oath, but for those who obey the law of the Savior's kingdom a simple yes or no is the bond of truth.

Bad people cannot be trusted on their oath, and good people speak the truth without an oath. People who can't be believed on their word certainly can't be believed on their oath. When people tell a lie, the next thing they usually do is swear they told the truth. When Peter lied, saying he did not know Christ, he took an oath that he was telling the truth (Matt. 26:69–75). So why must we preserve the needless taking of oaths? Christians should not yield to an evil custom, however great the pressure put on them. They should abide by the plain command of their Lord and King.

"You have heard that it was said, 'Eye for eye, and tooth for tooth.' But I tell you, Do not resist an evil person. If someone strikes you on the right cheek, turn to him the other also. And if someone wants to sue you and take your tunic, let him have your cloak as well. If someone forces you to go one mile, go with him two miles. Give to the one who asks you, and do not turn away from the one who wants to borrow from you." (38–42)

This law was founded in justice and worked far more fairly than the modern system of fines, for that method allows the rich to offend with comparative impunity. But when the law of eye for eye became the rule to be carried out by individuals, it fostered revenge, and our Savior would not tolerate that. A good law in court may be a very bad custom in personal relationships. Our loving King would have private dealings ruled by the spirit of love not by the rule of law.

Nonresistance and mercy are to be the rule among Christians. We are to endure personal abuse without coming to blows. We are to be the anvil when wicked people are the hammers. Thus we will overcome by patient forgiveness. In our everyday lives we do not follow the rule of the courts but the rule of the Cross and the all-enduring Savior. Yet many regard this as fanatical and even cowardly. The Lord our King would have us conquer by mighty patience. Can we do it? How can we prove we are Christ's servants if we do not show his patient spirit?

Let this person have all he or she asks, and more. It is better to lose a suit of clothes than be drawn into a lawsuit. The courts in our Lord's day were vicious, and his disciples were advised to endure wrong sooner than appeal to judges. Our own courts often furnish the surest method of solving a difficulty by authority, and we have known them to prevent strife. Yet even in a country where justice can be received, we are not to resort to law for every personal wrong. We should rather endure wrong than be forever crying out, "I'll sue you for this!"

At times this same rule of self-sacrifice may require us to take steps toward legal appeal, so that we may stop injuries that would fall heavily on others. But we ought to forego our own advantage when the main motive would be a proud desire for self-vindication.

Lord, give me a patient spirit, so that I may not seek to take my own revenge, even when I have a right to do so.

Governments in those days demanded forced service through their petty officers. Christians were to do twice as much as they asked rather than provoke ill words and anger. We ought not to evade taxation but stand ready to render to Caesar his due. *Yield* is our watchword. To stand up against force is not exactly our part. We may leave that to others. How few believe the patient, nonresistant doctrine of our King!

Be generous. A miser is no follower of Jesus. Discretion is to be used in our giving, lest we encourage laziness in others. But the general rule is, "Give to the one who asks you." This is the spirit of the Christian—to live with a view of doing service. Sometimes a loan may be more useful than a gift. Do not refuse it to those who will use it well. We are to be ready to help the needy by a gift or a loan, and we are not likely to err by excess in either direction.

"You have heard that it was said, 'Love your neighbor and hate your enemy.' But I tell you: Love your enemies and pray for those who persecute you, that you may be sons of your Father in heaven. He causes his sun to rise on the evil and the good, and sends rain on the righteous and the unrighteous. If you love those who love you, what reward will you get? Are not even the tax collectors doing that? And if you greet only your brothers, what are you doing more than others? Do not even pagans do that? Be perfect, therefore, as your heavenly Father is perfect." (43–48)

In this case a command of Scripture, "Love your neighbor," had a human opposite put on it by depraved minds: "and hate your enemy." Many professing Christians do not live up even to that. They hate their enemies and despise their neighbors.

The Jews assumed hatred for their enemies grew naturally out of the scriptural teaching of loving their neighbors. But their new teaching was wicked and a sad crime against the Word of God. The Holy Spirit will father only his own words. The "enemy" the Jews were commanded to "hate" was, in fact, their neighbor! Love is now the universal law, and our King who commanded it is the pattern of it. He will not see it narrowed down and placed in a context of hate. May grace prevent us from falling into this error!

It is our job to persist in loving, even if others persist in hatred. We are to render blessings for curses and prayers for persecutions. We are no longer enemies to anyone but friends to everyone. We do not merely cease to hate and then live in a cold neutrality, but we love where hatred seemed inevitable. We bless where the old nature told us to curse.

When this is seen in our practice, people will stand in awe of us. The theory may be ridiculed, but the practice is counted so surprising that people attribute it to a godlike quality in Christians. They admit that we are daughters and sons of our Father in heaven. Only the children of God can bless the unthankful and the evil, for in daily providence the Lord does this on a great scale, and no one but his children will imitate him.

To do good for the sake of the good done and not because of the character of the person benefited is a noble imitation of God. If the Lord sent the fertilizing shower on the land only of the saints, drought would deprive many of all hope of a harvest. We also must do good to evil people, or we will have a narrow sphere, our hearts will contract, and our child/parent relationship to the good God will be put in doubt.

Any non-Christian will love those who love him or her. Even tax collectors and the scum of the earth can rise to this shoddy virtue. Saints cannot be content with such a lowly style. "Love for love" is human, but "Love for hatred" is Christlike. Shall we not desire to live up to our high calling?

We are not to confine our greetings to those near and dear to us. Courtesy should be wide and still sincere, though it is general. We should speak kindly to all and treat every person as a brother or sister.

Christ can expect us to do more than others because we claim more. Claims should always be supported by facts. We also have more than others by virtue of our new birth in Christ. We also can do more than others. As Scripture says, "I can do everything through him who gives me strength" (Phil. 4:13).

Just what does Jesus expect us to do "more than others"? First, we are to set a more godly example. Our Lord has told us in this chapter that we are "the salt of the earth" (v. 13) and "the light of the world" (v. 14). Nonbelievers cannot live up to those descriptions.

Second, we are to excel others in purity, according to verses 21–30. Others may refrain from committing murder and adultery, but for us anger is a crime, and a lustful thought is a sin.

Third, we are to be more truthful than others, according to verses 33–37. Others must take an oath to prove their word, but we are to speak the truth because we can say nothing else.

Fourth, in verses 43–48, we must do more than others when it comes to love. Anyone will shake hands with an old friend, and even a dog will greet a dog. But we must love even our enemies and pray for those who persecute us.

"These are great responsibilities," you say.

Yes, but we have a great Spirit to help us!

Love is the bond of perfection. If we have perfect love, it will form perfect characters in us. Our goal is perfection like God's, and the way to attain it is to abound in love. Scriptural perfection is attainable, if not in degree, at least in proportion. A Christian's character may be "mature and complete, not lacking anything" (James 1:4), and yet such a believer will be the very first to admit that the grace within is in its infancy. Though that grace is as perfect as a child in all of his or her parts, it has not yet reached the perfection of full-grown adulthood.

What a standard is set before us by our perfect King! Lord, give what you command, then both the grace and the glory will be yours alone!

Jesus' Sermon on the Mount—Part 2

"Be careful not to do your 'acts of righteousness' before men, to be seen by them. If you do, you will have no reward from your Father in heaven." (1)

Our King here set his people right in the matter of "acts of righteousness." He took it for granted that we would do them. How could we be in Christ's kingdom if we did not? Acts of righteousness may be given publicly but not for the sake of publicity. It is important that we have a right goal, for if we are motivated by a wrong goal, our success will be a failure. If we do acts of righteousness to be seen, we will be seen, and that will be all there is to it. "You will have no reward from your Father in heaven." We will lose the only reward worth having. Even "acts of righteousness," if done for human applause, are spoiled.

But if we do them to please our Father, we will find the reward in his hands. When it comes to motive, we must "be careful," for no one does right without carefully trying to do so. Our acts of righteousness should be a holy duty, carefully done, not for our pleasure but for God's. Ask yourself, "How much have I done in the way my King commands?"

"So when you give to the needy, do not announce it with trumpets, as the hypocrites do in the synagogues and on the streets, to be honored by men. I tell you the truth, they have received their reward in full. But when you give to the needy, do not let your left hand know what your right hand is doing, so that your giving may be in secret. Then your Father, who sees what is done in secret, will reward you." (2-4)

We must not copy the loud charity of vain people. They are hypocrites who show off their gifts. Their goal is to be seen by people.

They are seen, and they get the reward they are after. But that is all their reward. They will never have any further reward in heaven. We cannot expect two rewards for the same action. If we have it now, we will not have it in heaven. Unrewarded charity alone will count in the record books of God.

Ours is an advertising age, and many are saying, "Look at my generosity!" Those who have Jesus as their king must wear his garment of humility, not the scarlet trappings of a purse-proud generosity that blows its own trumpet not only in the streets but even in the churches. To stand with a penny in one hand and a trumpet in the other is the posture of a hypocrite. "To be honored by men" is something that can be bought, but to be honored by God is far different.

Seek secrecy for your good deeds. Do not even see your own virtues. Hide from yourself all the admirable things you do, for the proud thought of your own generosity may tarnish all your charitable gifts. Keep them so secret that even you are hardly aware you are doing anything worthy of praise. Let God be present, and you will have enough of an audience. He will reward you as one who saw what you did and knew you did it entirely for him. If God rewards you, what a reward it will be! Any praise from his lips and any reward from his hands will be of priceless value.

Lord, help me when I am doing good to keep my left hand out of it, that I may have no sinister motive and no desire to win a present reward of praise from people.

"And when you pray, do not be like the hypocrites, for they love to pray standing in the synagogues and on the street corners to be seen by men. I tell you the truth, they have received their reward in full. But when you pray, go into your room, close the door and pray to your Father, who is unseen. Then your Father, who sees what is done in secret, will reward you. And when you pray, do not keep on babbling like pagans, for they think they will be heard because of their many words. Do not be like them, for your Father knows what you need before you ask him." (5–8)

Jesus also took it for granted that we would pray. No one will be in the kingdom of heaven who does not pray. A prayerless person is a Christless person.

Those with our Lord knew what he meant by the "hypocrites." They had often seen the proud man standing in public places repeating his prayers. Very likely they had also felt bound to hold such people in high regard for their superior sanctity. But here our Lord unmasked these hypocrites and showed us what they really are. They were not seekers of God but seekers of popularity. They twisted even devotion to God into a means of exalting themselves. They chose places and times that would make their prayers conspicuous. The synagogues and the street corners suited them admirably, for the goal was "to be seen by men." They were seen. They got what they were after. And that was their reward, and nothing more. Their prayer died where it was offered.

We ought to pray in the synagogues and on the street corners, but it is wrong to pray there to be seen by others. We should not be ashamed of our prayers, but neither should we put them on public display. They are intended for God's eye and ear.

Lord, let me never be so profane as to pray to you with the intent of getting praise from people.

Be alone. Enter into a little room into which no one else may intrude. Keep out every visitor by shutting the door, and there and then pour out your requests with all your heart.

"Pray to your Father." Prayer is mainly to be addressed to God the Father and always to God as our Father. Pray to the Father who is there with you, to the Father who alone can see you. If it is to God alone that you pray, no one else need be present. It would hinder rather than help your devotion to have a third person for a witness of your heart's private communication with the Lord. As the very soul of prayer lies in fellowship with God, we will pray best when all our attention is confined to him. We will also best reach the goal of being accepted by him when we have no concern for the opinion of anyone else.

Secret prayer is truly heard and openly answered in the Lord's own way and time. Our King reigns in secret. It is there he sets up his court and welcomes our approaches. We are not where God sees when we court publicity and pray to gain credit for our devotion.

To repeat a form of prayer many times has always seemed to the ignorantly religious to be worthy of praise, but it is not. It is a mere exercise of memory and the organs of noise. It is absurd to imagine that such a parrot exercise can please the living God. The Muslims and Catholics practice this pagan custom, but we must not imitate them.

God does not need us to pray for his information, for he "knows what you need before you ask him." Nor does he need us to repeat our prayer over and over before he will be persuaded to act, for as our Father he is willing to bless us. So let us not be superstitious and dream that there is virtue in babbling. In the multitude of words— even in prayer—sin abounds. Counting beads and the time we spend in prayer are both idle things. The prayers of Christians are measured by weight not length. Many of the most prevailing prayers have been as short as they were strong.

"This, then, is how you should pray:

"'Our Father in heaven, hallowed be your name, your kingdom come, your will be done on earth as it is in heaven. Give us today our daily bread. Forgive us our debts, as we also have forgiven our debtors. And lead us not into temptation, but deliver us from the evil one.'" (9–13)

After warning us about various vices connected to prayer, our Lord then gave us a model on which to build our prayers. The delightful prayer in verses 9–13 is short, devout, and full of meaning. Its first three petitions are for God's glory. Our chief prayers to God are to be for his glory. Do we begin with God in prayer? Don't we often put our daily bread (v. 11) before God's kingdom (v. 10)?

We pray not only as children to our Father but also as brothers and sisters, for we say, "Our Father." He is our Father, yet he is also "in heaven." He is in heaven and yet our Father. May his name be treated reverently, and may his Word and his gospel be regarded with deepest respect. If we walk before the Lord in all humility, others will see that we reverence the character of our holy God. We can truly pray, "Hallowed be your name," when we hallow it ourselves.

Oh, that our Father may reign over all hearts and lands! People have thrown off their allegiance to our God, and we pray with all our might that he may by his almighty grace subdue them with loyal obedience. We long for the coming of King Jesus, but in the meantime we cry to our Father, "Your kingdom come."

If the request for God's will to be done on earth had not been dictated by our Lord, we might have thought it was too bold. In heaven God's will is done joyfully, humbly, constantly, instantly, and without picking which commands should be obeyed and which should be ignored. Oh, that God's will might be done in those ways here on earth in our lives! But before God's will can be done, it must be known. So let us take the gospel of Christ to the ends of the earth.

We pray for food as a gift: "Give *us.*" We ask for providential supplies for ourselves and others: "Give *us.*" We request no more than the bread or food we need. Our petition asks only for a daily supply. We do not ask for the bread that belongs to others but only for what is honestly our own: "our daily bread." It is the prayer of a humble and contented mind, of a person so sanctified that he or she waits on God even for daily food, and of one who lovingly links others with self in prayer.

Give me, Lord, both the bread of heaven and of earth—the bread that feeds my soul and sustains my body. I look to you, Father, for everything.

No prayer of human beings could be complete without the confession of sin. Prayer that does not ask for pardon will fail, as the Pharisee's prayer did (Luke 18:9-14). Let proud people boast as they please, but we in Christ will always pray, "Forgive us our debts." Our Lord knew we would always have debts of sin and so would always need to cry, "Forgive us." This is the prayer of people whom the judge has absolved because of their faith in the great Sacrifice. Now to their Father they come as children for free forgiveness.

No one may pass one day without praying, "Forgive." And in our supplications we should not forget our fellow sinners. That is why we pray, "Forgive us." We should pray, "Lord, I pray for my forgiveness and the forgiveness of those who refuse or neglect to pray for theirs."

This pardon we can obtain only as we freely pass over the offenses of others against ourselves: "as we also have forgiven our debtors." This is a reasonable and a blessed requirement and a delight to fulfill. It would not be safe for God to forgive someone who would not forgive others.

Lord, I most heartily forgive all who have done me wrong. I am merciful to those who are indebted to me. And now with a hopeful heart I pray that you will forgive me, as surely as I now forgive all who in any sense are my debtors.

The forgiven person does not want to sin again. In the course of our lives the Lord tests our graces and the sincerity of our Christian faith. For this purpose he does sometimes lead us into temptation. Many are troubled by this, because it seems to contradict James 1:13: "When tempted, no one should say, 'God is tempting me.' For God cannot be tempted by evil, nor does he tempt anyone." But there is a vast difference between leading us into temptation and actually tempting us. When the Lord leads us into temptation, it is for our good. He leads us into battle not that we may be wounded and fall but that we may win glorious victories that will crown the head of our leader with many crowns and prepare us for future deeds of valor.

God leads us into temptation when he lets wicked people persecute us, for then we are tempted to strike back and to be afraid. God leads us into temptation even when he asks us to serve him, for we are tempted to disobey his order. Jonah is an example of that (Jonah 1:1-3).

So we ask God not to try us too severely. Temptation or trial will be for our good if we are delivered from Satan. But if we give in to the temptation, our misery will be great. So in prayer we must ask the Lord not to lead us into temptation, because we cannot keep ourselves from it.

Some cannot utter this prayer, because they already live in temptation. A man might pray to be kept out of the water, but a fish cannot, for it lives in it. Even so, if your native element is sin, you cannot pray, "Lead us not into temptation." The previous verse has a prayer for you: "Forgive us."

Lord, do not let my joys or sorrows become temptations to me. As I would not run into temptation by myself, I ask you not to lead me where I must inevitably meet it. But if I must be tried, Lord, deliver me from the Evil One who seeks to destroy my soul.

How perfect is this model prayer! So fit for us to pray, so suitable for us to lay before God's throne. Oh, that we may have grace to copy it all our days! Jesus our King will not refuse to present a prayer that he has drawn up and that is directed to the Father he loves to glorify.

"For if you forgive men when they sin against you, your heavenly Father will also forgive you. But if you do not forgive men their sins, your Father will not forgive your sins." (14–15)

This enforces Christian action by limiting the power of prayer according to our obedience to the command to forgive. If we refuse to forgive, we refuse to be forgiven. To succeed in prayer, our hearts must be purged from the spirit of revenge. This yoke is easy, and this burden is light (Matt. 11:30). It may be a blessing to be wronged, since it affords us an opportunity to judge whether we have received the pardon that comes from the throne of God. It is very sweet to pass by other people's offenses against us, for thus we learn how sweet it is to the Lord to pardon us.

"When you fast, do not look somber as the hypocrites do, for they disfigure their faces to show men they are fasting. I tell you the truth, they have received their reward in full. But when you fast, put oil on your head and wash your face, so that it will not be obvious to men that you are fasting, but only to your Father, who is unseen; and your Father, who sees what is done in secret, will reward you." (16–18)

Having dealt with prayer, our King now instructs us about fasting. Fasting took a leading place in devotion under the law, and it might profitably be more practiced now under the gospel. The Puritans called it "soul-fattening fasting," and many still find it to be so. We must, by order of our King, avoid all temptations to put this spiritual discipline on public parade.

Hypocrites went around with miserable and unwashed faces so that others would say, "Look how strictly they are fasting! What good people they must be!" But to look miserable to be thought holy is a wretched piece of hypocrisy. As it makes fasting a trick to catch human admiration, it destroys it as a means of grace. We cannot expect to get rewards both from the praise of our peers and from the pleasure of God. We have our choice. If we snatch at the minor reward, we lose the major. May it never be said of us, "They have received their reward in full."

Be diligent to conceal what it would be foolish to parade. Don't deny yourself personal cleanliness: "Put oil on your head and wash your face." If your fasting is for God, keep it for him. Act in seasons of extraordinary devotion as you do at other times, so that those with whom you come in contact may not know what special devotion you are practicing.

Your fasting may be discovered, but let it be no goal of yours that it be obvious to others that you are fasting. So when you fast from food, fast also from vanity, ambition, pride, and self-glorification. Fast in secret before the seer of secrets. Secret fasting will have an open reward from the Lord, but the fasting done out of ostentation will never be recorded in the books of the Lord. Now that our King has taught us how to pray, he goes on in the rest of this chapter to teach us how to live. In verses 19-34 he calls us away from worries about this life to a restful faith in God.

"Do not store up for yourselves treasures on earth, where moth and rust destroy, and where thieves break in and steal. But store up for yourselves treasures in heaven, where moth and rust do not destroy, and where thieves do not break in and steal. For where your treasure is, there your heart will be also." (19-21)

Don't set up your life for gathering wealth. This would degrade you as a servant of the heavenly kingdom. If you accumulate either money or clothes, your treasures will be exposed to moth and rust. Moreover, people may steal your money and clothes. The decay and possible theft of earthly things is an excellent reason for not making them the great objects of our pursuit. Accumulate for eternity and send your treasures into the land where you are going. To live for the sake of growing rich is a glossy death in life.

Even our love for family members is a treasure on earth we should not hoard. Our bereavements would not feel half as sharp if we always viewed our family members as on loan to us. A person does not cry when she or he has to return a borrowed tool.

Let our desires and efforts go after heavenly things. These are not in danger of any decay in themselves, nor can they be taken from us by force of fraud. Does not wisdom tell us to seek such sure possessions? Out of our earthly possessions what is used for God is stored up in heaven. What is given to the poor and to the work of evangelizing the world is deposited in the Bank of Eternity. To heaven we are going. Let us send our treasures ahead of us. There they will be safe from decay and robbery, but in no other place may we count them secure.

I heard of a man who said his religion did not cost him a dollar a year. No doubt his religion would have been expensive at that price. You can measure the value of a person's faith by how much that person is prepared to sacrifice for it.

Lord, let me be rich toward you. I had better send on to my treasure in heaven more of my substance than I have already sent. I will at once remember the church and its missions, orphans, aged saints, and poor. These are your treasure boxes, and I will bank my money there.

This is a great moral motive for keeping our desires above groveling objects. The heart must and will go in the direction we count precious. The whole being will be transformed into the likeness of what the person lives for. Our thoughts will naturally fly wherever we place our treasures. It will be wise to let everything we have act as a magnet to draw us in the right direction. If our very best things are in heaven, our very best thoughts will fly in the same direction. But if our choicest possessions are on the earth, our hearts will be earthbound.

"The eye is the lamp of the body. If your eyes are good, your whole body will be full of light. But if your eyes are bad, your whole body will be full of darkness. If then the light within you is darkness, how great is that darkness!" (22–23)

If the eyes of the soul are clear, the whole character will be right. But if they are polluted, the whole being will become defiled. The eyes of our understanding may also be here understood. If people do not see things in a right light, they may live in sin and yet think they are doing their duty. We should live up to our light, but if that light is itself darkness, what a mistake our whole lives will be!

If our religion leads us to sin, it is worse than no religion at all. If our faith is presumption, our zeal selfishness, our prayer a formality, our hope a delusion, and our experience infatuation, the darkness is so great that even our Lord holds up his hands in astonishment and says, "How great is that darkness!" Oh, for a good eye to God's glory, a sincere commitment to the Lord! This alone can fill our souls with light.

"No one can serve two masters. Either he will hate the one and love the other, or he will be devoted to the one and despise the other. You cannot serve both God and Money." (24)

Here our King forbade a double goal in life. We cannot have two master passions. If we could, it would be impossible to serve both. Their interests would soon conflict, and we would be forced to choose between them. We may serve two people, but neither one will be our master.

God and the world will never agree. However much we may attempt it, we can never serve both. Our danger is that in trying to gain money, or in the pursuit of any other goal, we should put it out of its place and allow it to master our minds. Gain and godliness cannot both be masters of our souls. You can live for this world or the next one, but it is impossible to live for both. Where God reigns, the lust of greed must go.

Oh, to be so decided that we may pursue one thing only! We need to hate evil and love God, despise falsehood and be devoted to the truth! We need to know how we are affected both by righteousness and by sin. When we learn this, we must not compromise our commitment. Money is the direct opposite of God. We must loathe its greed, its selfishness, its oppression, and its pride, or we do not love God.

Therefore I tell you, do not worry about your life, what you will eat or drink; or about your body, what you will wear. Is not life more important than food, and the body more important than clothes? Look at the birds of the air; they do not sow or reap or store away in barns, and yet your heavenly Father feeds them. Are you not much more valuable than they? Who of you by worrying can add a single hour to his life?" (25-27)

Therefore, that our one master may be served, we must cease from serving self and from the anxiety that self-seeking involves. We may be concerned about our lives, but worry is here forbidden. Our most pressing physical needs are not to engross our minds. Our lives are more important than the food we eat or the clothes we wear. God who gives us life will give us bread and clothing. We should care much more about how we live than how we eat. The spiritual should go before the physical, the eternal before the temporary. What we wear is of very small importance compared with what we are. Therefore let us give our primary concern to the one all-absorbing goal of our lives—the glory of God.

A little girl went into the country and told her mother, "Look at that poor bird. It has no cage!" But it was no loss to the bird. And if you and I were without our cages and their boxes of seed and glasses of water, we would suffer no loss, because we would be adrift in the glorious liberty of humble dependence on God. It is those cages of worldliness and those boxes of seed that we are always trying to fill that make the worry of this mortal life. But those who have grace to spread their wings and soar away into the open field of divine trustfulness may sing all the day.

God feeds the birds; will he not feed us? They are free from the fret that comes from hoarding and trading; why shouldn't we be? If God feeds the birds that "do not sow or reap or store away in barns," surely he will supply us when we use these means with trust in our Lord. For us to rely on these means and forget our God would be folly indeed. Our King would have his subjects give their hearts to loving and serving him and not worry themselves with groveling anxieties.

It is good for us that we have these daily needs, because they lead us to our heavenly Father, but if we worry about them, we twist them from their original purpose and make them into barriers to shut us out from the Lord. Oh, that we would be as good as the birds in trusting God, since in dignity of nature we are "much more valuable than they."

All the worry in the world cannot add a single hour to our lives. So why do we worry about things we cannot change? Worry may even shorten our lives, for many have worried themselves right into their graves. If anxiety were of any practical use, we would have an excuse for using it. But since it does us no good, let us cease from it.

"And why do you worry about clothes? See how the lilies of the field grow. They do not labor or spin. Yet I tell you that not even Solomon in all his splendor was dressed like one of these. If that is how God clothes the grass of the field, which is here today and tomorrow is thrown into the fire, will he not much more clothe you, O you of little faith? So do not worry, saying, 'What shall we eat?' or 'What shall we drink?' or 'What shall we wear?' For the pagans run after all these things, and your heavenly Father knows that you need them. But seek first his kingdom and his righteousness, and all these things will be

given to you as well. Therefore do not worry about tomorrow, for tomorrow will worry about itself. Each day has enough trouble of its own." (28–34)

We must not make clothes the goal of our lives, for even when we dress in our finest array, flowers excel us in beauty. We must not be anxious about how we will be dressed, for the lilies of the field not under the gardener's care are as glorious as the most pompous of monarchs, yet they enjoy life free from labor and thought. Lovely lilies, how you rebuke our worried hearts! The beauty of lilies comes without anxiety, so why do we kill ourselves worrying about the things that God gives to plants that don't worry?

My Lord, I want to grow to your praise as the lily does. I want to be content to be what you make me and to wear what you give me.

It is not merely that lilies grow but that God himself clothes them with surpassing beauty. When growing, these lilies appear only as "the grass," but Solomon could not excel them when God puts them in their full array of cloth of gold. Will he not be sure to take care of us, who are precious in his sight? If we doubt that, we show lack of trust in God. If what is so very short-lived is yet so bedecked by our Lord, depend on it, he will guard immortal minds and even the mortal bodies that house them.

"Little faith" is not a little fault, for it greatly wrongs the Lord and sadly grieves the worried mind. To think the Lord who clothes lilies will leave his own children naked is shameful. O little faith, learn better manners!

Here are the world's trinity of anxieties. These three questions are taken from the worldly person's catechism of distrust. The children of God may quietly work on them from day to day and cast all anxious cares from them.

We are to do better than "the pagans." Things they "run after" are not good enough for the children of God. People of the world seek earthly things and have no mind for anything beyond that. But we have a heavenly Father, and therefore we have higher goals and aspirations. Moreover, as our Father knows all about our needs, we need not be worried. He is very sure to provide for all our needs. Let the pagans hunt after their many carnal objects, but let God's children leave their temporary needs with the Lord of infinite grace, and then let them follow after the one thing they need.

Lord, help me to be free from worry. May I be so eager for heavenly things that I completely leave my earthly cares with you.

The "but" at the beginning of this verse links it to the warning against worry. Jesus seemed to be saying, "If you tend to worry, use it for a good purpose. Let your deepest, most intense and most thoughtful concern be for God's kingdom and his righteousness. If you want to worry, worry about your sins and your unrighteousness."

We should seek to enter God's kingdom, to enjoy it, and to extend it by winning people to Christ. If we seek first his kingdom and his righteousness, the rest will follow later. Spend your life on these two primary things, and it will be well spent. As for the twenty secondary things, they will be thrown in automatically. God who gives you heaven will not deny you bread on the road to heaven.

If you want a paper sack, you don't need to go into a shop to buy it. If you buy anything, you will get the paper sack thrown into the bargain. So when you go to God seeking first "his kingdom and his righteousness," the other things in our lives, which are like paper sacks, will be given to us in the bargain.

When I decided to enter college, revolving in my mind the joys of scholarship and the hope of being something in the world, Jeremiah 45:5 came to my heart: "Should you then seek great things for yourself? Seek them not." Then I thought of Matthew 6:33: "Seek first his kingdom and his righteousness, and all these things will be given to you as well." In that moment I gave up everything. I renounced my worldly ambitions. The finest prospects melted into thin air, merely on the strength of those two passages. I believed that God would most certainly fulfill his purpose if I could obey his command.

The argument leads up to a "therefore." Worry cannot help you (v. 27). It is useless and would degrade you to the level of a pagan (v. 32). There is no need for it (v. 33). "Therefore" do not anticipate sorrow by worrying about the future. Since we cannot live in tomorrow, we should not worry about it.

Our business is with today. We are to ask only for "daily bread," and only in sufficient supply for the day's consumption (v. 11). There can be no need to haul in cares from the future. To load today with trials that have not yet arrived and may never arrive would be to overload it with unbelief. When tomorrow brings sorrow, it will bring strength for that sorrow. Today will require all the strength we have to deal with its immediate evils. Worry is evil, but worry about things that have not yet happened is completely without excuse.

O my heart, what rest there is for you if you will give yourself up to your Lord and leave all your own concerns with him! Mind your Lord's business, and he will see to your business.

Jesus' Sermon on the Mount—Part 3

"Do not judge, or you too will be judged. For in the same way you judge others, you will be judged, and with the measure you use, it will be measured to you." (1-2)

Some people have an inclination to judge. They see nothing in others to praise but everything to blame. These people will find that they are condemned according to their own wicked rule. Others judge the people who like to judge.

Use your judgment, of course. These verses imply that you will judge in the right sense. Just do not be critical of others, as if you were set in authority and had a right to dispense judgment among your peers. If you impute motives and pretend to read hearts, others will do the same to you. A hard and judgmental spirit is sure to provoke revenge. Those around you will pick up the measuring cup you have been using and measure your flour with it. You do not object to people forming a fair opinion of your character, nor are you forbidden to do the same to them. But as you would object to them sitting in judgment on you, do not sit in judgment on them.

This is not the day of judgment, neither are we the judges God has appointed. Therefore we may not anticipate the time appointed for the final reckoning, nor may we usurp the privilege of the judge of all humanity.

Surely if I know myself well, I need not judge others, because there are many traitors in my own heart that can be judged in the court of my own conscience.

"Why do you look at the speck of sawdust in your brother's eye and pay no attention to the plank in your own eye? How can you say to your brother, 'Let me take the speck out of your eye,' when all the time there is a plank in your own eye? You hypocrite, first take the plank out of

your own eye, and then you will see clearly to remove the speck from your brother's eye." (3-5)

The judging faculty is best employed at home. Our tendency is to spy out the specks of sawdust in other people's eyes and not see the planks in our own. Instead of looking with gratified gaze at the fault of someone else, we should consider the greater faults in ourselves. It is the planks in our own eyes that blind us to our own faults. But such blindness does not excuse us, since it evidently does not shut our eyes to the little error of someone else. Rudeness pretends to play the eye doctor, but in fact it plays the fool. Imagine a man with a plank in his eye pretending to deal with so tender a part as the eye of someone else and trying to remove so tiny a thing as a speck!

At the bottom of all human judgment lies hypocrisy. Honest people will apply to themselves the judgment that hypocrites exercise against others. Jesus called that person a "hypocrite" who fusses about small things in others and pays no attention to great matters in his or her own personal life. Our reformations must begin with ourselves or they are not true and do not spring from right motives. We may rebuke sin, but not if we indulge it. We may protest against evil, but not if we willfully practice it. The Pharisees were great at finding fault as long as it was in others. Our Lord will not have his kingdom made up of hypocritical theorists. He calls for practical obedience to the rules of holiness.

After we ourselves are sanctified, we are bound to be eyes to the blind and correctors of unholy living—but not until then. Until we have personal piety, our preaching of godliness is sheer hypocrisy. May none of us provoke the Lord to say to us, "You hypocrite!"

"Do not give dogs what is sacred; do not throw your pearls to pigs. If you do, they may trample them under their feet, and then turn and tear you to pieces." (6)

If people are unable to understand the purity of a great truth, do not set it before them. They are like mere dogs, and if you put sacred things before them, they will then turn and tear you to pieces. Sacred things are not for the profane.

"Outside are the dogs" (Rev. 22:15). They must not be allowed in the sacred place. When you are in the midst of the vicious who are like pigs, do not bring forth the precious mysteries of the faith, for they will despise them and trample them under their feet in the mud. Silence is sometimes golden. Make sure you have golden silence as well as silver speech.

You should not provoke an attack on yourself or the gospel for no reason. You are not to judge, but neither are you to act without judgment. Do not count people as dogs or pigs, but when they admit that they are such or when by their conduct they act as such, do not give them opportunities to display their evil characters. Saints are not to be simpletons. They are to be neither judges nor fools.

Great King, how much wisdom your commands require! I need you not only to open my mouth but also sometimes to keep it shut.

"Ask and it will be given to you; seek and you will find; knock and the door will be opened to you. For everyone who asks receives; he who seeks finds; and to him who knocks, the door will be opened." (7–8)

Though you cannot always speak of heavenly things to people, you can to God! "Ask . . . seek . . . knock." Adapt your prayer to the case. Let it increase in intensity. Let it advance in the greatness of its goal. To receive a gift we asked for is simple. To find a treasure we sought is more enriching. To enter a palace after knocking on its door is best of all. Each form of prayer is rewarded by God.

A Christian may be hedged in, but a Christian cannot be roofed in. There will always be a path up to the throne of God. If you do not ask, you deserve to go without God's blessings. If you do not knock, you cannot be surprised that the gate of heaven is shut to you. A time will come when people will knock, and the door will not be opened for them. But now this verse is still God's gracious command and promise.

It applies to everyone who obeys the commands. They stand in contrast to the anxiety denounced in 6:25-34. They also encourage us to obey Jesus' commands concerning giving and nonresistance in 6:40-42, since the people who can have God for the asking may well give to others who ask and even yield to those who make unfair demands. So let us be neither stingy nor quarrelsome.

Lord, help me be done with fretting and to abound in asking, seeking, and knocking. In doing that, I will overflow with thanksgiving.

This rule is not always true in human relations. You may ask and not receive. You may seek and not find. You may knock and have no door opened for you. But when you deal with God, there are no failures or refusals. Why not try this and prove it to yourself? Ask God's people if this is true. They know the power of prayer, so let them tell you whether or not they have been deceived. As it has been with them, expect that it will be with you.

"Which of you, if his son asks for bread, will give him a stone? Or if he asks for a fish, will give him a snake? If you, then, though you are evil, know how to give good gifts to your children, how much more will your Father in heaven give good gifts to those who ask him! In everything, do to others what you would have them do to you, for this sums up the Law and the Prophets." (9–12)

In everyday things we make blunders and ask for what we think is bread when in fact it is a stone. We mistake a snake for an eel and beg for it as if it were a fish. Our heavenly Father will correct our prayers and give us not what we ignorantly seek but what we really need. The promise to give what we ask is here explained and set in its true light.

This is a gracious correction of the foolishness that would read our Lord's words in verses 7 and 8 in the most literal sense and make us dream that every whim of ours needs only to put on the dress of prayer before it can be gratified. Our prayers go to heaven in a Revised Version. It would be a terrible thing if God always gave us all we asked for. Your heavenly Father himself "knows what you need" (Matt. 6:8) far better than you know how to ask.

Though we are "evil," we correct our children's blunders when they ask us for the wrong things. Much more will our all-wise and all-good heavenly Father amend in his bestowals the errors of our requests. He will give the good that we did not ask and withhold the bad that we so unwisely requested. We know our children and use our knowledge for our children, yet we are evil creatures. Will not the perfectly good Father, who knows all things, arrange his gifts most graciously? Yes, we are sure he will!

"How much more," said our Lord, "will your Father in heaven give good gifts to those who ask him!" But Jesus did not tell us exactly how much more. He left that to our meditation. "We do not know what we ought to pray" (Rom. 8:26), but he knows how to give perfectly, and he will do that. He will give "good gifts," and especially his Holy Spirit (Luke 11:13), who is all good gifts in one.

Lord, I want to think more of you than of my own prayer, more of your Son than of my own faith, and more of your Holy Spirit than of all the good gifts in the world.

Everything that has gone before leads up to this last argument. This is the Golden Rule. Put yourself in someone else's place, and then act toward that person as you would want that person to act toward you under the same circumstances. This is a royal rule, a precept always at hand, always applicable, always right. Here you may be a judge and yet not judging others but judging for others. This is the sum of the Ten Commandments, the Law of Moses, and the whole sacred Word of God. Oh, that all people acted on it. Then there would be no slavery, no war, no striking, no lying, no robbing. All would be justice and love!

What a kingdom is this that has such a law! This is the sum of everything right and generous. We adore the King out of whose mouth and heart such a law could flow. This one rule is a proof that God is the author of Christianity. The universal practice of it by all who call themselves Christians would carry conviction to every unbeliever with greater speed and certainty than all the apologies and arguments that human wit or piety can produce.

Lord, teach me the Golden Rule! Write it on the documents of flesh in my renewed heart! Write it out in full in my daily life!

"Enter through the narrow gate. For wide is the gate and broad is the road that leads to destruction, and many enter through it. But small is the gate and narrow the road that leads to life, and only a few find it." (13–14)

Don't be ashamed to be called "narrow." During life's journey, if you are on the right road, you will find the gate somewhat difficult and very narrow, for it demands self-denial, strict obedience, and a watchful spirit. It is contrary to your human nature. It does not seem to hold any fascination. Nevertheless, "Enter through the narrow gate." Whatever its drawbacks because of few pilgrims or smallness of entrance, choose it and use it.

True, there is another road, wide and very busy with travelers. But it leads to destruction. People go to ruin along the freeway, but the way to heaven is a footpath. To be popular you must be broad in doctrine, morals, and spiritual life. But those on the small road will go straight to glory, and those on the broad road are all lost. All is well that ends well. We can afford to be small in the right way rather than large in the wrong way, because the first ends in eternal life, and the second hastens down to eternal death.

Lord, deliver me from the temptation to be broad. Keep me on the narrow road, though few find it!

Do not try to go with the majority. Truth is usually with the minority. Do not count heads, but prefer the option least liked by others. Only a few find the small gate and narrow road. Indeed, no one finds it unless grace first finds him or finds her. He who made that gate must go after the wandering sheep and bring them through it. They will never choose it by themselves.

"Watch out for false prophets. They come to you in sheep's clothing, but inwardly they are ferocious wolves. By their fruit you will recognize them. Do people pick grapes from thornbushes, or figs from thistles? Likewise every good tree bears good fruit, but a bad tree bears bad fruit. A good tree cannot bear bad fruit, and a bad tree cannot bear good fruit. Every tree that does not bear good fruit is cut down and thrown into the fire. Thus, by their fruit you will recognize them." (15–20)

Some honor all prophets. They esteem them as holding a high office, and they assume a prophet must be sent by God. But for that very reason there are many counterfeits whom God has never sent. So we must watch out for false prophets.

We need our judgments, and we must "test the spirits" (1 John 4:1) of those who profess to be sent by God. There are people of great gifts who are false prophets. They imitate the look, language, and spirit of God's people, but their desire is to devour souls, even as ferocious wolves thirst for the blood of sheep. They come to us as prophets with every outward commendation, but they are Balaams and will surely curse those they pretend to bless.

The false prophets look just like sheep. They have nothing in common with the sheep but the skin, and there is no connection between the skin and those who wear it. Hypocrites are goats in sheep's clothing, but false prophets are ferocious wolves in sheep's clothing, because they can do so much more harm and damage to the body of Christ.

Their teaching, living, and effect on our minds will be a sure test to us. Every doctrine may be tested in this way. If we pick grapes from them, they are not thistles. If they produce nothing but thistles, they are not grapes. Some object to this practical method of testing, but wise Christians will carry it with them as the ultimate touchstone. We must test modern theology by the spirituality, the prayerfulness, and the holiness of those who espouse it.

Grapes and figs are pleasant fruit. And holy living, true devotion, and fellowship with God are the things sweet to him and to spiritual people. They do not come from false teaching, nor are they seen in false prophets. Such prophets despise these things. They are for worldly ways. Not so the servants of God.

Everyone produces according to her or his nature. We cannot do otherwise. "Good tree—good fruit; bad tree—bad fruit. There is no possibility of the effect being higher than the cause. The truly good does not produce evil. It would be contrary to its nature. The radically bad never rises to produce good, though it may seem to do so. Therefore each may be known by its special fruit.

We are not to judge (v. 1), but we are to recognize (v. 16), and the rule for this recognition is as simple as it is safe. Such recognition of people may save us from great mischief that would come to us through associating with bad and deceitful persons. The ax and the fire are the end to which evil things are flowing. They await the ungodly, however fine they may look with the leafage of profession. Only let time enough be given, and everyone on earth who bears no good fruit will meet his or her doom. It is not merely the wicked—the tree that bears poison berries—who will be cut down but also the neutral. The one who bears no fruit of positive virtue will also be "thrown into the fire."

It is not our job to cut down or to burn the hypocrites, but it is our job to "recognize them." This recognition is to save us from coming under the shadow of influence of false teachers. Who wants to build a nest on a tree that is soon to be cut down? Who would choose a barren tree for the center of an orchard?

We cannot recognize false prophets by their bark, the spread of their branches, the greenness of their leaves, or the beauty of their blossoms in the spring. It is only by their fruit we can detect the false prophets. The Savior gives us this test, lest we be deceived, for many are deceived not only by their own sins but by false prophets who are among Satan's best agents.

We may recognize teachings as well as people by their fruits. The teachings that give a license to sin cannot be true, but those that lead to holiness are true. Truth and holiness of life will always run together.

Lord, remind me that I am to judge myself by this rule. Make me a fruit-bearing tree.

"Not everyone who says to me, 'Lord, Lord,' will enter the kingdom of heaven, but only he who does the will of my Father who is in heaven. Many will say to me on that day, 'Lord, Lord, did we not prophesy in your name, and in your name drive out demons and perform many miracles? Then I will tell them plainly, 'I never knew you. Away from me, you evildoers!'" (21–23)

No verbal homage will suffice. "Not everyone who says . . ." These people were sound in doctrine. They called Jesus "Lord." They worshiped him. They were earnest, for they said, "Lord, Lord," crying out to him again and again. But external utterances, however orthodox, and professions of faith, however sound, are not enough.

The true Christian is not the person who has only good words on the tongue but the one who has God's will on the heart and in the life. There must be holiness in us, for "without holiness no one will see the Lord" (Heb. 12:14). It is not knowing God's will but doing it that is the mark of God's people. Unless we carry out the commands of the Father, we pay no true homage to the Son. We may own our obligations to Jesus and so call him "Lord, Lord." But if we never practically carry out those obligations, what is the value of our words? Our King rejects from his kingdom those whose religion lies in words and ceremonies. He receives only those whose lives display the obedience of true discipleship.

Many *do* prophesy in the name of the Lord. So did Balaam. Was not Saul also among the prophets (1 Sam. 10:9–12)? Yet neither Balaam nor Saul was accepted by God but were castaways. You may be an eloquent preacher and have some blessing on your preaching, and yet be cast away forever. A thousand sermons would not prove you are a Christian, but one genuine prayer would.

There was one who drove out demons and was a devil himself, namely, Judas Iscariot, who also betrayed Christ (Matt. 10:1; John 6:70–71). He performed miracles in the name of Christ and then sold Christ for thirty pieces of silver.

We may do amazing miracles, yet be amazingly deceived. Not amazing works but holy works prove grace is in the soul. Not works that amaze people but works that please God. It is not attention to the miracles but to the essentials that marks a Christian, not the amazing things we do in public but the important things we do in secret.

These people will be unknown to Christ. Their motives were very different from his. Twice in the previous verse the people are described as those who do things "in your name." Yet the Lord, whose name they used so freely, so boldly, knew nothing of them and would not allow them to remain in his company. They knew Christ's name, but they didn't have his nature. Their tongues belied their hands. The Lord cannot endure the presence of those who call him "Lord, Lord" but are "evildoers." If Christ once knows you, he will never forget you. But at the judgment he will tell the hypocrites, "I never knew you."

How solemn is this reminder to me and to you! Nothing will prove us to be true Christians but sincere obedience to the Father's will. We may be known by everyone to have great spiritual power over demons and people, yet in that great day our Lord may not acknowledge us but may drive us out as impostors whom he cannot tolerate in his presence. These are solemn thoughts. Let them sink into your heart.

"Therefore everyone who hears these words of mine and puts them into practice is like a wise man who built his house on the rock. The rain came down, the streams rose, and the winds blew and beat against that house; yet it did not fall, because it had its foundation on the rock. But everyone who hears these words of mine and does not put them into practice is like a foolish man who built his house on sand. The rain came down, the streams rose, and the winds blew and beat against that house, and it fell with a great crash." (24–27)

Our Lord looks for the person who not only hears his words but also puts them into practice. This is more than some do today, for they sit in judgment on the teachings of the Lord. But hearing is not enough. You may hear the Word of God and only increase your condemnation, but to do what you hear is to have a good foundation. There must be practical godliness, or nothing is right inside us. The doing hearers have built a house with a stable foundation. This is the wisest, safest, most expensive, and most toilsome thing to do.

This man built his house on a rock, which implies he was not free from troubles. The next verse gives some examples of his troubles.

The rain typifies afflictions from heaven. God will send you showers of tribulations—as many as the drops of the rain. You will also have trials from the earth: "streams" of persecution from the enemies of Christ. Then there will come demonic trials typified by "the winds." The "ruler of the kingdom of the air" (Eph. 2:2) will assail you with blasphemous suggestions, horrible temptations, and artful insinuations.

No protection is given to the Christian. The rain came, the streams rose, and the winds blew and beat against that house. It was a substantial structure, but the tests became so severe that nothing could save the building unless it was the strength of its foundation.

Because the chief support was immovable, the entire building survived. "It did not fall." It may have suffered damage here and there, and it may have looked very weather-beaten, but "it did not fall." The more rain, the more streams, and the more winds, the more the house was admired for its stability.

Let the Rock of Ages be praised if, after terrible tribulations, it can be said of your faith, "It did not fall, because it had its foundation on the rock."

The mere hearer is also building a house. The hearing of the Lord's sayings starts him on a work designed to give him comfort and shelter. He built his house. He was practical and persevering and did not quit before completion. Yet though he was industrious, he was also foolish. No doubt he built quickly, for his foundation cost him no severe labor. His excavations were soon made, for there was no rock to remove. He built his house on sand.

Even if you live for Satan, you will not live without trials. Aren't all people "born to trouble" (Job 5:7)? The same kind of afflictions come to the foolish as to the wise. They operate in exactly the same way. But the result is very different.

Just when the tenant most needed shelter, the house fell. He did not need it so much until "the rain came down, the streams rose, and the winds blew and beat against that house." But then "it fell with a great crash." These are solemn words. It was a fine building, and it promised to stand for ages, but it fell. There were minor faults in the fabric, but its chief weakness was underground in the secret places of the foundation. The man built his house on sand. His fundamentals were wrong.

The house not only fell, but it fell "with a great crash." That's because it could never be set up again. Many heard the fall, and many more saw the ruins as they remained a perpetual memorial of the result of that foolishness that is satisfied with hearing and neglects obeying.

If you had looked at the two structures Jesus spoke of here, they would have seemed equally complete from basement to roof. Yet there was a great difference between them in a most essential point. The wise man's work was honest where human eyes could not judge it. The other's work was well built only above the ground. There was no reality in the hidden parts.

In the same way, many persevere in seeking salvation until they are sure they have found it. They remain for years in the full belief that they are saved. Yet a fatal error lies at the base of all their religion. Outward appearance is everything with people but nothing with God. The essential difference between the true child of God and the person who claims to be a Christian cannot be seen with the naked eye, but the Lord sees it.

When Jesus had finished saying these things, the crowds were amazed at his teaching, because he taught as one who had authority, and not as their teachers of the law. (28–29)

The Sermon on the Mount was now over. What came of it? Never was there so great a preacher, and never did he deliver a greater discourse. How many repented because of this sermon? How many were converted by it? We do not hear of any. Divine truth, even when preached to perfection, will not by itself lead the heart to conversion. The most overpowering authority produces no obedience unless the Holy Spirit subdues the hearer's heart.

"The crowds were amazed." Was that all? I fear it was. Two things surprised them: the substance and the manner of Christ's teaching. They had never heard such doctrine before. The commands he had given were new to their thoughts. But their main astonishment was at Christ's manner. There was a certainty, a power, a weight about it that they had never seen in the ordinary professional teachers.

Jesus did not raise questions or speak with hesitation. Neither did he cite authorities and their great names. "He taught as one who had authority." He spoke royally. The truth itself was its own argument and demonstration. He taught prophetically, as one inspired from above. People felt that he spoke like someone sent by God. It was not their fault they were amazed, but it was a serious crime to be amazed and nothing more.

My Savior, this was a poor reward for your royal discourse: "The crowds were amazed." Help me not to care to amaze people, but may I be enabled to win them for you. And if, with my utmost endeavors, I do nothing more than amaze them, may I never complain, for how should the disciple be above his Lord?

Get Ready for the Second Coming of Christ

Jesus left the temple and was walking away when his disciples came up to him to call his attention to its buildings. "Do you see all these things?" he asked. "I tell you the truth, not one stone here will be left on another; every one will be thrown down." (1–2)

Because he had finished his final discourse in the temple, Jesus left it, never to return. As his disciples moved away with him toward the Mount of Olives, they called his attention to the great stones with which the temple was built and its costly adornments. To them the appearance was glorious, but to their Lord it was a sad sight. His Father's house, which should have been a house of prayer for all nations, had become a den of robbers. Hence it would be destroyed.

Josephus told us that Titus at first tried to save the temple, even after it was set on fire, but his efforts were useless. Finally he gave orders that the whole city and temple be leveled, except a small part reserved for the headquarters. This was so thoroughly done that Josephus said, "Nothing was left there to make those who came believe it had ever been used."

We often delight in the temporary prosperity of the church as if it were something that must surely endure, but everything external will pass away or be destroyed. Let us consider substantial only that which comes from God and is his work. "What is seen is temporary" (2 Cor. 4:18).

As Jesus was sitting on the Mount of Olives, the disciples came to him privately. "Tell us," they said, "when will this happen, and what will be the sign of your coming and of the end of the age?" (3)

There are three questions here, the last two of which have been asked in every age since our Savior's day. The disciples inquired first about the time of the destruction of the temple, then about the sign of Christ's coming, and then the sign of the end of the age. Jesus' answers are somewhat vague. He told his disciples some things that related to the siege of Jerusalem, some that concerned his second coming, and some that would immediately precede the end of the age. When we have clearer light, we may possibly understand that all our Savior's predictions here had some connection with all three of these great events.

Jesus answered: "Watch out that no one deceives you. For many will come in my name, claiming, 'I am the Christ,' and will deceive many. You will hear of wars and rumors of wars, but see to it that you are not alarmed. Such things must happen, but the end is still to come. Nation will rise against nation, and kingdom against kingdom. There will be famines and earthquakes in various places. All these are the beginning of birth pains." (4–8)

Jesus was always practical. The most important thing for his disciples was not that they might know when the end of the age would come but that they might be protected from the specific evils of the time. They were to beware lest any of the false messiahs should lead them astray, as they would many others. A large number of impostors came forward before the destruction of Jerusalem, claiming to be anointed by God. Almost every page of history is blotted with the names of such deceivers.

In our own day we see some come in Christ's name, saying that they are Christ. These people seduce many, but they who heed the Lord's warning will not be deceived by them.

The news of "wars and rumors of wars" can be applied to any period of world history. There will be many of both until the time when "nation will not take up sword against nation, nor will they train for war anymore" (Isa. 2:4).

When Jesus said, "but the end is still to come," he implied that the destruction of Jerusalem was the beginning of the end, the great type and anticipation of all that will take place when Christ shall stand at the latter day on the earth. It was an end, but not the end.

We would think there would be enough sorrow in "famines and earthquakes in various places," but our Lord said all these were only "the beginning of birth pains." If famines and earthquakes are only the beginning of the world's birth pains, what must the end be? This prophecy should first warn us what to expect and then wean us from the world where these and greater sorrows will be experienced.

"Then you will be handed over to be persecuted and put to death, and you will be hated by all nations because of me. At that time many will turn away from the faith and will betray and hate each other, and many false prophets will appear and deceive many people. Because of the increase of wickedness, the love of most will grow cold, but he who stands firm to the end will be saved. And this gospel of the kingdom will be preached in the whole world as a testimony to all nations, and then the end will come." (9–14)

Our Lord predicted not only the general trial that would come on the Jews and the world but also the special persecution that would be the lot of his chosen followers. The New Testament gives abundant proof of the fulfillment of these words. Even in Paul's day, people everywhere were slandering Christianity (Acts 28:22). Since then has there been any land unstained by the blood of martyrs? Wherever Christ's gospel has been preached, people have risen up in arms against the messengers of mercy and killed them.

Persecution would reveal the traitors inside the church as well as the enemies outside. In the midst of the chosen ones successors of Judas would be found who would be willing to betray the disciples as he betrayed his Lord. Saddest of all is the betrayal of believers by their own relatives, but even this many have had to bear for Christ's sake.

What could not be accomplished either by persecutors outside the church or traitors inside it would be attempted by teachers of heresy. False prophets have risen in all ages. In these modern times they have risen in clouds, until the air is thick with them, as with an army of devouring locusts. These are the people who invent new teachings and seem to think that Christianity is something that they may twist into any form and shape that they please. How tragic that such teachers should have any disciples! It is doubly sad that they should be able to deceive many people. Yet when it happens, let us remember that our King predicted it.

If the reservoir is empty, you cannot expect much water from the pipes. If the heart grows cold, everything will be done coldly. When love declines, what cold preaching we have. It is all moonlight—light without heat, polished like marble but chilly. What cold singing we get—pretty music made by pipes and wind but no making of melody in the heart to God. And what poor praying! Do you call it praying? And what little giving! Does anything go as it should when love grows cold?

Is it any wonder that when wickedness increases, the love of most will grow cold? If the teachers deceive the people and give them a false gospel, it is no marvel that there is a lack of love and zeal. The wonder is that there is any love and zeal left after they have been subjected to such a chilling and killing process as that adopted by the advocates of modern destructive criticism.

Again our Savior reminded his disciples of their personal responsibility in the time of trial and testing they were about to pass through. He wanted them to remember that it is not the one who starts in the race who wins, but the one who runs to the goal.

If this teaching of enduring to the end so as to be saved were not supplemented by another, it would bring little good news to tempted and struggling saints. Who among us would persevere in running the heavenly race if God did not keep us from falling by his grace? We are "confident of this, that he who began a good work in you will carry it on to completion until the day of Christ Jesus" (Phil. 1:6).

The world is to the church as a scaffold is to a building. When the church is built, the scaffold will be taken down. The world must remain until the last chosen one is saved. "Then the end will come."

Before Jerusalem was destroyed, this gospel of the kingdom was preached in the whole world as far as it was known. But there will be a fuller proclamation of it as a testimony to all nations before the end will come, when the King will sit on the throne of His glory and decide the eternal destiny of the entire human race.

"So when you see standing in the holy place 'the abomination that causes desolation,' spoken of through the prophet Daniel—let the reader understand—then let those who are in Judea flee to the mountains. Let no one on the roof of his house go down to take anything out of the house. Let no one in the field go back to get his cloak. How dreadful it will be in those days for pregnant women and nursing mothers! Pray that your flight will not take place in winter or on the Sabbath. For then there will be great distress, unequaled from the beginning of the world until now—and never to be equaled again. If those days had not been cut short, no one would survive, but for the sake of the elect those days will be shortened. At that time if anyone says to you, 'Look, here is the Christ!' or, 'There he is!' do not believe it. For false Christs and false prophets will appear and perform great signs and miracles to deceive even the elect—if that were possible. See, I have told you ahead of time." (15–25)

This part of our Savior's words appears to relate only to the destruction of Jerusalem. As soon as the disciples would see "the abomination that causes desolation"—the Roman banners with their idolatrous symbols "standing in the holy place"—they would know the time had come for them to escape. Then they did "flee to the mountains." The Christians in Jerusalem and the surrounding towns and villages in Judea took the first opportunity to elude the Roman armies and fled to the mountain city of Pella in Perea. There they were preserved from the general destruction that overthrew the Jews.

There was no time to spare before the final investment of the guilty city. The person on the roof of the house could not come down to take anything out of the house. Nor could the person in the field return for her or his clothes. People had to flee to the mountains as soon as they saw "Jerusalem surrounded by armies" (Luke 21:20).

It must have been an exceptionally trying time for the women who had to flee their homes just when they needed quiet rest. How sympathetic was our Savior to them in their hour of need! The Lord knew exactly when they would be able to escape, yet he told them to pray that it might not be in the winter or on a Sabbath. The wise of the present day would have said that prayer was useless under such conditions. Not so the great teacher and example of his praying people. He taught that such a season was the very time for special prayer.

The great distress was the reason behind Jesus' command to pray. Read Josephus's history of the destruction of Jerusalem to see how truly our Lord's words were fulfilled. The Jews irreverently said concerning the death of Christ, "Let his blood be on us and on our children!" (Matt. 27:25). Never did any other people invoke such an awful curse on themselves, and on no other nation did such a judgment ever fall. We read of Jews crucified until there was no more wood for making crosses, of thousands of the people slaying one another in their fierce factional fights within the city, and of the fearful carnage when the Romans at last entered the doomed capital. The blood-curdling story exactly bears out the Savior's statement uttered nearly forty years before the terrible events occurred.

Jesus said these things not only as the prophet who was able to gaze into the future but also as the Lord of all events. He knew what a fiery trial awaited the unbelieving nation and that no one would survive unless those days should be cut short. If the horrors of the siege had continued longer, the whole race of the Jews would have been destroyed.

Jesus had the power to shorten those evil days, and he explained his reason for doing so: for the sake of the elect. Those who had been hated and persecuted by their own people became the means of preserving them from absolute annihilation. Thus it has often been since then. For the sake of the elect the Lord has withheld many judgments and shortened others. Non-Christians owe Christians more than they know or would even want to know.

"So if anyone tells you, 'There he is, out in the desert,' do not go out; or, 'Here he is, in the inner rooms,' do not believe it. For as lightning that comes from the east is visible even in the west, so will be the coming of the Son of Man. Wherever there is a carcass, there the vultures will gather." (26–28)

It is a grand thing to have such faith in Christ that you have none left for impostors. It is important not to distribute your faith too widely. Those who believe a little of everything will end up believing nothing of anything. If you exercise full faith in what is sure and steadfast, false Christs and false prophets will not be able to make you their dupes.

In one sense, the modern teachers of heresy are more successful than their Judean prototypes, for they do deceive even the elect, even though they can't perform great signs and miracles. One of the saddest signs of the times we live in is the ease with which even the elect are deceived by the smooth-talking false Christs and false prophets who abound in our midst. Yet our Savior expressly forewarned his followers against them: "See, I have told you ahead of time." To be forewarned is to be forearmed. Let it be so in our case. Our Savior's command may be fitly applied to the whole system of modern thought that is contrary to the inspired Word of God. "Do not believe it."

When Christ comes, we shall know who he is and why he has come. There will no longer be any mystery or secret about the coming of the Son of Man. There will be no need to ask any questions then. No one will make a mistake about his appearing when it actually takes place. "Every eye will see him" (Rev. 1:7).

Christ's coming will be sudden, startling, universally visible, and as terrifying as lightning to the ungodly. His first coming to judgment at the destruction of Jerusalem had terrors about it that until then had never been realized on the earth. His last coming will be even more dreadful.

Judaism had become a carcass, dead and corrupt, fit prey for the vultures of Rome. When Christ returns, there will be a dead church in a dead world, and the vultures of divine judgment will gather to tear them in pieces. The birds of prey gather wherever dead bodies are found, and the judgments of Christ will be poured out when religion becomes unbearably corrupt.

"Immediately after the distress of those days 'the sun will be darkened, and the moon will not give its light; the stars will fall from the sky, and the heavenly bodies will be shaken.'" (29)

Our Lord appeared to have perfectly mingled the prophecies of the destruction of Jerusalem with his own second coming. So there was nothing in his words to satisfy idle curiosity but everything to keep his disciples always on the watch for his appearing.

These verses apply primarily to the coming of the Christ at the last great day. There may have been a partial fulfillment of them in "the distress" that came on his guilty capital, and the language of the Savior might have been taken symbolically to set forth the wonders in heaven and the woes on earth in connection with that awful judgment, but we must regard Christ's words here as prophetic of the final return. There will be no further need of the sun or the moon or the stars when he who is brighter than the sun shines forth in all the glory of his Father (Rev. 21:23).

"At that time the sign of the Son of Man will appear in the sky, and all the nations of the earth will mourn. They will see the Son of Man coming on the clouds of the sky, with power and great glory. And he will send his angels with a loud trumpet call, and they will gather his elect from the four winds, from one end of the heavens to the other." (30–31)

Christ's coming will be the source of untold joy to his friends, but it will bring unparalleled sorrow to his foes. "All the nations of the earth will mourn," because Jesus will find them unsaved. As a result, horror will be their eternal portion.

Our Lord's first concern when he returns will be the security of his elect. He has gone to prepare a place for them (John 14:2–3), and when the place is ready, he will send his angels to gather them in.

What a contrast between the gathering of the vultures to devour the rotting carcass (v. 28) and the gathering of Christ's elect at the great trumpet summons of his holy angels. May you be in the latter company and look forward with joy to the Lord's coming!

"Now learn this lesson from the fig tree: As soon as its twigs get tender and its leaves come out, you know that summer is near. Even so, when you see all these things, you know that it is near, right at the door." (32–33)

Our Lord here apparently returned to the subject of the destruction of Jerusalem. In these words he gave his apostles warning concerning the signs of the times. He said they could learn this lesson from the fig tree. God's great book of nature is full of illustrations for those who have eyes to see them. The Lord Jesus, the great Creator, often made use of its illuminated pages to convey instruction to the minds of his listeners.

On this occasion he used a simple simile from the fig tree. "As soon as its twigs get tender and its leaves come out, you know that summer is near." They could not mistake so plain a token of the near return of summer. Jesus wanted them to read just as easily the signs that would herald the coming judgment on Jerusalem. O that people today were wise enough to learn the lesson of that fiery trial and seek the face of him whose wrath they cannot bear!

A generation had run its course when the Roman armies circled Jerusalem, whose measure of sin was then full and overflowed in misery, agony, and bloodshed such as the world had never seen before. Jesus was the true prophet. Everything he foretold was literally fulfilled. He confirmed what he had already said and what he was about to say by a solemn affirmation:

"I tell you the truth, this generation will certainly not pass away until all these things have happened. Heaven and earth will pass away, but my words will never pass away." (34–35)

Though the Lord appeared as a man and was crucified as a criminal, his words would endure when heaven and earth would have fulfilled their purpose and passed away. Christ's promises of pardon are as sure of fulfillment as his prophecies of punishment.

Our Lord's words will endure because they are divine, they are the revelation of the heart of God, they are pure truth, no power can thwart them, and God's honor is involved in their permanence.

"No one knows about that day or hour, not even the angels in heaven, nor the Son, but only the Father. As it was in the days of Noah, so it will be at the coming of the Son of Man. For in the days before the flood, people were eating and drinking, marrying and giving in marriage, up to the day Noah entered the ark; and they knew nothing about what would happen until the flood came and took them all away. That is how it will be at the coming of the Son of Man. Two men will be in the field; one will be taken and the other left. Two women will be grinding with a hand mill; one will be taken and the other left." (36–41)

Here the emphasis shifts to the last great coming to judgment. Some would-be prophets wrench this verse from its clear meaning when they say, "Though we may not know the day and hour of Christ's coming, we may know the year, the month, and even the week." If that is not blasphemous, it is foolish and betrays a disloyalty to the King. Jesus said not even the angels in heaven know when he will return.

We need not be troubled, therefore, by idle prophecies of reckless fanatics, even if they claim to interpret Scripture, for if the angels do not know when Christ will come back, neither does anyone else. Even Christ, in his human nature, so voluntarily limited his own capacities that he did not know the time of his second advent (Mark 13:32). It is enough for us to know that he will surely come. Our great concern should be to be ready for his appearing whenever it will be.

Though our King did not reveal the time of his coming, he declared plainly that history would repeat itself. "As it was in the days of Noah, so it will be at the coming of the Son of Man." When he comes, he will find many unprepared, even as the people were in Noah's day, when "the flood came and took them all away." Yet in both cases, sinners will have had ample warning. Noah was "a preacher of righteousness" (2 Peter 2:5) to the people of his day. And the gospel of Christ's kingdom will be preached to all nations before the end comes (v. 14).

Like the flood, Christ's coming will be sudden, unexpected, universal in its effects, and terrible to the ungodly. Yet they will be completely unconcerned, "eating and drinking, marrying and giving in marriage" until that day. These are lawful and right affairs, but they become a positive evil when they hinder a person's preparation for the coming of the Son of Man. Woe to those whose eating and drinking do not include the bread and the water of life. Woe to those who marry or are given in marriage but not to the heavenly Bridegroom!

The division between the godly and the ungodly at the coming of Christ will be precise. Companions in labor will be separated forever in that day. The believing laborer will be taken by the angels to join the hosts of the redeemed, while his unbelieving fellow worker will be left to the judgment that will be swiftly poured out on him.

The two women mentioned may be fellow servants in a rich person's mansion or mother and daughter or two sisters in a poor person's home. However closely they may be attached to one another, if one is saved by grace and the other is still under the sentence of condemnation, one will be taken and the other left. This separation will be eternal. There is no hint of any future reunion.

"Therefore keep watch, because you do not know on what day your Lord will come. But understand this: If the owner of the house had

known at what time of night the thief was coming, he would have kept watch and would not have let his house be broken into. So you also must be ready, because the Son of Man will come at an hour when you do not expect him." (42–44)

This is the practical conclusion of the whole matter. Our Lord's coming is certain and may be at any moment. We do not know when he will come. The title Jesus used gives greater force to the command to "keep watch," for it is our "Lord" who is coming.

If the owners of a house have reliable information that thieves are coming but do not know at what hour they will arrive, they will keep awake all night waiting for their appearance. But if they are told "at what time of night" the thieves will come, they will be especially on the alert then. Every little sound will attract their attention. They think they hear someone at the back door. No, the thieves are trying to enter by a front window! Wherever the thieves come, they will find the owners are listening and watching. The homeowners are ready to arrest them, for they have received timely warning of their coming. What a pity that people are not equally wise in watching for the coming of their Lord. We do not know, we cannot even guess at what time Jesus will come.

Christ's second coming will be like that of a thief in that it will be unexpected. Therefore, it will be when due preparations for his reception have not been made. But his followers will not let that day surprise them like a thief (1 Thess. 5:4). They will always be looking for his appearing.

Our Lord's warning to his disciples ought to have even greater weight with us who live so much nearer to the time of his second advent. We ought to be as watchful as if we knew he would come tonight. Though we do not know when he will come, we do know he may come at any moment. Oh, to be ready for his appearing, watching and waiting for him as servants whose Lord has been away from them for a long time and who may return at any hour!

This will not make us neglect our daily calling. On the contrary, we will be all the more diligent to attend to our earthly duties because our hearts are at rest about our heavenly treasures.

"Who then is the faithful and wise servant, whom the master has put in charge of the servants in his household to give them their food at the proper time? It will be good for that servant whose master finds him doing so when he returns. I tell you the truth, he will put him in charge of all his possessions." (45–47)

These words describe the ministry of a pastor, preaching the truth with all his heart and seeking to give to all over whom the Holy Spirit has made him an overseer their food at the proper time. Or they picture a teacher trying to feed the minds of the class with sound doctrine. Or they portray any servant of Christ doing the work the Master has entrusted to him or to her. This servant does the work as if knowing the Lord was coming at that moment to examine it. Such a servant of Christ is faithful and wise, a happy person to be found by the Lord doing so when he returns. May our Master find us thus occupied when he comes!

The master had formerly put the servant in charge of the servants. Now faithful and wise conduct in that job won a promotion to a higher post, so that the master put the servant in charge of all his possessions. Thus it is among the servants of King Jesus. There are rewards for faithful service—not of debt but of grace, not according to the rule of the law but the rule of love. Faithfulness in one form of service is rewarded by further service and increased responsibility. The servant whose mina gained ten more received authority over ten cities (Luke 19:16-17).

"But suppose that servant is wicked and says to himself, 'My master is staying away a long time,' and he then begins to beat his fellow servants and to eat and drink with drunkards. The master of that servant will come on a day when he does not expect him and at an hour he is not aware of. He will cut him to pieces and assign him a place with the hypocrites, where there will be weeping and gnashing of teeth." (48-51)

The servant's warning is not to the outside world but to those who profess to be servants of God. This is also a warning to pastors of the Word whom God makes rulers over his household.

This servant was wicked, a hypocrite who had intruded into an office he had no right to hold. His thoughts and words were wicked: "My master is staying away a long time." His conduct toward those under him was wicked: he began "to beat his fellow servants." His own life was wicked: he began "to eat and drink with drunkards." His wickedness would be suddenly cut short by his master's appearance. Immediate and terrible punishment would be meted out to him: "He will cut him to pieces and assign him a place with the hypocrites." He was one of those hypocrites. He pretended to be a servant of God when all along he was a slave of Satan, serving self and sin. Let him go to his own company.

Before they cut him to pieces, this counterfeit servant's heart was already divided. Outwardly he was a follower of Christ; inwardly he served his own lusts. When they cut him to pieces, it was only a righteous perpetuation of his own double-faced character.

Will people who follow in this servant's steps come to their end there? No. "There will be weeping and gnashing of teeth." What a destiny for one who was numbered among God's servants! As we read of this, let us in deep humility remember the solemn command of the apostle Paul: "If you think that you are standing firm, be careful that you don't fall!" (1 Cor. 10:12).

Christ's Resurrection and Great Commission

After the Sabbath, at dawn on the first day of the week, Mary Magdalene and the other Mary went to look at the tomb. (1)

We often forget that the first sinner was a woman. Christ took away that shame by giving women the honor of being the first at the empty tomb. And who but Mary Magdalene should be the first one there? Out of her Christ had cast seven demons (Luke 8:2), but here she acted as if Christ had sent seven angels into her. She had received so much grace that she was full of love for her Lord.

There was a violent earthquake, for an angel of the Lord came down from heaven and, going to the tomb, rolled back the stone and sat on it. His appearance was like lightning, and his clothes were white as snow. The guards were so afraid of him that they shook and became like dead men. (2–4)

This was no ordinary earthquake but a "violent" one. Death was going through an upheaval. All the bars of the tomb were beginning to burst. When the King awoke from the sleep of death, he shook the world. The bedroom in which he had rested for a little while trembled as the heavenly Lord arose from his couch.

Jesus was placed in the prison of the tomb as a hostage for his people. Therefore it was fitting that he not break out by himself. The angelic sheriff came with the warrant for his release and set the captive free. Jesus had been confined because of human debt, but the debt had been paid, so he had to go free.

When the angel rolled back the stone, he sat on it as if to defy earth and hell ever to roll it back again. When the angel sat on the stone, one greater than an earthly king sat on something better than a throne. That great stone seemed to represent the sin of all Christ's people that had shut them up in prison. It can never be laid again over the mouth of the tomb of any child of God. Christ has risen, and all his saints must rise too.

Are angels here with you and me now? Do they make a habit of coming where the saints meet together? I think they do. We have hints in Scripture that this is the case. Let us behave properly now "because of the angels" (1 Cor. 11:10). As they worship Jesus and count it their highest honor to serve him, let us also worship and adore Jesus.

Roman soldiers knew nothing of cowardice. Yet the sight of this angel caused them to shake and become like dead men. The angel said nothing as he rolled back the stone. He did not shake a sword at the guards to fill them with terror. The presence of perfect purity and heavenly glory is a terror to the ungodly. May you and I be such that our very presence in company will cast a hush over it. May there be in us enough of the heavenly to make the powers of evil quail before us.

The angel said to the women, "Do not be afraid, for I know that you are looking for Jesus, who was crucified. He is not here; he has risen, just as he said. Come and see the place where he lay. Then go quickly and tell his disciples: 'He has risen from the dead and is going ahead of you into Galilee. There you will see him.' Now I have told you." (5–7)

Though the angel said, "Do not be afraid," the women were afraid. Not even angels can speak so as to silence fears in trembling hearts, but Jesus can, as we shall see in a moment. One word from his lips has infinitely more power than all the words of angels or saints.

If you and I can truly say that we seek Jesus who was crucified, we can bear all the shame that philosophers gladly heap on the Cross, and we will have no cause for fear. The ridicule from ungodly people will not hurt us.

The angel reminded the women that Jesus had risen, "just as he said." He always does just as he said. He always gives just as he said. He always reveals himself just as he said. He never fails to fulfill a promise. Not only does he do what he said, but just as he said. In this case, "He has risen, just as he said."

Even the place where he lay is sacred to you. And if there is a place where you have ever had fellowship with Christ, you will remember it. You might bless the spot of ground where Jesus met with you. As you read the Bible, I hope you can see places where Jesus appears to you.

Jesus was buried in a tomb that belonged to Joseph of Arimathea. On his cross he borrowed our sins, and in his burial he borrowed another man's grave. Before his birth Christ lay in a virgin's womb, and after his death he was placed in a virgin tomb "in which no one had yet been laid" (Luke 23:53). So no one could say that another person rose, for no other body had been there.

In verse 6 the angel told the women to see, and in verse 7 he told them to go. You cannot tell the message until you know it. You who would serve God must first be taught. If you have seen, then go. Do not sit down and admire the sight and forget the thousands who have never seen it. We cannot afford to spend all our time in meditation, however heavenly it may be.

News this good ought to be spread quickly. "Go quickly and tell his disciples," for they were trembling and had fled. "He has risen" is good news for us now, though some may not feel the power of it. We have no dead Christ. We serve a living Savior. He has risen, and therefore he can come to us now and make us glad.

Christ's resurrection proves his deity. Because he was God, "it was impossible for death to keep its hold on him" (Acts 2:24). The empty tomb is a sign also of our forgiveness. If Jesus had not paid the debt for our sins, he would not have risen from the grave. The empty tomb also proves that we shall rise from the dead. Christ's same body rose; so shall ours. "Because I live, you also will live" (John 14:19). What is the grave? It is the bath in which Christians put the clothes of their bodies to have them washed. What is death? It is the place where the body, like Esther, bathes itself in spices, that it may be fit for the embrace of its Lord. Death is the gate of life, so we will not fear it.

The angel added, "[Christ] is going ahead of you into Galilee." That was the border land that touched the Gentiles. It was much despised as the place of illiterate people. There is a place where Jesus will meet his people in the border land between Jew and Gentile. He goes to the despised places, that he may lift up its people by the glory of his light.

So the women hurried away from the tomb, afraid yet filled with joy, and ran to tell his disciples. Suddenly Jesus met them. "Greetings," he said. They came to him, clasped his feet and worshiped him. Then Jesus said to them, "Do not be afraid. Go and tell my brothers to go to Galilee; there they will see me." (8-10)

What a mixture—fear and joy! Who would not fear who had felt an earthquake, seen an angel, and noticed the tomb broken open?

Yet who would not rejoice who had such an encouraging message and such an assurance that Christ had risen from the dead? The fear was not great, but the joy was. If now you have some fear, I hope you will be filled with joy. Then the bitterness of the fear will go away. A holy fear mixed with fullness of joy is one of the sweetest compounds we can bring to God's altar. These women brought other spices to the tomb, but the spices they took away from it were fear and fullness of joy. Some of us have brought those spices with us to this text.

While the women were on a mission to tell the disciples of Jesus' resurrection, suddenly Jesus met them. Happy are the pastors who meet the Lord as they walk up to their pulpits! Blessed are the teachers who meet Jesus when they walk into their classes! They will be sure to preach and teach well when that is the case.

Maybe the women clasped Jesus' feet because they feared he might again be taken from them. But this was also an act of humility. The women clasped the same feet that the nails had held three days earlier. They must have seen the nail prints before Thomas did as they held him by the feet and worshiped him. These women did not run to the angel. They shrank back from him. But they came to Jesus and clasped his feet. There must have been a new attraction about Christ after he had risen from the dead. Something more sweet about the tones of his voice. Something more charming about his face that had been so marred at Gethsemane, Gabbatha, and Golgotha.

The angel had talked of disciples (v. 7), but here Christ spoke of brothers. He always has the sweeter word. He wanted them to meet him in Galilee. He said nothing about classic Corinth, imperial Rome, or proud Jerusalem. If we will be humble, we shall meet Christ, who is "humble in heart" (Matt. 11:29).

While the women were on their way, some of the guards went into the city and reported to the chief priests everything that had happened. When the chief priests had met with the elders and devised a plan, they gave the soldiers a large sum of money, telling them, "You are to say, 'His disciples came during the night and stole him away while we were asleep.' If this report gets to the governor, we will satisfy him and keep you out of trouble." So the soldiers took the money and did as they were instructed. And this story has been widely circulated among the Jews to this very day. (11–15)

While good people were active, bad people were active, too. It is amazing to think of how much good and evil are being done at the same time. While holy women ran with holy messages for Christ, the guards went in to the vile chief priests.

These chief priests should have repented when the guards came and told them that Jesus had risen. They should have gone and fallen at his feet and begged for mercy. But instead, wherever money comes in, it seems to do harm. For money Christ was betrayed, and for money the truth of his resurrection was kept back as far as it could be. Money has had a hardening effect on some of the highest servants of God. Everyone who touches it has a need to pray for grace to keep from being harmed by it.

Roman soldiers would have committed suicide rather than admit they had slept while on guard. If they had been asleep, how could they have known what happened? How could they have known that they had even been asleep? Evidence given by men who were asleep at the time is not worth consideration. But when you have to tell a lie, any lie will do to slander the person you hate, just as any stick is good enough to beat a dog with.

Many a lie worse than this has been told to try to destroy the truth of God. The modern philosophy that casts a slur on the great truths of revelation are no more worthy of belief than this lie put into the mouths of the guards.

A pastor was once asked if he believed all the doctrines of his church. He replied, "Because my salary is so small, I can't be expected to believe them all." May none of us ever be swayed, as the Roman soldiers were, by thoughts of profit and loss in matters of Scripture, duty, right, and wrong.

You may start a lie, but you can't stop it. There is no telling how long it will live. Let us never teach even the least bit of error to a little child, for it may live on and become a great heresy long after we are dead. There is scarcely any limit to its life and power. Nothing lives as long as a lie—except the truth.

Then the eleven disciples went to Galilee, to the mountain where Jesus had told them to go. When they saw him, they worshiped him; but some doubted. (16–17)

Jesus had told his disciples to meet him in Galilee—a despised country known as Galilee of the Gentiles—and he did meet them there. Jesus always keeps his appointments. This may have been the occasion Paul referred to when he said Jesus "appeared to more than five hundred of the brothers at the same time" (1 Cor. 15:6).

Among them were some honest doubters. Their breed has been preserved ever since, only there are many more dishonest doubters than honest ones now. We can never expect to be quite free from doubters in the church, since even in the presence of the newly risen Christ some doubted.

Then Jesus came to them and said, "All authority in heaven and on earth has been given to me. Therefore go and make disciples of all nations, baptizing them in the name of the Father and of the Son and of the Holy Spirit, and teaching them to obey everything I have commanded you. And surely I am with you always, to the very end of the age." (18–20)

What a contrast this speech was to Jesus' groans in Gethsemane and his gloom at Golgotha! The complete authority his Father had given him was part of the reward for his self-humiliation (Phil. 2:6-11).

The Lord Jesus might have said, "All authority in heaven and on earth has been given to me. Therefore, take your swords and slay my enemies who crucified me!" But he had no thoughts of revenge. He might have said, "The Jews put me to death. Therefore, go immediately to the Gentiles, for these Jews shall never taste my grace." But no, he told his disciples to preach forgiveness "beginning at Jerusalem" (Luke 24:47).

Since Christ has all authority, let us not intrude another authority. Let us keep within the Master's house. Let us seek to know the Master's mind, to learn the Master's will, to study the Master's book, and to receive the Master's Spirit.

They were not to make the nations their disciples but Christ's disciples. He was still to be the teacher and Master. They were to do his work, not their own.

It is as much the duty of Christians to teach after baptism as before it. We must always be teaching. Hence believers are always to be learners. We are not to invent a gospel. We are not to change and shift and cut and shape it to keep up with the advancements of the age. The Great Commission is plain. We are to teach disciples to obey the commands Jesus has given.

The disciples had their commission, and the presence of Christ was the source of their power. They were to work in union with him. God grant that you and I, as we go out to teach Christ, may always have the sound of our Master's feet with us, even to the end of the age. May we realize Christ's presence with us until he calls us to be with him.

Since all authority has been given to Christ, let us obey him. Christ says, "Go." Then let us go at once out of respect for his word. Let us keep in fellowship with him, for he has promised, "Surely I am with you always." And let us be expecting his return. "To the very end of the age" suggests this thought.

The Death of Christ

Very early in the morning, the chief priests, with the elders, the teachers of the law and the whole Sanhedrin, reached a decision. They bound Jesus, led him away and handed him over to Pilate (1).

The whole Sanhedrin could be there very early in the morning only for an evil purpose like this. Wicked people are very diligent in carrying out their sinful schemes. How much more diligent ought the followers of Christ to be to give him their devoted service? It is a good thing to begin the day with united prayer and holy fellowship with his people. Let these wicked men who were so early in the morning seeking to secure the death of Christ make us ashamed that we are not more diligent in his blessed service.

As Isaac was bound before he was laid on the altar (Gen. 22:9), so Jesus, the great antitype, was bound before he was nailed to the cross. He could have snapped those bonds as easily as Samson snapped the Philistines' bonds (Judg. 15:13-14), but there were other invisible cords that bound him—the bonds of his own oath and promise, the bonds of his love for you and me. These constrained Jesus to yield himself to the Jews and Pilate as a lamb to the slaughter.

"Are you the king of the Jews?" asked Pilate.
"Yes, it is as you say," Jesus replied. (2)

Jesus did not look like a king as he stood before Pilate. He was wearing no royal robes, but simple clothes. Yet even in his humiliation there must have been so much majesty that even the governor was prompted to ask, "Are you the king of the Jews?"

There was no longer any reason King Jesus should conceal his true position, so he answered Pilate's question. The Jews rejected their King and refused to bow down to him. "His own did not receive him" (John 1:11), but he was still their King.

The chief priests accused him of many things. So again Pilate asked him, "Aren't you going to answer? See how many things they are accusing you of."
But Jesus still made no reply, and Pilate was amazed. (3–5)

Jesus never hesitated to speak when he could bless others, but he would not say a single word for himself. "No one ever spoke the way this man does" (John 7:46), and no one was silent as he was, either. Our Lord's silence was the index of his perfect self-sacrifice. He had dedicated himself as an offering for us. He could have cleared himself of every accusation brought against him, but that would have left the load of guilt on those whose place he came to take. So Jesus still made no reply. He was about to carry our sins, and there is no excuse for sin, so Jesus did not defend himself.

Silence was the best answer, the most eloquent reply that Jesus could give to his accusers. They deserved no other answer. Moreover, by his silence he was fulfilling the prophecy, "As a sheep before her shearers is silent, so he did not open his mouth" (Isa. 53:7). You will often find that your highest wisdom, when you are slandered, lies in the imitation of your Lord. Live a blameless life, and it will be the best reply to the false charges of the wicked.

Now it was the custom at the Feast to release a prisoner whom the people requested. A man called Barabbas was in prison with the insurrectionists who had committed murder in the uprising. The crowd came up and asked Pilate to do for them what he usually did. (6–8)

Pilate may have hoped that Jesus was so popular with the people that an appeal to the masses would result in a verdict in Christ's favor, especially since the choice was between "the king of the Jews" and Barabbas, a convicted criminal.

"Do you want me to release to you the king of the Jews?" asked Pilate, knowing it was out of envy that the chief priests had handed Jesus over to him. But the chief priests stirred up the crowd to have Pilate release Barabbas instead. (9–11)

Pilate hoped that the people, who were not moved by the same envy, would have chosen to have Jesus set free.

Lust is a Barabbas. Many indulge in its pleasure, even though it

means they must set Christ aside. Drunkenness is another Barabbas
that enthralls millions. If it was sinful for the Jews to choose a murderer (v. 7), what must it be for you to choose this cursed vice that
murders its hundreds of thousands? Sin is a Barabbas—a thief that
will rob your soul of its life and God of his glory. Sin is a Barabbas
also because it murdered our father, Adam, and slew our purity.

"What shall I do, then, with the one you call the king of the Jews?"
Pilate asked them.
   "Crucify him!" they shouted. (12–13)

There could be no danger of someone leading these people astray
when those very people were crying, "Crucify him!" It must have
been a transparent fraud. Pilate must have loathed them. Corrupt as
he was, he must have been able to see their corruption. The literal
translation of Psalm 14:1 reads, "The fool says in his heart, 'No
God!'" The desire to get rid of God shows the depravity of the
human heart. People will lust for that in the foolish hopes that they
can have it. This is what the crowd did here.

The Lord of glory had been sold by Judas for the price of a slave
(Matt. 26:14–16). Now a murderer is favored by the people over the
prince of life. Why didn't anyone speak up on behalf of Christ? Was
there no one out of all that multitude whose sickness Jesus had
healed, whose hunger he had satisfied, who would plead his case?
No, not one person.

"Why? What crime has he committed?" asked Pilate.
   But they shouted all the louder, "Crucify him!" (14)

The crowd did not answer Pilate's question. If they had, they
would have been forced to admit Jesus was innocent of any crime.
They only repeated the brutal demand, "Crucify him!"

If Jesus had really set himself up as a king in place of Caesar, these
people would not have cried out, "Crucify him!" Jesus would have
been their hero. Thus Pilate, by asking the question "Why? What
crime has he committed?" gave a powerful answer.

Wanting to satisfy the crowd, Pilate released Barabbas to them. He
had Jesus flogged, and handed him over to be crucified. (15)

Pilate thought that by having Jesus flogged, he could let him go.
But flogging was the most terrible of tortures. Many died under it.
It reduced the human body to a mass of bruised, bleeding, quivering

flesh. This flogging produced the wounds by which we have been healed (1 Peter 2:24). Yet for Christ it was only the beginning of the awful end.

Pilate knew Jesus was innocent of any crime (v. 14). He even spoke out for Christ, but he did not act for him, as he should have done. Many Pilates today would long ago have become Christians, except they lacked moral courage. Some would sooner be damned than laughed at.

The soldiers led Jesus away into the palace (that is, the Praetorium) and called together the whole company of soldiers. They put a purple robe on him, then twisted together a crown of thorns and set it on him. And they began to call out to him, "Hail, King of the Jews!" Again and again they struck him on the head with a staff and spit on him. Falling on their knees, they worshiped him. And when they had mocked him, they took off the purple robe and put his own clothes on him. Then they led him out to crucify him. (16–20)

The whole company of soldiers was called together that Jesus might suffer the full chorus of their ridicule. These men were hearty in their mockery of our Redeemer. When will we, his people, be as zealous in his praises? Should not the whole company of believers worship him? The soldiers were unanimous in mocking their prisoner. People are apt to go together when they go wrong. Watch out for sinning in a crowd. Beware of the notion that because many do it, there is less guilt for you.

The uniform of the Roman soldiers was purple, as if to indicate that they belonged to an imperial master. So when these soldiers in mockery put on our Lord the old cloak of one of their comrades, it clothed him with the royal purple that he was entitled to as King.

When you have gone up to the place of worship on Sunday and have only pretended to adore Christ, you have mocked him by a feigned worship and thus put the purple robe on him. That purple robe meant they made him a king in name only, and the homage they paid him was a mere show. Your Sunday religion, forgotten in the week, is a mere sham. You have mocked and insulted Christ even in your hymns and prayers, for your religion is a mere pretense.

The King of Kings was derided and made nothing of. He was treated as a mimic monarch by the vilest and most brutal people. In the time of his shame, no one had a good word for Jesus. That would be our condition if we had no share in Christ's substitutionary sacrifice. How ought we to love him for enduring our shame!

All this homage was paid to Jesus in mockery, yet what stern reality there was in that mockery! That band of soldiers really presented to Christ such honor as a wicked world could give him. Here was majesty in misery. Our Lord, the angels' King, was spit on by callous men. The men who drove the nails through Jesus' hands and feet did what they were ordered to do, but those who spit in his face performed an uncalled-for act.

It serves as a reminder to us that Jesus took the place of sinners. Sin deserves to be spit on. It deserves to be crucified. Because our Lord had taken our sin on himself, he had to endure this shame. If you want to see what God thinks of sin, watch these soldiers spit on his Son when he was made sin for us. The Master's face was full of spit because our faces were full of spots. If Jesus would save us, his face had to be full of spots too. He had none of his own, so those spots had to come from the lips of scoffers.

It seems as if Christ had to lean on those who led him out to his crucifixion. The Greek word translated "led" almost always signifies that. It is the word used for the leading of a child or a sick person who needed support. The Savior's weakness must have been very apparent by this time. After the agony and bloody sweat in Gethsemane, the night and morning trials, the scourging, mockery, and awful strain on his mind and heart in being made a sacrifice for sin, it was no wonder that he was weak. Besides, Jesus suffered much more than any ordinary human being would have done in similar circumstances.

A certain man from Cyrene, Simon, the father of Alexander and Rufus, was passing by on his way in from the country, and they forced him to carry the cross. (21)

John 19:17 tells us that Jesus started out carrying his own cross, but that didn't last long. The soldiers saw that he was about to collapse and were afraid he might die of exhaustion before they could crucify him. So they forced a man named Simon to carry the cross. You, too, can be a Simon and carry Jesus' cross if you become a Christian. If Christ will be your hope, his death will be your trust. You never become a true cross-bearer until you lay your burden down at his feet who carried the cross and curse for you.

Notice the blessings that came to Simon when he carried Jesus' cross. It brought him into fellowship with Christ. It helped him walk in Christ's steps. It linked him to the work of Christ. And it brought him the smile of Christ.

The man who carried Jesus' cross was Simon. Where was the other Simon? Simon Peter, another man has taken your place!

Sometimes the Lord's servants are remiss, and he finds other servants. Brother or sister, stay true to Christ. Don't let another Simon take your place! It was prophesied of Judas, "May another take his place of leadership" (Acts 1:20), but a true disciple will retain his or her office. Remember the word of our Lord, "Hold on to what you have, so that no one will take your crown" (Rev. 3:11). Simon Peter lost a crown here, and another head wore it.

Like Simon, the church is the cross-bearer behind Jesus. Our Lord did not suffer so as to exclude your suffering. He carried a cross not that you may escape it but that you may endure it. Christ exempts you from sin but not from sorrow, so expect to suffer. Though Simon had to carry the cross for a very little while, it gave him lasting honor. Even so, the cross we carry is only for a little while at most, and then we will receive the crown.

They brought Jesus to the place called Golgotha (which means The Place of the Skull). (22)

The Greek word translated "brought" implies that the soldiers had to lift and carry Jesus, for by this time he had almost fainted. Earlier they had led him out to crucify him but now they had to carry him.

Then they offered him wine mixed with myrrh, but he did not take it. (23)

The Romans always gave a cup of wine mixed with myrrh before crucifixion to ease the pain of the victim, but Jesus did not take it. Our Lord needed all his faculties in their clearest state to combat the dreadful powers of darkness. He had also come to earth to suffer. If a ransom is due, it must be paid in full. If one penny is left unpaid, the hostage is not totally free. If Jesus had drunk this cup of wine mixed with myrrh, the Atonement would have been incomplete. He had to feel the pain to the bitter end. Did Jesus refuse this drug because he loved to suffer? No, for in Gethsemane he prayed that the cup of suffering might pass him by (Mark 14:36). He refused the drug because he loved people.

Perhaps your husband or your wife has died, and your heart is broken. If you could have the cup of wine and myrrh offered to you, would you take it? If someone could tell you, "I will bring your pain to an end by bringing back to life your loved one," would you be able to say, "Not my will, but God's be done"?

And they crucified him. Dividing up his clothes, they cast lots to see what each would get. (24)

Jesus' clothes had to go to his executioners for two reasons: to carry out the full shame associated with his death and to fulfill the prophecy of Psalm 22:18: "They divide my garments among them and cast lots for my clothing."

The soldiers gambled for Jesus' clothes. Only gamblers could have cast the dice, all spattered with Jesus' blood, at the foot of his cross. No sin so hardens the heart as gambling, nor does any sin so swiftly send people to hell. Can gamblers pray? Can they meditate? Can they enjoy fellowship with the Lord Jesus? Can they be free from worry? Where is their faith? When gamblers have practically committed their fortune to the Devil, how can they trust in God? Worst of all, people who gamble help the Devil send others to hell.

It was the third hour when they crucified him. The written notice of the charge against him read: THE KING OF THE JEWS. *They crucified two robbers with him, one on his right and one on his left. Those who passed by hurled insults at him, shaking their heads and saying, "So! You who are going to destroy the temple and build it in three days, come down from the cross and save yourself!" (25–30)*

The third hour is equivalent to nine o'clock in the morning.

The King of the Jews. So he is, and so he always will be. Jesus has never left the throne! What a marvelous providence moved Pilate's pen! Any representative of the Roman emperor was unlikely to concede kingship to anyone, yet Pilate wrote that Jesus was "The king of the Jews," and nothing would make him change it. Even on his cross Christ was proclaimed King! The Jews will own him as their King when he comes again. Perhaps they will think more of Christ before then if we Christians think more of them.

As if to carry out the ordinary etiquette that gave the central place to the worst criminal, the soldiers put Jesus between the two robbers, thus giving him the place of greatest contempt and scorn. Wherever he is, Jesus always deserves the chief place. God's purpose for his Son is that "in everything he might have the supremacy" (Col. 1:18).

Jesus had sinners to the right of him, sinners to the left of him, and sinners all around him. They had sinned in the highest degree by putting to death the Son of God. You could not count the criminals on those crosses without counting Jesus. There were three, and the one in the middle could not be passed over as you counted the others, because he was carrying our sins. It is the hope of "lawless ones" now that Jesus was counted with them. Why did he willingly submit to this? So that the blessings of heaven could now descend on the sinners who accept him as their substitute and Savior.

Nothing torments a person in pain more than mockery. When Jesus most wanted words of pity and looks of compassion, they "hurled insults at him." Not just those who sat down to gloat their cruel eyes on Jesus' miseries, but even those who passed by hurled insults at him.

Perhaps the most painful part of ridicule is to have one's most solemn sayings turned to scorn. Jesus never said he was going to destroy the temple and build it in three days. He did, however, say concerning his body, "Destroy this temple, and I will raise it again in three days" (John 2:19). Sure enough, after they crucified him, he rose again on the third day. Precisely because Jesus was the Son of God, he did not come down from the cross, as these mockers asked him to do. He had to hang there until he completed the sacrifice for his people's sin. Jesus' cross is Jacob's ladder (Gen. 28:10-12) by which we mount up to heaven.

That is the Devil's old doctrine: "Save yourself! Live for self. Be selfish." But Jesus could never have acted like that. He had come to live and die for others (Mark 10:45).

In the same way the chief priests and the teachers of the law mocked him among themselves. "He saved others," they said, "but he can't save himself! Let this Christ, this King of Israel, come down now from the cross, that we may see and believe." Those crucified with him also heaped insults on him. (31–32)

What they said in bitter scorn was true. Mighty love had bound Jesus' hands, preventing him from saving himself. Found guilty of excess of love to us, he saved others and so could not save himself. Notice the testimony that Jesus' bitterest enemies bore even as they insulted him: "He saved others."

Again notice the confession our Lord's worst enemies made. They called him "King of Israel." They spoke the truth in scorn, but still the truth came out. The crowd wanted him to come down from the cross "that we may see and believe." That is always the world's way. But Christ's way is, "Believe, and you will see."

These scoffers claimed to be willing to believe in Christ as long as it was not the crucified Christ. Many today are willing to believe in Jesus as a good man but not the sacrifice for sin. But that would make Jesus an impostor, for he said he was the Son of God. You must either repudiate Jesus altogether or take him with his cross. It must be Christ crucified or no Christ at all. The crucified Christ is our great hope, especially since we know that this same Christ is now on the throne waiting for the time he will return to claim as his own all who have trusted in him.

Of all the people who might heap insults on the Lord Jesus, those crucified with him are the last we would expect, for they were dying fairly. But out of their foul hearts and mouths insults spewed.

At the sixth hour darkness came over the whole land until the ninth hour. And at the ninth hour Jesus cried out in a loud voice, "Eloi, Eloi, lama sabachthani?"—which means, "My God, my God, why have you forsaken me?" (33–34)

The sixth hour was high noon, when the sun had reached its zenith. So this was a supernatural darkness, contrary to the laws of nature. I wonder what people in other places thought when they saw the darkness. Perhaps they said, "Either the whole world is about to end, or God who made the world is in anguish." The sun could no longer look at its Maker surrounded by those who mocked him. It covered its face in very shame that "the light of the world" (John 8:12) himself should be in such terrible darkness. All lights are dim when Christ does not shine. The entire creation depends on him.

But in another sense, this miracle pictures the way the powers of darkness will always try to conceal the Cross of Christ. We fight with darkness when we preach the Cross. Nothing provokes the Devil like the death of Christ. Jesus had said to the Jewish leaders who arrested him, "This is your hour—when darkness reigns" (Luke 22:53).

When Jesus was born, midnight turned to midday, and when he died, midday turned to midnight. When he was born, heaven was lit up with splendor, but when he died, the heavens put out their brightest light.

This was the climax of Christ's grief—not merely to suffer intense agony of body, not only to be mocked by priests and people, but to be forsaken by his God. This was necessary as part of the penalty for sin. God must turn away from anyone who has sin. Since sin was laid on Christ, God had to turn his face away even from his beloved Son. See here the difference between the Christian martyrs and their Lord. In their dying agonies they were sustained by God, but Jesus was forsaken by God, because he suffered in the place of sinners.

There was a denser darkness over Jesus' spirit than over all the land (v. 33), and out of that darkness came his cry of agony. These were the bitterest words ever uttered by mortal lips. They expressed the quintessence of agony. It grieves me to think that my Savior should ever have had to say this when he hung on the cross, suffering and dying for me.

In his anguish our Lord did not look to his friends. Though God was angry, Jesus cried, "My God, my God." It is the only cry that fits a believer's lips. Even if God seems to forsake you, keep on crying out to him. Depend on it, he will help you sooner or later. He must do it. He cannot fail you. If faith gives up her God because he frowns, what kind of faith is that? Can't you believe in a frowning God?

Though Jesus knew his Father had forsaken him, he did not leave the cross. He could have unloosed the nails, but he did not. He did not leap down into the assembled mockers and chase them away. He kept on bleeding and suffering, even until he could say, "It is finished" (John 19:30).

If you die without trusting in Christ, he will forsake you forever. If you ask, "Why have you forsaken me?" he will answer, "You have forsaken me." But more awful than crying out "My God, my God, why have you forsaken me?" is to be apart from God and not care about it. I pity the agony of the non-Christian who cannot bear to be without God, but at the same time I can bless the Lord that he or she feels such an agony, for it proves to me that this individual's soul will never perish.

When some of those standing near heard this, they said, "Listen, he's calling Elijah." (35)

Did they misunderstand Christ's bitter cry of woe? Could they have mistaken what he meant? I do not think so. I fear it was a willful and cruel jest of what our Lord Jesus had just asked his Father in verse 34.

One man ran, filled a sponge with wine vinegar, put it on a stick, and offered it to Jesus to drink. "Now leave him alone. Let's see if Elijah comes to take him down," he said. (36)

Back in verse 23 Jesus refused the cup of wine mixed with myrrh because it was a drug that would have alleviated his suffering. But here he accepted this sponge with wine vinegar because it merely helped quenched his thirst. It fulfilled the prophecy of Psalm 69:21: "They . . . gave me vinegar for my thirst."

It seems strange that the sponge—the very lowest form of animal life—should have been brought into contact with Christ, the top of all life. As the sponge brought refreshment to the lips of our dying Lord, so may the least of God's living ones refresh him now that he has ascended from the cross to the throne!

With a loud cry, Jesus breathed his last. (37)

Jesus' strength was not exhausted, for his last words were uttered "with a loud cry," like the shout of a conquering warrior. We know from John's gospel that in this loud cry Jesus said, "It is finished" (John 19:30). There is nothing for us to do. We need not weep to receive salvation, for the work is finished. Religion says, "Do," but Christianity says, "Done!" There is no mortgage on the saints.

The curtain of the temple was torn in two from top to bottom. And when the centurion, who stood there in front of Jesus, heard his cry and saw how he died, he said, "Surely this man was the Son of God!" (38–39)

As if shocked by the sacrilegious murder of her Lord, the temple tore her garments. When the body of Christ was torn, the curtain of the temple also tore. This tearing of the curtain of the temple symbolized the end of Judaism, the opening of the mysteries of heaven, and the clearing of the way of access between God and humanity. In sum, this miracle showed that the Cross clears all obstacles out of our way. There is no obstruction between us and heaven. If our fear should invent one, the Christ who tore the curtain continues to tear it today.

The centurion probably said more than he understood. There was something so extraordinary about this central sufferer that the centurion could not understand who he could be unless he was truly "the Son of God." It was strange that this man should confess what the chief priests, scribes, and elders denied, yet since their day it has often happened that the most abandoned and profane have acknowledged Jesus as the Son of God while their religious rulers have denied his deity. Oh, the triumphs of the cross of Christ!

Some women were watching from a distance. Among them were Mary Magdalene, Mary the mother of James the younger and of Joses, and Salome. In Galilee these women had followed him and cared for his needs. Many other women who had come up with him to Jerusalem were also there. (40–41)

No woman is mentioned as having spoken against Jesus in his life or having had a share in his death. Jesus was "born of a woman" (Gal. 4:4) and anointed for his burial by a woman (Mark 14:3-9). A woman—Pilate's wife—pled for him (Matt. 27:19), and "women . . . mourned and wailed for him" (Luke 23:27). Women supported Jesus in his life (Luke 8:3), "prepared spices and perfumes" for his body (Luke 23:56), and were the first to meet him at his resurrection (John 20:10-16).

Where was Peter? We know from John 19:26-27 that John was near the cross, but James and the rest of the apostles were apparently in hiding. Yet these holy women were there.

It was Preparation Day (that is, the day before the Sabbath). So as evening approached, Joseph of Arimathea, a prominent member of the Council, who was himself waiting for the kingdom of God, went boldly to Pilate and asked for Jesus' body. Pilate was surprised to hear that he was already dead. Summoning the centurion, he asked him if Jesus had already died. When he learned from the centurion that it was so, he gave the body to Joseph. So Joseph bought some linen cloth, took down the body, wrapped it in the linen, and placed it in a tomb cut out of rock. Then he rolled a stone against the entrance of the tomb. Mary Magdalene and Mary the mother of Joses saw where he was laid. (42-47)

No doubt Pilate was very surprised that a member of the "Council" or Sanhedrin should come and ask for the body of Jesus, when, a little while before, he had put him to death by the mandate of that body of men (v. 1). In John 19:38 we learn that this "Joseph was a disciple of Jesus, but secretly because he feared the Jews." What brought him out into the open now? It was the power of the Cross! The shameful death of the cross had greater power over Joseph than all the beauty of Christ's life.

When Joseph asked for Jesus' body, he put himself at personal risk, brought on himself ceremonial pollution, and had to pay a great cost for the burial. Today Jesus does not need a burial, but he wants his gospel to be proclaimed in all the world. If you love him, do everything in your power to spread the knowledge of his name. If you have followed Christ secretly so far, throw secrecy to the winds.

The same centurion who had declared that Jesus was the Son of God (v. 39) here came forward to bear witness that he had seen him die. Then Pilate told Joseph that he might take the body.

This was probably the first time that "linen cloth" had touched the flesh of Christ. He had been accustomed to much coarser stuff in his lifetime.

Many believers say they would like to remain alive until the second coming of Christ. But if they do, they will be unable to enjoy fellowship with Jesus in his death and burial. If we are ever to lie in the tomb with Christ, we must be wrapped in the fine linen of holiness. This is the shroud of a person who is dead to sin.

Our proper response to this chapter describing the crucifixion of our Lord is to give him our repentance, faith, and love.

The Joy of the Trinity
When Lost People Become Found

Now the tax collectors and "sinners" were all gathering around to hear him. But the Pharisees and the teachers of the law muttered, "This man welcomes sinners and eats with them." (1–2)

The Pharisees and the teachers of the law formed the outside ring of Christ's hearers, but the inner circle consisted of the guilty, the burdened, the outcasts, and the lowly. They pressed as close to Christ as they could, that they might catch his every word. They could not have too much of it. There was an attractiveness about his manner that drew them to him. His mercy attracted their misery. They wanted him, and he desired them. However sunken they might have been, they knew their best friend who gladly smiled at them and lifted them up. So they formed clusters around him, like bees fly to the flower. It was thus a good match.

The Pharisees and the teachers of the law did not come too near. There will be an inner circle whenever the gospel is preached, and it will not consist of the self-righteous. They who are full will not press to the table on which the gospel feast is spread. The hungry will be found closest to the heavenly provision.

The muttering of the Pharisees and the teachers of the law was part of their nature. They were so wrapped up in themselves that they held others in contempt. They dared to despise the people whose shoes they were unworthy to untie. They did not want Christ themselves, but they murmured that other people should have him. They thought themselves too righteous to need a Savior, yet they complained when the physician came to his needy patients with healing medicine.

The Pharisees thought it disgraceful that Christ welcomed sinners, but our Savior could not have had a higher honor conferred on him. It is the exact portrait of his character. Christ does not welcome everybody. He does not have open arms for the self-righteous, who think they need no Savior. That was the attitude of the Pharisees in this verse. Jesus welcomes only those who confess that they have broken God's laws and have merited his displeasure.

The Pharisees did not say, "This man preaches to sinners," but, "This man welcomes sinners." It is a great blessing when the gospel is preached to sinners, but it is a far greater blessing when sinners run into Christ's welcoming arms! If you cannot come to Christ with a tender heart, come for a tender heart. If you cannot come to him with faith, come to him to get faith, for "this man welcomes sinners."

Nothing is said here about how the sinners came to Christ. Some came to him walking, others by limping, and still others on crutches. Jesus never turned away sinners because they came on crutches. One man came on his bed. He did not come on his own strength at all, for his friends brought him to Christ (Mark 2:1-12). But Jesus still welcomed him. The divine promise is, "Whoever wishes, let him take the free gift of the water of life" (Rev. 22:17). No matter how crippling your sins may be, if you wish to come to Christ, he will welcome you.

The deepest feelings of our Savior's heart seem to have been brought out by the two classes of people mentioned here. His compassion went out to notorious sinners and his righteous anger to the hypocrites. Yet even to this second group his heart was moved with pity, because they, too, were wandering. We owe a great deal to the complaints of the proud Pharisees, for by answering them, our Lord gave us some of the choicest parables ever heard.

Then Jesus told them this parable: "Suppose one of you has a hundred sheep and loses one of them. Does he not leave the ninety-nine in the open country and go after the lost sheep until he finds it? And when he finds it, he joyfully puts it on his shoulders and goes home. Then he calls his friends and neighbors together and says, 'Rejoice with me; I have found my lost sheep.' I tell you that in the same way there will be more rejoicing in heaven over one sinner who repents than over ninety-nine righteous persons who do not need to repent" (3-7).

There are three parables here, but because it is called "this parable," it is a picture in three panels, and we need all three panels to complete the picture. Each one represents the same scene from a different point of view.

The first panel of this threefold parable represents salvation in reference to the work of the Son of God as the great seeker and saver of the lost. In the second we have a picture of the work of the Holy Spirit in the church. In the third the work of the Father is revealed. Why wasn't the Father's work put first, since the Trinity is the Father, the Son, and the Holy Spirit? Because the love of Christ is the first thing a sinner understands.

Lost sinners are here compared to sheep, partly because of their stupidity and also because of their desire to wander. A sheep loves to stray. It is sport to a sheep to have liberty. It thinks nothing of the shepherd seeking it. The shepherd has wide-open eyes for the sheep, but the sheep has no eye for the shepherd. Until Christ finds sinners, they are thoughtless, careless, and indifferent about eternal things.

A sheep is also in constant danger of hunger, disease, and the wolf while wandering from its protector. In like manner, a sinner without the Savior is in danger of increasing her or his sin, being devoured by the Devil, and going to hell.

Jesus was justifying his seeking of lost people. The Pharisees' accusation was that he welcomed the riffraff and ate with them. "Yes," said Christ, "I do that, but I am a shepherd. Is it not the shepherd's business to look after the lost sheep? And does he not derive his highest joy from it?" The one sheep had a new importance in the shepherd's eyes when it became lost. Previously it was only one of a hundred sheep in the fold, but now it was distinct and separate from all the rest. The shepherd's thought was fixed on it.

The shepherd had no joy until he found his lost sheep. If someone had remarked, "That is a great load you are carrying," he would have answered, "I am glad to have it on my shoulders!" In the same way, when Jesus carried our sins, it was a great load, but a greater joy flashed before him when he thought of us being pardoned from the guilt of our sins. Hebrews 12:2 says that Jesus "for the joy set before him endured the cross, scorning its shame." That "joy set before him" was the joy of providing salvation for sinners.

What a picture of Christ finding willful and wayward people! They are lost to God, lost to society, lost to usefulness, lost to happiness, and perhaps lost to hope. In his incarnation Jesus went after us in our lost condition. In his ministry he continued to seek us. In his death he threw us on his shoulders and carried all our sins. In his resurrection he brought us home rejoicing. And throughout eternity he will make the angels in heaven glad by showing them the lost people he has found.

This is not to say that heaven holds one repentant sinner in greater esteem than ninety-nine saints who have stayed true by God's power. Jesus was saying to the Pharisees, "You think you are like the ninety-nine sheep that never went astray. Therefore, you can never give me as much pleasure as these notorious sinners who have wandered." Jesus' heart never leaped with delight over the self-righteous. Though they thought they were good, they did not yield to Christ the joy he felt when he found the tax collectors and other scandalous sinners.

A human being is far more valuable than a sheep. And if a shepherd will leave all his comfort to hunt for one stray sheep, then you and I, following Christ's example, ought to be ready for any self-denial by which we may also seek and save the lost.

"Or suppose a woman has ten silver coins and loses one. Does she not light a lamp, sweep the house and search carefully until she finds it? And when she finds it, she calls her friends and neighbors together and says, 'Rejoice with me; I have found my lost coin.' In the same way, I tell you, there is rejoicing in the presence of the angels of God over one sinner who repents." (8–10)

That one silver coin had no consciousness of its lost condition. It was just as happy to be in the dust on the floor as in the woman's purse with the nine other silver coins. It is just so with sinners who are spiritually dead in sin. They do not know or care that they are lost. This is what makes the Spirit of God so necessary in our ministry. We are dealing with insensible souls.

The woman's thoughts were all for that one lost coin. It had no more intrinsic value than the rest, but since it was lost, it called her attention away from the other nine. She valued it, lit a candle, swept the house, and sought diligently until she found it. This is a picture of the Holy Spirit's work in seeking lost people, all of whom bear the King's impress as coins of the realm. He takes the candle of the gospel, the broom of the law, and searches for the lost person.

The silver coin had lost none of its value, though it had rolled away into a mouse hole or into the cobwebs. It was the woman's job to seek diligently in every nook and cranny in the deserted and filthy places for that precious piece of money. And so we should give our utmost energy to seeking lost people. However degraded they may have become, they are still precious.

You may think no one cares about you, but this parable teaches that God does! You may say, "I am nothing. Just a castaway. Utterly worthless." No, you are not worthless to the Holy Spirit or worthless to the church of God. Do not think you will be unwelcome if you come to Christ. The Spirit of Christ is searching for you now! Christ, his Spirit, and his church will be glad to receive you!

She might never have called her friends together to rejoice that she had ten pieces of silver. She might even have hidden them away, and the joy she had in them might have been only her own—a solitary joy. But now that one piece had been lost and found again, she said, "Rejoice with me!"

If this woman rejoiced over finding her lost coin, how much more will God rejoice over a precious human being he finds through grace! There is joy in heaven and in all heavenly hearts when one sinner is found. We can scarcely imagine how much joy there is in heaven over the thousands and millions of sinners who repent!

Why don't the angels save their joy until the sinner dies and goes to heaven? Why do they rejoice over the sinner when he or she repents? Some would say this joy is premature, for they believe a person may be a believer today and a castaway tomorrow. They believe that tomorrow the angels may have to mourn over the same repentant sinners they sing over today. But the angels in heaven know better than that. They understand that when sinners are saved, they are secure forever, for they are in Christ.

The Pharisees and teachers of the law proved they were not friends of the soul-seeking Savior when they grumbled over the lost sinners who became found. If they had been anything like the angels in heaven—as they thought they were—they would have been glad that the Lord Jesus came to seek and find the lost. We may judge our fitness for heaven by this test: Do we rejoice over repentant sinners? Sometimes I think I could flog myself and bite my tongue because I often preach with a dry eye and a heart not half as earnest as it should be.

This verse does not say, "There is rejoicing among the angels," though no doubt that is true. It reads, "There is rejoicing in the presence of the angels of God." Who is in the presence of angels but God himself? What this means is that God himself rejoices so much that angels observe him and then join in his delight. The lost person is the great object of God's consideration. The application to us is that wherever the gospel is preached, the lost person is the most important one in the whole place.

What had this lost one done? Built a church? No. Preached a sermon? No. He or she had repented—that is all. But that is quite enough to set all the music of the angels' harps pouring forth the praise of God.

In the next verses we get the heavenly Father's part in the work of recovering the wanderer. This is perhaps the best loved of all the parables. It is the truest picture ever sketched of our folly and lost estate and at the same time the most wonderful picture ever painted of God's love and mercy.

Jesus continued: "There was a man who had two sons. The younger one said to his father, 'Father, give me my share of the estate.' So he divided his property between them." (11–12)

The younger son would have received his father's inheritance when his father died, but he demanded it in his lifetime. It was an unreasonable demand. Why did the father give in to him? Because God often lets people go their own sinful way.

"Not long after that, the younger son got together all he had, set off for a distant country and there squandered his wealth in wild living. After he had spent everything, there was a severe famine in that whole country, and he began to be in need. So he went and hired himself out to a citizen of that country, who sent him to his fields to feed pigs. He longed to fill his stomach with the pods that the pigs were eating, but no one gave him anything." (13–16)

The son left home "not long after that" because sin is rapid in its development, and sinners are often in great haste to get away from God. His heart was already far away when he asked his father to give him his share of the estate, even before he went into the distant country. He wanted to get away from his father, his authority, and his presence. The son's physical departure followed his spiritual departure.

His father's gift developed his son's latent evil. It is a sad commentary on human nature that divine love should lead to our sin. It is as when the sun shines in goodwill but makes weeds grow. The son could not have squandered his father's estate at home. His father's eye would have restrained him. People want to get away from God because they want to do wrong. At the bottom of all infidelity is the love of sin. People quarrel with divine truth because divine truth quarrels with them.

Did you ever look at an ungodly life as the squandering of a valuable estate? That is exactly what it is. The love that ought to go to God is wasted on lust. The energy that ought to be spent in righteousness is wasted on sin. The ability that ought to be laid at Jesus' feet is all used for selfish pleasure, and so it is squandered.

The boy "spent everything." There is an end to all carnal joy. We can go only so far with it. When we get to the bottom of the cup, it will not spring up like a fountain and fill itself again. Instead, "a severe famine" and other miseries come as messengers that God sends after wanderers.

Need was a new feeling for him. He had never been in need when he was at home. Nor had he been in need in his first robust days away from his father's house. But he was in need now. His greatest need was love.

The prodigal proved that the pleasures of sin last "a short time" (Heb. 11:25). Ungodly people are in need of everything good and worth having. Their souls are destitute. But if we stay close to our heavenly Father, we will have no need, for when "the LORD is my shepherd, I shall not be in want" (Ps. 23:1).

Feeding pigs was the most degrading work imaginable for a Jew, so sin leads to disgrace before it leads to death. Perhaps this job was the best the citizen of that country could have given the prodigal, for there was a famine in the land. When every person is pinched, there is not much any can do for another. And what can one poor sinner do for another? When the world does its best for a sinner, it gives the sinner a job feeding pigs. The Devil's best is always bad, so what must his worst be? If he lets his favorites feed pigs, what will he do with them when the time of his favor is over and they are forever in his power?

It does not say he could have satisfied his hunger with the "pods," only that he "longed to fill his stomach" with them, as if that might have choked his sense of need. Many people know that the world cannot satisfy them, but they indulge in it to take their thoughts away from their inward need.

Though the prodigal would have eaten pigs' food, he could not do even that, for he was a man and not a pig. Besides, generosity was unknown in that country. Of all the destitution in the world, the destitution of sinners who have grown sick of their own sin and can find no comfort anywhere else is the worst. The pleasures of the world have fooled many a person.

The prodigal had given his money to his friends, but they gave him nothing when he was in need. This was merciful, for if they had, he would not have returned to his father. There is nothing like a little gracious starvation to bring a person home to Christ. It is a blessed providence when rebels are starved by the Holy Spirit so that their only recourse is to return to God.

"When he came to his senses, he said, 'How many of my father's hired men have food to spare, and here I am starving to death! I will set out and go back to my father and say to him: Father, I have sinned

against heaven and against you. I am no longer worthy to be called your son; make me like one of your hired men.' So he got up and went to his father." (17–20)

Sin makes no sense. The prodigal had been out of his mind to rebel against his loving father. His insanity is clearly seen in what he did. He considered this mortal life all-important. He put eternity in the background. His interests had nothing to do with his loving father. He left the best home he could have had. After he spent everything, he should have returned to his father, but instead "he went and hired himself out to a citizen of that country" (v. 15). Let us pray for those we know who are spiritually insane.

It was merciful that the son's intention to return home did not end as a mere intention but led to his actual return. The thought that drew him home was that his father had "food to spare." That same thought ought to draw people to Christ. There is in the gospel "food to spare." Those who have lost hope of forgiveness and feel God is angry with them may reason, "God will not deny me the spare food, because he has no use for it. So I may well go to him and ask for it."

This son came to his senses and went to his father. Two verses before this he told himself, "I will set out and go back to my father." Resolves are good, like blossoms, but actions are better, for they are the fruit. The angels do not rejoice when a sinner says, "I will turn to God." They reserve their music for the sinner who actually repents.

"But while he was still a long way off, his father saw him and was filled with compassion for him; he ran to his son, threw his arms around him and kissed him." (20)

The father saw who it was and where he had come from. He saw the filth on his son's hands and feet, the rags he was wearing, and his repentant look. He saw what he had been, what he was, and what he would soon be. No one but the boy's father would have recognized the son, because he looked so different. God has a way of seeing us that you and I cannot understand. He sees right through us at a glance, as if we were made of glass. He sees our all past, present, and future.

At the beginning of this verse the prodigal "went to his father," but here we see a higher truth at the back of it: The father went to his son. And what a welcome he gave him! He showed reckless love for his reckless son. The son was half afraid to come to his father, but the father "ran to his son." Slow are the steps of repentance, but swift are the feet of forgiveness. The father was out of breath but not out of love. If we limp toward God, he will run toward us. He is "slow to anger" (Ps. 103:8) but quick to bless.

The father welcomed his son, though he had just come from a pigpen. So we should welcome forgiven sinners into the church and no longer look on them as dirty people who wear rags and smell like pigs. When his father saw him, it was with eyes of mercy. When he was filled with compassion, he showed a heart of mercy. When he ran to his son, it was with legs of mercy. When he threw his arms around him, it was in an act of mercy. When he kissed him, it was with lips of mercy.

If the father had stood at a distance and said, "I want to kiss you, but you are too filthy; I love you, but there is a limit to the display of my love," we would have understood. But before the boy was washed, his father "threw his arms around him and kissed him." I can understand how God shows his love to people who are washed in Christ's blood, but it is a miracle of love that he could throw his arms around filthy sinners and kiss them!

"The son said to him, 'Father, I have sinned against heaven and against you. I am no longer worthy to be called your son.'" (21)

The son gave up all ideas of justifying himself when he said, "Father, I have sinned." Earlier he would have said, "I have a right do whatever I want with my money. No one can tell me how to spend it. I am no hypocrite." If he had spoken that way, he would have aggravated his sin, for he would have denied that he had sinned at all.

He might have said, "I have sinned, but I am still your son." That would have been true, but he was too humble to say that. He gave up all his rights before his father. When you come before the heavenly Father, do not offer any excuses for your sins. Tell him, "I am lost. I flee from your justice and hide myself in the wounds of your Son."

"But the father said to his servants, 'Quick! Bring the best robe and put it on him. Put a ring on his finger and sandals on his feet. Bring the fattened calf and kill it. Let's have a feast and celebrate. For this son of mine was dead and is alive again; he was lost and is found.' So they began to celebrate. (22–24)

The prodigal did not get to say, "Make me like one of your hired men," as he had planned in verse 19 to say. The father's kiss (v. 20) prevented the son from saying that part of his speech. No doubt the prodigal also thought he would have to go on probation. He felt unfit to sit at the table as he had before. He expected his father to say, "Remember how badly you have lived, young man! It will be a long time before I trust you again!" The father, however, instead of speaking that way, called for a party. This was done at once, the same day the prodigal returned.

"What?" says someone, "can I enjoy the highest privileges of Christian fellowship as soon as I come to Christ?" Yes, that is God's way of welcoming sinners. Look at the dying thief. He went to paradise the same day he repented (Luke 23:39-43).

We never read that the party ceased, for the conversion of one person is enough to make eternal joy in the hearts of the righteous. Nor do we read that the father said, "Make my son eat." Instead, he said, "Let's have a feast," that is, "Let us eat." The best way to make another person eat is to dig in yourself. If the goal of your witness is to make a person eat the gospel feast, the best method is to begin feasting yourself. When the father and servants began eating, the prodigal found his appetite and so feasted too.

"Meanwhile, the older son was in the field. When he came near the house, he heard music and dancing. So he called one of the servants and asked him what was going on. 'Your brother has come,' he replied, 'and your father has killed the fattened calf because he has him back safe and sound.'" (25-27)

This older son represents the self-righteous Pharisee who hates to see prodigals become the center of attention. The party was a new thing to the older son, and apparently one he did not care much about, for he had a gloomy spirit. How had it come about that there was such noise, such joy?

If the younger brother had been allowed to come in through the back door and eat with the servants, his older brother would have been pleased. It did not seem right to him that the prodigal, who had acted so wickedly, should be honored. The older brother was the kind who did not believe in revivals, so he would not attend this one. He did not believe in many being converted, especially if they had been great sinners. He would have nothing to do with them.

Some churchgoers are like this older brother. When sinners come into the church, they say, "We'll see if they turn out to be genuine." Because the older members have not sinned in the same ways, they do not see how the new converts can be genuine. That is always their first thought.

The prodigal had come home "safe and sound." He had no broken bones, nor was his face disfigured. It is an amazing thing that sinners should come back to Christ safe and sound, considering where they have been. This is a wonder of grace.

"The older brother became angry and refused to go in. So his father went out and pleaded with him. But he answered his father, 'Look! All these years I've been slaving for you and never disobeyed your orders. Yet you never gave me even a young goat so I could celebrate with my friends. But when this son of yours who has squandered your property with prostitutes comes home, you kill the fattened calf for him!'" (28–30)

See the tenderness of the father. The same arms that embraced the sinning son were also ready to clasp the self-righteous one. I hardly know which to admire more—the father's love when he threw his arms around the prodigal (v. 20) or his love when he went out to talk with his older son. Our God is very good to us when we have an outburst of temper. If we begin to think we are holy people, that we have served God for many years, and that God ought to make the same fuss over us that he makes over great sinners who come into the church, our Father is very gentle. He comes out and reasons with us.

This older son was out of fellowship with his father, or he would not have talked as he did. We are all prone to become like him. If you have never had "a young goat" with which to celebrate with your friends, it is your own fault, for your Father never denied it to you. The older son complained, "I have had no banquets! I stayed at home, a patient worker, and have had no extraordinary joys." Those who try to earn their salvation by the law are unable to celebrate. They have to draw long faces—and well they may—for they have a long task before them.

I know even some Christian workers who are like the older son. They keep on and on in holy service and do well, but they seldom have indescribable delight. It is their own tragic fault, for they could have it if only they wanted it. There is a tendency to grow so absorbed in service that we are burdened by it, as Martha was. Then we miss out on the joy of Mary, who fellowshiped at the Master's feet (Luke 10:38-42).

Where does it say the prodigal son squandered his father's property with prostitutes? That is the older brother's version of it. I dare say it was true, but it is always a pity to give the worst interpretation to things. The younger son had "squandered his wealth in wild living"

(v. 13). When we are cross, we generally use the ugliest words we can. We may think we are speaking powerfully when we are speaking sinfully and not as our heavenly Father would want us to speak.

We do not read that the younger brother tried to repudiate the accusation of his older brother. It was not worth his while to try to do so, for he was right with his father, and he would be right with his brother one day. If you get right with God, even if some Christians should not believe in you, never mind. You will be right with them in due time.

"'My son,' the father said, 'you are always with me, and everything I have is yours. But we had to celebrate and be glad, because this brother of yours was dead and is alive again; he was lost and is found.'"
(31–32)

This is what our heavenly Father says to every believer when we get into a proud spirit like the older son. When we do not like to hear of sinners of the deepest dye coming to Christ, and when we disapprove of the excitement at revivals, the Lord says to us, "If you have had no joy, you could have had it if you had wanted it, for you are always with me. I have given you everything. What more do you want?"

How this statement reminds us of our privileges, if we would only appropriate them! It is ours to live always with our God and to know that all he has is ours. We ought to live in a perpetual festival. For us there should be one joyful Christmas season that lasts from the beginning to the end of the year.

The father felt compelled to rejoice, for he told his son, "We had to celebrate and be glad." We are happy when God forgives us but not as happy as God is. Since our Father's heart is much larger than ours, it is able to hold more joy. The only thing that could have made the father in this parable gladder was if his older son had found the prodigal.

The older son had said, "This son of yours" (v. 30), but here the father corrected him by saying, "This brother of yours." It was fitting and right that there should have been extraordinary joy over a returning sinner. After that reply, there was nothing more that could be said, even by the older brother. There ought to be, there must be, there shall be special music and dancing over sinners saved by the grace of God. May the Lord give us some today and make us glad over them!

If you do not take joy in the conversion of great sinners, listen to the gentle voice of God. You, as a believer, have everything. Christ and heaven are yours. You are always with God, and all that he has belongs to you. But it is fitting that when sinners return from the error of their ways, the bells of heaven should ring and a fuss should be made over them. They were dead but now are alive!

When Dwight L. Moody first came to England, a minister said, "I do not believe that Mr. Moody is sent by God, because many of the people converted under him have never gone to a place of worship before. Only the riffraff are brought in." That is the spirit of the older brother speaking. The riffraff were just the people we wanted to bring in. If they had never been to a place of worship before, it was high time they went. It was good that they were brought in. Instead of despising sinners, let us welcome them with all our hearts and praise the heavenly Father for lovingly taking them in.

Jesus, the Lamb of God

In the beginning was the Word, and the Word was with God, and the Word was God. He was with God in the beginning. (1–2)

The first words of this gospel remind us of the first line of Genesis: "In the beginning God created the heavens and the earth" (Gen. 1:1). Even then "the Word" was. Jesus Christ existed from all eternity. He is the eternal Son of the eternal Father. He is literally what Melchizedek was metaphorically: "without beginning of days or end of life" (Heb. 7:3).

"The Word" was as truly "God" as the Father was God and as the Holy Spirit was God. "These three are one" (1 John 5:7 KJV), and they always have been one. The Jesus we trust, worship, and adore is fully divine.

Through him all things were made; without him nothing was made that has been made. In him was life, and that life was the light of men. The light shines in the darkness, but the darkness has not understood it. (3–5)

He who was nailed to the cross was the Maker of all worlds. He who became an infant for our sakes was the Infinite. How low he stooped! How high he must have been that he could stoop that low! We cannot describe the deity of Christ in clearer language than John used. He had already said that Jesus was "with God" (v. 1), "was God" (v. 1), and existed with the Father "in the beginning" (v. 2). Now we read that Jesus did the works of God, for he was the Creator (v. 3). If you doubt Christ's deity, you must defy the language of Holy Scripture.

"The light" of Christ shined many times in "the darkness" that covered the world before his coming to live here in a physical body.

185

Yet very few people "understood" and rejoiced in that light. Christ's light shines more brightly now, but the dark, unenlightened human soul does not understand that brightness until the Holy Spirit raises it to newness of life and so gives sight to those who have been blind. Light will never understand darkness. You may sometimes call the darkness human ignorance or human sin. Some even call it human wisdom and human righteousness, but that is only another form of the same darkness.

Christ is still not understood. He is still unknown. How can darkness understand light when it opposes light? It has to flee before light, but it does not and cannot understand light. O God, work a miracle in dark hearts, and fill them with the light of Christ!

There came a man who was sent from God; his name was John. He came as a witness to testify concerning that light, so that through him all men might believe. He himself was not the light; he came only as a witness to the light. The true light that gives light to every man was coming into the world. (6–9)

How very different is the style of this verse from those that precede it. How grand, how sublime are the Evangelist's words when he spoke of Jesus. But here he dipped his pen in ordinary ink. Jesus himself said concerning John, "Among those born of women there has not risen anyone greater than John the Baptist" (Matt. 11:11), yet what a great climb it is from the greatest of the prophets to Jesus Christ, the Son of God! Still, it was a tremendous compliment to the forerunner of Christ when the writer spoke of him as "a man who was sent from God."

John's business is our business too. Each Christian is "a witness to testify concerning that light, so that through him all men might believe." This is our destiny. Oh, how often we go home and cry, "Who has believed our message?" (Isa. 53:1). We do not ask people to believe in us but in our Master, whose heralds we are. If we can lead you to faith in him, we will be truly glad! But if we do not lead you to trust in Christ, we will sorrow because we have missed our mark and failed in our purpose.

The only light from John came from what he reflected from his Lord. All light comes from Jesus. Everyone who comes into the world with any light borrows it from Christ. There can be no other light, for Jesus is "the light of the world" (John 8:12).

John could not give "light to every man . . . coming into the world." He was merely a witness to Christ (v. 7) who alone could do this. If we have saving light, true light, we get it through Christ.

There is no other light. All other light is just visible darkness. The light in which we see God comes from Jesus.

He was in the world, and though the world was made through him, the world did not recognize him. He came to that which was his own, but his own did not receive him. Yet to all who received him, to those who believed in his name, he gave the right to become children of God—children born not of natural descent, nor of human decision or a husband's will, but born of God. (10–13)

How sad that the Creator came to his own earth, and yet "the world did not recognize him." Jesus was a stranger in his own house. He was unknown by his own handiwork. People he had made made nothing of him. They mistook him, hated him, and crucified him whom they ought to have entertained with sacred hospitality and worshiped with holy loyalty. What terrible estrangement sin has caused between God and people! What dreadful ignorance sin has created in the human mind!

To those chosen as his own out of all the nations on the earth—the Jews who descended from Abraham, Isaac, and Jacob—Jesus came, yet they did not receive him. He healed many of them and fed thousands of them, yet they did not receive him. When Jesus taught them the words of God, "the Jews picked up stones to stone him" (John 10:31). After the Jews crucified our Lord, he could have gone into his glory, but he rose from the dead and stayed on earth forty more days to minister blessings to his people (Acts 1:3). Yet they still did not receive him.

We must not be too hard on the Jews, for we have shown the same ingratitude toward Christ. We set up thrones to other lords in our hearts. We give Jesus little service and lukewarm love. We have scorned his people, neglected his commands, and refused to trust him for our daily trials.

What does it mean that we have "believed in his name"? We get our clues from the names of Christ in this chapter. He is called "the Word" (v. 1). Words are a means of communication. God has spoken to us by sending Christ. Have you received Christ as God's Word, or message, to you? He is also called "the life" (v. 4). If you have believed in Christ as your life, you have confessed that you are dead in your sins. Christ is also called "the light" in this chapter (vv. 4–5, 7). Everything looks according to your light. If you have believed in Christ's name as light, you see everything in its true light.

Not all people are "children of God." The teaching of the universal fatherhood of God is utterly untrue. Only those who "received him, . . . who believed in his name" become God's children. The others are "children of wrath" (Eph. 2:3 KJV).

How do some people receive Christ when others reject him? A great inward change makes them different from others. That great inward change is the new birth. If you have "become children of God," show it to the world. And how do you do that? By showing how much God has made you like Christ.

Those who receive Christ, who truly believe on him, have been born in a way others have not—by a supernatural birth from heaven. Now they are set apart as those who have been created twice—first as human beings just like others, and then as new creatures in Christ Jesus. Human birth never makes anyone a Christian. If our ancestry should be a line of saints, we are still born sinners (Ps. 51:5). We must be "born again" (John 3:7) if we are to become saints. If we could trace our pedigrees to perfect parents—who don't even exist—our human birth would still do us no good. Children of God must be "born of God."

The Word became flesh and made his dwelling among us. We have seen his glory, the glory of the One and Only, who came from the Father, full of grace and truth. (14)

John and the other apostles had "seen his glory." Today we can see it by faith. Faith looks back to Christ who died for us and sees glory in his shame, honor in his disgrace, riches in his poverty, might in his weakness, triumph in his conflict, and immortality in his death. Faith sees the glory of the grace of Christ when he rolls away all our sins, when his blood reconciles us with his Father, and when his Spirit subdues our wills.

Make no mistake about this—Jesus Christ is worth knowing! You may be full of sins, but he is "full of grace." You may be full of ignorance, but he is "full of . . . truth." He can cleanse and teach. There is everything in him you need. You will not be deceived, for he is full of truth. Nor will you be rejected, for he is full of grace.

Those who saw Christ on earth were highly privileged, but it is a spiritual sight of him alone that is to be desired. We can have that even now. Christ is still full of grace and truth to all who are privileged to know him.

John testifies concerning him. He cries out, saying, "This was he of whom I said, 'He who comes after me has surpassed me because he was before me.'" From the fullness of his grace we have all received one bless-

ing after another. For the law was given through Moses; grace and truth came through Jesus Christ. No one has ever seen God, but God the One and Only, who is at the Father's side, has made him known. (15–18)

Jesus was not "before" John in human age, yet he had lived from eternity past. He was none other than the uncreated Son of God. He was also before John in rank and glory.

People of faith can say, "From the fullness of his grace we have all received—many times!" Let us hope to receive the fullness of God's grace again today, for it never declines. There was fullness of grace when the first sinner came to Christ, it is fullness of grace still, and it will be fullness of grace to the very end.

Our reception of the fullness of Christ implies that we were empty before we trusted in him. "In Christ all the fullness of the Deity lives in bodily form, and you have been given fullness in Christ" (Col. 2:9–10). There is fullness of cleansing power in his blood, for "the blood of Jesus Christ . . . purifies us from every sin" (1 John 1:7). There is fullness of pardon in him, for "There is now no condemnation for those who are in Christ Jesus" (Rom. 8:1). There is fullness of victory in his death, for by his death he destroyed him who held the power of death, the Devil (see Heb. 2:14).

How should we respond who have received Christ's fullness? First, we should be humble. I have sometimes heard of a proud Christian, but that is a contradiction in terms.

Second, we should be grateful. Jesus gives us blood and we give him a few tears. He gives us sweat and we give him cold service. He gives us groans and we give him languishing hymns. He gives us life and death, and we give him only what we can spare after we have put ourselves first.

Third, we should be full of praise for our Lord. Oh, let our tongues sing well of him to whom we owe everything!

And fourth, we should speak of him to others. If we have received Christ's fullness, let us pray and work so that others may do the same.

Like the waves coming in on the beach, we receive "one blessing after another." Each blessing becomes a stepping stone to something higher. The blessing of a broken heart leads to the blessing of repentance, which leads to the blessing of salvation, which leads to the blessing of a holy life, which leads to the blessing of intimacy with Christ, which leads to the blessing of becoming like Christ.

We know that "the law was given through Moses." The law has often burdened us, crushed us, convicted us, and condemned us.

Let us be equally clear that "grace and truth came through Jesus Christ." He is the channel between us and a loving heavenly Father.

When Moses had to prove he was sent by God, he took the rod in his hand and achieved marvels. But they were all miracles of judgment, not of mercy. Moses, the type of the law, had his credentials in judgment. How different from Jesus, who is full of grace and truth, and the seals of his ministry are acts of mercy. Unlike Moses, Jesus did not turn water into blood (Ex. 7:14-24) but into wine (John 2:1-11). He did not slay their fish (Ex. 7:20-21) but multiplied a few small fish and fed thousands (John 6:5-13). He did not ruin their fields with hail (Ex. 9:13-31) but multiplied their bread and gave them many blessings (John 6:5-13). He did not send boils (Ex. 9:8-12) but healed their sickness (Mark 1:32-34). Instead of striking the firstborn dead (Ex. 12:29-30) he healed the dying and rescued from the grasp of death some who had even gone down to the grave (Matt. 11:4-5).

The Father is too high, too spiritual, to be perceived by human senses. We do not even want to see God apart from Christ. I am perfectly satisfied to see the eternal light through his own chosen medium, Christ Jesus. Apart from that medium, the light would blind my eyes. It is easier to look directly at the sun than directly at God.

Christ does not hide the Father from us; he reveals him. Everything we need to know about God we may see in Christ— enough to save us, enough to make us holy, enough to make us all like Christ himself. There is no way of knowing God and being reconciled to him except as we receive Jesus Christ, his Son, into our hearts and learn through the Holy Spirit's teaching all that he delights to teach to us about the Father.

Now this was John's testimony when the Jews of Jerusalem sent priests and Levites to ask him who he was. He did not fail to confess, but confessed freely, "I am not the Christ." (19–20)

It must have been with indignation that John repelled the idea that he was "the Christ" or Messiah.

They asked him, "Then who are you? Are you Elijah?"
He said, "I am not."
"Are you the Prophet?"
He answered, "No." (21)

In a spiritual sense John was the "Elijah" who would come as a forerunner of the Messiah (Mark 9:13). Yet he was not the same man as the Old Testament prophet Elijah, which is what these questioners had in mind, so John answered, "I am not."

"The Prophet" they had in mind was the long-expected one Moses had promised in Deuteronomy 18:15: "The Lord your God will raise up for you a prophet like me from among your own brothers. You must listen to him."

To both questions asked in this twenty-first verse John gave short, sharp answers. He was not a man of dainty words and polished periods. He did not waste words, especially when dealing with people like this, who were critics.

Finally they said, "Who are you? Give us an answer to take back to those who sent us. What do you say about yourself?"

John replied in the words of Isaiah the prophet, "I am the voice of one calling in the desert, 'Make straight the way for the Lord.'" (22–23)

John did not pretend to be the Word. Jesus was that (vv. 1, 14). But John was "the voice" by which the Word was made known. Still, there was great power and wisdom in that voice. May you and I also be voices to make the Word of God sound across the desert of life!

Even as a voice John was not original, for here he quoted Isaiah 40:3. The straining after originality that we see so much today finds no warrant among the true servants of God. Even though John was only a voice, he was a voice quoting the Scriptures. The more of Scripture we can voice, the better. What are our words? Just air. But what is God's Word? It is grace and truth. May we continually lend our voices to the great words of God that have been given before.

Now some Pharisees who had been sent questioned him, "Why then do you baptize if you are not the Christ, nor Elijah, nor the Prophet?"

"I baptize with water," John replied, "but among you stands one you do not know. He is the one who comes after me, the thongs of whose sandals I am not worthy to untie." (26–27)

See the true humility of John, the faithful servant of Christ. He loved to hide behind his Master. He was a most worthy man, a truly great man, but he counted himself unworthy of the most menial service for Christ. John did not dream of putting his own name next to his Master's. The unloosing of thongs on his sandals was the work of a slave. It is better to be a slave of Christ than to rule vast empires. Those who truly serve Christ are glorified even in menial service.

How wisely God chooses his servants! John was just the man for his place. He was a "witness" (v. 7), and he lived up to his calling. He turned all attention away from himself to his Master, and he had such reverence for Christ that he put all honor and glory on him.

What are we worthy of doing for Christ? Nothing. Yet there are times when, if there is a thong to untie, we are too proud to stoop to do it. When there is something to be done that will bring no honor to us, we are too high and mighty to do it. The apostle Paul said he was "less than the least of all God's people" (Eph. 3:8). He ran away with a title that was very appropriate for us. Well, we must let him have it, so let us try to find another like it. May we never be ashamed to untie the thongs of Christ's shoes!

This all happened at Bethany on the other side of the Jordan, where John was baptizing. (28)

Was this the place where the Israelites crossed the Jordan? It is said to have been so. In any case, the place where we humble ourselves before Christ as John did is the place where we cross the Jordan—where we come out of the old Judaism into the true faith of the Lord Jesus Christ.

The next day John saw Jesus coming toward him and said, "Look, the Lamb of God, who takes away the sin of the world! This is the one I meant when I said, 'A man who comes after me has surpassed me because he was before me.' I myself did not know him, but the reason I came baptizing with water was that he might be revealed to Israel." (29–31)

John the Baptist lost no time. He no sooner discovered the Savior than he bore witness to him. "The next day," as soon as his eyes saw Jesus, he had this testimony ready for him. This was the text of John the Baptist's life sermon. In it he saw "the sin of the world" and "the Lamb of God." He preached a sacrificial, sin-bearing Savior. To carry the weight of the world would have been nothing compared with carrying the sin of the world.

You and I have nothing else to preach but Jesus as our substitute and God's Lamb and who takes away the sin of the world. Have you found Jesus? Then do what John did. Tell someone right away. Servants of God do not say, "Look to the priests. Look to the altar. Look to the sacraments. Look to yourself. Come and confess your sins, and I will give you absolution." No! The servants of Christ cry, "Look, the Lamb of God, who takes away the sin of the world!"

Our great difficulty is to get people's eyes off themselves—off their works, off their forms and ceremonies, off mere creedal religion—and to get them to look at the living Christ.

A day or two before I was to preach at the Crystal Palace, I went to decide where the pulpit should be placed. To test the acoustics of the building I cried in a loud voice, "Behold the Lamb of God, who takes away the sin of the world!" A man who knew nothing of what I was doing was working in one of the balconies. He heard the words, and they came like a message from heaven to his soul. He was struck with conviction for his sin, put down his tools, went home, and found peace and life by beholding the Lamb of God. Years later on his deathbed he told this story to a friend who visited him.

Jesus "was before" John—infinitely before him, for he had no beginning. Jesus was also before John in that he had a higher rank, a superior office, and a perfect nature.

When John first saw Jesus, he "did not know" he was "the Lamb of God, who takes away the sin of the world" (v. 29). It was by baptism that Christ was thus revealed. John knew more of Jesus Christ than anyone else, yet he did not know him to be "the Son of God" (v. 34) until he baptized him.

Then John gave this testimony: "I saw the Spirit come down from heaven as a dove and remain on him. I would not have known him, except that the one who sent me to baptize with water told me, 'The man on whom you see the Spirit come down and remain is he who will baptize with the Holy Spirit.' I have seen and I testify that this is the Son of God." (32–34)

I do not doubt that John was morally certain that Jesus was the Messiah. He had been brought up with him. He knew his mother. He had heard of his wondrous birth. John and Jesus must have been together often. Surely he had guessed with confidence that Jesus was "he who will baptize with the Holy Spirit." But John had nothing to do with guesses. He was a witness for God (v. 7), and he was not to know anyone as the Messiah until he received the token that God had told him to look for, which was the descent of the Holy Spirit. When John saw that token in Jesus' baptism (Matt. 3:16–17), he knew unquestionably who Jesus was, and he bore instant witness.

Has God given you a token that Jesus is the Savior? Do you know Christ by the witness of the Holy Spirit? Then go and speak of him to others. The witness that John bore, which we should repeat to people we know, is revealed in these verses:

The next day John was there again with two of his disciples. When he saw Jesus passing by, he said, "Look, the Lamb of God!" (35–36)

Since John's time many others have given similar testimony. We also have received Christ, and we rejoice to say he has baptized us with the Holy Spirit. All that John said of Christ is true—and much more. Because he is the Son of God, "therefore he is able to save completely those who come to God through him" (Heb. 7:25). Oh, that all men and women, boys and girls, would receive the testimony concerning Christ that we find in this blessed book! We delight to repeat it all in his name!

Earlier in verse 29 John pointed to Jesus and said these same words: "Look, the Lamb of God!" John had no new metaphor or figure with which to set forth Christ. He believed that striking the same nail on the head twice would do more good than bringing out a new nail. The mention of "the next day" tells us that John preached Christ as the Lamb of God two days in a row. If you proclaim the crucified Christ two hundred days in a row, you will not preach him too often. Some very seldom speak of Christ as carrying the sin of the human race, so others of us must do it all the more.

John told people merely to "look" to Christ. Is that all a sinner has to do? Yes. No sinner in hell ever looked at Christ with the eye of faith, and everyone in heaven entered there simply by looking at the slain Lamb who takes away the sin of the world. Look out of the corner of your eye if that is all you can do. Look through your blinding tears. Look through the mists and clouds that surround you, but look to Christ! As every dying person bitten by the snakes who looked to the bronze snake lived (Num. 21:4–9), so every sick person who looks to Christ will live. This is the gospel. As we read in Isaiah 45:22, "Look unto me, and be ye saved" (KJV).

When the two disciples heard him say this, they followed Jesus. Turning around, Jesus saw them following and asked, "What do you want?"
They said, "Rabbi" (which means Teacher), "where are you staying?"
"Come," he replied, "and you will see."
So they went and saw where he was staying, and spent that day with him. It was about the tenth hour. (37–39)

It is hard preaching when you preach away your congregation, but John did that on purpose. He wanted these two disciples no longer to be his disciples but to become the disciples of Jesus. John had mastered the meaning of his own words, "He must become greater; I must become less" (John 3:30).

These two disciples went beyond John, their teacher. And what a mercy it is if our hearers can go far beyond us in the direction of Christ! John was well content to be left behind if they followed Jesus, and so may any minister of Christ rejoice if the listeners will follow him, even if they go beyond the minister's accomplishments.

Jesus desires intelligent followers, so he asked, "What do you want?" How would you answer that question? Do you want forgiveness? You can find it in Christ (Acts 13:38). Do you want peace? Jesus will give you rest (Matt. 11:28). Do you want a pure heart? Jesus will send you his Holy Spirit (John 16:7).

Still today, Jesus' answer to inquirers is, "Come, and you will see." If you want to know Christ, you are perfectly welcome to come and see all that he has to show you. He wants you to learn by experience—to "taste and see that the LORD is good" (Ps. 34:8). He wants you to go beyond merely hearing what he has to say. He invites you to come and see. Come and see Christ in the reading of Scripture. Come and see him in the preaching of the gospel. Best of all, come and see Christ by trusting in him.

The best part of the day was the part these two disciples spent with Jesus. It was the best day they had ever enjoyed, for they "spent that day with him." It was also the beginning of better days for them, for now that they had spent one day with Jesus, they learned never to spend another day without him.

Andrew, Simon Peter's brother, was one of the two who heard what John had said and who had followed Jesus. The first thing Andrew did was to find his brother Simon and tell him, "We have found the Messiah" (that is, the Christ). And he brought him to Jesus (40–42).

Andrew is the pattern for all believers. When a person begins to follow Christ, the first thing he or she should do is to bring others to him. Where should missionary work begin? A brother should begin with his brother, a sister with her sister. It is good to have a desire to go to the heathen in Africa, but if you can't begin work as a missionary where you are, you will not do well in Africa. Those who cannot win to Christ a brother or a sister are not likely to win anyone else. Andrew, who would later bring many to Christ, began at home. If we are unfaithful with one or two relatives, how can God trust us with a pulpit and a congregation? As Andrew found Simon, one convert must make another. And each convert must make another the same way Andrew did with Simon: "He brought him to Jesus."

Simon would be worth ten Andrews, as far as we can gather from
the gospel accounts. Like Andrew, you may have very little talent,
but God may use you to bring a mighty worker to Christ. You may
speak a word to a child who will grow up to be an evangelist who
will stir the Christian church in years to come. You do not know
how much God can do through you. Verse 42 continues:

*Jesus looked at him and said, "You are Simon son of John. You will be
called Cephas" (which, when translated, is Peter).*

There was a meaning in the change of names, for there was about
to be a change of character. The timid son of a dove would soon
become a very rock for the church. Christ changes not only people's
names but their natures. He can make the most fickle of us firm and
steadfast. Oh, that he would work by his grace on us in this way!

*The next day Jesus decided to leave for Galilee. Finding Philip, he said
to him, "Follow me." Philip, like Andrew and Peter, was from the town
of Bethsaida. Philip found Nathanael and told him, "We have found
the one Moses wrote about in the Law, and about whom the prophets
also wrote—Jesus of Nazareth, the son of Joseph." (43–45)*

Bethsaida, the city of Andrew and Peter, was a poor, miserable vil-
lage, but God greatly honored it. Great works often begin in little
places. The best of human beings came out of the despised town of
Nazareth (v. 46), and three of the best men—Philip, Andrew, and
Peter—came out of Bethsaida.

True faith may make blunders. Jesus was not "the son of Joseph,"
except by reputation. And he was Jesus of Bethlehem as much as
"Jesus of Nazareth." But God accepts true faith, though it makes
some mistakes, for it believes God's Word and God's Son.

Here Philip did not say, "We think we have found the Messiah"
or "We hope we have found him." He spoke without the slightest
hesitation or doubt: "We have found the one Moses wrote about in
the Law, and about whom the prophets also wrote." We may be just
as positive as Philip was. No spiritual comfort will be ours until we
are sure of our salvation.

Two verses earlier we read that Jesus found Philip, but here Philip
claimed to have found Jesus. When I was a little child, I saw a needle
moving across the table. I was old enough to understand that some-
body was making it move by means of a magnet underneath the
table. Thus the Lord, with his mighty magnet of grace, is often at
work on the hearts of people, and we think their desire for God and

their faith in Christ come from themselves. But there is a divine force at work on them producing these results. Philip said he had found Jesus, but behind the veil it was Jesus who had found Philip.

If you have found Christ, tell others about him, even as Philip told Nathanael in this verse. As a Christian you are not to keep Christ to yourself. Again, if you have found Christ, never part from him. Philip became one of Jesus' disciples, then one of his apostles, and now he is with Christ forever. Let it be so with you.

"Nazareth! Can anything good come from there?" Nathanael asked. "Come and see," said Philip. (46)

The gospel is something we have to see. John the Baptist had said, "Look" (vv. 29, 36). Jesus had said, "Come, and you will see" (v. 39). And here Philip said, "Come and see." Faith is that blessed sight by which we discern the Savior. Whoever looks to Christ by faith will live. When Philip said, "Come and see," he uttered the same words that Jesus said back in verse 39. It is always right to follow the example that the Lord Jesus has set.

When Jesus saw Nathanael approaching, he said of him, "Here is a true Israelite, in whom there is nothing false." (47)

Jesus was saying, "There is no craftiness or deception in Nathanael, as there was in Jacob, whose name was changed to Israel. Nathanael is like Israel at his best." Traitors like Judas are carved out of the ebony of deceit, but Nathanael was different. He doubted that anything good could come from Nazareth (v. 46), but at least he was honest about it. Even in his doubts he was willing to examine the claims of Christ, for here he came to see him.

"How do you know me?" Nathanael asked.
Jesus answered, "I saw you while you were still under the fig tree before Philip called you." (48)

We do not know what Nathanael had been doing "under the fig tree." Possibly he had been meditating, or he may have been praying. Whatever it was, only Jesus and Nathanael knew. It was a secret between the two of them, and it was the plainest proof Nathanael could have had that Jesus could see all things and read human hearts. Christ knows you who seek him in a prayerful spirit. And whenever you are seeking him, be sure that he is also seeking you.

Then Nathanael declared, "Rabbi, you are the Son of God; you are the King of Israel." (49)

Because Jesus had seen what Nathanael was doing in secret, it convinced Nathanael that he was "the King of Israel."

Jesus said, "You believe because I told you I saw you under the fig tree. You shall see greater things than that." He then added, "I tell you the truth, you shall see heaven open, and the angels of God ascending and descending on the Son of Man." (50–51)

Those who are ready to believe Christ on what seems to be slender evidence will have even clearer evidence. "You shall see greater things than that." This is the first personal promise our Lord spoke in his ministry. He did not give it to the most talented but to the most simple-hearted of his disciples. His promise to us is "Blessed are those who have not seen and yet have believed" (John 20:29). They will gaze on a wonderful sight some day!

Nathanael had seen the omniscience of Christ at work. What "greater things" could there be than that? I suppose Jesus meant, "Nathanael, you have seen my omniscience, but you will also see my omnipotence. You have discovered that I can read your heart, but you will also learn that I can change your heart."

Because Nathanael was "a true Israelite" (v. 47), he would have Israel's vision. He would see the same sight that Jacob, who became Israel, saw when he fell asleep with a stone for his pillow (Gen. 28:10–15)—except Nathanael's vision would be far more glorious than Jacob's. He would see literally what Jacob saw only in a dream when the stairway of light leading from earth to heaven appeared before him. Jesus by his manhood and Godhead bridges the distance between us and God. Christ always knows how to meet the needs of our hearts and to give us something in accordance with our own expressions and to make his answers fit our requests. And he always does "immeasurably more than all we ask or imagine" (Eph. 3:20).

A Life-Saving Message to Dying People

I SUPPOSE THAT MORE people have been saved through the reading of
this chapter than through almost any other portion of the Bible. If
you were visiting a dying person who did not know the gospel and
you wanted to select a chapter in the Bible that would set the truth
before him or before her very briefly and clearly, you could not make
a better choice than this third chapter of John's gospel. And what is
good for dying men and women is good for us all, for that is what we
are. No one can tell how soon she or he may be at the gates of death.

*Now there was a man of the Pharisees named Nicodemus, a member
of the Jewish ruling council. He came to Jesus at night and said,
"Rabbi, we know you are a teacher who has come from God. For no
one could perform the miraculous signs you are doing if God were not
with him." (1–2)*

The old saying has it, "Better late than never." And so it was for
Nicodemus. It is better to come to Christ in the dark, as he did,
than not to come at all. It may even have been the best time to come
to Christ, for the business of the day was over, and all was quiet.
Perhaps Nicodemus was prudent, not wishing to commit himself
until he had heard what Christ taught. Maybe Nicodemus was himself busy during the day. In any case, all hours are convenient for
Christ. When everyone else is asleep, Jesus is still awake. He is quite
willing to be the physician of your soul even if you ring him up at
midnight.

Nicodemus did use good reasoning. He had not yet learned to
believe in Christ as the Savior, but he did at least admit that he was
"a teacher who has come from God" and that God was "with him."
The miracles of Christ proved that to Nicodemus. He admitted the
truth as far as he could see it.

Always be willing to go as far as you can in the pursuit of truth. If you do not yet know Christ, make sure you don't trifle with what you do know about him. If you cannot see everything at once, see all you can see. If you are troubled with unbelief, believe as much as you can, and then cry, "I do believe; help me overcome my unbelief!" (Mark 9:24). Be teachable, as Nicodemus was. Thank God if you know as much as Nicodemus knew, and ask him to teach you more.

Our Lord Jesus could read all hearts. He needed no one to tell him what was there. Yet for our sakes he set the example of letting Nicodemus speak first. So when nonbelievers come to see you, do not begin by talking to them. Let them begin by telling you what they want to say, for it will probably guide you in what you will reply to them.

In reply Jesus declared, "I tell you the truth, unless a man is born again, he cannot see the kingdom of God." (3)

Jesus' formula "I tell you the truth" was a new style of speech for the Pharisees to hear. They quoted Rabbi this and Rabbi that, but Jesus gave himself as his own sufficient authority. He had an egoism that could not be blamed and that no true disciple of his ever questions, for Christ is himself the truth (John 14:6). Christ speaks with an authority that no human can ever possess.

It seems our Lord was saying, "Nicodemus, you speak of my 'miraculous signs' (v. 2). The greatest one of all is the new birth that I can give you. The miracles you have heard about are physical, but this is spiritual. And if you have the new birth, you will 'see the kingdom of God.'"

"The kingdom of God" is such a mystery that our old nature cannot "see," or understand, it. We must have new eyes. We must be new people. We must be "born again." Do you understand that you cannot polish yourself up to a certain point and then be admitted into the kingdom of God? There must be a radical change in you, a new birth from heaven, if you are even to "see the kingdom of God."

Because of this, our most lucid explanations of the gospel are completely lost on unregenerate men and women. However bright a light God may make your ministry, bright light is of no use to blind people. They must be born again before they can see the kingdom of God.

Nicodemus was a Pharisee, apt to put too much importance on the outward form of religion, so observe how the Savior dealt with him by dwelling on the inner part of it—the necessity of the new birth. Our main business in dealing with people's spiritual lives is not to teach them what they want to know but what they need to know. They may not find it palatable, but it will be profitable.

"How can a man be born when he is old?" Nicodemus asked. "Surely he cannot enter a second time into his mother's womb to be born!" (4)

This question proved Nicodemus could not see the kingdom of God (v. 3). The idea of the new birth is simple to us who have experienced it, but it was very difficult to Nicodemus. He misunderstood the metaphor Christ used. The unregenerate heart can no more understand the gospel than a horse can understand astronomy. But just because Nicodemus misunderstood Jesus' metaphor, did our Lord therefore refuse to give him any further instruction? No!

Jesus answered, "I tell you the truth, unless a man is born of water and the Spirit, he cannot enter the kingdom of God. Flesh gives birth to flesh, but the Spirit gives birth to spirit. You should not be surprised at my saying, 'You must be born again.' The wind blows wherever it pleases. You hear its sound, but you cannot tell where it comes from or where it is going. So it is with everyone born of the Spirit." (5–8)

To "enter the kingdom of God" we must be cleansed—"born of water." If the "water" here relates to baptism—which I greatly question—then it shows the way for a believer to enter the visible kingdom of God publicly through the church. But if it relates to the purifying power of God's Spirit—as I believe it does—it teaches that we cannot enter the kingdom of God and share its privileges—which is far more than seeing it (v. 3)—except the Spirit of God purifies us from sin as water purifies our flesh. This takes place when we are "born again" (v. 3).

We must be born not only "of water" but also of "the Spirit." Since the Holy Spirit cleanses us from sin, possibly the word *Spirit* defines the word *water*. If so, this verse could be translated, "Unless a man is born of water—that is, the Spirit—he cannot enter the kingdom of God."

However godly your father, however gracious your mother, you are just like the children of the most ungodly parents, for "flesh gives birth to flesh." There is no such thing as inherited godliness. Anything that comes to us by our first birth is mere "flesh," for you can get nothing better than flesh out of flesh. The only evolution that comes out of it is corruption. This is why Paul said, "Flesh and blood cannot inherit the kingdom of God" (1 Cor. 15:50).

Only "the Spirit gives birth to spirit." Everything is according to its birth and nature. There must be, then, a birth from the Holy Spirit, or you have no spirit. You do not belong to the spiritual realm, and you cannot enter the spiritual kingdom. Only the "new creation" in Christ (2 Cor. 5:17), whose "birth" comes from "the Spirit," can possess the spiritual things that belong to the kingdom of God. The flesh cannot enter the spiritual kingdom. Only spiritual people can. Hence our need of the new birth, that God's Spirit may be created in us.

Nicodemus was surprised at this strange teaching, so Jesus told him, "You should not be surprised." Since the first birth can only give you "flesh," we must have a second birth to bring us into the realm of spiritual realities.

Everyone "must be born again," for Jesus addressed this message to a man who might have been exempt from the new birth, if anyone might have. He was "a man of the Pharisees" (v. 1). The Pharisees practiced fasting, tithing, giving to the needy, and regular prayer. Nicodemus was also "a member of the Jewish ruling council" (v. 1) and "Israel's teacher" (v. 10). He had studied Scripture very carefully. Yet it is not the study of Scripture but having Christ formed in us that brings salvation.

You may be rich or poor, but "you must be born again." You may be intelligent, educated, or talented, but "you must be born again." Many things are desirable, but this one thing is absolutely necessary.

Some think they are Christians because they live in England or America. Is a rat a horse because it lives in a stable? That is just as good reasoning. If you are not born twice, you must die twice, because you are no Christian.

How do you know if you have been born again? You will repent of your sins, put your faith in Christ, pray from your heart, and show the world the change Christ has made in you. Since you must be born again, bow yourself down and say, "Then, Lord, I will be born again."

We use the expression "free as the wind." It can blow in any direction at any time. The Holy Spirit is like that. Tomorrow he may save a prince and the next day a backslider. The last thing expected in Jerusalem was that Saul of Tarsus would be converted, but he was (Acts 9:1–19). The wind of God's Spirit may blow on those willing to go to church to hear the gospel but unwilling to be changed by it. Oh, that God would send us a cyclone of his Holy Spirit!

You cannot see the wind or tell where it begins, where it goes, or where it ends. The Holy Spirit is mysterious like the wind, and so is the person born of the Spirit. Spiritual people often cannot understand themselves. How, then, can they understand how that wondrous new life is created within them? There are heights to which the spiritual life can carry them of which they have never dreamed. All we know is that this is a new creation, as much the work of eternal power as our first creation. We have seen mysteries in nature, and we experience this mystery in grace. Though we cannot completely understand this, we can completely enjoy it!

"How can this be?" Nicodemus asked. (9)

Many a person has asked this same question in different words. "How can I become a new creature?" Only God, who makes all things, can make all things new. The new birth is as great a wonder as creation itself. There is as much to be done in you to make you a Christian as there has been done in you to make you a human being.

Our Savior is an example to all of us who preach. He shows us the wisdom of not keeping back the mysteries of the kingdom. I greatly fear that many preachers would have begun by talking to Nicodemus about some point that Judaism and Christianity had in common, and then they would have apologized for the mysteries of Christianity. All that would have been a waste of breath—and worse than that. Speak the truth boldly, and let the Holy Spirit make use of it as he pleases.

"You are Israel's teacher," said Jesus, "and do you not understand these things? I tell you the truth, we speak of what we know, and we testify to what we have seen, but still you people do not accept our testimony. I have spoken to you of earthly things and you do not believe; how then will you believe if I speak of heavenly things? No one has ever gone into heaven except the one who came from heaven—the Son of Man. Just as Moses lifted up the snake in the desert, so the Son of Man must be lifted up, that everyone who believes in him may have eternal life." (10–15)

Jesus was saying, "You teach others, yet have you never been taught this first great spiritual truth? You know the law of God, so why are you ignorant of the Spirit of God?" Nicodemus was not the last rabbi who failed to understand the new birth. No doubt there are many who teach others the Bible who have never experienced this all-important change. Many who have earned the highest degrees a university can grant do not know what is means to be born again. The Lord have mercy on them! It would be better to be ignorant of all other things and to know this one thing than to have all possible human learning and yet miss the most essential knowledge of all—how to be born again.

Spiritual people do not preach theories but facts. We do not speculate; "we speak of what we know," because we have passed through the second birth. "We know" and "have seen" spiritual realities, and we have a right to be believed, for we are not liars but honest people. Though others have not experienced the new birth, we have. If a judge wanted six witnesses in court to establish a fact, I am sure the judge could not desire better witnesses than those who say they are born again.

Yet often our witness is rejected. Though our testimony would be believed if we gave it concerning anything else, we are not believed when we give it concerning the higher and better life. We need not be surprised at this, for it was the same with our Master.

If these elementary truths about the new birth stagger Nicodemus, what is the use of a Bible teacher going on to anything higher? If at the entrance to the kingdom of heaven you say, "How can this be?" what will you say if I take you into the central metropolis of truth and introduce you to the great King himself? You would be at a total loss. Should a boy be taught the classics if he will not study his spelling book? The primary teachings of the new birth must be believed before the more advanced doctrines of our election and God's sovereignty can be revealed.

Now Nicodemus must have been completely puzzled. Jesus was a man who had come "from heaven" and had "gone into heaven," yet he was at that moment talking to Nicodemus! Without the Spirit of God to explain this mystery, he could not make top or bottom of it. Jesus, the only one who has come from God, is the only one who knows all his secrets. He can teach all truth, for he has been in heaven.

You and I are on the stairway between heaven and earth. Christ has come down and gone up, yet he is always with us. We can go up by prayer, and blessings can come down. In both cases, Christ is there.

Jesus refers to the story in Numbers 21:4–9, when the people of Israel were invaded by poisonous snakes. But that was nothing compared to poisonous lusts. The snakes infused poison into the blood, but lust infuses damnation into the soul. The only cure for the snake bites was for Moses to lift up a bronze snake on a pole, so that people might look to it and live. And the only cure for sin is to look in faith to the Savior, who was lifted up on a cross when he died in our place and became sin for us.

No doubt some in Moses' day looked to their physicians. Others looked to their sores. But they all died. And you will perish unless you look away from human teachers and your own sinful condition to the bleeding Savior. The only purpose for which Jesus died on the cross was that you could look to him in faith and be saved from your sins. So do not say the gospel is not for you.

Let us who call ourselves Christians remember that we are not to lift up doctrine, the church, or our denomination. "The Son of Man must be lifted up." Let us make it our business to preach Christ so that our listeners see him exalted.

The last verse is the gospel in a nutshell, the whole Bible in a line. Through faith in Christ we have eternal life that will outlast the world, the sun, the moon, and the stars! Note the word "everyone" (v. 15). It means you, and it means me! You may be at death's door, crushed and broken, bruised and mangled. Still, look to the crucified one, and by looking you will find that there is eternal life for you! Though your soul has been ready to choose strangling rather than your life, there is a better life for you by trusting in Christ. Choose that, and rest in him! Say from your heart the lines of the hymn:

> Jesus, to your arms I fly;
> Save me, Lord, or I will die!

Eternal life is given for a look to the crucified Savior. Look to him, then, in the preaching of the gospel. As surely as those who were bitten by the snakes in the wilderness were healed the moment they looked at the bronze snake, so will everyone who looks in faith to Christ be saved at once and forever.

"For God so loved the world that he gave his one and only Son, that whoever believes in him shall not perish but have eternal life. For God did not send his Son into the world to condemn the world, but to save the world through him. Whoever believes in him is not condemned, but whoever does not believe stands condemned already because he has not believed in the name of God's one and only Son. This is the verdict: Light has come into the world, but men loved darkness instead of light because their deeds were evil. Everyone who does evil hates the light, and will not come into the light for fear that his deeds will be exposed. But whoever lives by the truth comes into the light, so that it may be seen plainly that what he has done has been done through God." (16–21)

The verb gave is in the past tense, though when Jesus said this he had not yet died. In the heavenly Father's eternal purpose "he gave his one and only Son" before the world was created. I believe God is still giving away his Son today. Oh, that many would accept "his indescribable gift" (2 Cor. 9:15)!

Some say that believers in Christ may later perish, but there is no such teaching in Scripture. We who believe in Christ are members of his body (1 Cor. 12:27). Will Christ lose his bodily parts? Will he be maimed in heaven? How could he be perfect if he loses even his little finger? If you were trying to drown me, you could not drown my foot as long as my head was above water. This is why we shall not perish. We are united to Christ, and we must live because he lives.

I sometimes think that if I never had a gleam of love from God's face again, I would live on John 3:16. This one verse has saved thousands of people. I have known several hundred who have been guided into spiritual liberty by this text. The constellation in the heavens called the Great Bear has two pointers that direct the eye of the observer to the pole star. This verse is the Great Bear of Scripture. Its two pointers are the new birth and faith in the Savior. These point to Christ so clearly, so distinctly, that many have found him. And in finding him, they have found life.

These two truths—our need for the new birth and salvation through faith in Christ—are in perfect harmony with each other. May you know them both by personal experience! Never talk of reconciling these two truths, for they have never parted ways from one another.

Condemnation does come to the world through Christ, because the world rejects him. But that was not part of God's purpose in sending him. His goal was only "to save the world." Oh, that more might believe and so fulfill God's purpose in sending his Son!

This is very good teaching for any who have recently come to Christ or for those seeking him. And it is the same teaching that will bring comfort to the best instructed saint. How I love continually to begin with Christ over again as I began at the beginning of my Christian life! They say when someone is sick, it is good to take that person to his or to her native land. And when the souls of true believers get weak and unbelieving, let them breathe the air of Calvary over again.

The educated Grotius, who had spent most of his life in theological debates—not always on the right side—when he was dying, said, "Read me something." They read him the story of the Pharisee and the tax collector (Luke 18:9–14). He said, "I am that poor tax

collector. God be merciful to me, the sinner!" That was the word
with which that great scholar entered heaven. That is also the way
in which you and I must come to God. May the Holy Spirit help us
to come to him that way!

Believers are very faulty. Their consciences accuse them, but in
spite of every sin they have ever committed, they are not condemned. Why? Because their acceptance depends not on themselves
but on the perfect righteousness of Christ. They may displease God,
but for that they are not condemned. They will be disciplined by the
Father (Heb. 12:6) but not condemned. They are assaulted by Satan
but not condemned.

Our reason for trusting in Christ is not that we feel our need of
him but that we have a need of him. It is not our soft hearts that
entitle us to believe. We believe in Christ to renew our hard hearts,
and we come to him with nothing but our sins.

If an angel should say to me, "Charles Spurgeon, I have come
from heaven to tell you that you are pardoned," I would reply,
"I know that without your telling me anything of the kind. And I
know it on a greater authority than yours." If he asked me how
I knew it, I would answer, "The Word of God is better to me than
the word of an angel, and he has said, 'Whoever believes in him is
not condemned.' I do believe in Christ, and therefore I am not condemned, and I know it without an angel telling me so."

Go to bed tonight saying, "If I die in my sleep, I cannot be condemned!" If you wake up tomorrow morning, go into the world
saying, "I cannot be condemned!" When the Devil howls at you, tell
him, "You may accuse me, but I cannot be condemned, for I believe
in Christ!"

The person who refuses to believe the witness of God is by that
very fact condemned already. If that person had no other sin, it
would be enough to sink him or her to the lowest hell for making
God a liar by refusing to believe in Jesus Christ his Son.

There was no need for Christ to come to condemn us, for we
were condemned already by our sin. There is no need to point out
your evil words and acts. There is no need to bring out your diary
and turn over the record of your life. If you have not believed in
Jesus Christ, it shows a lack of love to the loving God. By that evidence you are condemned already.

Human beings are not in a state of probation with God. That
probation passed away in the days of Adam and Eve. Humans are
not prisoners at the bar about to be tried for their lives. Their trial
is over, their sentence is passed, and they are condemned already. By
contrast, every believer is forgiven already. Surely they deserve the

deepest hell who will not have heaven on these terms.

Oh, believe me, if you could roll all sins into one mass—if you could take murder, blasphemy, lust, adultery, fornication, and everything that is vile, and unite them all into one vast globe of foul corruption, they would not equal even then the sin of unbelief. This is the monarch sin, the quintessence of guilt, the mixture of the venom of all crimes, the dregs of the wine of Gomorrah. It is the A-1 sin, the masterpiece of Satan, the chief work of the Devil!

Those who love their sins cannot love the Savior at the same time. They must love the one and hate the other. If people did not hug their sins, they would embrace the Savior. Trace hatred for Christ home to its den and lair, and you will find that it is bred by the love of sin. It is a terrible choice when people reject Christ, who is light, and choose the outer darkness of sin and woe.

Those who do evil hate the Light. This is the reason behind all opposition to God. There is no more damning sign of people's condition than their avoidance of divine light. If you do not like those parts of the Word of God that judge you and make you tremble, be sure that your heart is not right. The person in business who cannot bear to look at the books probably has good reason to be afraid of them. Whatever you trifle with, don't trifle with your soul!

People do not see because they do not want to see. They do not want to see because they would be uneasy in their sins. So they kick against Christ and try to put out the light of his gospel, lest it rebuke and correct them.

Are you a person who comes into the light—the light of Scripture? If so, good. God help us not to shun that light. Instead, may we feel that it is our friend, and may we desire to walk in it. Those who seek the light will find it in Jesus Christ.

After this, Jesus and his disciples went out into the Judean countryside, where he spent some time with them, and baptized. Now John also was baptizing at Aenon near Salim, because there was plenty of water, and people were constantly coming to be baptized. (This was before John was put in prison.) An argument developed between some of John's disciples and a certain Jew over the matter of ceremonial washing. They came to John and said to him, "Rabbi, that man who was with you on the other side of the Jordan—the one you testified about— well, he is baptizing, and everyone is going to him." (22-26)

John would not have needed plenty of water if he had merely sprinkled these people in baptism. He practiced immersion.

John was busy until he was put in prison. He would not waste an hour while he had an opportunity to do good, and he did it with all his heart. Be like John! Spend every moment in the service of Christ while you can.

Isn't it sad that there was arguing over ceremonial washing? After reading about looking to Christ and God's love for the world, here we find an argument. The church will always have its idle quarrels about the pastor's clothes, the mode of administering the communion elements, and other matters.

These people brought John what they thought was bad news—that people were leaving him. They grieved that John's influence appeared to be on the decline. But John was a stranger to this feeling. He loved to see his Master grow, even at the cost of his own decrease in popularity.

To this John replied, "A man can receive only what is given him from heaven. You yourselves can testify that I said, 'I am not the Christ but am sent ahead of him.' The bride belongs to the bridegroom. The friend who attends the bridegroom waits and listens for him, and is full of joy when he hears the bridegroom's voice. That joy is mine, and it is now complete. He must become greater; I must become less." (27–30)

No spiritual power, no ability to bless others, comes except from God. Shall I quarrel with God, therefore, if he gives someone else more power than he gives me? It is God's sovereign will, and he does whatever he wants. Each Christian has her or his appointed place. John had no desire to usurp the place of another, least of all that of his Lord. The truth stated in this verse should act as a cure for envy.

John's friends were vexed, but he was joyful. He loved to hear of Jesus prospering. John was clear on this point. It is good for all Christians to be equally sure that they have never exalted themselves but have always exalted Christ alone.

The job of "the friend who attends the bridegroom" is to introduce him. Since John had done that, his new job was to disappear from the scene.

"He must become greater; I must become less." This is just what happened. As the morning star fades when the sun rises, so it was the joy of Christ's herald to lose himself in the supreme radiance of his Lord's appearing. After this John preached no more sermons recorded in the New Testament. He had to go to prison and there lie in a silence he could scarcely bear. It was very hard for John to be quiet. He had an active, noble mind, and he became the victim, we fear, of doubts when he was in prison. The breezy air of the wilderness suited him much better than the dull, heavy atmosphere of a prison.

You may feel in despair, like John. Do not automatically attribute it to spiritual causes. It may be the result of the atmosphere that surrounds you. We must not think too much of our feelings, for even the wind can change them.

"The one who comes from above is above all; the one who is from the earth belongs to the earth, and speaks as one from the earth. The one who comes from heaven is above all. He testifies to what he has seen and heard, but no one accepts his testimony. The man who has accepted it has certified that God is truthful. For the one whom God has sent speaks the words of God, for God gives the Spirit without limit. The Father loves the Son and has placed everything in his hands. Whoever believes in the Son has eternal life, but whoever rejects the Son will not see life, for God's wrath remains on him." (31–36)

However good a person may be, he or she "belongs to the earth." Even if we handle heavenly things, our earthiness peeps out every now and then. Christ had no earthiness in him. He was "above all."

The news that people were going to Christ pleased John, but when virtually no one accepted Christ's testimony, John's heart must have been grieved.

What was Christ's testimony? In this chapter alone, he testified that God is to be approached only in a spiritual way (vv. 3, 7), that God gives salvation to everyone who believes in Christ (v. 16), and that believers in him are not condemned (v. 18). We would have thought that the moment this testimony was given, the whole world would have gladly welcomed it. But the reverse happened. Virtually no one accepted Jesus' testimony.

John eagerly turned people's hearts and minds to the Savior. He was willing to be nothing so that they would believe in Christ as God's truth incarnate. All who love people must desire the same thing for them, for only as Jesus is received in the heart can people be saved.

Didn't the Holy Spirit descend and remain on Christ "without limit"? Yes. And there was an infinite spiritual power in the words of Christ. They were the words of God. Today the Holy Spirit concentrates all his energy in those words.

The believer in Christ has eternal life now. If that believer could lose it, it would not be "eternal life," for eternal life lasts eternally. We have a life that must continue forever and ever!

The person who rejects Christ will not even know what eternal life is. All unbelievers are blind to spiritual things. As such, they "will not see life."

So John's last words were thunder. His dying speech has in it the message most terrible to all who do not believe in Christ. "God's wrath remains" on them. If this verse said, "God's wrath remains on prison inmates," most people would assent to that. If it declared, "God's wrath remains on prostitutes," most of us would say, "Amen." It is true that God's wrath rests on open sinners, but here the truth declared is that God's wrath remains on even virtuous people who have not believed in Jesus Christ.

Many reject the teaching of God's wrath, but as for me, I have never been able to believe in a little hell, because I cannot find in the Bible any trace of a little heaven, a little Savior, a little sin, or a little God. I believe in drawing my theology to scale.

Do Not Let Your Hearts Be Troubled

THIS CHAPTER IS THE epitome of comfort and a river of delight. Jesus knew his absence would greatly upset his disciples, and therefore on this night before he died he poured out a stream of consolations. Many thousands of true believers have been comforted by these gracious words. All Scripture is a garden of sweet flowers, but this fourteenth chapter of John may be compared to the rose, because it has marvelous beauty and sweetness.

"Do not let your hearts be troubled. Trust in God; trust also in me. In my Father's house are many rooms; if it were not so, I would have told you. I am going there to prepare a place for you. And if I go and prepare a place for you, I will come back and take you to be with me that you also may be where I am. You know the way to the place where I am going." (1–4)

You will be troubled. That cannot be helped. But "do not let your hearts be troubled." You are like a ship, and all the water in the sea cannot hurt the ship if it is kept outside of her. The waves may beat all around your boat, but do not let the boat take in the water and leak. There is no cure for heart trouble but heart trust. Twice in this verse our Savior used the word "trust." He seemed to say, "Take another dose of faith every time you are troubled." Faith is a double cure when we are "troubled." It delivers us from the trouble, and it helps us find sweetness in it as long as we have to endure it.

We can paraphrase our Savior's words as follows: "You trust in God, whom you have never seen. Trust also in me when you will no longer see me. Trust in me as still working for your good. You trust in God's providence; now trust in my atonement. You have come close to God already; come even closer to him through me. Your faith deals with some things; now let it deal with more things. Your past troubles have been endured by trusting in God; now endure the present by trusting in me as well."

Wicked people may shut you out of your Father's house on earth, but "we have a building from God, an eternal house in heaven, not built by human hands" (2 Cor. 5:1). Since our "Father's house" contains "many rooms," there is room for many people. So there is room for you there—if you believe in Christ.

The reason the disciples were "troubled" (v. 1) was that their Master was leaving them. Yet he was going for their good. He left with a specific purpose, and the same reason still keeps him away from us. We are not to mourn for Christ as we might for one slain in battle, as if he will never come back for us. He has gone briefly to his Father's house on the most gracious and necessary errand: "to prepare a place for you." The Spirit of God is down here to prepare us for the place, and the Son of God is up there to prepare the place for us. Thus heaven is a prepared place for a prepared people. How does Jesus prepare a place for us? Simply by going there. When he went to heaven, that made it heaven! His glory makes it fully glorious!

Jesus keeps this promise in many senses. He has already come back by his gracious Spirit. He has also come back by his divine presence with us. When we die, he will come back to meet us. And if we do not die, we will see his promise fulfilled to the greatest possible extent, for Jesus will come back for us physically.

"I will come back and take you to be with me" remains one of the sweetest promises ever given to believers by the Lord Jesus. He did not say, "I will take you into heaven." He promised something far better than that: "I will . . . take you to be with me." Oh, what bliss it will be to have Christ take us personally to himself and to be with him forever! It is sweet to know we will always be with the Lord if we die before he comes, but another sweet hope is his personal return.

This is the first and last fact about heaven. Wherever it is, we will be with Christ. Do not tell me about purgatory for Christ's people, a limbo in which they lie while being prepared to share his glory. No. He will come and take us to himself. His promise is "that you also may be where I am." Do you want a better rest than that after your life here? Doesn't this truth encourage you on earth's journey? When you die, you will not be plunged into the great unknown. You will be with Christ.

He had taught "the way" to his disciples. He had explained to them that he was the goal of their way and the way to their goal, that he was going to the Father, and that he was the way to the Father.

If a mother says, "I have missed my boy for twelve months and have never heard from him," that is sad. But when she adds, "I know where he has gone, why he has gone, and what he went for," she is greatly comforted. So we are comforted in knowing where Jesus went. Since "you know the way," use it often by praying to Christ.

Thomas said to him, "Lord, we don't know where you are going, so how can we know the way?" (5)

Thomas was contradicting his Master, and he should not have done that. Be careful that you do not contradict Christ. Our unbelief would be shamed out of us if we were to examine it carefully. Faith in God is nothing but sanctified common sense. At least Thomas brought his confusion to the Lord. When we put our troubles down in black and white, we sometimes get rid of them. But to bring them to the Lord in prayer is a better plan still.

How much ignorance there often is when there ought to be much knowledge! It is not always the person who lives in the sunlight who sees the most. Thomas had been one of the twelve apostles for several years. During all that time he had Christ for his teacher, yet he learned very little. With such poor teachers as we are, it is no wonder that our students learn very little from us. But they ought to learn much from Christ, though they and we learn nothing even from him except under the teaching of the Holy Spirit.

Jesus answered, "I am the way and the truth and the life. No one comes to the Father except through me. If you really knew me, you would know my Father as well. From now on, you do know him and have seen him." (6–7)

The way, the truth, and the life: here are three mixed metaphors to describe Jesus, but we are obligated to use them when we talk of Christ, for he is the mixture of everything delightful and precious.

Let us link this to our Lord's discussion of heaven in the previous verses. He is "the way" to heaven, "the truth" of heaven, and "the life" of heaven. He is heaven's everything. It is impossible to describe our Lord in human language. He was going away, yet he was himself "the way." He is also "the Beginning and the End" (Rev. 21:6). He is everything to his people. Jesus is everything we could want on "the way" to heaven. He is "the truth" that will make heaven for us and "the life" that we will enjoy forever in heaven. He gives us all this while we live here on earth.

Many people are not coming to God; they are running as far as they can from him. But as for us who want to come to the Father, we cannot do it in faith or in prayer or in fellowship or in worship except through Christ. No music is sweet to God unless Christ tunes the harp. If there is no blood on the harp, there will be no music that God can accept. Martin Luther used to say very wisely, "I will have nothing to do with an absolute God. I must come to him through Christ."

If I want to go up to the top of the house and a ladder goes only halfway, it does me no good. If I want to go to God, I need a ladder that reaches all the way up to God. Christ is that ladder, for he is God.

Christ is also the "Mighty God" and "Everlasting Father" (Isa. 9:6). "In Christ all the fullness of the Deity lives in bodily form" (Col. 2:9), and he is "the radiance of God's glory and the exact representation of his being" (Heb. 1:3). Whenever we see the Son, we see the Father. When we come to Christ, we come to the Father.

I hope it can be said of you, as Jesus said of his disciples, "You do know [the Father] and have seen him." The main point of knowledge with us is to know God. He is the most excellent of all sciences.

Philip said, "Lord, show us the Father and that will be enough for us." (8)

Thomas was not the only dunce among the disciples. Philip also betrayed his ignorance. He had not yet grasped the idea of the perfect union of the Father and the Son. What a comfort these men should be to us. We are not the only dolts in Christ's school! If he could bear with them, he can bear with us. Like them, we retain so little of what Christ teaches. We are taught much, but we learn little. Our memories hold little and our understanding even less. We are too apt to want something we can see, as Philip did when he asked, "Lord, show us the Father and that will be enough for us."

Jesus answered: "Don't you know me, Philip, even after I have been among you such a long time? Anyone who has seen me has seen the Father. How can you say, 'Show us the Father'? Don't you believe that I am in the Father, and that the Father is in me? The words I say to you are not just my own. Rather, it is the Father, living in me, who is doing his work. Believe me when I say that I am in the Father and the Father is in me; or at least believe on the evidence of the miracles themselves. I tell you the truth, anyone who has faith in me will do what I have been doing. He will do even greater things than these, because I am going to the Father. And I will do whatever you ask in my name, so that the Son may bring glory to the Father. You may ask me for anything in my name, and I will do it." (9–14)

God has given us a life-size example of himself in Jesus. In all God's works of creation we have no more than a mere miniature picture. If only we knew Christ more, we would know the Father! We who understand Christ's character understand God as much as any human can. We know more of God from the life of Christ than from any other source. Yet until the Spirit of God illumines our minds we learn little even from the best of teachers. God was in Christ most evidently, yet Philip did not perceive it.

Say, "Yes, Lord, I believe that you are in the Father and that the Father is in you. This is a doctrine about which I have no question at all."

Even our Lord Jesus did not claim to preach his own words. How much more should preachers today be careful not to preach their own philosophies but only the Word of God!

Jesus urged his disciples to believe. Again and again he returned to this vital point. There is no relief from heart trouble except by believing the eternal truth of God, and especially by trusting in him who is "the truth" (v. 6). Only the believer has true peace of heart. The unbeliever is tossed around by the waves of the great ocean of doubt.

What can be the meaning of this verse if Jesus is not divine? No clearer statement of his oneness with the Father could be given.

Christ's very absence would let loose a greater power than the disciples could have experienced when he was here. As God, Jesus could delegate his infinite power to others. His apostles did "greater things" because they spread out all over the world and brought more converts to the faith by their testimony than the Lord himself called during his own personal ministry.

We cannot add anything to Christ's atonement, for he has said, "It is finished" (John 19:30). That work must stand as complete and unique. But we can do his work of teaching and blessing people. The Lord Jesus never preached a sermon that yielded three thousand converts in one day. But Peter did after the ascended Christ poured out his Spirit on him (Acts 2:14–41). There are still many more "greater things" we can do today through the Holy Spirit.

Mark the breadth of prayer: "You may ask me for anything," and also the limit of prayer: "in my name." This is the only limit to true, believing prayer. There are some things we could not ask in Christ's "name." There are some wishes and whims we may cherish and we think we can pray about, but we do not have Christ's name or authority to warrant us to expect we will receive them. Therefore we cannot ask for them in his name.

To say, "For Christ's sake" is one thing, but to say, "I ask in Christ's name" is quite another matter. It is the difference between doing my own business for someone else and doing someone else's business because that other person has authorized me to do so. To pray in Christ's name is to feel that, as Christ stood in your place, you dare to stand in his place. It is to feel that what you have prayed for is what Jesus would have prayed for. Jesus never authorized us to make use of his name about everything. There are only certain things about which we can sign his name on the checks of our prayers. These are the biblical promises of God. When you pray for one of them, you will prove Christ's words in verse 14 to be true.

I have heard some say that prayer is helpful to those who offer it, but it has no effect on God. They think we are idiots. Would anyone but an idiot go on praying if he or she did not believe it would prevail with God? I would just as soon stand and whistle out my bedroom window for half an hour as kneel down and pray for half an hour if I felt no result would come from it. So would every sensible person.

Some of God's children have very little power with him in prayer. Since they do not listen to God's words, he does not listen to theirs. Yet he still gives them the necessities of life, even as you give your disobedient children what they need.

"If you love me, you will obey what I command. And I will ask the Father, and he will give you another Counselor to be with you forever—the Spirit of truth. The world cannot accept him, because it neither sees him nor knows him. But you know him, for he lives with you and will be in you. I will not leave you as orphans; I will come to you. Before long, the world will not see me anymore, but you will see me. Because I live, you also will live. On that day you will realize that I am in my Father, and you are in me, and I am in you. Whoever has my commands and obeys them, he is the one who loves me. He who loves me will be loved by my Father, and I too will love him and show myself to him." (15–21)

Some Christians, out of supposed love for Christ, have attempted acts of fanaticism. In many cases they were sincere, but they were also unwise. Some wish Jesus had said here, "If you love me, become a preacher, a missionary, or a martyr." But he did not say that. He told us, in effect, to obey him by exhibiting his character wherever he has placed us in life. True "love" for Jesus always shows itself by obedience. All other love is a thing only of the lips and betrays a hypocritical heart. Are we daily giving proof of our love to Jesus by obeying his commands? ·

Jesus implied that our love precedes our obedience. He did not say, "Obey my commands, then love me." We must not expect pure streams until the fountain is cleansed. Love for Christ is the best reason for obeying him. Personal affection will produce personal obedience, and obedience is the best proof of love. If there is a commandment of Christ that you do not relish, let that be a warning to you that your heart needs to be set straight.

The disciples' trouble that day was that Jesus was leaving them, but the other "Counselor" would make it up to them. He will also make it up to you, believer, when you have trouble. Is it a physical problem? The infirmity of old age? A feeling of depression? Losses and crosses at home? Crooked things that can't be made straight? Whatever it is, your Lord's promise still stands good.

The word *Counselor* could also be translated "Comforter," "Helper," or "Advocate." This "Spirit of truth" knows the truth, can teach us the truth, and can apply the truth to our hearts. The Holy Spirit as "another Counselor" implies that Jesus is also our Counselor and that the Spirit is just like Christ. We do well to treat the Holy Spirit as we would treat Jesus if he were still among us. Our Lord's disciples told him their troubles. Let us trust the Counselor with ours. In all your learning ask him to teach you. In all your suffering ask him to sustain you. In all your teaching ask him to give you the right words. In all your witnessing ask him to give you boldness. In all your service depend on him for help.

The Holy Spirit is here called "the Spirit of truth" because he never teaches anything but the truth, and he works truthfulness in God's children. They are honest, sincere, and open-hearted.

The world is always receiving one form of falsehood or another. Tossed back and forth, it never stays long in one belief. People cry, "This is truth!" or "That is truth!" or "Now we have the truth!" This is proof of Christ's statement regarding the Holy Spirit: "The world cannot accept him, because it neither sees him nor knows him. But you know him."

Worldly people can hear the gospel, but they know nothing of the inward Spirit who speaks it. They are unaware even of the Holy Spirit's existence. They say there may or may not be such a divine being, but they have never come across his path. This, then, is one test of true believers. They have received a new nature that enables them to recognize the existence of the Spirit of God and to feel the influence of his work.

A doctor once told a Christian there was no soul. He asked, "Did you ever see a soul, hear a soul, smell a soul, taste a soul, or feel a soul?" The Christian answered no to each question except the last, to which he replied, "Yes, I can feel my soul inside me."

"Well," said the doctor, "you have four senses against you but only one for you."

"Very well," said the Christian. "Did you ever see a pain, hear a pain, smell a pain, taste a pain, or feel a pain?" The doctor answered just as the Christian had—the first four times no and the last time yes. The Christian replied, "You also have four senses against you but only one for you." Still, the doctor insisted that was enough.

So worldly people say there is no Holy Spirit, because they cannot see him. But we can feel him, and that is enough to convince us he lives.

Without our Lord, we are "as orphans"—unhappy and lonely. Orphans have dead parents, but we have a death-conquering Christ. Orphans are left without the instruction they need. But we have the Holy Spirit as our teacher (v. 26). Father and mother may leave us as orphans, but Jesus will not. Friends we love may turn their hearts against us, but Jesus will not. Judas may play the traitor, but Jesus will always be true to us.

Remember to whom our Lord originally spoke these words. "Peter, you will deny me, but I will not leave you as an orphan. Thomas, you will doubt me, but I will not leave you as an orphan."

Their spiritual sight that discerned the presence of the Holy Spirit with them would also discern the continuing presence of Christ after he had ascended back to heaven. Children of God always see Jesus spiritually. We have life in a look, and our continued sight of Christ brings us continued life through Christ.

If you see Christ with the eye of faith, remember three things: The Holy Spirit made you see him. This sight will lead you to other sights. This sight makes up for many other things we do not see. "At present we do not see everything subject to him. But we see Jesus" (Heb. 2:8-9).

"Because I live, you also will live." Oh, what a rich promise! How, then, can Christ's people ever perish? Until Christ himself perishes, no child of his can ever be lost. Because he lives, there is a living, lasting union between us and Christ.

A trinity of unities we can "realize" is that Christ is in the Father, we are in Christ, and Christ is in us. What a wondrous combination of the Father, Christ, and us! Each truth is a mystery and yet something we can "realize."

Jesus did not say that "the one who loves me" will "preach my commands" or "brag about obeying my commands." The true lover of Christ "obeys" the Lord's commands. If we claim to love Christ, we must prove it by obeying his commands. Be on the lookout for disobedience. It is part of God's discipline that when we disobey, he withdraws from us his comfortable presence. Oh, that we might carefully watch our thoughts, words, and acts, lest we grieve our Lord. He will "show" himself to us when we yield ourselves to him.

Then Judas (not Judas Iscariot) said, "But, Lord, why do you intend to show yourself to us and not to the world?" (22)

The Holy Spirit is careful to preserve the name of the gracious Judas from being confused with that of the traitor. Our characters are safe in his keeping. Often when overwhelmed with a sense of the Lord's love to us, we have been ready to ask a question similar to Judas's here: "Why did you choose me, Lord? Why me?" It is an unanswerable question.

In this verse large-hearted Judas wanted all the privileges enjoyed by God's children to be shared with the King's enemies, but that could not be. Judas felt that Jesus was not extending his kingdom far enough when he showed himself only to a few poor fishermen, but if he would show himself in all his glory to the world, surely they would be overwhelmed, and the kingdom would come. But this was not Christ's way. He does not care about the world's glitter. His concern is to bless his disciples.

Jesus replied, "If anyone loves me, he will obey my teaching. My Father will love him, and we will come to him and make our home with him. He who does not love me will not obey my teaching. These words you hear are not my own; they belong to the Father who sent me." (23–24)

Where the grace of God has created a love between us and Christ, there is a window through which the Father and Christ will come to us. Our Lord and his Father are sure to reveal themselves to those who love and obey Christ, but how can they reveal themselves to someone who does not love and obey him? That person cannot see Christ, would not appreciate him if he or she could see him, and has no spiritual taste with which to enjoy him.

The Father and the Son love to abide where they are welcomed by humble and affectionate hearts, for these are habitations they have themselves prepared for their own indwelling. All the universe cannot contain either the infinite Father or the infinite Son, yet they both live in a loving and obedient heart. Jesus' promise that the Father and he "will come to him and make our home with him" implies that the distance caused by sin is now removed. How honored is the person who gets to receive the Father and the Son as guests!

There is much talk of love for Christ by those who disobey his teachings. The teachings of his apostles in the pages of the New Testament are the teachings of Christ. They are an extension of what our Lord taught. He will not allow us to say we love him if we do not obey his teaching.

This is a wonderful denial of originality by Jesus. If anyone could have spoken his own words, it was surely the Christ of God. But he was a messenger, and he delivered his heavenly Father's message.

Since this is true of Christ, it is also true of us. We ought to be careful not to deliver our own thoughts or philosophies. If the Lord Jesus Christ did not do that, what fools his servants must be if they pretend to do it! If a teaching is not revealed in Scripture, it will not be taught by me, nor should it be received by you. Our only power lies in the Word of God. When we speak a message that is not ours but the Father's, we can feel safe about it and sure of its success. Whereas, if we made up our own message, we would often question the truth of our statements. When we can fall back on the Word of God and prove it from what the Father has said, we no longer feel responsible. To some this may look like weakness, but it is real strength.

"All this I have spoken while still with you. But the Counselor, the Holy Spirit, whom the Father will send in my name, will teach you all things and will remind you of everything I have said to you. Peace I leave with you; my peace I give you. I do not give to you as the world gives. Do not let your hearts be troubled and do not be afraid." (25–27)

Since the Father sends the Holy Spirit in Christ's "name," shouldn't we do everything in his name? God would certainly want us to act on the same principle that he acts on. The Father glorifies Christ by sending the Spirit in his name. Let us glorify Christ by offering our prayers and praises in that same lovely name.

The Holy Spirit will not reveal anything fresh to us. He will only "remind" us what has already been written in the inspired Word of God. The canon of Scripture is closed. No one can add to it without a curse. The biblical pages convey to us the outward sense, but the Holy Spirit gives us the inward meaning. The embodiment of truth we have in the Bible, but the truth itself, which deals with the conscience, heart, and spirit, must be laid home by the author of the book, the Holy Spirit.

Divine power is never exerted unnecessarily. Since God has given us the Holy Spirit as our teacher, we can conclude that we need him. When you and I have read our Bibles through so often that nothing in it interests us, it is high time we asked God to teach us how to read it. It is a sign of a lack of grace when we feel the Bible is a dry book.

Do we sufficiently look to the Holy Spirit for divine teaching? With great diligence we may read our Bibles, as well as books that help us understand the Bible. But do we look up to the Holy Spirit and ask him distinctly and immediately to teach us the meaning of Christ's words and to remind us of everything he has said to us? I wish we did this more than we do.

Earlier Jesus told his disciples "Let not your hearts be troubled" (v. 1). Now he went further and left them and us his precious legacy of peace. His own deep peace in us is unbroken even when enemies persecute us. Christ does not say, "'Peace, peace,' . . . when there is no peace" (Jer. 6:14). He puts his hand into his heart and takes out the choicest jewel it contains—his own peace—and he says, "Wear that on your finger. It is the seal and token of my love."

Are you at peace right now? "I am very troubled," someone says. Well, you will have tribulation here, but Jesus will give you peace with it.

A Christian martyr once said to his executioner, "Put your hand on my heart and then on your heart. Feel which heart is beating fast because it is troubled." The executioner was awestruck when he found the Christian's heart at peace and his own in a state of agitation. We defy the world to rob us of our peace, because we have the very peace of Christ.

The world gives scantily, half-heartedly, hypocritically, with a selfish motive, with an expectation of getting a reward in return, and sometimes with a desire to take back. But Christ gives us his peace generously, sincerely, freely, and forever.

Jesus was near the time when he would suffer, but his main anxiety was to encourage the hearts of the dear ones he was about to leave. He had no selfish thought.

Let me suggest four reasons our hearts do not need to be troubled and afraid. First, we are forgiven. We are like a convicted murderer on death row who receives a presidential pardon. Second, our troubles do not come by chance. Third, "our light and momentary troubles

are achieving for us an eternal glory that far outweighs them all"
(2 Cor. 4:17). Fourth, our troubles will soon be over, and then the
bliss of heaven will begin!

My one regret is that these reasons do not apply to everyone.
Jesus does not say to unconverted people, "Do not let your hearts
be troubled and do not be afraid," for they ought to be more afraid
than they are. But though they are troubled and afraid, they may
have the Savior.

*"You heard me say, 'I am going away and I am coming back to you.'
If you loved me, you would be glad that I am going to the Father, for
the Father is greater than I. I have told you now before it happens, so
that when it does happen you will believe. I will not speak with you
much longer, for the prince of this world is coming. He has no hold on
me, but the world must learn that I love the Father and that I do
exactly what my Father has commanded me.*

Come now; let us leave." (28–31)

Jesus knew his disciples loved him, but they were not showing it.
So he asked them to act in love by rejoicing that he was going to the
Father. Let us rejoice that Jesus is not physically here with us. If he
were, he would still be in his humiliation, but now he has returned
to his glory.

The heavenly Father was greater than Christ in the sense that
Jesus "made himself nothing" (Phil. 2:7), took "the very nature of
a servant" (Phil. 2:7), "humbled himself" before the Father (Phil.
2:8), and became the stepping-stone between people and God. But
now he was going back to take his own natural dignity again. We
ought to rejoice in his gain. Though you may think it a loss not to
have Jesus' physical presence, would you like to call him away from
the heavenly harps that ring out his praises and the perfect fellowship of the Father with whom he reigns supreme? Oh, no, blessed
Master, stay where you are!

Jesus warned his disciples of all that would happen in his death
and his departure. I believe the Spirit of God often gives warnings
to God's people of troubles to come, so they may be prepared for
the trouble when it comes.

How many answers to prayer have you received? How many deliv-
erances from trouble? How many helps in time of need? Have you
believed all the more because of them?

Jesus would have very few words, for he was going to the bloody
sweat and scourging and death. It was right that his words were few,
for his actions would speak louder than mere words.

Still, Christ would have enough to do to meet that archenemy and endure all that would come on him during that dreaded encounter.

With unfaltering steps Christ advanced to his agony. He did not wait to be seized. He was a willing victim who went forward to take up his cross. After Jesus said, "Come now; let us leave," his disciples followed him to Gethsemane, the garden of his agony. Let us be willing to follow wherever our Lord calls us. Whether it be to service or suffering, if he leads the way, we can follow.

Christ Is the Vine; We Are the Branches

SOME OF THE CHOICEST sayings of the Lord Jesus to his disciples are found in John 15. Jesus spoke these words of cheer and counsel while on his way from the Upper Room in Jerusalem, where he had instituted the Last Supper, to the Garden of Gethsemane, where he would be betrayed. As we read this chapter, may the savor of these words abide in our hearts as the letter of them abides in our memories.

"I am the true vine and my Father is the gardener. He cuts off every branch in me that bears no fruit, while every branch that does bear fruit he prunes so that it will be even more fruitful. You are already clean because of the word I have spoken to you. Remain in me, and I will remain in you. No branch can bear fruit by itself; it must remain in the vine. Neither can you bear fruit unless you remain in me." (1–4)

Many questions have been raised about what is the true church. The Savior here provides the answer: He is the "true vine." The church will never die, for it is Christ. Everyone united to the ever-living Savior is a member of the true church.

We tend to think that the burden of all the churches lies on our shoulders, but that is a great mistake. Jesus here said that his Father is the gardener. He will take the best possible care of the vine, for it is very dear to him. All preachers and teachers are just the pruning tool in the hand of the great "gardener." There is not a branch in the vine that the Father does not love with infinite affection. And as for the majestic stem, Jesus, "the gardener" loves him beyond measure.

Real saints are in Christ, they remain in Christ, and they bear fruit for Christ. When these traits are absent, you have a counterfeit

225

Christian, and such a person God "cuts off." The removal of super-fluous shoots is a necessary part of caring for the vine. Too much wood prevents the bearing of fruit and is a waste of strength. And so in the church some are in Christ by outward profession, but they bear no fruit. For a while they appear to be fresh and green, and they who assist the gardener dare not cut them off, but the Father does.

God is continually cutting off from the church, in some way or another, those who bear no fruit. They do not truly belong to Christ, for fruit must come from vital union with him. It is a trial to the church to have branches that bear no fruit. These are taken away, sometimes by death, sometimes by the open discovery of their secret sin, and sometimes by God's final judgment. But side by side with this action another process is going on: pruning.

Two similar people are mentioned in this section. Both are branches connected to Christ, but only one bears fruit. "By their fruit you will recognize them" (Matt. 7:16). Let us search our lives to see if there is any spiritual fruit. And what is that fruit? Galatians 5:22-23 explains: "The fruit of the Spirit is love, joy, peace, patience, kindness, goodness, faithfulness, gentleness, and self-control."

The Father cuts off the fruitless branches but prunes the fruitful ones. If the branch were dead, what good would it do to prune it? Are you suffering under the pruning knife? Accept it joyfully. How much better that the knife should cut off your excess wood than that it should cut you off!

Many Christians, when they are sorely afflicted, think God is punishing them for secret sin. Sometimes, however, affliction is an evidence of virtue, for only the fruit-bearing branch gets pruned. Look at Abraham, Isaac, and Jacob. Didn't these men of God feel the knife? Consider Moses, David, Jeremiah, and Daniel. Who among them escaped the pruning process?

If you are being pruned, rejoice to think you are so good a branch that God wants to make you better. You have such capacities for bearing fruit that he wants to develop those capacities even more. If you bore no fruit, you would be left unpruned, because the knife would do its sterner work on you by taking you completely away. If you really are "fruitful" for God, you must expect to have trials, troubles, and afflictions—not because God is condemning you but because he is preparing you to be "even more fruitful."

God wants us to be even more fruitful in three ways: in variety, in quantity, and in quality. Perhaps you will not pray more, but you will pray more earnestly. You may witness no more often, but you will share the gospel with more compassion for unbelievers.

The word Jesus spoke sorely grieved his disciples. So he had to say to them more than once in the previous chapter, "Do not let your hearts be troubled" (John 14:1, 27). They had felt the sharp edge of the pruning knife, so Jesus reassured them that they were "clean"—ready to bear fruit.

If we were more willing to feel the edge of God's Word and let it cut away things that may be very dear to us, we would not need so much pruning by affliction. It is because the first knife of Christ's "word" does not always produce the desired result that the second sharp tool of affliction is used to prune us.

The pruning does no good without us remaining in Christ. You may suffer again and again, but no good can come of it unless you have vital, continuous fellowship with Christ. You cannot take a branch away from the vine and then put it back again. Its life depends on it remaining in the vine. So it is with us and Christ. The branch is in the vine, and the vine is in the branch. The sap of the vine is in the branch even as the branch is part and parcel of the vine.

The main thing is not restless activity, running here and there, doing this and that. It is remaining in Christ—persevering in our faith and constantly clinging to him. The true heir of heaven is not the one who says, "I was converted twenty years ago"; it is the person who remains in Christ. Do not merely find a temporary shelter in Christ, as a ship runs into a harbor in stormy weather and then comes out again when the gale is over. Cast your anchor in Christ, as the vessel does when it reaches its desired haven.

You may hurry, flurry, and worry, but you will be the loser for that. Keep close to Christ. Never let your heart be severed from intimate fellowship with him. This is the only way you will "bear fruit."

"I am the vine; you are the branches. If a man remains in me and I in him, he will bear much fruit; apart from me you can do nothing. If anyone does not remain in me, he is like a branch that is thrown away and withers; such branches are picked up, thrown into the fire and burned." (5–6)

We must not pretend to be the vine. If God blesses us and makes us a blessing to the church, let us not dream that we are the root and stem of the church. At best we are the branches.

The double remaining of us in Christ and Christ in us brings a double harvest of much fruit. It is easy to grow spiritually cold in this cold world. It is hard to maintain a holy spiritual fervor, but without it there is no spiritual health. I trust that we are bearing some fruit for Christ, but the test of us remaining in Christ and him remaining in us is that we "bear much fruit."

No saint, no prophet, no apostle would say this. It is impossible to conceive that Jesus Christ could say these words if he were anything less than God.

Beware of a Christless Christianity—of trying to be a Christian without living daily in Christ. The branch may just as well try to bear fruit apart from the vine as for you to maintain the reality of Christian life without continual fellowship with the Lord Jesus Christ. Jesus did not say, "Apart from me you can do very little" or "almost nothing," but "Apart from me you can do nothing." We can do nothing good, nothing spiritual, nothing acceptable, if we are apart from Christ.

Think of this: The world dying around us, and we can do nothing! Africa in darkness! China perishing! Hindus sunk in superstition, and the church can do nothing! Christian, the world is dying for the gospel, and "you can do nothing" if you are apart from Christ.

It is the beginning of apostasy when someone wants to be independent of Jesus. My heart says, "There is nothing I want to do apart from my Lord. If I can do without Christ, I am sorry to possess so dangerous a power. I am happy to be deprived of all strength except that which comes from him. It charms and exhilarates my soul to think that Jesus is my all!"

If even Christians "can do nothing" apart from Christ, how much more is this true of our Lord's enemies! If his friends can do nothing fruitful without him, his foes can do nothing harmful against him!

We as branches prove our salvation by our fruitfulness. The branch is good for nothing but bearing fruit. If it does not bear fruit, it is good only to be burned. Other trees yield timber and are useful for various purposes. But as the prophet Ezekiel said of the fruitless vine, "It was not useful for anything when it was whole" (Ezek. 15:5). So with us. If we are fruitless, we are useless.

According to one of Jesus' parables, there is a sad future in store for people who are like weeds (Matt. 13:24–30). But there is a much sadder lot reserved for those who are in some sense branches, who make a profession of faith in Christ but are not vitally united to him. In everyday life evil people may contribute something good to society, but members of the church of Christ who do not bear fruit are of no use whatever. There is nothing to be done with them but to gather them up with the autumn leaves and burn them in the corner outside the wall.

How painful is the smoke that comes from such a burning! We

pastors sometimes get it into our eyes, and it fills them with bitter tears. I know of nothing more grievous to us than the excommunication of unworthy church members.

"If you remain in me and my words remain in you, ask whatever you wish, and it will be given you. This is to my Father's glory, that you bear much fruit, showing yourselves to be my disciples." (7–8)

This is not a promise of unlimited answers to prayer, for an "if" qualifies it. People who remain in Christ and in whom his words remain will be so influenced by the Holy Spirit that they will ask for nothing contrary to the mind of God. Some talk about a spiritual attachment to Christ while they shoot their poisoned darts against his teachings, but that will not do. Christ's words of doctrine, precept, and promise must "remain" in everyone who claims to be his disciple.

The secret to successful prayer is that Christ listens to your words because you listen to his words. If you are conformed to his will, he will grant you your will. Those who have their wills at the throne of grace are disciples who have done God's will in other places. When disobedient children pray, they may expect to get the rod for an answer. In true kindness God may refuse to listen to them until they are willing to listen to him. Our power in prayer will decrease as our obedience to Christ decreases.

Just as the fruit will come out of the vine branch with no conscious effort on the part of the branch but simply because of its living union with the stem, so prayer is the natural fruit of a person who remains in fellowship with Christ. As stars shine, so the person who clings to Christ prays.

What a wonderful vine that must be whose branches glorify God! Have you ever heard of such a thing? The very branches do this by bearing much fruit. How this ought to spur us on to desire to bear Christian graces, to do Christian service, and to submit ourselves to the Lord's will, for those are the clusters that hang on this vine.

"Much fruit" should be produced by the disciples of the much-doing Christ. Since "the true vine" (v. 1) is full of fruit, we cannot expect others to believe we are branches of that vine if we produce only a little fruit. Jesus himself was no moderately good man. He was more than a little useful in this world. He was perfectly consecrated and abounded in every good work. Unless we are the same by bearing much fruit, how will people know we are his disciples? If we are going to prove our discipleship to Christ, we must do everything possible for him as our Lord. When we do, God will strengthen us to serve Christ beyond our natural abilities.

"As the Father has loved me, so have I loved you. Now remain in my love." (9)

As truly as the Father loves the Son, Jesus loves us. Even more than that, for Jesus loves us in the same manner as the Father loves him. That is, without beginning, without ending, without change, and without measure. There are many great texts in the Bible, but I have often questioned whether there is a greater one than this. Oh, drink this nectar down! Here is the choicest pearl of truth ever dissolved into a single verse.

Recognize Christ's love, enjoy it, live in it as a fish lives in the stream, and show it to others.

If you obey my commands, you will remain in my love, just as I have obeyed my Father's commands and remain in his love. I have told you this so that my joy may be in you and that your joy may be complete. My command is this: Love each other as I have loved you. Greater love has no one than this, that he lay down his life for his friends. You are my friends if you do what I command. I no longer call you servants, because a servant does not know his master's business. Instead, I have called you friends, for everything that I learned from my Father I have made known to you. You did not choose me, but I chose you to go and bear fruit—fruit that will last. Then the Father will give you whatever you ask in my name. This is my command: Love each other." (10–17)

It is an idle tale for people to talk of mystical, visionary love for Christ that does not result in obedience to his will. If we do not keep his commands, we cannot say to him with Peter, "Lord, you know all things; you know that I love you" (John 21:17). Christ was not here threatening to cast away his people if they are disobedient to him but to take from them the sweet sense of his love.

Everything Jesus speaks is meant to produce joy in his people. Christians never fully realize what Christ came to do for them until they have grasped the joy of their Lord. Christ wants his people to be happy with a holy joy. It is not a second-rate joy but the very joy of Christ himself. And it makes us "complete."

If Christ is not pleased with us, we cannot be glad. If he has no joy in us, we cannot have joy in him. These two things rise and fall together. When a father looks with joy on his boy, the boy is happy.

But when the father has no joy in his son, the son has no joy in his father. May we never grieve God, for that would grieve us. We would not want it to be otherwise. Oh, that we might so live that Christ's joy may be in us, for then our joy will be complete. When this takes place, there is no room for any other joy, nor is there any room for sorrow.

This chapter gives us some hints as to how our "joy may be complete." First, by remaining in Christ (v. 4). Second, by bearing much fruit (v. 8). I am not surprised that some Christians have so little joy when I remember how little joy they are giving to Jesus, because they are bearing so little fruit to his glory. Third, our joy is complete when we "love each other" (v. 12). Fourth, we have complete joy when we keep Christ's commands (v. 14).

Are you loving others, Christians? Do you refuse to pick holes in the other believer's character? Do you never judge another Christian harshly? If you are guilty of these things, chide yourself, and cease from this evil habit at once. We can never love each other too much, for we are here commanded to do it as Christ loved us.

If there is anything about which Christians are sure, it is the love of Christ. If we preach as we should, we are sure to have something of the savor of Christ's love in our preaching. Christ showed great love when he came from heaven to earth and when he called his disciples. But when he died for his friends, he showed the greatest love of all. When he died, his heavenly Father forsook him (Mark 15:34), yet love for us made him endure that.

When Jesus laid down his life for his friends, he proved he had the greatest of all loves. Yet his love went beyond even that, for he died for his enemies. The friendship was all on his side when he died. He called us his "friends," but we called him our enemy, for we were opposed to him. He loved us, but we did not love him. "He was despised and rejected by men" (Isa. 53:3).

The death of Christ may be viewed in many aspects, but we have learned to cherish its substitutionary character. Many people have died for others, but they have not carried their sins. They were willing to take the punishment of the other person but not the guilt. But Christ did both. Since he has proven the greatest of all loves for us, let us make it our goal to prove our superlative love for him.

We are not the friends of Christ until we cease to delight in sin and turn into the path of holiness. This applies to all of Christ's commands. We are not to omit one of them or neglect what seems to be a small duty. I wish we would remember that every sin is an act of unfriendliness toward our best friend. Sin also harms us, for neglected duties, even of the smallest kind, act on us like little stones in the boot of a hiker. They may not prevent us from walking, but they make us limp and mar our comfort on the road.

We are friends of Jesus but not on an equal footing, for we must do what he commands. Genuine friends of Christ do not command themselves; they are servants of Christ. If you call yourself the friend of Jesus, remember that you are not your own master or guide. You have submitted your mind and will to the supremacy of the Lord Jesus Christ.

Whenever you are uncertain about something you are thinking of doing, ask yourself, "If I do this, will I be acting as Christ's friend? Will my conduct honor him?" If it will, be glad to do it. If it will dishonor Christ, have nothing to do with it.

Obedience to Christ's commands implies that we are not to let anyone else command us. "You have only one Master" (Matt. 23:8). No church may control your mind, for the church may be wrong, but Christ is "head over everything for the church" (Eph. 1:22), and he is never wrong.

The laborer works in a building and is content to lay part of a line of bricks or stones. Perhaps he has never seen the design of the structure, nor does he wish to. But you and I have the great architect constantly coming to us and telling us what the building will be. This helps us serve with greater pleasure than mere laborers, for the very heart of Christ is laid bare to us.

Our Lord is not interested in spasmodic piety—the religion that can be kept up only by popular preaching, great meetings, much excitement, and all that sort of thing. Christ was here speaking of the life that bears clusters of fruit tomorrow as well as today and even months and years from now.

Because when we bear "fruit that will last," power in prayer will last also. If we are constantly living for God, we will find ourselves privileged to have the ear of God, and when we pray to him, he will grant us the desires of our hearts.

Our Lord here repeated the command he had given in verse 12, because he knew how prone we would be to disobey it. This command is so comprehensive that all the other commands are fulfilled in it (see Rom. 13:8-10; Gal. 5:14).

"If the world hates you, keep in mind that it hated me first. If you belonged to the world, it would love you as its own. As it is, you do not belong to the world, but I have chosen you out of the world. That is why the world hates you. Remember the words I spoke to you: 'No servant is greater than his master.' If they persecuted me, they will persecute you also. If they obeyed my teaching, they will obey yours also. They will

*treat you this way because of my name, for they do not know the One
who sent me. If I had not come and spoken to them, they would not be
guilty of sin. Now, however, they have no excuse for their sin. He who
hates me hates my Father as well. If I had not done among them what
no one else did, they would not be guilty of sin. But now they have seen
these miracles, and yet they have hated both me and my Father. But
this is to fulfill what is written in their Law: 'They hated me without
reason.'" (18–25)*

It is no new thing when ungodly people hate the followers of
Christ, so let us not be surprised if it happens to us. It will be our
honor to be treated as our Master was.

It ought to be quite sufficient for servants to be treated as their
Lord was. What higher honor than that could we wish to have?

Some of these people professed to know God and even thought
they were rendering acceptable service to him when they rejected his
Son he had sent them.

It is as if all other sins would hardly have been sin at all in comparison with the sin against the Light that people committed after
Christ had "come and spoken to them." If you have been near the
kingdom and your conscience has been aroused and your mind
impressed with the truth and yet you have gone back to your sin,
you have multiplied that sin a thousandfold. What an amazing thing
that the very words of Christ, which created everything good,
should, through the depravity of the human heart, also result in evil!

People who have heard Christ speak through the gospel "have no
excuse for their sin." Someone might say, "I did not know I was sinning when I did such and such." But you who have heard the Word
of God cannot say that. God by his law has told you what is wrong.

Again, you might say, "When I sinned, I did not know how great
the punishment would be." But again you have no excuse because
of the gospel. Did not Jesus tell you that those who reject him will
be cast into "eternal punishment" (Matt. 25:46)?

People may say they love God and despise Christ, but it cannot
be so. Christ is so truly God that those who hate Christ would hate
God if they knew him.

Our Lord did not mean that they would have been sinless if he
had not done his miracles in front of them. Rather, because they
had seen his miracles and then hated him and the Father who sent
him, they had enormously increased and intensified their sin.

Never was anyone more lovely than the Savior, yet no one ever
endured more persecution than he. He was no sooner ushered into
the world than the sword of Herod was ready to cut him off (Matt.

2:16). If I want to tell you of people's sin, I will say it is
Christicide—the putting to death of the world's Messiah. This is the
very pinnacle of the terrific pyramid of mortal guilt.

Since our Master was "hated . . . without reason," do not expect
to be treated any better in this world. Again, make sure that if the
world hates you, it hates you "without reason." The world is bitter
enough without us putting vinegar in it. Let us pray that those who
hate Christ may soon love him.

*"When the Counselor comes, whom I will send to you from the Father,
the Spirit of truth who goes out from the Father, he will testify about
me; but you also must testify, for you have been with me from the
beginning." (26–27)*

As the Holy Spirit is "the Comforter" (KJV), Christ is the comfort. The Holy Spirit consoles us, but Christ is the consolation. The
Holy Spirit is the physician, but Christ is the medicine. The Spirit
heals our wound by applying the holy ointment of Christ's name
and grace.

Here is the mark by which you may know whether a teaching
comes from "the Spirit of truth": If it does not testify about
Christ—if he is not the beginning and end of it all—there is nothing
in it for you to accept. If anyone comes to you with a revelation and
it is not all about Christ, that person was not sent by the Spirit of
God.

There is no bearing witness for Christ unless we have first been
with him. The witness of the Holy Spirit continues today, and
Christ's disciples are still privileged to be cowitnesses even with the
Holy Spirit himself. What can we testify about? The peace we find
in the precious blood of Christ, the change Christ has made in us,
how our love for others has increased, how God's grace has renewed
us, and the comfort we receive from Christ's presence. Let us be
eager to avail ourselves of this privilege whenever we can.

The Real Lord's Prayer

CAN WE FIND IN all the writings of humanity anything to match the record of our Savior's great intercessory prayer? This chapter ought to be known as the real "Lord's Prayer." It is the Holy of Holies in the Word of God. Christ seemed to pray here as if he already stood within the veil, not pleading in agony as he did in the Garden of Gethsemane but speaking with the authority that clothed him when his work on earth was done.

There is as much of the divine as of the human in this prayer. It is remarkable that in it our Lord made no confession of sin in his people. The burden of his prayer was that he might be glorified and that his Father might be glorified in him. The words of the prayer are the simplest that could have been selected, but what depths lie beneath them! I think that none of us may know the full meaning of this chapter this side of heaven. May the Holy Spirit graciously grant us a glimpse of the glorious truths revealed here.

After Jesus said this, he looked toward heaven and prayed: "Father, the time has come. Glorify your Son, that your Son may glorify you. For you granted him authority over all people that he might give eternal life to all those you have given him. Now this is eternal life: that they may know you, the only true God, and Jesus Christ, whom you have sent. I have brought you glory on earth by completing the work you gave me to do. And now, Father, glorify me in your presence with the glory I had with you before the world began." (1–5)

What a sight it must have been to see the divine intercessor in this his last great prayer before he poured out his soul to death! We must die and enter heaven before we can fully grasp all that Christ meant when he said, "Father, the time has come." It was the time of darkness, suffering, and death. When our time comes—and we shall all have times of darkness—may we have nothing on our minds but glorifying God. We shall not dread suffering, because suffering often gives opportunities for us to glorify God in our patience.

Did Jesus look on his suffering as his glory? He did not merely pray, "Sustain your Son," but "Glorify your Son." Our Lord's lowest stoop was his highest glory. There was no way he could go into his glory except by passing through tears, blood, agony, and death. He was never more radiant than when he hung on the cross. That was his true spiritual throne.

The death of Christ glorified the Father. We see his love and justice given more glory in the death of Christ than they would have been by any other method. The great goal of Christ all through his life on earth was to glorify his Father. He came to save his people, but that was not his chief aim. His goal was to glorify his Father through the salvation of myriads of people.

The only reason Jesus asked the Father to glorify him was "that your Son may glorify you." When you pray, let your motive be not your own self-advancement but your heavenly Father's glory. Do you pine to have your health back? Be sure you want to spend it for him. Do you desire advancement in your career? Desire it that you may promote God's glory. Do you long for growth in grace? Ask for it only that you may glorify God.

Here we have both the general and the special aspects of redemption. The purpose of the rain is to water one particular field, but God is so generous that the rain falls everywhere. The aim of Christ's atonement is to purchase eternal life for those whom the Father gave him, namely, people who trust in Christ. But Christ has also obtained "authority over all people." He can convict every living person of sin if he so wills. He has authority also to make those who are not convicted of their sins serve his purposes.

When Adam and Eve sinned, humanity lost the knowledge of God. Out of this ignorance many idolatries grew, for people must have a god as surely as a dog must have a master. They cannot be happy without one.

See how Christ put himself side by side with God the Father as no mere human could have done. Only he who was equal with the Father could have dared to pray this way. The knowledge of God that brings eternal life is not an awareness of God's existence. It is to know God the Father as your best friend and Jesus Christ as your personal Savior. It is to love them, delight in them, and talk with them as naturally as you talk with anyone else.

This knowledge of God and Christ does not mean mere head knowledge but knowledge in the heart and soul. God without

Christ does not bring eternal life, and if Christ were not sent by God, he would not bring eternal life to us. But knowing God in Christ is eternal life. No one who is ignorant of God and Jesus Christ his Son has eternal life. Have you been brought into such a knowledge of God that you have accepted his Son Jesus Christ as your Savior and Lord? Then you will never perish, for you have eternal life, and eternal life will never end.

Our Savior made a leap of holy faith. He foresaw that he would pass through his suffering, that all the work of his people's redemption would be fully accomplished, and in this, his final prayer on earth to the Father, he could truly say, "I have completed the work you gave me to do."

Again, no mere human could have prayed those words. Even Adam before he sinned did not complete his work. If he had, it would not have become marred. The most gracious people who have ever lived could not in their final moments say, "I have completed the work God gave me to do," for it was still imperfect. There were many things they wanted to do and many errors they wanted to have corrected. But as more than human, our Lord could say, "I have brought you glory on earth by completing the work you gave me to do."

After the finished work, Christ was to have the glory. If you are a servant of God, do not seek glory before your work is done. Do not expect honor from people because you have begun with zeal. Plod on until your work is finished, then the glory shall come. Our Lord said of the hypocrites who sought public praise, "I tell you the truth, they have received their reward in full" (Matt. 6:5). But you have not yet received your reward. It is still to come. Wait for it—it is sure to come.

"I have revealed you to those whom you gave me out of the world. They were yours; you gave them to me and they have obeyed your word. Now they know that everything you have given me comes from you. For I gave them the words you gave me and they accepted them. They knew with certainty that I came from you, and they believed that you sent me. I pray for them. I am not praying for the world, but for those you have given me, for they are yours. All I have is yours, and all you have is mine. And glory has come to me through them. I will remain in the world no longer, but they are still in the world, and I am coming to you. Holy Father, protect them by the power of your name—the name you gave me—so that they may be one as we are one. While I was with them, I protected them and kept them safe by that name you gave me. None has been lost except the one doomed to destruction so that Scripture would be fulfilled." (6–12)

How tenderly Jesus spoke of his disciples! He said the best he could of them. They were full of faults and weaknesses, but he said, "They have obeyed your word." So they did. May you and I do the same and not be swept away by the drift of the current of unbelief. If we are imperfect, if we fail in some respects, yet may the Master be able to say of us to God, "They have obeyed your word." Do you make God's Word the guide of your whole life? The token of God's people is obedience to his Word.

How the blessed Christ loves to lay aside all honor to himself even in his own gospel! He said the truths he had taught his disciples were not his own but had come from his Father. The Father always honored the Son, and the Son was careful always to honor the Father.

Our Lord Jesus Christ made no claim to being an original thinker. On the contrary, he said to his Father concerning his disciples, "I gave them the words you gave me." I would rather repeat the Word of God, syllable by syllable, than think for myself apart from the revealed will of God. What are human thoughts but vanity? If we feed others our own words, we mock their hunger and dishonor God. But the Word of the Lord is spiritual food that glorifies God. It shall remain when heaven and earth have passed away.

If Jesus acted this way, how much more must the messengers of God receive the Word from their Lord's mouth and pass it on? Fellow pastor, when we come to die, may you and I be able to say to the Lord concerning our people, "I gave them the words you gave me."

Perhaps nothing makes people so angry as the statement that Jesus did not pray for the world. They cannot bear to think God would give his gifts according to his will, but it is true. There is an intercession of Christ for all the world, but his choicest prayers are for his own people. If he did not pray for us, our faith would fail.

Jesus said to his Father, "They were yours." Here he said, "They are yours." The transference of believers to the Son made no change in the Father's relation to them. They still belonged to the Father.

I can understand someone saying to God, "All I have is yours." But no mere human dares to say to God, "And all you have is mine." Because Jesus is both God and human, he can say both these things.

If Christ had said, "I will glorify them," I could have understood it. If he had said, "I am pleased with them," I might have set it down to his great kindness. But when he said, "Glory has come to me through them," it was amazing!

Every true child of God glorifies Christ. If you cannot say you are glorifying Christ, you should question whether you really belong to him. If you are his, this is true of you: "Glory has come to me through them." We glorify Christ by our patient suffering, our bold witness, our efforts to extend his kingdom, our Christian virtues, and our faith in him. Christ is more glorified by a sinner's humble faith than by a seraph's loudest song.

Perhaps you say, "How insignificant I am! The church would not miss me if I were taken away, and the choirs of heaven do not need me." Oh, but your Lord is glorified in you! In your very weakness he finds opportunity to glorify his strength. In your emptiness his fullness is glorified.

When God keeps us, he keeps us in unity. Our divisions are not the result of his work. While we are in the world, we shall never all think alike, but let us all think alike about our Lord and gather to his name and "make every effort to keep the unity of the Spirit through the bond of peace" (Eph. 4:3). The soldiers at Calvary tore Christ's seamless robe, and it still remains torn through the schisms and errors that divide his people from one another. When we get away from his keeping and his Word, we are torn in heart from both him and one another.

Sheep never outgrow their need of being protected and kept by their shepherd. If the Eleven required this, you and I do, too. We need to be "kept . . . safe" from error, for the world swarms with false doctrines, as Egypt did with frogs in the day of her plague (Ex. 8:1–15). We also need to be kept from sin, for if we are not, we saints will soon become sinners.

I wonder if we can hope that in our churches there would be found as few as one in twelve who are not in heart with Christ. The Scripture was fulfilled in both the preservation of our Lord's people and the destruction of the traitor. God's Word will be fulfilled one way or another. May it be to us a fragrance of life to protect us and not an aroma of death, as it was to Judas. He was blinded by the light that shone on him. The brilliant light that beat around the King of Kings fell on him and blinded him eternally. God save us from such an awful doom!

An unbeliever outside the church may batter against the walls with little result, but inside she or he would be like the hidden soldiers in the wooden horse who opened the gates of Troy to the besiegers. Only an apostle could be "the one doomed to destruction," as Judas was. So beware if you profess to follow Christ. Your position gives you great potential both for usefulness and for doing damage to the cause of Christ.

"I am coming to you now, but I say these things while I am still in the world, so that they may have the full measure of my joy within them. I

have given them your word and the world has hated them, for they are not of the world any more than I am of the world. My prayer is not that you take them out of the world but that you protect them from the evil one. They are not of the world, even as I am not of it. Sanctify them by the truth; your word is truth. As you sent me into the world, I have sent them into the world. For them I sanctify myself, that they too may be truly sanctified." (13–19)

I think I see the look on the Savior's face as he said this to his Father. May that same look be on your face when your last moments come. Our Lord thought nothing of the bloody way by which he would go to the Father. What if the cross and nails and spear were in the road? By comparison he thought little of all those terrible things. He looked beyond them and said, "I am coming to you now." These are appropriate words in the mouth of a dying believer. When the time comes for you to look away from the dear ones you must leave as Jesus left his disciples, may you be able to say, "I am coming to you now."

Our divine Lord thought nothing of his sufferings. While he drained the cup of sorrow to the dregs and went forward to all the agonies of the cruel cross, Jesus wanted his disciples to have the full measure of his joy in them. The "man of sorrows" (Isa. 53:3) was the happiest person who ever lived. Have you ever received this blessing that Christ requested for you—not only of joy, not only of his joy, but the full measure of his joy in you?

If nobody hates you for being a Christian, are you a Christian at all? If you find that you run with the crowd and swim with the current, can you be a follower of Christ, who was despised and rejected by the world? These words do not have in them the tone of trying to please the world, to adapt our method to the spirit of the age, to dabble in its politics and join in its schemes. Our Lord called us to be different.

Never did anyone more thoroughly mix with people than Jesus did, and never did anyone have greater sympathy for human beings than he had. Yet he was never "of the world." Here he said that his disciples were like him. We are to be not so much unworldly as other-worldly. Christ's people have a life that others do not have. They are swayed by motives that others do not understand. They are journeying to a holiness that others have no desire for. So we are not of this world, and the world treats us as hated, speckled birds.

There are two senses in which we can understand Christ's prayer not to take them out of the world. First, Christ asked the Father not to take us out of the world into solitude. Some hermits think that if they live alone, they will be more devoted to God. That may be the way to serve self by dressing ourselves in the clothes of self-satisfaction, but it cannot be the way to serve God. We are not to shut ourselves up in monasteries and convents.

Perhaps on Mondays you say, "I am sorry Sunday is over. I have to go back to my business. I wish it were always Sunday." Does Jesus agree with that? No, for he asked the Father to keep us in the world.

The second way to understand this petition is that Christ asked the Father not to take us out of the world straight into heaven. A little stay on earth will make heaven all the sweeter. If Christ and his people had gone out of this world at the same time, it would have left the world destitute, with no help whatever.

Sometimes in great pain of body or in deep depression of spirit, believers, like Elijah, request that they may die (1 Kings 19:4). If you ever say such a prayer, utter if softly, for the Master does not authorize it. It is a matter that must be left to the Lord of life and death.

Our Lord leaves us in this world that we may serve him in the place where we sinned against him. If I were converted today and the Lord were to open the gates of heaven and say, "Come in," I think I would step back and reply, "Dear Master, may I stay here just a little while to undo some of the damage I caused in my ungodly state?"

Just as God permitted Job to be tempted by the Devil so that all the world might see how God can enable someone to triumph through adversity, so he keeps us here to let the Devil and all people see that his grace can make saints out of sinners.

Sin is the real evil in the world, where Christ wants us to serve. The danger is that we will become entangled in worldly customs or drop into the evil ways of an ungodly generation. Christ did pray that we will be protected from the evil in the world. So we may pray that the Lord will protect us from all the evil around us, and especially from the Evil One himself, who seeks to destroy us (1 Peter 5:8). There is no less power needed for our preservation than for our salvation. The protection of a saint is a constant miracle that can be secured only by God himself.

You cannot make Christ worldly. If you twist his character, you must still see that he is otherworldly. So let it always be with his people. We are of another race. We are swayed by other motives and have another destiny. Is this true of you?

Many think the difference between a Christian and a worldly person is that one goes to church and the other does not. One pays attention to holy things and the other does not. But the distinction between a Christian and a worldly person is not external but internal. The difference is one of nature, not of act. A Christian is as different from a worldly person as a dove is from a raven or a lamb from a lion. Yet it would puzzle the angel Gabriel if he were sent down to the world to pick out the Christians from the worldly people. None but God can do it, for in these days of worldly religion they are so much alike.

We are not of this world. We are protected from the Evil One. Yet we need to be sanctified. Without sanctification how can we be saved, since "without holiness no one will see the Lord" (Heb. 12:14)? Without sanctification we lose our testimony, for if we live as others, what witness do we bear? Without sanctification we are unfit for service and unable to enjoy the sweets of our holy faith, for the unsanctified are full of doubts and fears.

We will always need sanctifying until we reach our heavenly home, where sin cannot enter. Every day we need the sanctifying influence of Scripture to lead us into holiness. Only the truth of God can create holiness. False teaching is never the medium of sanctification. You can tell the false teachings from the true by our Lord's own test: "By their fruit you will recognize them" (Matt. 7:16). The same people who reject the old-fashioned doctrines also rebel against the old-fashioned lifestyle. Loose living generally goes with loose doctrine.

Thank God for this: "Your word is truth." Not "Your word contains truth with some error mixed in" or "Your word has some truth in it." Not only is God's Word true, it is truth.

We can draw four lessons from this truth that Christ has sent us into the world. First, we are not guilty of intrusion when we speak of him. Second, we dare not run away. If Jesus commands us to go forward, we must not retreat. Third, Christ is sure to help us. Our King never sends his servants on an errand in their own strength. And fourth, we will give an account to the Lord who sent us.

This eighteenth verse shows the original missionary society and the model for all others. As the Father took Jesus out of the bosom of his love and told him to go as his missionary to this world, so Jesus keeps us for a while away from the bosom of his glory that we may stop here to be missionaries. Are we fulfilling a calling that is not for ourselves but for our Master? Are we justifying the commission Jesus gave us (Matt. 28:19–20)? How dare we call ourselves Christians if we have no mission to anyone! If you are living here for yourself alone, how can you belong to Christ, who never lived a moment for himself but always lived completely for others?

When Christ came into this world, it meant the complete submission of himself to the Father's will. It also meant the end of his rest, for he left his throne from which he reigned to serve the Father here on earth. Again, it meant that Jesus had to forego heaven itself. Therefore, we must not sigh for heaven while so much is to be done on earth. If Christ had not come, the whole world would have perished. Your work is also indispensable.

Christ's prayer for sanctification means, "I dedicate, devote, and commit myself wholly for their salvation, that they may be dedicated, devoted, and committed to the truth." Have you realized that you are dedicated by Christ and to Christ? Every breath you take, every thought you think, every word you speak, every act you do should all be done for him. He lived for you alone. Live for him alone.

"My prayer is not for them alone. I pray also for those who will believe in me through their message, that all of them may be one, Father, just as you are in me and I am in you. May they also be in us so that the world may believe that you have sent me. I have given them the glory that you gave me, that they may be one as we are one: I in them and you in me. May they be brought to complete unity to let the world know that you sent me and have loved them even as you have loved me." (20-23)

We would have expected Christ to say, "I pray also for those who will believe in me through my message." Indeed, it is his message that leads sinners to repent and believe. Yet Christ put the honor on those who speak his message out of the fullness of their hearts. They have by experience made it their own message, so he called it theirs. Thank God that Christ will bless our word as well as his own Word! When our word is based on his Word, when we simply expound what Christ has given us to say, people will believe in him through our word. Until Christ returns, he will always rely on our witness.

When Jesus prayed this, there were only a few disciples, but you could not tell what a multitude would believe in him through their witness. There were only twelve apostles, but Christ saw 144,000 of all the tribes of the children of Israel (Rev. 7:1-4). And after that he saw a great multitude that no one could number, from all nations and languages and people. They were all standing before the throne of the Lamb, clothed with white robes (Rev. 7:9). Hence when Jesus prayed this, he looked with the eyes of faith.

What great events spring from little causes! Whenever you minister for Christ, remember not only those who are immediately saved but also the others who will be blessed through them. Christ prayed for us before we believed, and we believed in answer to his prayer.

The church will never know her true glory until she knows her perfect oneness. When Christians, who are one in Christ, shall become one in heart, life, and faith, what glad days we may hope to see! Let us lay aside everything that divides, especially the evil heart of unbelief, pride, and self-seeking. May we realize that all of us in Christ must live as one because we are one. If we are members of one body, one blood courses through our veins and gives us life. One Spirit is in the one body of Christ. There cannot be two lives within the one body of Christ. All true believers must be one. If we speak much to one another about our Lord and much to God in prayer, we will see that we are one.

Are you a part of this great unity? I did not ask, "Are you a member of a Christian church?" Do not look for all the saints in one room but in Christ. Have you been born into God's family? Have you passed from death to life? If not, though you were in the visible body of Christ, you would be a gangrene that brings pain and suffering and should be cut off.

Does the Father love his people as he loves Christ? Then his love to them must be without beginning, without end, without change, and without measure. It would ravish your heart and carry you away to the highest heaven if you could grasp the truth that God loves you as much as he loves Christ! You cannot fully comprehend this, but believe it.

"Father, I want those you have given me to be with me where I am, and to see my glory, the glory you have given me because you loved me before the creation of the world." (24)

This is Christ's last will and testament, for he said, "Father, I will" (KJV). It was not merely his prayer, but he made this as one clause in his will, that everyone the Father gave him should be with him to see his glory. And it will be so. He will not lose one of his own. He will never drop from that dear pierced hand any part of the Father's eternal gift. He is a bridegroom who cannot be satisfied unless his bride shares his joy. As a head cannot be content to be crowned while the rest of the body is disgraced, so neither can Christ be content without us sharing his glory.

Some talk of the saints going for a while into limbo in purgatory so they can be made ready for heaven. But Jesus prayed that we might be with him in glory. We already know a little of what it means to be with Christ. Sometimes I have said to myself, "If this isn't heaven, it is next door to it," and I have thought I was dwelling in the suburbs of the celestial city. Yet the most we ever have of

Christ here on earth is just a sip from the well. What will we do in heaven? We will see his glory. That will be something worth looking at and something to delight us forever!

"Righteous Father, though the world does not know you, I know you, and they know that you have sent me. I have made you known to them, and will continue to make you known in order that the love you have for me may be in them and that I myself may be in them." (25–26)

Here are two groups: the world and the church. Here is what divides them: "The world does not know you" and "They know that you have sent me." What stands between these two groups? "I know you." Christ himself comes between the world and the church like the pillar of cloud and the pillar of fire—black with darkness to the Egyptians and bright with light to the Israelites. Oh, to have Christ between you and the world! It is the best form of separation.

The last petition of our Lord's prayer concerns love. He asks not that the Father's love may be on us or near us but that it may be in us. From our hearts it should go out to Christ and then to all the world. Here the doctrine becomes experience. This prayer is for you and me as much as for the twelve apostles. May we never rest until we get the full experience of it, that the love God gives to Christ may be found in our hearts as the Holy Spirit pours it out. If Christ prayed this way for us, we ought to pray this way for each other!

The Birthday of the Church

WE CANNOT TOO OFTEN read the story of this wondrous outpouring of the Holy Spirit on the day of Pentecost. Let us never read it
without asking the Lord to manifest to us the fullness of the Spirit's
power. We may not have a repetition of the miraculous gifts that
were then bestowed on the apostles, but we must have the gracious
influence that will convict and convert those who gather to hear the
Word of God. Our success in preaching the Word depends entirely
on the presence and working of the Holy Spirit. Therefore, let our
prayer be:

> Lord God, the Holy Ghost,
>   In this accepted hour,
> As on the day of Pentecost,
>   Descend in all Your power.
> The young, the old inspire
>   With wisdom from above;
> And give us hearts and tongues of fire
>   To pray and praise and love.

When the day of Pentecost came, they were all together in one place.
Suddenly a sound like the blowing of a violent wind came from heaven
and filled the whole house where they were sitting. They saw what
seemed to be tongues of fire that separated and came to rest on each
of them. All of them were filled with the Holy Spirit and began to speak
in other tongues as the Spirit enabled them. (1–4)

As these believers were unified, so we must be before we can
expect a revival. The Spirit of God will not bless and visit a church
where there is strife.

The Jews believed that Pentecost marked the time when God gave the Law. Since at that time there was a marvelous display of power on Sinai, it was to be expected that when the Holy Spirit was poured out, there would be some special unveiling of his divine presence.

Here the Holy Spirit came as "a sound like the blowing of a violent wind." This would teach the believers that the Spirit of God was given not to be hidden in their hearts as a silent guest but to be heard throughout the world as the voice of God. To their ears the speaking hurricane would say, "We, a handful of disciples, are to sweep around the globe like a violent wind and compel people to hear the sound of mercy."

The Spirit came also as "tongues of fire." God wanted to have believers speak the gospel of Christ with fire in their hearts. We are not to speak of Christ coldly, as if we had tongues of ice; nor learnedly, as if with tongues of gold; nor arrogantly, as if with tongues of brass; nor sternly, as if with tongues of iron; but earnestly, as if with tongues of fire. Our word should consume sin, scorch falsehood, enlighten the darkness, and comfort the poor.

There were two immediate results of the Pentecostal miracle. First, "All of them were filled with the Holy Spirit." We are empty things by nature and useless while we remain so. We need to be filled with the Holy Spirit. When we are, there will be no room for anything else in us. Fear will be banished, minor motives will be expelled, and the desires of the flesh will find no room in our hearts. If we are "filled with the Spirit," we will be empty of self.

The second Pentecostal result was utterance. As soon as the Spirit filled these people, they began to speak. They could not help it. It was quite surprising that people were able to speak in foreign languages they had never learned. The sound was heard outside the Upper Room where they were gathered. Many pressed to the door to listen and then went away to tell the strange news.

Now there were staying in Jerusalem God-fearing Jews from every nation under heaven. When they heard this sound, a crowd came together in bewilderment, because each one heard them speaking in his own language. Utterly amazed, they asked: "Are not all these men who are speaking Galileans? Then how is it that each of us hears them in his own native language? Parthians, Medes and Elamites; residents of Mesopotamia, Judea and Cappadocia, Pontus and Asia, Phrygia and Pamphylia, Egypt and the parts of Libya near Cyrene; visitors from Rome (both Jews and converts to Judaism); Cretans and Arabs—we hear them declaring the wonders of God in our own tongues!" Amazed and perplexed, they asked one another, "What does this mean?" (5-12)

These men, far from being able to speak many languages, could not even speak one correctly. The Galilean dialect was a corruption of the true Jewish language, so that the Galileans were always the objects of sneers. So it was strange that they were able to speak in foreign languages.

One man would have asked another, "Where do you come from?"

"Parthia. And I am astonished to hear these Jews speak the Parthian language."

"And you, sir?"

"I am from Media, and I am amazed to hear them speak the language of the Medes. This is very strange! How is it we hear them speaking in the language in which we were born?"

Babel's curse was now removed. Thus was fulfilled the promise of Jesus, "Anyone who has faith in me will do what I have been doing. He will do even greater things than these, because I am going to the Father" (John 14:12). For Jesus never spoke with many tongues, nor did he enable his disciples to do so.

Don't overlook the content of the message that these Spirit-baptized men spoke. It was "the wonders of God." That included redemption, the putting away of sins, and the creation of new life by the Holy Spirit. Oh, that to your dying day your only topic might be "the wonders of God"!

Some, however, made fun of them and said, "They have had too much wine." (13)

These people heard languages they did not understand as well as those they did, so they put the worst possible interpretation on the event by saying the speakers were drunk. It is a sign of wicked minds when people are ready to give an evil explanation to something they cannot understand. Let us never do that but always be ready to believe all the good of people that we can.

Then Peter stood up with the Eleven, raised his voice and addressed the crowd: "Fellow Jews and all of you who live in Jerusalem, let me explain this to you; listen carefully to what I say. These men are not drunk, as you suppose. It's only nine in the morning! No, this is what was spoken by the prophet Joel: 'In the last days, God says, I will pour out my Spirit on all people. Your sons and daughters will prophesy, your young men will see visions, your old men will dream dreams. Even on my servants, both men and women, I will pour out my Spirit in those days, and they will prophesy. I will show wonders in the heaven

above and signs on the earth below, blood and fire and billows of smoke.
The sun will be turned to darkness and the moon to blood before the
coming of the great and glorious day of the Lord. And everyone who
calls on the name of the Lord will be saved.'" (14–21)

This was a twelve-man ministry concentrated into one voice—
Peter's. The twelve apostles were twelve witnesses to the
resurrection of Christ, for they had seen and eaten with him after he
had risen. They made up a jury of twelve honest and true men with
Peter as their foreman. He "stood up with the Eleven" and gave
their verdict.

We might have thought it beneath our dignity to respond to the
crowd's insulting remark, but Peter knew how to meet them on
their own ground. He began where they left off, but he went on to
say what they least expected to hear.

Peter was speaking to Jews, so he began by quoting the Old
Testament. He was wise to win their attention by a passage from one
of their own prophets. It said that every member of the Christian
community should be anointed by the Holy Spirit. The blessing
would be given not just to one here and another there, but a wonderful outpouring would fall on the whole multitude of believers.

The Scripture Peter quoted also spoke of people who would "see
visions" and "dream dreams." My dream is that a very large number of people will spring up in our churches whose highest ambition
will be to give themselves to the work of Jesus Christ on the foreign
mission field.

What a connection: a darkened sun, a blood-red moon, yet
"everyone who calls on the name of the Lord will be saved." There
are no exceptions, for the text says "everyone." When the worst
comes to worst, prayer will still be heard, and faith will lead to salvation. They say drowning people will catch at a straw. This is no
straw but a gloriously strong lifeboat. Whoever will get into this
boat will certainly sail to glory. Everyone who calls out to God in
repentance, faith, and prayer not only may be but will be saved.

"Men of Israel, listen to this: Jesus of Nazareth was a man accredited
by God to you by miracles, wonders and signs, which God did among
you through him, as you yourselves know. This man was handed over
to you by God's set purpose and foreknowledge; and you, with the help
of wicked men, put him to death by nailing him to the cross. But God
raised him from the dead, freeing him from the agony of death,
because it was impossible for death to keep its hold on him. David said
about him: 'I saw the Lord always before me. Because he is at my right

hand, I will not be shaken. Therefore my heart is glad and my tongue rejoices; my body also will live in hope, because you will not abandon me to the grave, nor will you let your Holy One see decay. You have made known to me the paths of life; you will fill me with joy in your presence.'" (22–28)

Peter did not begin with the deity of Christ. He would get to that soon, but like a wise speaker he started with the points upon which they were all agreed. They knew that God had affirmed Christ's mission, so he appealed to them for confirmation: "as you yourselves know."

How boldly Peter stated the truth, for he was no doubt addressing many of the same people who had put his Lord to death. He was once such a coward that he trembled before a little maid (Matt. 26:69–72), but here in the fullness of the Spirit he boldly charged this crowd with murdering the Son of God.

Peter brought home the murder of Christ to them, yet he skillfully softened it by the mention of "God's set purpose and foreknowledge." It never occurred to Peter that God's set purpose overruled the responsibility and guilt of people's actions. Neither need it ever occur to you. Peter would have been a bad prosecutor if he had introduced into his argument something that could easily have been made into an excuse for those he was accusing.

There is no excuse in it. This verse shows that everything is predetermined and foreknown by God, yet when people act wickedly, they are responsible for it. No one knows where these two great truths of human free agency and divine predestination meet. Some deny the first truth, others deny the second. Believe them both, yet do not pretend you can reconcile them.

Perhaps in heaven, with a larger capacity of mind we will be able to reconcile these two truths. I am not sure we will be able to do so even then. I am not sure that even angels understand this great mystery, but it is a grand thing to exercise faith where we cannot comprehend what is revealed to us. People who believe only what they can understand will have a very short creed, and soon they will have none at all. But those who believe what they cannot understand simply because it is taught in Scripture are those who walk humbly with their God. They will be accepted. I thank God for the mystery that conceals so much from us. Where would we have room for faith if all things were as plain as A B C?

It was possible for Christ to die but impossible for death to keep its hold on him. He had his father's promise, quoted in verse 27, that he would not remain in the tomb or see decay. Again, if death had kept its hold on Christ, we would have had no assurance of our own resurrection. We could have said only, "Yes, Christ carried our sins, but we do not know that he conquered them. We know he accepted our debt, but we are not sure he paid it."

Since Christ was more than a match for death, who or what can ever stand against him? No one! Nothing! Again, since it was impossible for death to hold Christ in its bonds, it is impossible to keep in bondage us who belong to him, for we are his body. You wonder how you will ever get rid of your guilt for your old sins. If you fully trust in the precious blood of Christ, your sins will vanish, and you will be freed from guilt. Even if Satan assaults you, just resist him, firm in your faith (1 Peter 5:9).

Note how Peter kept to the Old Testament. Those quotations added force to his argument, for his hearers believed the ancient Scriptures to be the very voice of God, and therefore Peter gave them a lot of it. In the Psalms David spoke of someone who would die yet never feel in his body the natural result of death, namely, decay. Having quoted from the Psalms, Peter went on to make this comment on David's words:

"Brothers, I can tell you confidently that the patriarch David died and was buried, and his tomb is here to this day. But he was a prophet and knew that God had promised him on oath that he would place one of his descendants on his throne. Seeing what was ahead, he spoke of the resurrection of the Christ, that he was not abandoned to the grave, nor did his body see decay. God has raised this Jesus to life, and we are all witnesses of the fact. Exalted to the right hand of God, he has received from the Father the promised Holy Spirit and has poured out what you now see and hear. For David did not ascend to heaven, and yet he said, 'The Lord said to my Lord: "Sit at my right hand until I make your enemies a footstool for your feet."'" (29–35).

With the eleven apostles and the greater company of disciples behind him, Peter made the noble utterance: "God has raised this Jesus to life, and we are all witnesses of the fact." It must have been an impressive sight as they all stood up bearing witness that they had seen the crucified Christ alive after his death. It was a wonderful public testimony to the greatest of all facts—the resurrection of Christ.

Peter was saying, "This is a mystery to you, but it is the result of Christ's exaltation to the right hand of his Father." Was not that enough to convince them, for they had seen and heard the proofs of the working of the Spirit among them? It must have been very striking to have been there and to have heard and seen these tokens of God setting his seal to the work of Jesus.

When we read of our Lord at the "right hand" of God, we understand that Christ enjoys infinite ecstasy, for David said there are "eternal pleasures at your right hand" (Ps. 16:11).

"Therefore let all Israel be assured of this: God has made this Jesus, whom you crucified, both Lord and Christ." (36)

How Peter's listeners must have jerked when he came to the point at which he had aimed all along: "God has made this Jesus, whom you crucified, both Lord and Christ." This was not an original or sensational sermon. There was no fine oration in it, no garnishing of poetry. It was a heart-moving argument, entreaty, and exhortation. In plain language Peter proved that it was Jesus Christ of whom David spoke in the Psalms. This is exactly what the people wanted to have proved. Many of them were ready to receive such a proof, and they did receive it.

Let us remember that whatever we think of Jesus, God thinks everything of him, for he has made him "both Lord and Christ."

When the people heard this, they were cut to the heart and said to Peter and the other apostles, "Brothers, what shall we do?" (37)

The pointed truth had gone home to their hearts, and they were pierced by it. They felt a stirring of emotion and a movement of love to Christ. Where did the power of Peter's sermon lie? It lay partly in Peter's faith. People respect someone who believes what he or she is saying. Its power also lay in being full of Scripture. Most of all, Peter's message was powerful because that very day he was "filled with the Holy Spirit" (Acts 2:4).

Peter's listeners had to be "cut to the heart," because true Christian faith begins there. Unlike religion, the gospel does not try to change people from the outside. "Rend your heart and not your garments" (Joel 2:13). If people are not "cut to the heart," the impression will not last. They will be like Judah, to whom God said, "Your love is like a morning mist, like the early dew that disappears" (Hos. 6:4). The reason so many backslide is that they build their faith on the sand of a counterfeit gospel that does not cut to the heart.

Before God uses us to convert people, he must use us to do the exact opposite. It is idle to try to heal those who have not been wounded, to attempt to clothe those who have never been stripped, and to make rich those who have never realized their poverty.

The chief instrument God uses for cutting to the heart is the dying love of Jesus Christ. Nothing wounds like the cross of Christ. A bleeding Savior makes hearts bleed. When he is pierced, they are pierced.

A comforting thought is that the Holy Spirit, who alone can cut to the heart, is called "the Comforter" (John 14:26 KJV). He who wounds is the one who heals. The Spirit who convicts consoles. Though one of his hands holds a sharp dagger, the other hand carries the remedy with which to heal the wound. As God says in Deuteronomy 32:39, "I have wounded and I will heal."

Others who were cut to the heart stoned the preacher (Acts 7:54–60), but these wanted to obey God. They were the same people who had mockingly said, "They have had too much wine" (v. 13). They had begun badly but ended well. They were in doubt about what they should do, but they were resolved to do whatever they were told to do. Happy the person whose sin has been killed through the deadly wound inflicted by the sword of the Spirit, which is the Word of God.

I hope you have not read these words to mock. But if you have done so and then become cut in your heart by the truth you have heard, it will be better than coming to church in an attentive frame of mind and then going out unimpressed, as many do. May God give us grace to yield a sweet obedience to his will when he cuts into our hearts.

Peter replied, "Repent and be baptized, every one of you, in the name of Jesus Christ for the forgiveness of your sins. And you will receive the gift of the Holy Spirit. The promise is for you and your children and for all who are far off—for all whom the Lord our God will call." (38–39)

Peter told them to change their minds entirely—to repudiate what they had done—then to confess their faith by baptism. This is the full proclamation of the gospel. We have no more right to leave out the call to baptism than the call to repentance. Peter was unafraid to exhort a sinner because the sinner is spiritually dead. He promised his listeners that if they did what he said, they would share in the wonder that had astounded them—the reception of the Holy Spirit.

What promise did Peter have in mind? The promise in verse 21: "Everyone who calls on the name of the Lord will be saved." That promise is also given to you and to everyone far off, even in the most distant pagan country. It is for "all." So do not shut yourself out or try to shut others out, but believe the promise, call on God, and you will be saved. When God heals the disease of sin, he can remove the very scars it has left behind.

The promise of this thirty-ninth verse is also fulfilled in the giving of the Holy Spirit in verse 38. We need the Holy Spirit to illumine us, for we are blind. We need him to instruct us, for we are ignorance itself. We need the Spirit to soften our hearts of stone. We need him to make us alive, for by nature we are "dead in . . . transgressions and sins" (Eph. 2:1).

Thus we have a twofold promise from God, and many have come to Christ with far less encouragement. Salvation is founded on God's promise, not our merit. That is what grace is all about. God does not say, "You must do this, and feel that, and be something else," but "I will give, and you will receive." In this thirty-ninth verse Peter did not say, "The law is for you," but "The promise is for you."

With many other words he warned them; and he pleaded with them, "Save yourselves from this corrupt generation." Those who accepted his message were baptized, and about three thousand were added to their number that day." (40–41)

Peter first bore witness to the truth, then pled with his hearers to receive his testimony. All true ministers will both testify and plead. Some are always pleading. They cry, "Believe! Believe!" But they do not tell their hearers what they should believe. Others are always testifying. They preach good doctrine, but they do not like to plead with sinners to repent and believe the gospel. Each of these is a one-legged ministry, but we must have two legs to ours. Like Peter, we must warn and plead.

Peter didn't say, "Save yourselves from hell." Only Christ can do that for you. Peter said, "Save yourselves from this corrupt generation." That is to say, "Leave the world behind, take on yourselves the distinctive mark of a Christian, and escape for your lives to the Savior's side!"

Peter's listeners showed obedient faith. When Peter said, "Repent," they did repent. When he told them to be baptized, they did it gladly. This is the true scriptural order, first to accept the gospel message, then to be baptized.

When these people joined the church, they could not hide their convictions. It is a strong temptation to many to say, "I have believed in Jesus, but that is a private matter between God and me. I do not need to tell anyone else. Can't I be a Nicodemus, who came to Jesus at night, or a Joseph of Arimathea, who was a secret disciple?"

Not if it means you are going to be a coward. You can be a Nicodemus if you go with him when he carries spices to the grave of Jesus. You may be a Joseph of Arimathea if you go with him when he boldly asks Pilate for the body of Jesus. Neither of these two men were ashamed to identify with Christ after the cross had been set before their eyes.

Why not three thousand converts in one day again? Why not thirty thousand? Why not three hundred thousand? There is nothing too great for us to request nor for God to grant.

They devoted themselves to the apostles' teaching and to the fellowship, to the breaking of bread and to prayer. Everyone was filled with awe, and many wonders and miraculous signs were done by the apostles. All the believers were together and had everything in common. Selling their possessions and goods, they gave to anyone as he had need. Every day they continued to meet together in the temple courts. They broke bread in their homes and ate together with glad and sincere hearts, praising God and enjoying the favor of all the people. And the Lord added to their number daily those who were being saved. (42–47)

These new converts did not try to go to heaven by some underground railway without confessing Christ. Instead, having confessed their faith in Christ, they showed their devotion to the apostles' teaching, the fellowship, the breaking of bread, and prayer. It is a great blessing to have such well-balanced spiritual lives.

What a notable example of the power of divine grace! O that we had more of this generous spirit today!

I believe that wherever two or three disciples of Christ meet together, it is proper for them to celebrate the Lord's Supper. It is not a church ordinance to be confined to the official assembling of all believers. Christ is in the midst of two or three disciples who meet in his name. And where he is, there the emblems of his broken body and shed blood may be shared in memory of him.

Does anyone besides the Lord ever add converts to the church? Yes. The Devil also thrusts in his servants. Sometimes the names of people are "added" to the church, but the people themselves are subtractions. They are added like figures on paper, but they do not augment the church's strength. Because the church is the body of Christ, a divine operation is necessary to add to it.

The church can also be compared to a tree. To add to it, you cannot take a dead bough and tie it on. Instead of adding to the tree, that encumbers it. To add to a tree, grafting must be done. A live branch must be knit to the living trunk by a living union, so that the vital sap of the tree will flow in the grafted bough. May the Lord so add to all our churches, and he will have the glory forever.

From No Condemnation to No Separation

THIS EIGHTH CHAPTER OF Romans begins with no condemnation and ends with no separation. Everything between is full of grace and truth. Happy are the people who share in this double blessing, and unhappy are those who know nothing of it. What a banquet this chapter has proved to be to the souls of God's hungry servants! It is the very cream of the cream of Holy Scripture. May it be so now to us as we read it.

Therefore, there is now no condemnation for those who are in Christ Jesus, because through Christ Jesus the law of the Spirit of life set me free from the law of sin and death. For what the law was powerless to do in that it was weakened by the sinful nature, God did by sending his own Son in the likeness of sinful man to be a sin offering. And so he condemned sin in sinful man, in order that the righteous requirements of the law might be fully met in us, who do not live according to the sinful nature but according to the Spirit. (1–4)

Each of us is by nature under God's condemnation. Because of our sin we are "condemned already" (John 3:18). The sweet words in this verse are the little ones: "There is now," at this very moment "no condemnation" that will lie in the court of your conscience or in the court of God's heaven. If we are "in Christ Jesus," not only is part of our condemnation removed but all of it is gone.

We have many doubts but no condemnation, many disciplines but no condemnation, even apparent frowns from our Father's face but no condemnation. There is a great deal of accusation and a great deal more of tribulation, but there is not the least hint of any condemnation for those in Christ Jesus.

One of the martyrs, when brought before the judge, was told,

"Since you are dying for heresy, you will be condemned." But the good man answered, "No, for 'there is now no condemnation for those who are in Christ Jesus.'" He caught the very spirit of this verse!

Not only does sin no longer condemn us but also it has lost its power to rule us. We are free from it, for we are now under the new and higher "law of the Spirit of life." It alone can "set me free from the law of sin and death." By nature we are all under bondage to the law of sin and death. It is so powerful that even when we want to do good, we cannot get away from evil. Only the higher law of the Spirit of life can liberate us.

The Law never made anyone holy, and it never will. It says to us, "This is what you must do, and you will be condemned if you don't do it!" Then it gives us no power to enable us to obey it. The Law says to the lame, "You must walk!" and to the blind, "You must see!" But it does not enable them to walk or see. On the contrary, when the Law issues its commands, my sinful nature disobeys them. There are some sins we never would have thought of doing if the Law had not commanded me not to do them. So the Law is weak and unable to produce righteousness—not because of the wickedness of its own nature but because of the wickedness in my nature.

But the Lord Jesus Christ by his death has put away my sin. Now I love him who has delivered me. This love becomes the force that inclines me toward holiness. What a blessed system this is that saves me from the love of sin, delivers me from sinning, gives me a new nature, and puts the right spirit in me!

God found a way to condemn sin without condemning me! The law could not condemn sin so truly and thoroughly as God did when he condemned sin in the person of Christ. O believer, don't let your sins grieve you, for they have been condemned in Christ. They may have been enormous, but if you are in Christ, you are free, for Christ was punished for you, and God's justice does not ask for a second punishment for one offense. If you are a believer in Christ, there is no way you can be condemned. So do not fear.

No one keeps the law as well as the person who does not hope to be saved by it. This person renounces all confidence in good works, accepts the righteousness of God through faith in Christ, and is moved by gratitude to a height of dedication and purity of obedience that mere legalism can never know. The child will obey better without desire of reward than the slave will under fear of the lash or in hope of a wage. The most potent motive for holiness is free grace. A dying Savior is the death of sin.

Christians do more than talk "according to the Spirit" (v. 4); they "walk" (KJV) that way. Many can talk religion whose lives are ungodly.

Those who live according to the sinful nature have their minds set on what that nature desires; but those who live in accordance with the Spirit have their minds set on what the Spirit desires. The mind of sinful man is death, but the mind controlled by the Spirit is life and peace; the sinful mind is hostile to God. It does not submit to God's law, nor can it do so. Those controlled by the sinful nature cannot please God. (5–8)

Everything is according to its nature. The wolf devours. The sheep patiently feeds. And people "who live according to the sinful nature have their minds set on what that nature desires," which is sin. Judge whether or not you belong to God by this test: What are you living for? Is your mind set on what the sinful nature desires or on what the Holy Spirit desires?

The great thing, then, is to be brought under the control of the Holy Spirit and the new nature he gives. Then we try to rise to our source, and we rise much higher than human nature ever can. The new nature can do what the old nature can't. Spiritual joys, spiritual hopes, spiritual pursuits belong only to people who are spiritual. Spiritual people live for something nobler than the worldly person's trinity: "What shall we eat?" and "What shall we drink?" and "What shall we wear?" (Matt. 6:31). That life befits only a beast, a bird, or an insect. But when we become spiritual, we live for divine things: holiness, righteousness, and Jesus himself. This is real life!

The sinful nature must die. Its tendency is corruption. But the spirit never dies. Its tendency is growth, advance, and immortality. You may think that because you have never been guilty of any vice, you do not require the new birth. But "the mind of sinful man," though it may be whitewashed until it looks spiritual, "is death." Though you may plant a few good garden seeds with the flowers of morality, "the mind of sinful man" will still yield nothing but damnation in the end.

The "sinful mind" or old nature is so depraved that it is hopelessly evil. There is no mending it. It is not only "hostile to God" but "enmity against God" (KJV). It is not merely at enmity, but absolute enmity. However polished and polite people may be, if they have not been born again, they are "hostile to God." So what should we do with the old nature? Improve it? No. Just let it die.

Many teach that people can be saved whenever they want and that if they are unsaved, it is not because of any personal defect. But I do not understand the meaning of this verse if that is correct.

Some say people can repent if they want, but that is just the point. They never will want to repent unless they are constrained to desire repentance by the grace of God. A hog could lick himself clean like a cat if he wanted to, but that is contrary to his nature. Until you could change the swine's nature, it will never lick itself clean. This verse says the same of human beings. The lesson coming out of this is that from first to last, the work of salvation is all of grace. This humbling truth is far more useful than the other doctrine that puffs people up with pride by telling them they can do what they cannot do.

As long as you are "controlled by the sinful nature," there is no pleasing God. Whatever you do, there is an essential impurity in your nature. As long as you are "controlled by the sinful nature," you cannot please God by church attendance or moral living. Virtues in unregenerate people are nothing more than whitewashed sins. The best performance by an unchanged heart is worthless in God's sight, because it lacks the stamp of grace and is thus a false coin.

You may wash "the sinful nature," clothe it, decorate it, and educate it, but no evolution can produce grace out of a sinful nature. The natural person may be well dressed, but he or she is still dead inside. Ask Christ to give you his Spirit so that you may be spiritual, and then you can please God.

You, however, are controlled not by the sinful nature but by the Spirit, if the Spirit of God lives in you. And if anyone does not have the Spirit of Christ, he does not belong to Christ. But if Christ is in you, your body is dead because of sin, yet your spirit is alive because of righteousness. And if the Spirit of him who raised Jesus from the dead is living in you, he who raised Christ from the dead will also give life to your mortal bodies through his Spirit, who lives in you. (9–11)

What a wonderful fact! The Spirit of God can live in us! I do not know which of two mysteries to admire most: God in the flesh in the person of Christ, or the Holy Spirit indwelling us. These are the miracles of miracles.

It does not matter what you call yourself. You may be a pastor or a bishop, but if you do not possess the Spirit of Christ, you do not belong to Christ. Do you have the Spirit of Christ directing you, guiding you, teaching you, comforting you, and supporting you? Do you have the Spirit's gentleness, purity, and goodness? If not, you do not belong to Christ. It is one thing to profess religion and quite another to possess the Spirit of Christ.

You may sit at the communion table, but if you do not have the Spirit of Christ, you are a counterfeit Christian. What a fearful thing it is to not belong to Christ! To such people he will say, "I never knew you" (Matt. 7:23). The highest point that human nature can reach still falls short of being in Christ. Unless the Spirit of God lives in us, we do not belong to Christ. But God is gracious and full of mercy. Even if you are the worst of sinners, if you trust in Christ, God will send his Spirit into your heart.

Hence come those aches, pains, weariness, decay, and infirmities of age. We experience these things as long as we live with this body of death before the resurrection. The body must see corruption unless the Lord comes. Even when he does come, our bodies must undergo a wondrous change.

Unlike our bodies, our spirits triumph even in the midst of pain and weakness. The spirit will not die, and it enables us to rejoice in spite of our afflictions, trials, and depressions.

There is coming a time when our bodies will experience redemption. God does not say he will give you new bodies. Instead, he will "give life to your mortal bodies." That is, the same bodies now subject to death will be brought to life at the resurrection.

When Pharaoh agreed to let the people of Israel go to worship the Lord, he told Moses, "Leave your flocks and herds behind" (Ex. 10:24). But Moses replied, "Not a hoof is to be left behind" (Ex. 10:26). So no particle of our real humanity will be left under the power of sin and death. Our souls have already been emancipated, and our bodies will be redeemed too.

Therefore, brothers, we have an obligation—but it is not to the sinful nature, to live according to it. For if you live according to the sinful nature, you will die; but if by the Spirit you put to death the misdeeds of the body, you will live, because those who are led by the Spirit of God are sons of God. (12–14)

What do we owe the old nature? Nothing. It drags us down and ruins us. The only thing we owe the sinful nature is to be masters of it. So let us not serve it, consult it, or even consider it. Let us just give it a decent burial. Let it be buried with Christ in baptism.

This is because "the sinful nature" is a dying thing. If you live after its dying fashion, you will die. If you live to gratify your ambition, feed your greed, or please yourself, you will be disappointed, for both you and your hope will die.

Shall the dying body be your master? Shall the cravings that come from the sinful nature dominate your spirit? God forbid! If you seek by the Spirit's power to kill sin, to crush all sinful desires, if you keep evil with a rope around its neck so that you can put it to death, "you will live."

Leading implies following, and those who follow the divine Spirit have one evidence of childhood. It is not those who say they are sons of God but those who prove they are by being influenced and gently guided by the Spirit. You may have many weaknesses, but if you follow the divine leadership of God's Spirit, you are a child of his. Judge yourself by that test.

The so-called doctrine of the universal fatherhood of God is rubbish. No others but "those who are led by the Spirit of God are sons of God." This is the essential thing to sonship, that we have the Spirit of God within us. Since "God is spirit" (John 4:24), his children are spiritual. To be "sons of God" is more than anything that ungodly kings and emperors can boast.

For you did not receive a spirit that makes you a slave again to fear, but you received the Spirit of sonship. And by him we cry, "Abba, Father." The Spirit himself testifies with our spirit that we are God's children. Now if we are children, then we are heirs—heirs of God and co-heirs with Christ, if indeed we share in his sufferings inorder that we may also share in his glory. (15–17)

We had that fear once, and it led to a good result in us for the time being. We were under the Law and made to feel its curse, but that made us go to Christ for freedom. Now we who were slaves to sin are children of God, and we are not afraid of our Father. We have reverence for him, but it is mixed with love, and "there is no fear in love. But perfect love drives out fear" (1 John 4:18).

What a blessing to utter the choice word that no slave may ever pronounce: "Abba!" It is the kind of word little children utter when they first open their mouths to speak. It runs the same both backwards and forwards: AB-BA. Oh, to have a childlike spirit with God!

The apostle began this part of the verse with "you" but here changed to "we," because he felt so much of the spirit of adoption in his own heart that he could not talk of it as belonging to others alone. Woe to the preachers who can preach an adoption they never enjoyed! Woe to any of us if we can teach others about the Spirit of sonship but never feel it crying in our own souls, "Abba, Father."

You make a profession of being a Christian. Does your own spirit say that is true? Our Lord Jesus said, "If I testify about myself, my testimony is not valid. There is another who testifies in my favor, and I know that his testimony about me is valid" (John 5:31–32). Likewise the witness of our spirit must not stand alone. It must be backed up by "the Spirit himself."

What better testimony can we have than that of these two witnesses: first our own spirits, which have been changed so as to be reconciled to God, then the Holy Spirit, who first of all gives us life, then bears witness that we are children of God? "A matter must be established by the testimony of two or three witnesses" (Deut. 19:15).

God is the Father only of those who are spiritual. We are born into his family by the new birth. Not all children are heirs in earthly families. But it is so in God's family!

What a heritage to be a coheir with God! We are not only heirs of what God chooses to give but also heirs of God himself. God himself becomes our heritage. So we can say with the psalmist, "You are my portion, O Lord" (Ps. 119:57). We inherit all that God has and all that he is.

We are with Christ both "in his sufferings" and "in his glory." If we shun the path of humiliation with Christ, we may expect him to deny us in the day of his glory. The rule for us who are in Christ is "Share and share alike." Are you willing to take a share in Christ's sufferings? If not, you will not share in his glory. To receive the crown, you must take up the cross.

The sufferings of Christ are spiritual as well as physical. Do you ever feel pressed down when you see abounding sin? Are your eyes ready to be flooded with tears at the thought of the destruction of the ungodly? Then you are sharing in the sufferings of Christ, and you will one day share in his glory.

I consider that our present sufferings are not worth comparing with the glory that will be revealed in us. The creation waits in eager expectation for the sons of God to be revealed. For the creation was subjected to frustration, not by its own choice, but by the will of the one who subjected it, in hope that the creation itself will be liberated from its bondage to decay and brought into the glorious freedom of the children of God. (18–21)

Paul made our present sufferings a matter of simple arithmetic. He added them all up and saw what the total was. He was then about to say what an equal sum of glory would be, but he gave it up and just said, "Our present sufferings are not worth comparing with the glory that will be revealed in us." Did they stand as one to a thousand? No, for then they would have been worthy of comparison. Even if our sufferings equaled one millionth of our future glory, they would have been worth comparing. But Paul saw that there was no proportion whatever to them. The sufferings were as a single drop and the glory as the boundless ocean.

Do we suffer now? Then let us wait for something better in the future. In the meantime our lot is trouble and perplexity, moaning and groaning. But one day "glory . . . will be revealed in us." Think of that! Now we see the revelation of Scripture, but then we'll see the revelation of God's glory in us. We will be full of glory!

There is something that the "creation" is waiting for on tip-toe, as it were, and it cannot come until God's children are manifested, until his glory is revealed in them. We live in a world cursed by human sin. It is a beautiful world, but the slime of the serpent is on all our Edens now.

There is a future even for material things. The dark cloud we live in will be illuminated with the light of God. These poor bodies that are like dust of the earth and subject to pain and weakness and death are still to be brought into "the glorious freedom of the children of God."

We know that the whole creation has been groaning as in the pains of childbirth right up to the present time. Not only so, but we ourselves, who have the firstfruits of the Spirit, groan inwardly as we wait eagerly for our adoption as sons, the redemption of our bodies. For in this hope we were saved. But hope that is seen is no hope at all. Who hopes for what he already has? But if we hope for what we do not yet have, we wait for it patiently. (22–25)

The whole creation is in its birth pangs, and its complete deliverance can never come until God's children are revealed in their glory. The globe itself is wrapped in swaddling bands of mist and fails to shine out like its sister stars in its pristine brightness and splendor. What does the fog mean? What does the general sighing and mourning of the air all through the winter mean? What about the volcanoes, earthquakes, and hurricanes? It is the creation groaning and waiting for the new heaven and new earth.

Some pretend not to groan inwardly, but we will make no such claim. It is a sign of grace and a mark of God's children that they do not think they are perfect, but they groan after perfection. These bodies of ours still lie in a sense under the curse of sin.

Here is what "we wait eagerly for . . . the redemption of our bodies." We will not wait in vain, for Christ is the Savior of our bodies as well as of our souls. Our souls have been born again, but our bodies have not. We have the first fruits of it and the promise of it, but it is not yet ours to enjoy. The day will come when our bodies will be free from pain, weakness, weariness, sin, and death. We may well look forward to that happy day with the loftiest anticipation!

If we could be all we want to be, there would be no room for hope. If we had everything we will one day have, hope, which is one of the sweetest of the graces, would have no room to exercise herself. It is a blessing to have hope. I have heard that faith and hope will not be found in heaven, but I question that. I think they will never die. "These three remain: faith, hope and love" (1 Cor. 13:13). In heaven there will surely be room for hope in the second coming of Christ, the conquest of the world, and the bringing of all God's elect to glory.

Yet this life is the main sphere of hope, so let us give it full scope. When other graces seem to be at a low ebb, let us still hope. I believe in New Zealand the word for hope is *swimming thought,* because hope will swim when everything else is drowned. Happy the person whose hope swims on the crest of the stormiest wave, who can accept sorrow as an introduction to the joy that is to come from God's mysterious hand!

You would gladly have heavenly joy on earthly ground, but that would be a mismatch. You will have earthly sorrow in earthly ground, and you will have heavenly bliss on the heavenly shore—but not until then. For now "we wait for it patiently."

In the same way, the Spirit helps us in our weakness. We do not know what we ought to pray for, but the Spirit himself intercedes for us with groans that words cannot express. And he who searches our hearts knows the mind of the Spirit, because the Spirit intercedes for the saints in accordance with God's will. (26–27)

Oh, how many weaknesses we have! Ignorance, pride, coldness of heart, lack of faith and zeal—these are some of our weaknesses. But thank God, we have the omnipotent Spirit of the Lord to help us! We are blind to many of our weaknesses. We may think we're strong when we are very weak. The Spirit of God spies out the weakness and puts the help where the strength is required.

Our weakness is most easily seen in our prayer lives. How few of us prevail with God, as Elijah did (James 5:17–18). Aaron and Hur held up the hands of Moses (Ex. 17:12), but the Holy Spirit himself "helps us in our weakness."

We might have expected this to say, "but the Spirit himself teaches us what to pray for." But the Spirit goes beyond that and prays "for us." God not only answers our prayers when we make them but also makes our prayers for us. The awesome things in prayer that can never be expressed in human language the Holy Spirit translates into "groans." And so we are made to groan when we cannot speak, and those groans bring us blessings that words cannot express. Have you been in your prayer room lately and felt that you could not pray? We often pray best when we think we are praying worst. When there is the most anguish, sighing, and crying in prayer, there is most of the very essence of prayer.

There are other things we desire for which we cannot ask. Sometimes we do not even know what we want. We have a vacuum in our hearts, but we don't know what will fill it. There is a hunger in our spirits, but we do not know what the bread is. But the Holy Spirit can articulate our unuttered groans.

So if you find it hard to pray, don't give up praying. The Devil tells you that such poor prayers as yours can never reach God's ear. Do not believe him. The Spirit helps your weaknesses, and when he helps you, you will succeed. I fear that people who know nothing of the "groans that words cannot express" will never know anything of "the glory" that words cannot express (v. 18).

When we ourselves do not know the mind of the Spirit, God, who searches our hearts, knows it. When we feel that we cannot pray, God's Spirit intercedes for us and blesses us. Often groaning, wrestling believers have no inkling of the full significance of their own prayers. But God does!

This is the philosophy of prayer. Whatever God's will is, the Holy Spirit writes it on the hearts of praying saints, and they pray for the very thing God wants to give. As the barometer often predicts the coming rain, so the Holy Spirit in the Christian is the barometer that indicates when showers of blessing will fall from heaven. The spirit of prophecy is on the person who knows how to pray, for the Spirit of God has moved that individual to ask for what God is about to give.

The Holy Spirit is not the only one helping us. God the Father "searches our hearts." This explains what to many is the mystery of prayer. Since the Holy Spirit is God, he knows the secret purposes of the divine will. Therefore he moves the saints to pray in accordance with that will and grants their pleas through his own intercession. The Spirit knows what we need. God knows what the Spirit is asking for. And so our prayers make the complete round, and God sends us the blessing.

And we know that in all things God works for the good of those who love him, who have been called according to his purpose. (28)

This is not a matter of opinion. This is scarcely a matter of faith. "We know." We are sure of it. We have proved it in our own experience. We are not agnostics who must say, "We do not know," or even philosophers who say, "We think." God gives us the assurance to say, "We know."

To us almost everything in this world seems to be in confusion, but to God's eye everything is in order. Jacob said, "Everything is against me!" (Gen. 42:36). But he was speaking in unbelief, and later he knew better.

There is nothing inactive in God's providence. "In all things God works." There is a divine unity in all events. God works in all things for our good. "All things" includes your present trouble, your aching head, and your heavy heart. God's purpose for his people is good and nothing but good. Though some things may hurt us, yet if we love God, he works through them for our good.

Do you love God? Can you say with Peter, "Lord, you know all things; you know that I love you" (John 21:17)? If so, then God is at work in all things for your good. Not only will he work, but he is working now for our good. The reason God works for the good of those who love him is that he loves them.

If God works even the bad things for our good, what about the good things? If God makes us sing in the dungeon, how much more sweetly will we sing in heaven!

For those who do not love God, however, he works in all things for their calamity. Are they prosperous? They are as the beast fattened for the slaughter. Are they healthy? They are as the blooming flower that ripens for the mower's blades. Do they suffer? Their sufferings are the first drops of the eternal hailstorm of divine vengeance. Everything to those who do not love God—if they could see it—has a dark aspect.

Of course God works all things for the good of those who have been called according to his purpose, for infinite love is the purpose for which God called them. This is not the common call that God sends out to other people. This is his special call. When the hen is in the yard, she keeps on calling. But when she wants her own little ones to come and run beneath her wings, she has a special cluck for them. They know it and run to hide beneath her. We who trust in Christ have responded to God's call and are safe beneath the wings of our heavenly Father.

But how are we to know who are those who have been called? We cannot peer into the pages of the Lamb's Book of Life, yet we can tell by this simple test if our names are recorded there: Do we truly love the Lord? "Those who love him" are the same as those "who have been called according to his purpose." If we love God, all things—visible and invisible, friendly and unfriendly—are working for our present and eternal good.

*For those God foreknew he also predestined to be conformed to the like-
ness of his Son, that he might be the firstborn among many brothers.
And those he predestined, he also called; those he called, he also justified; those he justified, he also glorified. (29–30)*

God looked upon us with pleasure and delight before the creation
of the universe. He loved and called us to be his own even then.
Those whom God "foreknew" or foreloved, he has ordained, determined, predestined to be made like his Son.

Our likeness to Christ is something we and others can see. Since
we are "co-heirs with Christ" (v. 17), what a joy it is to share his
nature and be made like him! Christ will be reflected in all his people.
The glory of heaven will be that whatever way you look, you will see
either Christ himself or his likeness in his people. If you have ever
stood in a room full of mirrors, your likeness has been revealed
everywhere. Heaven will be a mirror chamber in which Christ will
be seen in every one of his people.

Note the word *he,* which occurs six times in verse 30. All of them
refer to God. It is God who works our salvation from beginning to
end. "Salvation comes from the LORD" (Jonah 2:9).

We cannot yet see the last link, which is glorification. It is in the
excessive brightness of the future, just as God's divine election is in the
brightness of the past. These are two columns on the shores, but the
swinging bridge between them is our calling and justification. These
are joined in one. If you have either God's calling or justification, you
may know your predestination and future glorification.

There is no break in this chain of five links. Each link is welded
to the next, and where God gives one of these blessings, he gives
the rest. The foreknown are predestined, the predestined are called,
the called are justified, and the justified are glorified. You cannot
read God's foreknowledge, nor can you enter into the secrets of predestination, but you can tell if you are "called" and "justified." If
you can hold these links, you have a grip on that endless chain that
is firmly fastened to the granite rock of eternity past and eternity
future. Whoever grasps this chain anywhere has all of it, for
"Scripture cannot be broken" (John 10:35).

Has God "called you out of darkness into his wonderful light"
(1 Peter 2:9)? Have you been "justified through faith" (Rom. 5:1)?
If so, you may rest assured you have been predestined and that in
due time you will be glorified.

Shall we complain of our physical sufferings? No. We will speak
about the wonders of grace and mountains of mercy! It exceeds our
understanding. The only thing we can say in response to this is

something practical that will encourage our hearts, as Paul did in the next verse:

What, then, shall we say in response to this? If God is for us, who can be against us? He who did not spare his own Son, but gave him up for us all—how will he not also, along with him, graciously give us all things? Who will bring any charge against those whom God has chosen? It is God who justifies. Who is he that condemns? Christ Jesus, who died—more than that, who was raised to life—is at the right hand of God and is also interceding for us. Who shall separate us from the love of Christ? Shall trouble or hardship or persecution or famine or nakedness or danger or sword? As it is written: "For your sake we face death all day long; we are considered as sheep to be slaughtered." (31–36)

We can get through all our trials if God is on our side. The whole world may be against us, but if God is for us, we count them as nothing. Our hearts may be against us, but "God is greater than our hearts" (1 John 3:20). The Devil is against us, and he is mighty, but God is almighty, and he "will soon crush Satan under your feet" (Rom. 16:20). "If God is for us, who can be against us?" Who may be against us? Who dares to be against us?

There is an opposite to this. If God is against you, who can be for you? If you are an enemy to God, your blessings are curses to you. Whether you have adversity or prosperity, if God is against you, you can never truly prosper.

There can be no end to the generosity of God once he has given his Son. He who has given the jewel of the universe, the very eye of heaven, will surely give us everything else we need and give it freely! In giving us Christ, the Father has already given us all things. What encouragement this gives us for believing prayer! Christ is the golden key of God's treasuries. Use him properly, and whatever you need will be yours.

Paul did not say merely that God will "graciously give us all things" but that he will give us all things "along with him." We will get all things along with Christ, but without Christ we will get nothing, for all other gifts come in this one. First God gives us his Son; then he gives us everything in him.

Here is true boldness. Paul called himself "the worst" of sinners (1 Tim. 1:15), yet he dared to challenge anyone to bring a charge against those God has chosen. Paul had good reason to ring out these confident challenges to earth and hell. Christ is our judge who died for us. Will he who died condemn? No! Because he is now "at the right hand of God and is also interceding for us" as our representative; he has carried us into heaven. His eternal pleas silence all the accusations of the Devil.

The most dreadful thought of all is the fear of being condemned by God. No wonder Belshazzar's "face turned pale and he was so frightened that his knees knocked together and his legs gave way" (Dan. 5:6), for God had condemned him with his handwriting on the wall.

You might answer Paul's question by saying, "My conscience condemns me. The Word of God condemns me. Satan condemns me." But our real judge is Christ, and will he who died for us and accepted us by faith condemn us? No. If he, our judge, is unable to condemn us because of all he has done for us, no one can!

Why was Paul sure Christ would not condemn him? Because he had never sinned? No, for his hands were red with the blood of the martyrs. Was it because Paul had become a missionary? No, for all his good works he considered "rubbish" (Phil. 3:8). Paul's chief ground of assurance that he would not be condemned was that Christ had died.

Since we who are in Christ will not be condemned by God, we are accepted by him, loved by him, dear to him, pure and precious in his sight.

Will Christ blow hot and cold, first interceding for us and then with those same lips condemning us? It cannot be. Still, Satan will ask us, "What if Christ died for all your past sins? What about your present sinfulness?"

We answer, "Christ is 'interceding for us' now in heaven."

Our motto in every trial is, "Who shall separate us from the love of Christ?" The seven things listed in verse 35 have been tried on the saints for ages, but they have not kept Christ from loving them or them from loving Christ. Saints have been beaten like wheat on the threshing floor, but Christ has loved them just the same in spite of all the suffering he has allowed to fall on them. When they have been in famine or poverty, has Christ ever forsaken his saints? No. He has loved them all the more. Instead of separating them from Christ, these things have made them cling all the more to him.

John Bunyan was a good example of this. When his persecutors told him he could go free from prison if he would promise not to preach Christ, he replied, "I will lie in prison until the moss grows on my eyelids rather than make such a promise. If you let me out of prison today, I will preach tomorrow by the grace of God." Persecution could not separate John Bunyan from Christ's love for him or his love for Christ.

In Paul's day they were being hunted to death by the tens of thousands. Were they separated from Christ's love? No! The enemy grew tired of persecution before the saints were wearied by it. In the days of the Roman Empire, Christians came to the judgment seat to confess Christ even when they were not sought after, as if they were tempting their enemies to throw them to the lions. They didn't know fear. Though emperors were worse than brutes, the Christians defied them, outbraved them, and vanquished them. That's why Paul could say:

No, in all these things we are more than conquerors through him who loved us. For I am convinced that neither death not life, neither angels nor demons, neither the present nor the future, nor any powers, neither height nor depth, nor anything else in creation, will be able to separate us from the love of God that is in Christ Jesus our Lord. (37–39)

Paul did not say, "In some of these things we are more than conquerors," but "in all" of them. Again, he did not say we are mere "conquerors" but "more than conquerors." We are more than conquerors in the sense that we lose nothing by the fight. Our faith, though tried, grows stronger. Christ is our representative. If he our head has triumphed, we the bodily members will surely share in the victory. While the head is above the water, you cannot drown the body.

Someone once asked me, "What persuasion are you of?" I replied, "I am persuaded that neither death, nor life, nor angels, nor principalities, nor powers, nor things present, nor things to come, nor height, nor depth, nor any other creature, shall be able to separate us from the love of God, which is in Christ Jesus our Lord" (KJV).

We cannot be separated from God's love, because we are members of Christ's body. Will Christ lose his hands and feet? Will one of his fingers be lopped off? Will one of his eyes be plucked out, leaving him half blind? No! We cannot imagine a deformed Christ. Since we are one with Christ, nothing good or bad, hard or fearful, can separate us from God's love in Christ Jesus our Lord!

Are you convinced of God's love for you? Do you believe not only that he is love but that he loves you? Two things join God and a believer. The first is God's love for the believer, and the second is the believer's love for God.

The Resurrection of Christ

THE SILVER THREAD OF all God's blessings runs through the resurrection of Christ and binds them together.

The deity of Christ finds its surest proof in his resurrection, since the apostle Paul told us that Jesus "was declared with power to be the Son of God by his resurrection from the dead" (Rom. 1:4). It would be reasonable to doubt that our Lord was divine if he had not risen from the dead.

Jesus' lordship also depends on his resurrection, for Scripture affirms, "Christ died and returned to life so that he might be the Lord of both the dead and the living" (Rom. 14:9).

Again, our justification hangs on Christ's resurrection, according to Romans 4:25: "He was . . . raised to life for our justification."

Our new birth also depends on Jesus' resurrection, for Peter wrote, "In his great mercy he has given us new birth into a living hope through the resurrection of Jesus Christ from the dead" (1 Peter 1:3).

And certainly our ultimate resurrection rests here, for "he who raised Christ from the dead will also give life to your mortal bodies through his Spirit" (Rom. 8:11).

Now, brothers, I want to remind you of the gospel I preached to you, which you received and on which you have taken your stand. By this gospel you are saved, if you hold firmly to the word I preached to you. Otherwise, you have believed in vain. (1–2)

This is capable of two interpretations. Paul may have meant that "this gospel" brings salvation unless we have a false faith, a mere mental assent. Or he may have meant that if the gospel itself is a myth, we exercised our faith in a phantom, and so we have "believed in vain." When Paul preached the gospel, these hearers received it and held "firmly to the word." It is essential to salvation to hear the gospel, receive it, and then cling to God's Word in sacred trust.

For what I received I passed on to you as of first importance: that Christ died for our sins according to the Scriptures, that he was buried, that he was raised on the third day according to the Scriptures, and that he appeared to Peter, and then to the Twelve. After that, he appeared to more than five hundred of the brothers at the same time, most of whom are still living, though some have fallen asleep. Then he appeared to James, then to all the apostles, and last of all he appeared to me also, as to one abnormally born. (3–8)

The preacher of Christ must not make new doctrines. We are not to be our own teachers. We must first receive God's truth and then deliver it. The Christian teacher takes the lamp out of God's hands and passes it into the hands of his people. Originality in preaching is good, but only when it comes to the manner in which we present the Word of God. If we try to get original with the message, we preach false doctrine, and it is not worth listening to. We are not makers or inventors; we are messengers. We must tell our Master's message just as he gives it to us in Scripture.

Martin Luther said, "Jesus Christ never died for our good works. They were not worth dying for. But he died for our sins." That is the gospel. It is made up not so much of doctrines as of facts. Christ took our sins on himself. He took the death penalty for us. This is "according to the Scriptures." There are plenty of Old Testament Scriptures that teach the gospel prophetically. The best example is Isaiah 53.

Christ's burial was necessary as a proof of his death and as the groundwork of his resurrection. The grand fact of Christ's resurrection is rightly put after his substitutionary sacrifice. This is the keystone of the gospel arch. Christ died, was buried, and "was raised on the third day." Now he lives forever. We must dwell on these points, for they are the essentials of the gospel. We do not believe the gospel until we accept the great truth of Christ's resurrection.

Our Lord was careful to show himself after his resurrection to those who knew him before his death and so would be able to identify him. Had he shown himself only to strangers, they would have been able to say they had seen a man, but they could not have affirmed that he was the same person who had died and been buried. But when Christ showed himself to people like Thomas, whom he invited to put his fingers into the print of the nails and thrust his hand into his wounded side (John 20:26–27), he gave the most absolute proof of his resurrection and received from the most competent witnesses the surest evidence that no deception had taken place.

Though it was at first difficult to make the eleven apostles believe that Christ had risen from the dead, it was impossible to make them doubt it later. The witnesses had nothing to gain but everything to lose by their testimony. They were cast into prison, stoned, burned at the stake, and crucified for believing the evidence of their own senses and affirming what they knew to be true.

As uneducated men, they were unfit to invent a hoax. Their evidence was so clearly substantiated by the absence of the body of Christ from the tomb that the Jewish leaders had to invent an incredible story to account for it (Matt. 28:12-15).

Jesus was seen after he had risen from the dead—in different places, at different hours, sometimes by one person, sometimes by eleven, and by "more than five hundred of the brothers at the same time." It was not as if only a few people saw the risen Christ. The time when these many witnesses were "still living" was when this letter was written.

There is no fact in all history so well attested as the resurrection of Christ. Whether there ever was such a person as Julius Caesar or Napoleon Bonaparte might be contested, though there were, no doubt, thousands of witnesses who saw them and many who wrote about them. But as to whether Christ rose from the dead, no candid mind can entertain a doubt. He was seen by great companies of believers and by various individuals who had known him most intimately. They had many opportunities to judge whether or not they were deceived.

Christ's resurrection not only is well attested but also is the most important fact that ever happened in the history of the world, as Paul went on to show in the remainder of this chapter.

Paul did not try to defend the doctrine of the resurrection by any arguments from reason. He proved it by the convincing evidence. If I had to prove the existence of a cedar tree, I would not use logical arguments. I would simply produce a number of witnesses who had seen a cedar, and I would have proved my point. If the evidence of honest men were unacceptable, we would have to throw out not only Christianity but all the sciences, and you and I would be left to wander in a maze of doubts.

The words "abnormally born" literally mean "an abortion." Paul was referring to the time of his conversion, when Jesus spoke to him out of heaven and plainly revealed himself to him (Acts 9:1-6). Because Paul's conversion occurred in such an unusual way, he felt he was hardly worth mentioning. Yet he had seen the Lord after his resurrection from the dead. He was not a man to be deceived, for he had persecuted the church. He overflowed with anger against the Messiah. So when he said he had seen Jesus of Nazareth and was converted by the sight, we may be quite sure it was so. Paul was not a man to undergo all the sacrifices he had to endure for the sake of a mere dream.

An example today of being "abnormally born" would be a person who is converted after the spiritual parent is dead. I wish that your godly mother in heaven, who prayed for you for years yet died leaving you unsaved, would come to your remembrance now, and that God would honor her memory to bring you to Christ.

For I am the least of the apostles and do not even deserve to be called an apostle, because I persecuted the church of God. But by the grace of God I am what I am, and his grace to me was not without effect. No, I worked harder than all of them—yet not I, but the grace of God that was with me. Whether, then, it was I or they, this is what we preach, and this is what you believed. (9–11)

It was hard for Paul to forgive himself. He knew God had forgiven him and made him an apostle, but he knew he did not even deserve it. No doubt the tears gushed from his eyes when he wrote this verse.

This confession, suitable on the lips of Paul, is equally fitting in the mouths of us who have known and proved the grace of God. Let this be our comfort, that the same grace that made Paul an apostle has made us Christians. If there is anything good in us, we must confess that God put it there. He taught our souls to pray. He made us feel our need of grace. He stripped us of our boastful pride. He delivered us from our refuges of lies. He opened our blind eyes and showed us the beauty of Christ. He gave us the first glimmer of faith.

Everything we are we owe to God's grace. We are chosen by God, and this election is of grace. We are redeemed, and our redemption is the mighty masterpiece of grace. We are called, and our calling is of grace. We are kept secure in Christ, and this too is of grace.

The truth that we are what we are by the grace is God is meant to teach us four virtues. First, humility. We will soon be in the storm if we do not see God's grace in the sunshine. Second, it teaches us love. Why should I be harsh toward those who are not what I am, when it is by God's grace that "I am what I am"? Third, it should teach us hope for others. There is a drunk. You think she or he can never be converted. But why not? The grace that saved you can save that drunk. God's almighty power knows nothing of degrees. Fourth, we should learn from this text to be thankful. Those who owe everything to grace can never forget to praise their God. Along with Robert Robinson we must say, "O to grace how great a debtor, daily I'm constrained to be!"

If Paul could say, "By the grace of God I am what I am," ask yourself, "What am I?" Has God's grace ever changed you? If not, what has made you what you are?

What humble tones Paul spoke in here! He did not deny what had been done in him and by him, but he gave all the credit to "his grace." We are not to shut our eyes to the gracious change that God's Holy Spirit makes in us. We may speak of it often, but let us always guard against taking any honor to ourselves and be careful to put the crown on the right head.

No one could be more thoroughly with Christ, heart and soul, than Paul, who before had been the bloodthirsty Saul of Tarsus. His witness may well be believed, and in light of all he had done before his conversion, we may put away all doubt that Christ was crucified, laid in the tomb, raised from the dead by the power of God, and seen alive.

There was no doubt about this. All the apostles and the early Christians preached the resurrection of Christ, and the Corinthians believed it when they became Christians.

But if it is preached that Christ has been raised from the dead, how can some of you say that there is no resurrection of the dead? If there is no resurrection of the dead, then not even Christ has been raised. And if Christ has not been raised, our preaching is useless and so is your faith. More than that, we are then found to be false witnesses about God, for we have testified about God that he raised Christ from the dead. But he did not raise him if in fact the dead are not raised. For if the dead are not raised, then Christ has not been raised either. And if Christ has not been raised, your faith is futile; you are still in your sins. Then those also who have fallen asleep in Christ are lost. If only for this life we have hope in Christ, we are to be pitied more than all men. (12–19)

Had these readers gone so far as to call themselves Christians, yet they doubted the truth of the resurrection of the dead? Yes, they said it was to be interpreted spiritually, not literally. They made it into a myth or fable, yet they called themselves Christians. It was normal for the heathen not to believe in the resurrection, but it was a strange thing that those who professed to believe that Christ had risen from the dead doubted the resurrection of his people, for Christ is their representative. Everything he did was for them. If Christ rose from the dead, all the members of his body will also rise. Prove that Christ rose, and you prove that his people rise, for they are one with him.

Yet it was proven by hundreds of credible witnesses that "Christ has been raised." Therefore the Corinthians were being illogical when they said, "There is no resurrection of the dead."

If Jesus Christ did not rise from the dead, we are preaching "useless" doctrine, and you are believing it. Our preaching and your faith evaporate if Christ did not come out of his tomb. Christianity stands or falls with the resurrection of its founder. Pull the resurrection away, and the whole structure of our faith crashes.

These were strong words, but not too strong. Paul seemed to say, "You know me to be an honest man. I have no selfish motive in what I declare to you. But if Christ did not rise from the dead, I have proclaimed a gross lie to you and led you to put your trust in a counterfeit. Therefore, Christ must have risen, for if he had not, you would have remained sinners as you once were."

Between Christ and his people there is a union that can never be broken. If he rose from the dead, they must rise. If we are one with him, who can drive a wedge between us? And if we cannot be separated, we must share everything with him. If Jesus did not rise "from the dead," the whole system of Christian thought crumbles into dust.

Paul put the emphasis on what Jesus is and not what we are. He did not say, "If you are not in a good moral condition" but "If Christ has not been raised." Our hope rests not in what we are spiritually but in what he is. When you are depressed and say to yourself, "I am afraid I am not really converted," continue to believe in him who rose from the dead. When you see your sins and feel as if you were lost, hold on to Christ, who loved you and gave himself for you and rose again from the dead for you. If we are to be saved, we must look beyond ourselves to Christ in faith.

If Jesus Christ has not risen, he has done nothing for you. You are unsaved, unforgiven, and unregenerate. Christianity is all a myth, all a piece of deceit. If we give up the fact that Christ rose from the dead, everything connected with salvation must be given up. Can you bear the thought that "you are still in your sins"?

You cannot be a Christian if you deny the resurrection of Christ. You must give up Christianity completely and confess that your faith in it was a delusion. Let it always be most clearly understood that what Christ is, his people are. There is an unbroken union between the head and the bodily members, so that if he lives, they live, and if they do not live, he does not live.

If Jesus did not rise, those who died resting in him were deceived and have found no advocate at the bar of God. They are therefore lost forever. Both nature and grace revolt against this statement. All the godly saints died resting in the risen Christ, but if he did not rise from the dead, they all died under a delusion and have now perished. If Christ were still dead in his grave, how could he give us life? If he did not rise, how could he raise believers who have died? They would still be lost.

We who believe in Christ are miserable dupes if he has not risen from the dead. We are believing and resting all our hopes on a lie. It makes us happy, but if you can take away our hope by persuading us that it is grounded on a lie, you have made us pitiful people. If we could lose a hope so brilliant as the resurrection of Christ, a sense of loss so great would fall on us that no one in the world could be as pitiful as we would be. Besides, if the apostles constantly lived in poverty, persecution, and the fear of martyrdom all for a lie, they were "to be pitied more than all men."

To be born into the Christian life, which gives great pain and sorrow, would be a miserable thing if it were not compensated by the hope of glory that we have in Christ. People who have always been poor can bear their poverty, but let them taste wealth and luxury for a while and then go back to poverty, and how keen is the pang they feel! In the same way, if we come alive in Christ and know God, yet then are told there is no resurrection, we are to be pitied more than all men.

There is an implied contrast to verse 19 that warns unbelievers. It is this: If in this life there is a genuine hope of a resurrection, unbelievers are to be pitied more than all people. Do you see where you will be in the next life? You will go before the great judge and be condemned to hell. In the name of my Lord and Master, I urge you to flee from your sins to Christ! Do not fling away eternity! Do not play the fool with such a solemn issue as this! Look to the bleeding Savior, trust him, and lay hold of eternal life!

But Christ has indeed been raised from the dead, the firstfruits of those who have fallen asleep. For since death came through a man, the resurrection of the dead comes also through a man. (20–21)

Paul had been arguing from every angle, and here he came back with his own positive witness that Christ was risen. You remember that Jesus died at the time of the Passover as the one great Passover lamb. But he rose again on the first day of the week. That was the Feast of Firstfruits with the Jews. They brought handfuls of wheat from the fields to show their gratitude to God and to receive a blessing on all their crops. Paul used Christ's rising on that particular day as a symbol. He lives and is "the firstfruits," so the full harvest will follow. All who are in him will rise from the dead, for he is one with them. No one can separate them from him. They died in him, and they live because he lives.

Christ must always come first, and here he is our "firstfruits." God's purpose is that "in everything he might have the supremacy" (Col. 1:18).

For as in Adam all die, so in Christ all will be made alive. But each in his own turn: Christ, the firstfruits; then, when he comes, those who belong to him. (22–23)

This does not mean that everyone will be saved but that "all" will be raised from the dead. Or this verse could mean that as all who were in the first Adam died as a result of his sin, so all who are in the last Adam, Christ, will live as the result of his righteousness. Are you in the last Adam? Faith unites you to him. If you are trusting in him by a living faith, his rising from the dead secures yours. If you have no living faith in Christ, you will rise, but only to shame and eternal contempt.

Then the end will come, when he hands over the kingdom to God the Father after he has destroyed all dominion, authority and power. For he must reign until he has put all his enemies under his feet. The last enemy to be destroyed is death. (24–26)

Why is it that Jesus "must reign" (v. 25)? First, because his reign over us is based on truth. Second, because it is based on love. Third, because it is the one remedy this sad world requires. The world will never rest until it rests in Christ. Fourth, Christ must reign because divine justice demands it. Fifth, Jesus must reign because he alone is fit to rule the world. No one can rival him. Finally, he must reign because the power to reign belongs to him alone. "All authority in heaven and on earth has been given to" Christ (Matt. 28:18).

How this ought to comfort us! If Christ must reign, then every soldier who fights for him is contributing to the victory. Everyone who advances the cause is working with sure and great results. You have not wasted those many silent prayers and bitter tears. Our foes are as tall as Goliath, as mighty as Pharaoh, and as proud as

Nebuchadnezzar, but in the name of Christ we will destroy them!

Does Christ reign in your heart? If not, you will find his reign as terrible as it is sure. He will reign over you, with or without your loving consent. Which will it be?

"Death" is well called an enemy (v. 26), for it does an enemy's work against us. Its goal is to destroy and kill us. The greatest conquerors have been only death's slaughtermen, apprentice butchers working in his shambles. War is nothing more than death holding carnival. Those who have stood around a fresh grave and buried half their hearts can tell you what an enemy death is. It takes the friend from your side, the child from your heart, and it cares nothing for your tears.

Why will death be "the last enemy to be destroyed"? Because Christ can make great use of it. Some of us have learned valuable lessons from death. It also gives us an opportunity to show our love for Christ. Love for Christ has triumphed most in the death of the martyrs who were burned at the stake and thrown to the lions. Death also allows us to be more conformed to Christ, because he died. Again, death is useful to our Lord, because it brings us home to heaven.

For he "has put everything under his feet." Now when it says that "everything" has been put under him, it is clear that this does not include God himself, who put everything under Christ. When he has done this, then the Son himself will be made subject to him who put everything under him, so that God may be all in all. (27–28)

To solve the great problem of sin, Jesus was appointed a mediator over the world. He will continue in that position until all his enemies are destroyed and sin is crushed under his feet. Then Christ—as mediator and not as Lord—will deliver up his kingdom to his Father. Then the great shout will be heard: "Hallelujah! For our Lord God almighty reigns!" (Rev. 19:6). Christ as God, as one of the divine persons of the Trinity, will still be as glorious as ever, but his reign as mediator will then be over, because he will have fulfilled all its purposes. Then we will rejoice in the God who is "all in all."

May God be our all in all even now in every hymn. Let us make God our all in all in our joy, our hope, and our thoughts. May God be all in all in all of us. May we all be redeemed, delivered from the power of sin, and summed up in Christ.

Now if there is no resurrection, what will those do who are baptized for the dead? If the dead are not raised at all, why are people baptized for them? (29)

This is a most difficult verse, and many meanings have been given to it. I think the most likely is this: As soon as a member of the early Christian church was given up to the lions or to the stake, another convert would step forward and say, "Let me take his name and place." Though it was almost certain that this person also would soon be put to death, there were always found people bold enough to come forward to be "baptized for the dead." But Paul was saying, "What advantage is there in heroism if the dead do not rise?"

And as for us, why do we endanger ourselves every hour? I die every day—I mean that, brothers—just as surely as I glory over you in Christ Jesus our Lord. If I fought wild beasts in Ephesus for merely human reasons, what have I gained? If the dead are not raised, "Let us eat and drink, for tomorrow we die." (30–32)

Why were the apostles always subjecting themselves to cruel persecution if there were no resurrection to look forward to? Suffering Christians are the greatest fools if there is no resurrection.

Paul was so hunted by his persecutors that there was not a day in which his life felt secure. So he asked, "Why should I endure all that if there is no world to come?"

In a physical sense we can all say with Paul, "I die daily." The moment we begin to live we begin to die. We are like hourglasses. There are fewer sands left to run from the very moment they begin to trickle down. This is not the land of the living but the land of the dying. This so-called life is just one protracted act of death. We fly like arrows to that common target of humanity—the grave.

But to die daily in a spiritual sense, we must come each day to the cross of Christ as poor guilty sinners and rest in him, just as we did at conversion. This will prepare us for the day of physical death. No one will find it hard to die who has died every day.

It was quite possible that Paul was thrown to the lions in the theater at Ephesus and that he fought with wild beasts there and defeated them. "But why," he asked, "did I try to save my life for future labor and suffering if the resurrection is a mere dream?"

If there is no resurrection, the philosophers of pleasure are right. If we are to come to an end when we die, let us enjoy life while we can. If it is to be a short life, let it be a happy one. You see to what a conclusion this theory would lead us, so let us jerk back from it in horror. The logical consequence convicts the statement of falsehood. There is a future state, and there is a resurrection of the body.

Do not be misled: "Bad company corrupts good character." Come back to your senses as you ought, and stop sinning; for there are some who are ignorant of God—I say this to your shame. (33-34)

Living among philosophical skeptics, the Corinthian Christians had learned to doubt. Paul here warned them of the danger of such "bad company." He also rebuked them for bringing "shame" on their holy faith by calling into question the fundamental teaching of the resurrection. God save us from the bad company that "corrupts good character."

But someone may ask, "How are the dead raised? With what kind of body will they come?" How foolish! What you sow does not come to life unless it dies. When you sow, you do not plant the body that will be, but just a seed, perhaps of wheat or of something else. But God gives it a body as he has determined, and to each kind of seed he gives its own body. All flesh is not the same: Men have one kind of flesh, animals have another, birds another and fish another. There are also heavenly bodies and there are earthly bodies; but the splendor of the heavenly bodies is one kind, and the splendor of the earthly bodies is another. The sun has one kind of splendor, the moon another and the stars another; and star differs from star in splendor. (35-41)

Paul seemed at first to have lost his patience in answering this question. He called the person "foolish" who asked, "How are the dead raised?" The questioner was implying that a dead body decays and cannot be raised again. Once you grant the existence of God, you need never ask, "How?" Almighty God can do what he wants, and they are fools who ask "How?" after they have believed in God.

Would you take the seed into your hand and begin to argue, "How can that little seed ever become a flower?" Could you guess, apart from observation, what kind of flower would come out of that seed? You would make a hundred foolish guesses if you tried. So it is concerning the resurrection of the body. In due time we will know, but until then we must wait and trust.

Here you have a plant three feet high, bearing many grains of wheat. The other day you had a little shriveled grain, yet no one doubts that the two are the same. That is the way it will be in the resurrection. The body we have now is a shriveled seed. There is no beauty in it. It is put in the grave like wheat sown in the earth. There it rots and decays, but God preserves in it a life germ that is immortal, and when the trumpet of the archangel sounds, it will expand to the full flower of humanity and blossom from the earth a far more glorious form than the humanity that was buried.

We cannot tell by looking at a seed what the plant will look like. Neither can we tell by looking at our present bodies what we will look like in glory. How lovely is the flower compared to the shriveled grain! How beautiful will our bodies be in comparison with these trembling frames!

As all these things differ from each other, so will the resurrection body differ from the body we now live in. It will be the same body as to identity, yet it will be far improved "in splendor."

So will it be with the resurrection of the dead. The body that is sown is perishable, it is raised imperishable; it is sown in dishonor, it is raised in glory; it is sown in weakness, it is raised in power; it is sown a natural body, it is raised a spiritual body. (42–44)

We are like crawling caterpillars—a creature that eats and drinks and is easily stepped on. In a few weeks that caterpillar will spin itself a shroud, lie down, become inactive, and sleep. That is a picture of what we will do. We will spin our winding sheet and be laid in a grave. But after a while the corpse will burst its sheath. The chrysalis will fall off and the insect will fly out equipped with glittering wings. So will we, after passing through our wormlike state here to our chrysalis condition in the grave, burst our caskets and mount up like the angels in heaven.

No matter how much honor we pay to our departed loved ones, it is a "dishonor" to them to have to lie encased in a casket in the cold dirt of a cemetery. Their bodies are "sown in weakness" in that they cannot get into their own resting places but must tenderly be laid there by others.

If there is a natural body, there is also a spiritual body. So it is written: "The first man Adam became a living being"; the last Adam, a life-giving spirit. The spiritual did not come first, but the natural, and after that the spiritual. The first man was of the dust of the earth, the second man from heaven. As was the earthly man, so are those who are of the earth; and as is the man from heaven, so also are those who are of heaven. And just as we have borne the likeness of the earthly man, so shall we bear the likeness of the man from heaven. (44–49)

The spiritual body is the one fitted for the new spirit we receive when we experience new life in Christ. As the first Adam was the representative of the human race when he sinned in the Garden of Eden, so Christ, "the last Adam," is our covenant head. Whatever Christ did was for the whole body of his church. We were "crucified with Christ" (Gal. 2:20). We were "buried with him . . . and raised with him" (Col. 2:12). As if that weren't enough, God has "seated us with him in the heavenly realms" (Eph. 2:6). In these ways God has "made us accepted in the beloved" (Eph. 1:6 KJV), namely, in Christ.

You and I have every evidence that we are "of the earth." But we also belong to Christ through faith in him, and already the heavenly light has begun to shine on us. We are getting ready soon to put on the clothes of immortality.

The head and the members share the same nature. They are not like the monstrous image that Nebuchadnezzar saw in his dream. Its "head . . . was made of pure gold, its chest and arms of silver, its belly and thighs of bronze, its legs of iron, its feet partly of iron and partly of baked clay" (Dan. 2:32-33). Christ's mystical body is no absurd combination of opposites. The members were mortal, and therefore Jesus died. The glorified head is immortal, and therefore the body is immortal too. Thus the record stands, "Because I live, you also will live" (John 14:19).

A chosen head and chosen members. An accepted head and accepted members. A living head and living members. If the head is pure gold, all the parts of the body are pure gold also. When we think of how far Jesus stooped to unite our wretched condition to his glory, how can we fail to be amazed?

I declare to you, brothers, that flesh and blood cannot inherit the kingdom of God, nor does the perishable inherit the imperishable. Listen, I tell you a mystery: We will not all sleep, but we will all be changed—in a flash, in the twinkling of an eye, at the last trumpet. For the trumpet will sound, the dead will be raised imperishable, and we will be changed. For the perishable must clothe itself with the imperishable, and the mortal with immortality. When the perishable has been clothed with the imperishable, and the mortal with immortality, then the saying that is written will come true: "Death has been swallowed up in victory. Where, O death, is your victory? Where, O death, is your sting?" The sting of death is sin, and the power of sin is the law. But thanks be to God! He gives us the victory through our Lord Jesus Christ. (50–57)

We will not all die, for some will be alive when Christ returns to this earth, but "we will all be changed," if not by the process of death, by some other means. Those who are alive when Jesus comes must undergo a transformation before they can enter heaven. "We will be changed."

There is no sting left in death for the believer. As for its aches and pains and groans, we know that all these things work together for our good (Rom. 8:28). As for its gloom and horror, we know that since Christ is with us, we will walk through the valley of the shadow of death and fear no evil (Ps. 23:4). When death robs us of the sights of earth, we gain the sights of heaven. When death closes our ears, they open to the music of heaven's angels. Do we lose by losing earth? No, for in gaining heaven the loss is all forgotten!

Sin puts a sting into death because sin brought death into the world. People would be more content to die if they knew it was not a punishment. Also, "the sting of death is sin" because unforgiven sin makes death terrible.

Before you can destroy sin, you must somehow satisfy the law. Since "the law is spiritual" (Rom. 7:14), it is impossible for us to live without sin. If the Law related simply to overt acts, I question even then if we could live without sin. But when I read in the Ten Commandments, "You shall not covet" (Ex. 20:17), I know it refers even to the wish of my heart. Our very thoughts are crimes. Thus has the Law put potency in sin.

Again, "the power of sin is the law," because the law says to everyone who breaks it, "I will not forgive you." For every transgression the Law has a punishment.

Observe what Paul did not say: "Let us cry our hearts out. Let us throw down our weapons. It is no use to continue our spiritual warfare, for we must all die." No! Instead, he wrote, "Thanks be to God! He gives us the victory through our Lord Jesus Christ."

How does our Lord Jesus give us the victory over sin? First, he has removed the Law. "You are not under law, but under grace" (Rom. 6:14). The principles of do or be punished and do and be rewarded are not the motives of a Christian's life. Our principle is God has done so much for me; what can I do for him?

Second, Jesus gives us the victory over sin in that he has completely satisfied the Law. The Law demands a perfect righteousness. Christ says, "Law, try to find fault with me. I am the sinner's substitute. Haven't I perfectly kept your commandments?"

The assurance of our victory in Christ gives us confidence beyond the grave. At Stratford-on-Bow, in the days of Queen Mary, a stake was erected for the burning of two martyrs, one of them a lame man and the other a blind man. One said to the other, "Be brave, brother. This fire will cure us both!" So can the righteous say of the grave, "I will bravely endure it, for it will cure me of all my infirmities!"

Therefore, my dear brothers, stand firm. Let nothing move you. Always give yourselves fully to the work of the Lord, because you know that your labor in the Lord is not in vain. (58)

Stand firm in your doctrine. Hold the truth of the resurrection with an iron grip. Stand firm in holiness. Stand firm in your faith. Temptations will come, but stand firm! Do not be moved from your faith by the world's persecutions or its smiles. God help you to be faithful to death. "Let nothing" of the world's customs "move you." It is sad when professors of our holy faith begin to live like people of this world.

Every Christian should be involved in "the work of the Lord." What are you doing for Jesus Christ? If nothing, repent of your laziness and escape from it, for talents wrapped in pieces of cloth will be terrible witnesses against you (Luke 19:20). If you serve the Lord, don't become proud, but remember that it is the work of the Lord rather than our own work. Whatever we accomplish is achieved by the Lord in us. As Jesus said, "Apart from me you can do nothing" (John 15:5).

What confidence we who trust in Christ may have! Paul said, "You know." What gives us this confidence? The knowledge that Christ has risen and we will rise with him. The Lord's people may die, but his church never dies. The Lord himself, the ever-living one, is always with us! This confidence that our "labor in the Lord is not in vain" should be the practical outcome of receiving the great truths of this chapter. God grant that it may be so in our lives!

Every Spiritual Blessing in Christ

IN THIS CHAPTER WE find the Christian's true Promised Land of spiritual blessings. May we have faith enough to enter into full possession of it. Here we find the possessions and privileges of those who believe in the Lord Jesus Christ.

Paul, an apostle of Christ Jesus by the will of God,
  To the saints in Ephesus, the faithful in Christ Jesus. (1)

Paul was not made an "apostle" by any human being, nor did he take the office on himself. He became "an apostle of Christ Jesus by the will of God."

This is written not just "to the saints in Ephesus" but to everyone who is "faithful in Christ Jesus."

Grace and peace to you from God our Father and the Lord Jesus Christ. (2)

The wish of the apostle and the will of God is that we abound in "grace and peace." Your mind may be filled with anxiety, yet our Lord says to you, "Peace I leave with you; my peace I give you" (John 14:27). God knew that you would have trials, but he willed that in Christ you would have peace.

There is no peace apart from grace. First grace changes us; then peace quiets us. As we read in Isaiah 57:21, "'There is no peace,' says my God, 'for the wicked.'" Those who have peace that does not own grace as its parent have a false peace. Only when we have God's grace do we have the right to enjoy his peace.

Praise be to the God and Father of our Lord Jesus Christ, who has blessed us in the heavenly realms with every spiritual blessing in Christ. (3)

When we view God the Father properly, he becomes the object not of our dread but of our praise. How dear the Father is when we view him in association with our Lord Jesus Christ. The saints seem to delight most in God when they see him that way. Then he is inexpressibly lovely to us, and we preach him with joy and delight.

It is right that we should praise God, because he has so richly blessed us. Well may we praise him with our feeble thanks who has blessed us with his mighty mercies! Nothing makes people praise God like God blessing them.

How has God blessed us? "With every spiritual blessing in Christ." We have nothing apart from Christ, but we have "every spiritual blessing in Christ." We have not only some blessings but all we want. We are as rich as Christ is when we are united to him by the living bond of faith. We have no need—either in time or in eternity—that God cannot meet in Christ. There is no blessing outside of Christ. If you want to be blessed, you must come to Christ for your blessing. There is nothing but spiritual deprivation in this world, but "every spiritual blessing in Christ" is found "in the heavenly realms." The phrase "every blessing" suggests that we do not have one blessing that God did not give us in Christ. We could never earn or create one blessing on our own.

For he chose us in him before the creation of the world to be holy and blameless in his sight. (4)

This is the first of all God's blessings to us. Paul did not ignore the doctrine of election. He delighted to meditate on it and speak of it. I am sorry that some Christians are afraid of it. This is the fountain from which the living waters flow. There would have been no stream of blessing to us if it had not been for this first primeval choice of us by God. As Jesus said to his disciples, "You did not choose me, but I chose you" (John 15:16).

Did the Lord choose me "before the creation of the world"? Then I choose him with all my heart to be my Lord and my all. Did he love me that long ago? Then I will love him with all my soul and strength, and I will pray that my heart may be enlarged to love him more.

We were chosen not because we were holy but that we might "be holy." God's purpose will not be fulfilled until we are holy. If you do not have a holy character, you cannot talk of being chosen in Christ. Holiness is the most noble goal for which we could have been elected. Isn't it the highest of our hearts' desires "to be holy and blameless in his sight"? Then why does any Christian quarrel with the doctrine of election?

I have met people who say they are perfectly holy, but I believe they are under a delusion. No doubt those who know them do not think they are perfect. We make no claims to be holy and blameless in our own sight, but through Christ God has made us holy and blameless in his sight. It would be something to be "blameless" before the Devil, as Job was (Job 1:8-11). It would also be something to be perfect in the eyes of people who are ready to criticize us. But to be holy and blameless in his sight whose eyes read our thoughts is a far higher accomplishment. Only God can do this for us, and only through Christ. So our "praise" (v. 3) belongs to him.

In love he predestined us to be adopted as his sons through Jesus Christ, in accordance with his pleasure and will. (4-5)

Many believe in the universal fatherhood of God, but here we see that God has "adopted" us "through Jesus Christ." Parents do not adopt their own natural children. By nature we are "children of wrath" (Eph. 2:3 KJV), not children of God. Still, when God adopts us, we can cry, "Abba, Father" (Gal. 4:6) just as much as if we were his natural sons and daughters! That is because we not only have the name of God's children but also "participate in the divine nature" (2 Peter 1:4).

When children are adopted, they are released from the old family they left behind. In the same way, the moment we are taken out of Satan's family, he is no longer our father and we are no longer his sons and daughters. We are God's children.

We hear much about the free will of men and women, but this verse speaks of the free will of God. You would think from the talk of some that God is our debtor and must do everything according to our will. That is not so. He is a sovereign who gives his grace where he chooses, and he wants us to know that our adoption is the result of his predestination. It is based not on our merits but "in accordance with his pleasure and will." Romans 9:15 is still true: "I will have mercy on whom I have mercy, and I will have compassion on whom I have compassion."

People do not like the doctrine of predestination. It galls them terribly, but there is little gospel preached when predestination is denied. God is the King who will sit on his throne, and no one will drag him from it. We marvel that some of us should be regarded in error because we preach predestination, for in former times the opponents of that glorious doctrine were labeled heretics. Turn to all the great creeds in church history, and you will find predestination mentioned. It is the glory of the church that it has a Calvinistic creed.

To the praise of his glorious grace, which he has freely given us in the One he loves. (6)

No truth is more plainly taught in Scripture than the salvation of sinners being entirely dependent on the "grace" of God. What a wonderful expression is used here—not only "grace," not only "glorious grace," but "to the praise of his glorious grace." Every attribute of God has its glory. God's justice is glorious, and we sometimes tremble to think how awfully glorious it is in the lowest pit of hell. But here we read of "his glorious grace."

Grace is glorious if we consider its antiquity. It is not a piece of new cloth put on an old garment. Grace is not a change in God's original plan. It was born in eternity past and will reign in the eternal future. God's grace is also glorious in that it never changes. Even the sun and the oceans change, but grace never has and never will. Again, God's grace is glorious in its freeness. It is as free as the air we breathe. If you ask whether you may believe in Christ, I answer that you not only may, but God commands you to believe.

Three words in this sixth verse have the same thrust: "grace . . . freely given." Some say this is redundant. So it is, but it is a blessed redundancy, for it makes the meaning emphatically clear. We feel no regret in ringing such a silver bell three times: "Grace . . . freely given"! So that no one will think that grace can be earned, we will continue to say not only "grace," not only "free grace," but, "grace freely given"! Since God's grace is freely given, there is nothing to prevent you from having it.

This grace is never given apart from Christ. God does not deal with you as an individual but only "in the One he loves." Everyone in God's family is loved, but Christ is "the One he loves."

In him we have redemption through his blood, the forgiveness of sins, in accordance with the riches of God's grace that he lavished on us with all wisdom and understanding. (7–8)

Here the apostle insisted that we have both "redemption" and "forgiveness of sins" only in Christ. His five wounds are the sacred fountains from which a world of blessing flows to needy sinners. No one but Christ can bless us.

This is one of twelve times in this chapter that Paul wrote, "in him" or "in Christ" or "in the Lord Jesus." We can look at it in several different ways. First, we are in Christ's heart. When we fell in Adam, we did not fall out of Christ, for even then he loved us. Second, we are in Christ's book. Because our names are recorded there, we will not be thrown into the lake of fire (Rev. 20:15). Third, we are in Christ's hand. He has said of us, "I give them eternal life, and they shall never perish; no one can snatch them out of my hand" (John 10:28). Fourth, we are in Christ's person, for we are members of his body (1 Cor. 12:27). What a breathtaking thought—we are in Christ! How sad, then, is the state of those outside of Christ.

The proof of our being in Christ is spiritual fruit, for Christians are represented as being in Christ as the branch is in the vine (John 15:5). Do you love Christ? Do you want to be like him? People in Christ say, "Yes!"

Paul's fondness for the theme of us being in Christ shows that he did not have a teaching apart from Christ. He did not mention a single blessing or a single mercy without the Lord Jesus. I believe there is no way of preaching gospel doctrines apart from the Master. In the first century if you had asked one of Christ's disciples what he believed, he would have pointed to Christ and said, "I believe in him." Let us then also always trace our mercies to Jesus and look upon every blessing as being purchased by his blood.

We are no longer in bondage but in Christ. How was our "redemption" secured? "Through his blood." What is the result? "Forgiveness of sins." What is the measure of our liberty? "In accordance with the riches of God's grace."

If you want to see the riches of God's grace, read the Father's heart when he sent his Son to earth to die. Read the lines on the Father's face when he poured his wrath on his beloved Son. Look at others who have been saved, though they scoffed at their mothers' love, would not be melted by their mothers' prayers, and wished only to commit more and more sin. Some of these prodigals are our finest preachers of the gospel today! So no one out of hell has sinned too much for "the riches of God's grace" to save.

God does not drown us with floods of his grace but hands it out to us as we are able to take it in its lavishness. We have the riches of his grace, but God uses "all wisdom and understanding" while he teaches us little by little as we grow. He raises us by degrees up from one level of grace to another, as our poor bodies can endure the joy.

And he made known to us the mystery of his will according to his good pleasure, which he purposed in Christ, to be put into effect when the times will have reached their fulfillment—to bring all things in heaven and on earth together under one head, even Christ. (9–10)

Even the knowledge of "his will" is "made known to us . . . according to his good pleasure." If your eyes have been divinely opened, you will see the will of God coming in everywhere and ordering all things to his gracious and unerring purpose.

There are things in Christ "in heaven" and things in Christ "on earth," and "all" of them will be gathered "together." None will be left out. There will be no failure on any point. Believing Jews will no longer be divided from believing Gentiles. Today the church is separated—disfigured and weakened by sects and parties—but it will not always be so. All the redeemed will come as one great host to bow before the throne of the infinite Majesty.

We should remember that God's glory is a greater object than even our salvation. God gave his Son not so much to save us as to honor himself and glorify his Son. The gospel has for its chief aim the glory of all God's attributes.

Some foolish people have twisted verse 10 to prove the absurd doctrine of the salvation of all the lost. They have said that even the fallen angels in hell will be restored. We do not find that in this text, for it speaks only of "all things in heaven and on earth" but not in hell. Once we die, our destiny can never be changed.

In him we were also chosen, having been predestined according to the plan of him who works out everything in conformity with the purpose of his will, in order that we, who were the first to hope in Christ, might be for the praise of his glory. (11–12)

God not only has a will, but also he "works out everything in conformity" with it. Part of that will is that we have "been predestined." Some people are dreadfully afraid of that word *predestined,* but the apostle loved to harp on this theme. It is to be wisely handled, but it is not to be gagged and set in a corner, as some do. There is no truth in Scripture that should not be taught. If we keep back any precious truth of God's Word, we will be held accountable on the Judgment Day.

Predestination boils down to this: God is King, and he will have his divine will. He rules and reigns and will do so in our world. All of God's loyal subjects want him to rule. Whether or not you want that, the Lord will reign.

The early Christians "were the first to hope in Christ." They led the way in front of God's army, and still today they are "for the praise of his glory." Now we follow them as they followed Christ.

It appears that God's predestination deals not just with salvation but also with its details. Its ultimate purpose is "that we . . . might be for the praise of his glory." Paul did not say, "that we might sing for his glory" or "that we might suffer for his glory" or "that we might work for his glory" but "that we . . . might be for the praise of his glory." Our very existence is to praise him.

And you also were included in Christ when you heard the word of truth, the gospel of your salvation. Having believed, you were marked in him with a seal, the promised Holy Spirit, who is a deposit guaranteeing our inheritance until the redemption of those who are God's possession—to the praise of his glory. (13–14)

First we "heard the word of truth," then we "believed" in Christ, and then God gave us "the promised Holy Spirit" to live in our hearts. The Spirit is God's "seal." The Holy Spirit does not bring the seal with him; he is the seal. Where he lives, the seal of God's love is found.

Many people crave something to see or feel before they will believe in Jesus, but God will not put his mark on a blank piece of paper. There must be the writing of faith on the heart, then the Spirit comes in as God's seal.

Even our sealing is "in him," that is, in Christ. In John 6:27 we read of Christ, "On him God the Father has placed his seal of approval." Since our sealing is in Christ, it must be the same sealing he had. The seal put on our Lord was God's Spirit. So it must be with us. We cannot be known by our fellow Christians except by the possession of the Spirit of God.

In light of this, let us remember Ephesians 4:30: "And do not grieve the Holy Spirit of God, with whom you were sealed for the day of redemption." If you are not a Christian, do not look for seals. Your only business is to seek Christ, not seals.

The Holy Spirit is first God's "seal" and then his "deposit." This is different from a pledge. A pledge is given and then taken back when the condition is carried out. But a deposit is part of the full price to be paid. The person who receives a deposit gets a few dollars on Thursday instead of taking all his pay on Saturday. The worker never returns the deposit; it is part of the wage. And so the Holy Spirit is part of Christ. When we have the Spirit, we have Christ.

In verse 14 heaven is described as "our inheritance." An inheritance cannot be purchased with money, earned by labor, or won by conquest. It comes to us by birth. People receive their inheritances not because of any special merit in them but because they are the sons or daughters of parents who have given it to them. So it is with heaven. We cannot obtain it by obeying God's law or trying to be good. It is given to us graciously when we are born into God's family through faith in Christ.

In verse 12 Paul spoke of "the praise of his glory," and now here again in verse 14. In verse 6 he also said, "to the praise of his glorious grace." The true gospel glorifies God.

For this reason, ever since I heard about your faith in the Lord Jesus and your love for all the saints, I have not stopped giving thanks for you, remembering you in my prayers. I keep asking that the God of our Lord Jesus Christ, the glorious Father, may give you the Spirit of wisdom and revelation, so that you may know him better. I pray also that the eyes of your heart may be enlightened in order that you may know the hope to which he has called you, the riches of his glorious inheritance in the saints, and his incomparably great power for us who believe. That power is like the working of his mighty strength, which he exerted in Christ when he raised him from the dead and seated him at his right hand in the heavenly realms, far above all rule and authority, power and dominion, and every title that can be given, not only in the present age but also in the one to come. And God placed all things under his feet and appointed him to be head over everything for the church, which is his body, the fullness of him who fills everything in every way. (15–23)

Is this the way we pray? Do we give thanks for people in our prayers? It is good to do that. It is a good plan to keep a list of people for whom we ought to pray and to put it before us and go over the names when we draw near to God. I know one man who has kept a debtor and creditor list with God for many years. He puts his requests down in the book, and when they are answered, he puts that down. If they are not answered, he repeats the prayers. It is a wonderful book.

He told me there is one name of a person for whom he has prayed who is still unconverted and that out of many for whom he began to pray, only this one man has not yet trusted in Christ. My friend prays on with the same confidence that this man will be converted that I have that Christmas will come in December. I wish we did business with God that way. Our prayers are too shadowy. God, teach us how to pray!

As a Christian you already know Christ. Now God wants you to "know him better." You can scarcely have a higher privilege than that. The knowledge of Christ crucified is the most excellent of all sciences. It is better to be well acquainted with Christ than to be a very Solomon concerning all other things and not know him.

God has given you "eyes" in "your heart." Divine things are seen better by your heart than by your physical eyes or your mind. When you put the telescope of faith over the eyes of your heart, you can see much more than you have ever seen.

What are some examples of our "hope"? We expect a stormy voyage in this world, but because Christ is at the helm, we "hope" that all things will work together for our good. We expect to be slandered, but we hope to be cleared. We expect to be tried, but we hope to triumph. We expect to stand at the judgment seat of Christ, but we hope to receive a perfect justification and enjoy eternal happiness in heaven.

The second reality that God wants us to know is that he makes "riches" out of poor sinners, by pouring his rich love on them, investing his infinite wisdom in them, and spending a life of suffering on them. The third reality God wants us to know is that it takes nothing less than "his incomparably great power" both to make a believer and to sustain a believer.

See how high Christ is raised! The same power that "raised him from the dead and seated him at his right hand in the heavenly places" works for the salvation of every believer. Nothing less than omnipotence at its very best in the glorification of Christ is needed for the securing of our salvation.

The "rule" here may refer to angels, and the "authority" to demons. Good angels have no glory compared to Christ, and demons have no power to resist him. Our Lord is not only "above" them but "far above" both the angels and the demons. And so are we! As for angels, they are "ministering spirits sent to serve those who will inherit salvation" (Heb. 1:14). And as for demons, "the God of peace will soon crush Satan under your feet" (Rom. 16:20). So in Christ we are "far above all rule and authority."

We rejoice to think that our sins are under Christ's feet! He "will tread our sins underfoot" (Mic. 7:19).

When Christ is our "head over everything," we become wonders of grace. What a "glorious inheritance" (v. 18) Christ will have when the church all over the world operates as one, because Christ is our head!

The church's highest honor is that until Christ is finally united to us, he considers himself in some measure incomplete, for what "head" (v. 22) is complete without its "body"? If the very least believer will be absent on the final day, Christ will be maimed. All the sheep of the Good Shepherd will be gathered into the heavenly fold. We rejoice to know there is such a connection as this between ourselves and Christ. It is our glory, our boast, and our trust.

Do you belong to those to whom Paul spoke in this chapter? At the start he addressed "the faithful in Christ Jesus"—that is, those full of faith in Christ. If you are trusting completely in the Lord Jesus, all the privileges mentioned in this chapter belong to you.

Christ Is Supreme Over All Things

Paul, an apostle of Christ Jesus by the will of God, and Timothy our brother,
To the holy and faithful brothers in Christ at Colosse:
Grace and peace to you from God our Father. (1–2)

Kindness is the very breath of Christianity, so the apostle did not begin his subject until he wished the Colossian Christians the best of all blessings. It is the very spirit of our holy faith to wish others God's blessing, and I am sure we cannot have a better wish for our dearest friends than "grace and peace."

Grace will save you, and peace will make you know you are saved. Grace is the root of every blessing; peace is the sweet flower that makes life so fragrant. May you have both of these blessings "from God our Father" and thus know your adoption and redemption.

We always thank God, the Father of our Lord Jesus Christ, when we pray for you, because we have heard of your faith in Christ Jesus and of the love you have for all the saints—the faith and love that spring from the hope that is stored up for you in heaven and that you have already heard about in the word of truth, the gospel that has come to you. All over the world this gospel is bearing fruit and growing, just as it has been doing among you since the day you heard it and understood God's grace in all its truth. You learned it from Epaphras, our dear fellow servant, who is a faithful minister of Christ on our behalf, and who also told us of your love in the Spirit. (3–8)

Paul graciously blended his giving of thanks and his constant prayer for these Christians. Let us imitate his example. Let us also not only pray for those who have no faith but allow the presence of faith in believers to lead us to pray for them. Where there is life in the seed, and it begins to sprout, let us water it with our prayers and thanks.

Here are the three sisters—"faith . . . love . . . hope"—that should always go hand in hand. We must never be satisfied unless we see in ourselves and in our fellow Christians these three delightful fruits of the Spirit of God. Note the order here: faith, love, then hope. Perhaps the Colossians were a little deficient in this last grace, so the apostle prayed constantly for their hope, because faith and love would spring from it. When we were lost in sin, Satan came and wrote over the doorposts of our hearts, "No Hope," for we were "without hope and without God in the world" (Eph. 2:12).

If there is a way of knowing God's grace in vain, it is when it is not known in truth. That is, when a person has only head knowledge and not heart knowledge. But when the grace of God sinks into the soul and changes a person's nature, it is an experience for which we may well give thanks to God.

We know the grace of God in truth when it yields spiritual fruit in us. We do not really know it unless it affects our lives and produces faith, love, and hope. That is, faith that lifts us above the world, love that prevents selfishness, and hope that keeps us from discouragement in all our trials.

I like to read of godly men like Paul and Epaphras speaking well of each other. In our day it is thought to be a distinguishing mark of faithfulness to be able to pick holes in the coats of our fellow Christians. We cannot help perceiving their defects, and sometimes it is our duty to confront them faithfully, but let us also observe all the virtues that are to be found in them. Otherwise we may despise the work of the Holy Spirit and rob him of his glory.

How kindly Paul spoke of Epaphras, and how kindly Epaphras spoke of the church at Colosse! He first told them of Paul's prayers for them, and when he came back from Colosse, he told Paul of their great love in the Spirit.

For this reason, since the day we heard about you, we have not stopped praying for you and asking God to fill you with the knowledge of his will through all spiritual wisdom and understanding. And we pray this in order that you may live a life worthy of the Lord and may please him in every way: bearing fruit in every good work, growing in the knowledge of God, being strengthened with all power according to his glorious might so that you may have great endurance and patience, and joyfully giving thanks to the Father, who has qualified you to share in the inheritance of the saints in the kingdom of light. For he has rescued us from the dominion of darkness and brought us into the king-

dom of the Son he loves, in whom we have redemption, the forgiveness of sins. (9–14)

The apostle asked for them something more than even faith, love, and hope. He prayed that they might be filled with the knowledge of God's will. This shows how valuable it is to know and understand the will of God.

If you have the graces of the Spirit, it is important that they should be deepened and should grow by being fed with divine nourishment. As water helps a plant grow, so knowledge of God's will causes our gifts and graces to develop. They grow and become fruitful as we understand more and more what God delights to do and what he wants us to do.

Mark the positive tones in which the apostle wrote. There are no uncertainties here. Concerning eternal matters, nothing but certainties will do for us. Allow uncertainties about your estates if you will, but we must have positive assurance about eternal things. Nothing short of this will satisfy our spirits. Can you say, "God has rescued me from the dominion of darkness and brought me into the kingdom of the Son he loves, in whom I have redemption, the forgiveness of sins"?

Being rescued from the "dominion" or power of sin is just as much the work of God as being saved from the guilt of sin. If God has rescued us from the "dominion of darkness," he will certainly help us in our daily trials.

Here the apostle was handling the string he most delighted to touch. He was at home with everything that concerns the welfare of saints, but when he began to talk of his Lord and Master, he seemed to ride in a chariot of fire with horses of fire, and he grew eloquent under the inspiration of the Spirit of God.

He is the image of the invisible God, the firstborn over all creation. For by him all things were created: things in heaven and on earth, visible and invisible, whether thrones or powers or rulers or authorities; all things were created by him and for him. He is before all things, and in him all things hold together. And he is the head of the body, the church. He is the beginning and the firstborn from among the dead, so that in everything he might have the supremacy. For God was pleased to have all his fullness dwell in him, and through him to reconcile to himself all things, whether things on earth or things in heaven, by making peace through his blood, shed on the cross. (15–20)

Notice how Paul harped on one string—Christ. See how much he focused on the divine person of the blessed Lord Jesus. He could never praise Christ enough. He kept heaping up glorious titles to magnify the blessed name. Paul truly was in the Spirit of God when he did this, for it is the work of the Spirit to bring glory to Jesus Christ. As our Lord himself said of the Spirit, "He will bring glory to me" (John 16:14). The Holy Spirit does that by making Christ great in our hearts and then by enabling us to make him great by our words and acts.

How can anyone read these verses and say that Christ Jesus is only human? By what twisting of words can such language as this be applied to the most eminent prophet or apostle who ever lived? Surely he must be God by whom all things were created and by whom all things hold together.

This is to us the sweetest of Paul's words in this chapter. The head is necessary for the body to live. "Christ . . . is your life" (Col. 3:4). "In him was life, and that life was the light of men" (John 1:4). So separation from Christ is spiritual death. Without him the church is a corpse, deprived of all its glory. The head gives orders to the body. Each of us should ask, "Am I yielding my obedience to my head, Jesus Christ?"

Are we giving Christ the supremacy in all things? Our theology must be false if it puts Jesus in second place or even lower than that. Our experience is wrong if it does not always put Christ in the forefront. In all things he must always stand first.

If all God's fullness dwells in Christ, why are we so weak and unhappy? Christ's fullness allows us to rise to the heights of grace. I delight to think that God's fullness is placed in Christ, because he delights to receive sinners. Perhaps the sweetest thought is that "all his fullness" is fitly placed in Christ, because he alone is able to distribute it to each one of us. Let our praises remain where his fullness remains.

As the sun is to be seen mirrored not only in the face of the water but in every little drop of dew that hangs on each blade of grass, so is the glory of Christ to be seen not only in his universal church but in every separate individual in whom his Spirit has wrought holiness.

Once you were alienated from God and were enemies in your minds because of your evil behavior. But now he has reconciled you by Christ's physical body through death to present you holy in his sight, without blemish and free from accusation—if you continue in your faith, established and firm, not moved from the hope held out in the gospel. This is the gospel that you heard and that has been proclaimed to every creature under heaven, and of which I, Paul, have become a servant. (21–23)

This is a verse that ought to be read and pondered every day by the many unstable professing Christians in the church: "if you continue in your faith, established and firm," like a building wall that will have no further settlements, no more moving of the stones, no more cracking of the walls, because your foundation is secure, and you are firmly built on it.

The "hope held out in the gospel" is the hope of full salvation, of resurrection, of the return of Christ, and of being with him forever. The ground of that hope is the grace of God, the merit of Christ, and the promise that "whoever believes in him shall not perish but have eternal life" (John 3:16).

How delighted Paul was to have such a gospel to preach and such a hope to proclaim! If you had to creep from a sickbed or come up from a dungeon, if you were aching in every bone of your body, and if you were depressed in soul, this ought to be enough to make you overflow with joy, that we have such a Christ to preach and such a fullness of blessing to declare to humanity.

How blessed is the person who has so mastered self that suffering for fellow Christians becomes a matter of rejoicing! That believer not only accepts suffering and bears it patiently, but he or she says:

Now I rejoice in what was suffered for you, and I fill up in my flesh what is still lacking in regard to Christ's afflictions, for the sake of his body, which is the church. I have become its servant by the commission God gave me to present to you the word of God in its fullness—the mystery that has been kept hidden for ages and generations, but is now disclosed to the saints. To them God has chosen to make known among the Gentiles the glorious riches of this mystery, which is Christ in you, the hope of glory. (24–27)

There is nothing "lacking" in the atoning work of Christ's sufferings, but there is much yet to be endured so that all the elect may be brought to Christ. Some must suffer through extraordinary labors in preaching the gospel, others through bearing reproach for the truth's sake. Paul was glad to take in his mortal body his share of the sufferings to be endured for the sake of Christ's mystical body, the church.

The King James Version says in this verse that Paul was "made a minister." What a wonderful expression! The true minister is of God's making. A self-made minister must be a poor creature, but a God-made minister will prove his calling.

"Christ in you" is glory begun, a sure pledge and down payment of a glory greater than you can ever conceive. If Christ is in you, you have the beginnings of heaven. You have the excellence and flower of heaven, for there is no heaven but the glory of Christ. "Christ in you" means Christ accepted by faith, Christ experienced in all his power, Christ reigning in your heart, Christ filling your personality, Christ seeking sinners through you, Christ comforting believers through you, and Christ working through you.

We proclaim him, admonishing and teaching everyone with all wisdom, so that we may present everyone perfect in Christ. To this end I labor, struggling with all his energy, which so powerfully works in me. (28–29)

It is not so much what we proclaim as whom we proclaim—Jesus. We preach not just salvation but a living Savior.

Perfection is absolutely necessary for all who hope to enter heaven. We may have lost perfection through sin, but that does not alter God's demand for it. It may be impossible for us to reach perfection in ourselves, but God demands perfection all the same. Our only hope is to be "perfect in Christ."

The realization of this truth gives us the greatest sense of peace. Why be down in spirits when we are perfect in Christ? Though the wind may blow between the rags that cover us, if we can say, "I am perfect in Christ," we can be content with poverty. Though we are in pain and tossing in bed, if we can say, "I am perfect in Jesus," it will be like medicine to soothe our spirits. And when grim death appears, we need only look him in the face and say, "I am perfect in Christ," and death will change into an angel, pain will be turned into bliss, and sorrow into immortal glory.

If God's people strive mightily, it is because God works mightily in them. Nothing can come out of people except what God puts in them. We work to will and to do when he works in us according to his good pleasure. Oh, for more of the agonizing of the Holy Spirit within us, that there might be more agonizing in our spirits for the glory of God! No mighty work will come from us unless there first be a mighty work in us. No one truly labors for souls unless the Holy Spirit first performs a mighty work of grace in his or in her life.

The Heroes of Faith

THIS IS A VERY familiar chapter, but it is no less precious. In it we
read of the heroes of faith. I have never read a chapter setting forth
the heroes of unbelief. Unbelief is barren, impotent, a curse, a
mere negation. But faith bears fruit, produces good works, and
achieves marvels. If not for the faith that moved these people to
accomplish such valiant deeds as described in this chapter, we
might not have known anything about them. May you and I possess the same precious faith that we read about here in Hebrews
11. Without it we can neither enter heaven nor fight our way
through this world.

*Now faith is being sure of what we hope for and certain of what we do
not see. This is what the ancients were commended for. (1–2)*

Though we only "hope for" and "do not see" these things now,
the eye of faith can see them, and the hand of faith can grasp them.
Faith gets a grip on what it hopes for and keeps it in its hand. Faith
is mightier than any of our senses or all of them combined. Faith is
to us like the hair of Samson—our great strength lies in it. It is our
Moses' rod, dividing seas of difficulty. It is our Elijah's chariot, in
which we rise above the earth.

The only thing "the ancients were commended for" was their
faith. Their commendation was given that we might be encouraged
to live by faith as they did. They believed their God and everything
he revealed to them by his Word. Doubt gives people a bad reputation. It is only believers who obtain commendation from the Holy
Spirit.

*By faith we understand that the universe was formed at God's com-
mand, so that what is seen was not made out of what was visible. (3)*

302

Only by believing the inspired record can we obtain a true understanding of the wondrous works of creation. Science says the universe evolved out of something that existed before. Evolution is a rank lie against revelation. The world was not made out of the world, for "what is seen was not made out of what was visible." People like to have everything laid down according to the rules of science, but God, who himself is unseen, asks them to believe that "what is seen was not made out of what was visible."

Reason is all very good, but faith mounts on the shoulders of reason and sees much farther than reason with its best telescope will ever be able to see. It is enough for us who have faith that God has told us how he made the world, and we believe it. The real foundation of everything made is God's command. Material things are not our foundation. They are mere shadows.

By faith Abel offered God a better sacrifice than Cain did. By faith he was commended as a righteous man, when God spoke well of his offerings. And by faith he still speaks, even though he is dead. (4)

The first in a long line of martyrs triumphed by faith. Abel was a better man than Cain, and his offering was better than Cain's. But the main difference between these two brothers was that Abel had faith, and Cain did not. Faith teaches us to worship correctly. The most gorgeous ceremonies are nothing in God's sight. He accepts only the faith of our hearts. It was the sacrifice of believing Abel that pleased God. And though his brother Cain out of jealousy and malice slew him, his good reputation continues even to this day.

Only this way of living enables people to go on speaking for God even after they die. Abel spoke by faith when he lived, and that faith makes him speak now that he is dead. If you want to follow in the steps of Abel and have your life speak out of the grave, its voice must be the voice of faith.

The first saint to enter heaven entered it "by faith," not by works. Rest assured that is true to the last person. No one will enter heaven but those who believe. Oh, that we may have Abel's faith and offer to God "the Lamb"—Jesus Christ—that our sins may be taken away (John 1:29).

By faith Enoch was taken from this life, so that he did not experience death; he could not be found, because God had taken him away. For before he was taken, he was commended as one who pleased God. And without faith it is impossible to please God, because anyone who comes to him must believe that he exists and that he rewards those who earnestly seek him. (5–6)

Faith either conquers death or avoids it. There is scarcely anything that faith cannot do, for faith ranks itself on the side of the omnipotent God. Enoch accomplished one of the greatest acts ever—to leap from this life into the next and to bypass the grave—and he did it "by faith," not by works. He shows that the way to please God is to believe him. You cannot be an Enoch unless you please God, and you cannot please God unless you have faith in him.

We never read of an unbeliever who pleased God. If any non-believer had been lifted up to heaven as Enoch was, we would have been able to point to a great feat accomplished apart from faith. But it has never been so.

A very little sin greatly provokes our holy God, but faith knows how to please him. I am not surprised that Enoch avoided death. It was far easier to go to heaven alive than to please God. To live for three hundred years in constant fellowship with God, as Enoch did, was a mighty triumph for faith (Gen. 5:22). May God grant that during all our years, however few or many, we may so live as always to please him! If we cannot bypass death on our way to heaven, as Enoch did, at least let us please God, as he did. If we do, we will conquer death, for we will triumph over the grave.

This verse says Enoch "could not be found." That implies that people missed him and looked for him. When Elijah went to heaven alive, fifty men searched for him (2 Kings 2:16–18). We want to live so that others will miss us. Enoch was missed when he was gone, and so will you be, if you live by faith and walk with God, as Enoch did (Gen. 5:22, 24).

Enoch's departure was also a witness to people that there is a future state and that God rewards the righteous.

It does not say, "Without faith it is difficult" or "barely possible" to please God. It says, "It is impossible." Let us not attempt the impossible. To attempt a difficulty is laudable, but to rush upon an impossibility is insanity. We must not hope to please God by any labor of our own. This is not a popular teaching, but neither do we wish to teach a popular theology.

Only "the fool says in his heart, 'There is no God'" (Ps. 14:1). But even the demons believe that God exists, and they shudder (James 2:19). So we must make the Lord our personal God. Many believe in a hazy, imaginary power they call God. But they never think of him as a person, nor do they suspect he thinks of them. We must believe that God exists as truly as we do. He must be as real to us as our marriage partners and our children.

How earnestly do you seek God in the Scriptures? How earnestly do you seek him in prayer? How much have you lived for God's glory this past month? Have you tried to win someone to him? If you believe God "rewards those who earnestly seek him," do not despise the reward.

How does God reward people of faith? By giving himself to them. Of the millions of Christians who have died, not one has sat up on her or his deathbed and said, "I am sorry I ever served the Lord. I regret that I was so diligent in seeking him, for I found no reward in it. My life would have been happier if I had served myself or lived for this world. But I made a mistake by living for God."

By faith Noah, when warned about things not yet seen, in holy fear built an ark to save his family. By his faith he condemned the world and became heir of the righteousness that comes by faith. (7)

In verse 5 we read of Enoch who "was taken from this life, so that he did not experience death." He never saw the flood nor heard the wailing of those swept away by the waters. But Noah stands in contrast to Enoch. He represents those who live through the evil days faithfully.

Noah built an ark on dry land. How could water be brought there to float it? Faith that believes in a probability is anybody's faith. Faith that believes in something barely possible is better. But the faith that is unconcerned with possibilities but rests solely on the Word of God is the faith of God's people. God deserves such faith, "for nothing is impossible with God" (Luke 1:37).

Adam was the first great father of humanity, and Noah was the second. In the flood, all died except Noah and his family. Noah's faith looked to "things not yet seen." Faith never relies on the human senses.

Noah's faith was also moved by "holy fear." There is an unholy fear that perfect love drives out (1 John 4:18). But holy fear dwells most happily with faith. Noah had it, and it moved him to build an ark, which became the instrument for the salvation of his family. Hence faith and fear can live in the same heart. In Noah's case, faith molded him and fear moved him to build the ark. A holy faith in God and a holy fear of disobeying him are sweet companions. When we are moved by that fear, our faith becomes practical. When true faith lives in us, it masters our fears and all our other emotions.

As in Noah's life, so in ours, faith outlives a deluge that drowns the whole world. It has an ark even when God's wrath sweeps everyone else away.

Faith has a condemning power toward an ungodly world. You do not need to be telling worldly people they are doing wrong. Let them see clearly the evidence of your faith, and that will bear the strongest witness against their unbelief and sin. If you want to show how crooked a stick is, do not waste words describing it. Just place a straight stick by its side, and you will make your point. Noah's faith was that straight stick that condemned a crooked world.

By faith Abraham, when called to go to a place he would later receive as his inheritance, obeyed and went, even though he did not know where he was going. By faith he made his home in the promised land like a stranger in a foreign country; he lived in tents, as did Isaac and Jacob, who were heirs with him of the same promise. For he was looking forward to the city with foundations, whose architect and builder is God. (8–10)

Though Abraham "did not know where he was going," God knew, and that was enough for the Patriarch. From that day on, Abraham had no one but God as his protector. That was surely a masterpiece of faith. As a little child is willing to be led by his or her parent, so Abraham was willing to be led by God, even though that meant leaving his own country and people and going to the distant land that God wanted to give him.

We are not to ask for full knowledge before we obey the Lord's will. We are to obey in the dark, even as Abraham did. It is better to have the faith that obeys than the faith that moves mountains.

Wherever God may lead us, if we do not know where we are going, at least we know with whom we are going. We do not know the road, but we know the guide. One of our hymns speaks of this:

> So on I go—not knowing—I would not if I might;
> I'd rather walk in the dark with God
> Than go alone in the light;
> I'd rather walk by faith with him
> Than go alone by sight.
> Where he may lead I'll follow,
> My trust in him repose;
> And every hour in perfect peace I'll sing,
> "He knows! He knows!"

An evidence of true faith is its perseverance with no visible signs of assurance. Abraham's faith was like that in this verse. Like his faith, ours knows that the land it treads on belongs to it, yet in another sense it cannot claim a solitary foot of it. It knows that it is at home, even as Abraham was in his own land, yet like him, faith knows it is a "stranger in a foreign country," and it is content with that.

I think Abraham was sent to Canaan as a stranger to be a witness for God. These people were soon to be destroyed, but a man of God lived among them. You, my Christian friend, are a stranger here, and you are living in this world for the good of those around you. Be like Abraham, who lived "like a stranger" to show people what God could do for those who trusted in him.

What a depth of meaning is found in those four words: "the city with foundations"! It implies that all other cities have no foundations. They come and they go as if they were molehills raised on the surface of the earth or little mounds of sand made by a child's wooden spade on the seashore but which the next tide will wash away. What vast numbers of cities have already been destroyed! Archaeologists are constantly picking up the pieces of them. But we are on our way to "the city with foundations." It is founded on eternal power and will last as long as God himself exists.

Many we know have looked for this same city and gone to it. Others of us wait here until our dear Lord's hand will reach out to us and his voice will say, "Come up here" (Rev. 4:1). We are looking for that heavenly city. There is nothing in this world worth looking for.

By faith Abraham, even though he was past age—and Sarah herself was barren—was enabled to become a father because he considered him faithful who had made the promise. And so from this one man, and he as good as dead, came descendants as numerous as the stars in the sky and as countless as the sand on the seashore. (11–12)

Sarah's faith was not like Abraham's, but it was true faith, and God loved it. Therefore her name appears among faith's heroes. Faith turned Sarah from a barren woman into a joyful mother. Still today, when barren people catch the blessed influences of faith, they begin at once to bear fruit for God.

This was literally true of Abraham's natural descendants. They are "as countless as the sand on the seashore." It is also true in a spiritual sense, for "he is the father of all who believe" (Rom. 4:11). They are the multitude "as numerous as the stars in the sky."

All these people were still living by faith when they died. They did not receive the things promised; they only saw them and welcomed them from a distance. And they admitted that they were aliens and strangers on earth. People who say such things show that they are looking for a country of their own. If they had been thinking of the country they had left, they would have had opportunity to return. Instead, they were longing for a better country—a heavenly one. Therefore God is not ashamed to be called their God, for he has prepared a city for them. (13–16)

This verse is the epitaph God has carved over the resting places of his faithful ones. Will it be the record of your life? God gives us faith not that we may escape death but that we may die with our trust in Him. "All these people" lived by faith to the end of their lives. I have been told that you can be a child of God one day and a child of the Devil the next. I do not believe it.

Though the promises could be seen only from a distance, the faith of these people had such long arms that it "welcomed" them as loving relatives who have not seen each other in years welcome each other at a family reunion. So may we see God's promises and be persuaded that they belong to us. May we welcome them as we would a special guest in our homes.

God's people not only "were aliens and strangers on earth," they "admitted" it. Confessed faith is indispensable. If you, like Nicodemus, come to Christ at night, be ashamed that you are ashamed of him. Come out and boldly confess what you are!

They were aliens and strangers here, so they were "looking for a country of their own." Everyone wants a country. If we do not have one beneath the stars, we seek it above them.

The proof of faith lies in its perseverance. True pilgrims never think of going back. If they have a chance to return, they still have no wish to. They know that whatever difficulties and trials lie ahead of them, there are far greater ones in "the country they . . . left."

John Bunyan's Christian was resolved not to go back to the City of Destruction, whatever perils he might have to face on his way to the Celestial City. Almighty grace will not permit God's people to turn aside and find their rest anywhere else. The only coercion to keep someone a Christian is the coercion of love for Christ.

The "better country" people of faith long for is "a heavenly one." We desire something better than this world. It has never satisfied us. Perhaps it did when we were dead in sin. A dead world may satisfy a dead heart, but we will never find our heaven here.

The Old Testament saints' "longing for a better country" was implanted in them by God himself. "He has prepared a city for them" that will more than satisfy their highest desires. Because the saints were not ashamed to be called God's people, he was "not ashamed to be called their God." They were looking for a city, and he prepared one for them. God and his people have an agreement. They want heaven, and he is preparing heaven for them and them for heaven.

By faith Abraham, when God tested him, offered Isaac as a sacrifice. He who had received the promises was about to sacrifice his one and only son, even though God had said to him, "It is through Isaac that your offspring will be reckoned." Abraham reasoned that God could raise the dead, and figuratively speaking, he did receive Isaac back from death. (17–19)

This was one of the grandest achievements of faith. It was also a figure or type of God's offering up "his one and only son" on almost the same spot.

The greatest problem Abraham overcame was not his fatherly instinct that would prevent him from slaying his son. It was this question: How can God keep his promise to give me descendants through Isaac if I obey his command to slay him? But by faith Abraham obeyed! He knew his plain duty was to obey God's command and not worry about how the Lord would fulfill his promise. Perhaps he had also learned, through his mistake concerning Ishmael (Gen. 16), that God's way of fulfilling his promise might not be his way and that God's way was always best.

Though almost driven to desperation, Abraham did not give up his faith in God. He was forced to believe two apparently opposite things. First, that through Isaac he would have many descendants, and second, that he must offer Isaac as a burnt sacrifice. But he bridged the two by believing another grand truth: "God could raise the dead." Thus God would keep his promise to Abraham. Whenever you find two things in Scripture that you cannot reconcile, you may believe that between them lies something more glorious that your dim eyes can scarcely yet perceive.

In Abraham's day no one had ever been raised from the dead, yet he believed it would happen to Isaac. His faith laughed at an impossibility. It was not Abraham's business to keep God's promise for him. That was God's business, and he did it. You remember how Rebekah tried to make God's promise come true for Jacob and what a mess she made by her plotting and scheming (Gen. 27). When we give our attention to obeying God and let him fulfill his own promises, all will be well.

The doctrine of the resurrection is a precious jewel that faith wears as a ring on her right hand. "God can raise the dead," says faith, and it finds comfort in that truth. If you are grieving the loss of a loved one, wear that ring! If you fear death, wear that precious jewel! It will be better than any lucky charm that a superstitious person ever wore.

By faith Isaac blessed Jacob and Esau in regard to their future. (20)

Your faith can bless others as well as yourself. It not only comforts your own heart but also enables you to speak words of love and comfort to your children, as Isaac did when "by faith" he "blessed Jacob and Esau." Isaac was so old and blind, he could not tell one of his sons from another, yet "by faith" he could look into the futures of his sons. Oh, what sharp eyes faith has, even when our physical eyes are dim! We may see far more by faith than we can by sight.

"Isaac blessed Jacob and Esau" with blundering faith, for Jacob deceived his father, and Isaac himself made mistakes in giving his blessing. Yet even his mistakes were all right in God's sight. It was by faith that he blessed his sons, and therefore I gather that a faith that blunders, if it be faith in God, is an acceptable faith.

By faith Jacob, when he was dying, blessed each of Joseph's sons, and worshiped as he leaned on the top of his staff. (21)

Death is a thorough test of faith, but Jacob passed his test, for "by faith Jacob, when he was dying," was a blessing to his grandchildren. You remember Jacob's discernment, how he crossed his hands so he would lay the right hand on the younger son (Gen. 48:13–14). Faith is always giving a blessing to others, and it knows which way to give it.

Jacob's staff had been Jacob's companion on many memorable occasions. With it he had crossed the Jordan (Gen. 32:10), and he had leaned on it when he came back from the place of his wrestling with God, limping on his dislocated hip (Gen. 32:22–32). So it was most fitting that he should lean on that same staff while worshiping God. He offered the worship of gratitude, testimony, and reverent love.

By faith Joseph, when his end was near, spoke about the exodus of the Israelites from Egypt and gave instructions about his bones. (22)

This was a sure proof that Joseph believed God's people would come out of Egypt, for he insisted that he not be buried among the pharaohs, though a prominent place would have been assigned to him there. Why was it important for Joseph to have his bones buried with his ancestors? Because he never forgot that he belonged to God's chosen nation. He refused to be an Egyptian.

This would encourage the faith of others. Every time an Israelite thought of Joseph's bones, he would say to himself, "We are to leave this country one day." Perhaps he was prospering in business, but he would tell himself, "I will have to part with this. Joseph's bones are to be taken out of Egypt. I will not be here forever."

By faith Moses' parents hid him for three months after he was born, because they saw he was no ordinary child, and they were not afraid of the king's edict. (23)

It is a great blessing when both parents in a family have faith in God. Faith made Moses' parents unafraid to brave the consequences of disobeying Pharaoh's command to slay their infant son (Ex. 1:15-16). Later in this chapter we read of how the faith of others "conquered kingdoms, . . . shut the mouths of lions" (v. 33), "quenched the fury of the flames, and escaped the edge of the sword" (v. 34). But the faith of Moses' parents moved them to do a simple thing—hide their infant son. Faith not only rides the whirlwind; it threads the needle. It not only climbs up to God's throne; it stands by a baby's cradle. There is nothing faith cannot make noble when it touches it.

Their faith acted on slender encouragement, for don't all parents think their baby is "no ordinary child"? Moses' parents had no Bible. The man who was to write the first book in the Bible was their own little baby. If sometimes, like Moses' parents, you have very little encouragement for your faith, do not let go of it.

"The king's edict" to kill the infant Hebrews boys made all the people of Egypt tremble, but faith made Moses' parents fearless in the face of Pharaoh's threat of punishment. The whole history of Israel rested on the hiding of that little child. Even the divine babe of Bethlehem was connected with Moses. We do not know all we are doing when we do little things by faith. Great wheels turn on little axles. If you have faith in Christ, show it by overcoming all fear of the consequences of doing right.

By faith Moses, when he had grown up, refused to be known as the son of Pharaoh's daughter. He chose to be mistreated along with the people

of God rather than to enjoy the pleasures of sin for a short time. He
regarded disgrace for the sake of Christ as of greater value than the
treasures of Egypt, because he was looking ahead to his reward. By faith
he left Egypt, not fearing the king's anger; he persevered because he saw
him who is invisible. By faith he kept the Passover and the sprinkling
of blood, so that the destroyer of the firstborn would not touch the first-
born of Israel. (24–28)

Moses was a man of education and rank. As "the son of
Pharaoh's daughter" he was the prince of Egypt. If Pharaoh had no
sons and his daughter had only Moses as a son, he was the heir to
the Egyptian crown.

No doubt that when he "refused to be known as the son of
Pharaoh's daughter," some told him he was acting unkindly to his
adoptive mother. "She drew you out of the water. She saw that you
were nursed and cared for. She has given you everything your heart
has desired." But Moses' faith made him do the right thing. Jesus
said, "Anyone who loves his father or mother more than me is not
worthy of me" (Matt. 10:37). Moses teaches us that we ought to
abhor the thought of obtaining honor in this world by compromis-
ing our faith.

Nothing but faith could have brought Moses to that decision. No
one would choose to be mistreated, but to be mistreated along with
the people of God is completely different. God's people "are they
who have come out of the great tribulation; they have washed their
robes and made them white in the blood of the Lamb" (Rev. 7:14).

In Moses' day the followers of God were not in themselves a lov-
able people. They were wretchedly poor, engaged in brickmaking,
and utterly spiritless. They were literally a herd of slaves, broken
down, crushed, and depressed. Only faith could have led Moses to
side with them. Moses teaches us to take our place with those who
follow Christ and the Scriptures, even if they are not all we would
like them to be. Moses left honor (v. 24), the pleasures of sin (v.
25), and now wealth, for he gave up "the treasures of Egypt." Faith
makes us willing to part with everything for Christ. If we are unwilling, we are not his disciples, for Jesus said, "Any of you who does
not give up everything he has cannot be my disciple" (Luke 14:33).
An unbeliever would not choose disgrace for the sake of Christ as of
greater value than the treasures of Egypt, but neither does an unbeliever live by faith.

Like Moses, let us get into fellowship with Christ, give ourselves
to him without reserve, and see life in an eternal light, looking ahead
to the reward. Here is the obedience of faith. It takes the hand and

follows the leading of "him who is invisible." Faith is the soul's eye that enables it to see the Lord.

By faith the people passed through the Red Sea as on dry land; but when the Egyptians tried to do so, they were drowned. (29)

This is because faith can do what unbelief must not try to do. When unbelief tries to follow in the footsteps of faith, it becomes its own destroyer. You must have real faith in God or you cannot go where faith would take you. But with faith you may go through the sea and find yourself safe on the other side. This is the difference between faith and presumption. Faith goes through the sea; presumption is drowned in the sea.

By faith the walls of Jericho fell, after the people had marched around them for seven days. (30)

You could not have seen faith at work on those solid walls. Those huge ramparts and battlements seemed to stand fast and firm, yet "by faith" they fell, after the people had marched around them for seven days. Faith can do better than battering rams or dynamite.

By faith the prostitute Rahab, because she welcomed the spies, was not killed with those who were disobedient. (31)

What? Is the prostitute Rahab listed among the heroes of faith with people like Abraham, Isaac, Jacob, and Joseph? Yes. God the Holy Spirit records her faith and hides her fault. Her faith caused her to unite with God's people. She "was not killed with those who were disobedient," because she had come out from them and allied herself with God's people when she hid the spies (Josh. 2).

Rahab had singular faith, for she alone in Jericho believed in the Lord. She possessed stable faith, for it stood firm when the walls of her city collapsed. She showed daring faith, for she risked her life for the sake of the spies. It was also a sanctifying faith, for she did not continue as a prostitute after she believed.

And what more shall I say? I do not have time to tell about Gideon, Barak, Samson, Jephthah, David, Samuel and the prophets, who through faith conquered kingdoms, administered justice, and gained what was promised; who shut the mouths of lions, quenched the fury of the flames, and escaped the edge of the sword; whose weakness was turned to strength; and who became powerful in battle and routed for-

*eign armies. Women received back their dead, raised to life again.
Others were tortured and refused to be released, so that they might
gain a better resurrection. Some faced jeers and flogging, while still
others were chained and put in prison. They were stoned; they were
sawed in two; they were put to death by the sword. They went about in
sheepskins and goatskins, destitute, persecuted and mistreated—the
world was not worthy of them. They wandered in deserts and mountains, and in caves and holes in the ground. (32–38)*

Here are some names we would not have expected to see. Some of
these people were badly disfigured by serious faults and flaws and fail-
ings, but the distinguishing feature of faith was in every one of them.
Perhaps no one had such childlike faith as Samson. Who but a man
of faith would have hurled himself on a thousand enemies with no
weapon in his hand but the jawbone of a donkey (Judg. 15:15-16)?
That weak, strong man had an amazing confidence in God. Though
that did not excuse his faults, it put him in the ranks of the believers.
Happy is the man or the woman who believes in God! In the Old
Testament there were multitudes of others besides those named here.

Is it as great an exploit to have "wrought righteousness" (v. 33,
KJV; "administered justice," NIV) as to have "conquered kingdoms"?
Yes. To preserve a holy character in such a world of temptation as
ours is a far greater achievement than to conquer any number of
kingdoms.

Think of Shadrach, Meshach, and Abednego, and remember how
they "quenched the fury of the flames" that Nebuchadnezzar ignited
to destroy them (Dan. 3). Unlike them, you may not be able to defy
the fury of the flames, but often you have been a person "whose
weakness was turned to strength."

Faith works equal wonders in women as in men. We have already
seen examples in this chapter from the lives of Sarah (vv. 11-13),
Moses' mother (v. 23), and Rahab (v. 31).

Is it a feat of faith to refuse to be released? Yes, for instead of
showing their faith by putting their enemies to flight, these people
proved it by enduring all kinds of torture without shrinking. It took
great faith to sustain the saints through the tortures they experienced. The story harrows our hearts even to read it. What must it
have been like to endure it?

Why does God permit his people to endure such persecution? It
acts as a sieve to sift the church of its hypocrites. It reveals the reality of our conversion experiences. It also does us good, for painful
as our persecutions are, they drive us to prayer. Again, we must be
persecuted, for the life of the church is the life of Christ drawn out

in his people. And once more, persecution makes us fit for the life to come, since it builds in us holy character.

We have seen the works of faith and the sufferings of faith. Now we read of God's appraisal of faith. He places a far higher value on believers than on unbelievers.

These were all commended for their faith, yet none of them received what had been promised. God had planned something better for us so that only together with us would they be made perfect. (39–40)

This is the grandest roll call of heroes who ever lived. Every one of them was a man or woman of faith. Faith made them mighty. They were not greater or better than the rest of us, but they believed in God. They were firm in faith, and this became the basis of their conquering characters, and thus their names are indelibly recorded here in Hebrews 11. They did not win a military medal, but they did bear the cross for their Lord, and he has honored them with a crown that can never perish or be taken away.

In each of the people listed in this chapter, faith worked differently. Faith is able to work in a variety of ways. It is good at everything. Faith can fulfill everything God calls us to do.

They passed away before Christ came, so they did not see the fulfillment of the promises of his coming. Since the coming of Christ, equally noble exploits have been performed by the heroes of faith.

We who bring up the rear of the army of faith are necessary to its completeness. It cannot be perfect without us. There would be empty seats in the heavenly orchestra and gaps in the sacred choir. The heroes of faith are in heaven, but the perfect number of the divine family of love will never be made up until we who have believed go there to join all those who have had the same precious faith. It was never God's intention that any part of his church should be able to do without the rest of it. By God's grace, we will be there that they with us may "be made perfect."

Let us agree that if we are to bring to perfection the history of the church of Christ, we must be no less heroic than the Old Testament saints were. A good poem gathers force as it grows. Its waves of thought roll in with greater power as it nears its climax. So should the mighty poem of faith's glorious history increase in depth and power as it gets nearer to its grand consummation. In this way God will be glorified more and more through all his believing children.

Do you have the faith seen in this chapter? If you do, you are blessed. If not, what hope is there for you either in this life or in eternity?

Jesus Christ in All His Glory

The revelation of Jesus Christ, which God gave him to show his servants what must soon take place. He made it known by sending his angel to his servant John, who testifies to everything he saw—that is, the word of God and the testimony of Jesus Christ. Blessed is the one who reads the words of this prophecy, and blessed are those who hear it and take to heart what is written in it, because the time is near. (1–3)

The apostle John shared the same spirit with his Master. He lived in very intimate fellowship with his Lord. Therefore, the choicest revelation was made to him. The Lord does not reveal his secrets to uncongenial minds. Those who will do his will may know God's secrets. If we lived nearer to God and walked more in the love of Christ, how much more we would know and see! If we did not see visions, yet God would grant inward perceptions to our hearts.

Twice in verse 1 the title "servant" is used. This is a revelation to Christ's "servants," made first to his "servant" John. There is no higher honor under heaven than to be a servant of such a Master. His servants we are this day, and we find in that service perfect freedom and the highest imaginable delight. The Book of Revelation, then, is written to us.

At the cross the apostle John both saw and gave his testimony (John 19:35). So now it was fitting that the same man should both see and testify about the ascended Christ. No eyes were so fit to see the glory of Christ as those that saw him in his humiliation.

The Book of Revelation is not meant for the shelf. Its promise is not, "Blessed is the one who understands the words of this prophecy." I am afraid very few would receive that benediction. Instead, the blessing is for the one "who reads" this book and "those who hear it and take to heart what is written in it." It is a blessing to hear our Father speak, even when we cannot understand him. When you were a little child, how did you learn to understand your father but by at first hearing him say many things that were way over your head?

I love to read those parts of God's Word that I cannot yet understand, because I remember there are some parts that I now understand that I did not understand before, and it was by reading, hearing, and thinking over them that light gradually broke into my mind. Why, then, should I not go on reading this Book of Revelation, though as yet I may be unable to understand it?

But notice this. The doctrine of this book is often used as a sort of astrologer's text to tell us about the future instead of being used in a practical way to humble us before God and to teach us to trust in the wisdom of God, who knows all things. Oh, that we might use the teaching of the second coming of Christ in a more practical way—not to speculate on it, but to be warned by it to be ready for the coming of our Lord!

John,
To the seven churches in the province of Asia:
Grace and peace to you from him who is, and who was, and who is to come, and from the seven spirits before his throne, and from Jesus Christ, who is the faithful witness, the firstborn from the dead, and the ruler of the kings of the earth. (4–5)

The two blessings of "grace and peace" come in that order. Peace that is not built on grace is a false peace. But if you have grace, you have a right to peace. Grace and peace come from our heavenly Father, Yahweh, the I am, who lives in all tenses and fills all time.

You need not be afraid of the Holy Spirit in his sevenfold ministry. He is the Spirit of burning, for he will burn up nothing in us but what ought to be consumed. He is the Spirit of judgment, for he will judge nothing in us but what ought to be judged and condemned, so that peace may come to us.

Since Jesus Christ is the faithful witness, he always tells us the truth, his witness can be trusted, and he deserves our faith. Along with the Father and the Holy Spirit, Jesus now is also identified as the source of "grace and peace" (v. 4). What a wondrous fountain of grace and peace his resurrection is to us! Also his divine sovereignty—his rule over all events, people, and nature—what grace and peace may we who love Christ find there! Never let us forget that even to this day Christ is "the ruler of the kings of the earth." The president rules, and the queen reigns, but it is still more true that "our Lord God Almighty reigns" (Rev. 19:6).

To him who loves us and has freed us from our sins by his blood, and has made us to be a kingdom and priests to serve his God and Father— to him be glory and power for ever and ever! Amen. (5–6)

John had hardly begun his message to the seven churches when he felt that he had to lift up his heart in a joyful doxology. The very mention of the name of the Lord Jesus Christ fired John's heart. He could not sit down coolly to write even what the Spirit of God dictated. He had to rise, fall on his knees, bless, and magnify the Lord Jesus.

Leave it to "the disciple whom Jesus loved" (John 21:20) to praise Christ as the one "who loves us." The best work we can do on earth is to adore Christ. We are blessed in prayer but seven times more blessed in praise. One thing adoration does is help us see, and when we close our eyes in adoration, we see more than when we have them open in any other way.

John's praise was not to the love of God, an attribute or an emotion, but "to him who loves us." I am very grateful for love, but more grateful for him who loves me. It is an amazing mercy that Christ should ever do anything with sin except punish it. Jesus "freed us from our sins" not by some influence outside himself but "by his blood." The twelve disciples were bound to love the hands that took the basin and poured water on their feet (John 13:5), but as for the washing Christ gave us with his blood, how will we ever praise him enough? Well might we join in the heavenly song, "You are worthy . . . because you were slain, and with your blood you purchased men for God" (Rev. 5:9). People are willing to shed the blood of others by entering into war, but Christ was willing to shed his own blood that we might be saved.

Note the order in this verse. First Christ "loves us," and then he "freed us from our sins." One of the glories of Christ's love is that it comes to us while we are defiled with sin and even dead in sin (Eph. 2:1). I can understand that Jesus pities us as filthy sinners, but that the Lord of glory "loves us" is a deep and heavenly thought that my finite mind can hardly hold. His heart is knit with our hearts, and his happiness is bound up with ours.

Since Christ "freed us from our sins by his blood," we must hate sin. It murdered our Lord. It cost him his life to save us. How, then, dare we toy with it? We are "freed . . . from our sins." Sin no longer holds us captive. The chains are dissolved by the blood of the Atonement. Then how can we go about as if we were still slaves to it?

If we speak this benediction, we must make it personal and say, "To him be the glory and power in my life." Each person is a little empire of three kingdoms—body, soul, and spirit—and it should be a united kingdom. Make Christ the King of it all. We do well also to say, "To Christ be the glory and power in the lives of others." Begin at home, and do not be satisfied until you see your children saved. Then pray for opportunities to lead your neighbors to Christ.

Look, he is coming with the clouds, and every eye will see him, even those who pierced him; and all the peoples of the earth will mourn because of him. So shall it be! Amen. (7)

This is a grand doctrine, and it should never be put in the background. The Scriptures are incomplete unless we understand that there is something still to come. The Old Testament without the first coming of Christ is a riddle without a key, and so is the New Testament without the second coming of Christ.

Every eye will see him—that includes your eye and mine. Whatever in the future we will not see, we will see Christ. This part of the verse implies that Christ's coming will be a literal coming, an actual sight. If our Lord's return were to have a spiritual fulfillment, this verse would have said, "Every mind will perceive him." But that is not what we read here.

What a sight it will be for those that pierced him—not only the Romans and Jews who put Christ to death physically, but for all of us who by the sins of our evil words and backsliding have pierced him and put him to shame.

Though the wicked will weep when Christ returns, the saints must give consent to the judgments of God as well as to his mercies. We will say, "So shall it be! Amen." When I was young and rebellious, my praying mother said to me, "My son, if at the Judgment Day you are condemned, remember that your mother will say 'Amen' to your condemnation." That stung my heart.

"I am the Alpha and the Omega," says the Lord God, "who is, and who was, and who is to come, the Almighty." (8)

These are the words of the Father, yet later in this book the Lord Jesus also calls himself "the Alpha and the Omega" (Rev. 21:6; 22:13). We cannot always draw the line between the voice of God and the voice of the God-man, Christ Jesus, nor do we wish to do so. Yet it is always true that Christ is so truly God that Scripture can speak of him either as the absolute God or as the God-man.

I, John, your brother and companion in the suffering and kingdom and patient endurance that are ours in Jesus, was on the island of Patmos because of the word of God and the testimony of Jesus. On the Lord's Day I was in the Spirit, and I heard behind me a loud voice like a trumpet, which said: "Write on a scroll what you see and send it to the seven churches: to Ephesus, Smyrna, Pergamum, Thyatira, Sardis, Philadelphia and Laodicea." (9–11)

How sweet it sounds when John, who was full of visions, who had seen the broken seals (Rev. 6:3–8:5) and the poured-out bowls (Rev. 16), and who was familiar with the infinite God, identified himself as our "brother and companion."

What an amazing link between "the suffering and kingdom and patient endurance that are ours in Jesus"! We must have the cross and crown together. We get the kingdom of Christ, but not without the suffering of Christ. The Cross is marked on all the treasure trove we find in Christ. It is not genuine if it is not marked with the Cross.

John was exiled to the island of Patmos because he preached the gospel. It was an attempt to silence his eloquent tongue and to prevent his loving teachings from building up the church.

The Lord's Day is the first day of the week, especially set apart for the Lord's worship. Though John was on a desert island and far away from all Christian companionship, he was careful to spend Sunday in worship, to draw near to God. Let us, then, never make excuses when we are traveling and far away from home on vacation. "The Lord's Day" is just as much the Lord's Day to us in one part of the world as another. Let us be careful that we use it properly. God has put a fence around it for our benefit. It is not a day of bondage but a day of holy joy and rest. Let us not miss the ripe blessings of this day.

God allowed John to be "in the Spirit" on this special day of worship. God's Spirit enabled John to hear "a loud voice," which we learn in the following verses was the voice of Christ! May this be the experience of all God's people when they worship on the Lord's Day.

There were churches in each of these places. It is not the custom of the Holy Spirit to talk of the church of England, but he would speak of the church of London, the church of New York, and the church of Los Angeles. These are separate and independent churches. They are one in Christ, yet each church is in itself complete if it is under the orders of God.

I turned around to see the voice that was speaking to me. And when I turned I saw seven golden lampstands, and among the lampstands was someone "like a son of man," dressed in a robe reaching down to his feet and with a golden sash around his chest. His head and hair were white like wool, as white as snow, and his eyes were like blazing fire. His feet were like bronze glowing in a furnace, and his voice was like the sound of rushing waters. In his right hand he held seven stars, and out of his mouth came a sharp double-edged sword. His face was like the sun shining in all its brilliance. (12–16)

When we hear a voice, we like to see the person who speaks. That is why John turned around, but even more, he turned around because he recognized the voice as that of Jesus, with whom he had lived for more than three years.

The lampstands were not, as in the Old Testament, one great seven-branched golden candlestick but seven distinct candelabra, for these seven churches were separate. Each had its own individuality. And the same "son of man" John had known during our Lord's earthly ministry was present, but John could say only, "like a son of man." This majestic figure was "like" the Jesus John knew, but also unlike him, for he was now glorified. We are never to forget that though Christ is glorious in his deity and majestic in all his sublime offices, he is still most surely human. What a sweet and consoling thought!

The robe and the sash point to the excellence of our Lord in all his offices. He is a prophet. A prophet of old wore a leather sash, but our Savior wears "a golden sash," for he is vested with authority far above the prophets. Let us therefore submit to him. This piece of attire also shows his power, for men wore a sash when they received an office. Eliakim was given a sash when he received authority (Isa. 22:20–21). You remember how our Lord once took a towel and washed his disciples' feet (John 13:5). The golden sash here shows that he is still ready to serve his servants. Let us follow his example and be ready to serve.

Christ's hair was white for he is "the Ancient of Days" (Dan. 7:9), and all the wisdom that is supposed to belong to gray hairs is with him. His eyes were discerning and burning into everything and everyone. His feet are burning. "His face was like the sun shining in all its brilliance" (v. 16). That speaks of his glory. But here "his feet were like bronze glowing in a furnace." That suggests trials. I think we may understand by these "feet" the church on earth, for "you are the body of Christ, and each one of you is a part of it" (1 Cor. 12:27). As long as we live in this world, we can expect to endure trials of our faith.

The mention of Jesus' "right hand" proves that he is still a person. The hand pierced by the nail on the cross is not paralyzed; it has strength to hold "seven stars." The hand that worked for our redemption has not ceased to work for us.

The "seven stars" are generally understood as the pastors of the seven churches of Asia. Christ holds in his hand what he bought with the blood of his heart. It is specially mentioned that these stars are not in Christ's left hand but his right hand, as if the Lord intended to put special honor on his faithful servants. We who preach the gospel should not seek our own honor. It is enough for us if Jesus honors us by holding us in "his right hand."

Does not the mention of these seven pastors in Christ's right hand teach us that each person is completely dependent on him? Other stars may shine in their own natural spheres, but Christ's stars can shine only as he holds them up, holds them out, and holds them tight. Do not rely on yourself at all; depend only on that right hand of power and skill that will hold you up until the end.

We see here our security as well, for who can extinguish a star whose sphere is in the right hand of God? I see the Devil puffing against these stars until his cheeks are about to burst, but he does not make them even flicker. Who can harm those whom Jesus holds? When we are in the right hand of Christ, we are not shooting stars that soon melt away.

The doubled-edged sword came out of his mouth and is therefore to be identified as the Word of God. As a sword cuts, pierces, pricks, and wounds, so does Scripture. It cuts the throat of our sins. It kills our self-righteousness. It lays our lusts dead at Christ's feet. It completely subdues our hearts. I am not surprised that people are angry with the Word of God. Who wouldn't be angry when cut with a sharp double-edged sword? Nor am I surprised when others weep as if their hearts would break. Who would not weep when the sword cuts into the flesh and touches the very marrow? There is nothing so sharp as the Word of God. It is also double-edged. There is no handling this weapon without cutting yourself. The Word of God has no back to it; it is all edge. I have often noticed that when I have been preaching for the comfort of God's people, even then some sinners have been wounded.

In Christ's right hand he held seven stars, yet how insignificant they appeared when John caught the sight of his face! You cannot see seventy thousand stars, much less seven, when the sun shines in all its brilliance. When you go to a house of worship, always try to see the Lord's face rather than the stars in his hand. The best of his servants are only stars, but Christ is the sun.

If Christ's face is "like the sun shining in all its brilliance," we know where to trace all the light and all the glory we have ever seen. If there is any beauty in the landscape, it is the sun that gives it beauty. As darkness is the grave of beauty, so the absence of Jesus would be the end of all human virtue. We who look into the face of Jesus may rejoice, for by doing so our faces will also shine with his brilliance!

When I saw him, I fell at his feet as though dead. Then he placed his right hand on me and said: "Do not be afraid. I am the First and the Last. I am the Living One; I was dead, and behold I am alive for ever and ever! And I hold the keys of death and Hades." (17–18)

John had seen Christ on earth, but then his glory had been overshadowed by his humanity. Here John saw him in all his glory, and it made John fall at his feet as though dead. Jesus desires us all to see him as John did, for he prayed, "Father, I want those you have given me . . . to see my glory" (John 17:24). John was not literally dead, but "as though dead." He could no longer see, for the blaze of Jesus' face had blinded him. He could no longer hear, for Jesus' "voice was like the sound of rushing waters" (v. 15), and it had stunned him. No bodily faculty retained its power.

It is an infinite blessing when we are utterly emptied, stripped, spoiled, and slain before our Lord. Our strength is our weakness, and our life is our death. When both strength and life are gone, we begin to live. To lie at Jesus' feet is a good experience. To lie there sick and wounded is better. But to lie there "as though dead" is best of all. It does not matter what condition we are in, as long as we are at Jesus' feet. It is better to be dead there than alive anywhere else.

If I might see Christ at this moment on the terms of instant death to my fallen nature, I would gladly accept the offer. The bliss would far exceed the penalty. How the "I" dies when Christ is seen! How we sink! And yet our joys rise indescribably and immeasurably high.

Was not John "the disciple whom Jesus loved" (John 21:20)? Yes. But here he seemed to have forgotten his Lord's love for him, for he was afraid of him. Our Lord wants us not to be afraid of him but to be confident around him. Our comfort comes not from what we are but from what he is. At this point in history we are the last, but Christ will always be both the First and the Last.

No other hand could have revived John but the right hand that had been pierced for him on Calvary's cross. The right hand is the hand of favor and power. God gives strength to those who have none. Oh, Lord, if we are dead in a sense worse than John was—if we have fallen into sin—lay your pierced right hand on us and make us live! Touch us with your right hand of love and power. Then, like John, we will be able to hear what you say, and we will obey your command!

Because Jesus "was dead" and is now "alive for ever and ever," he will carry on his heavenly work of interceding for us (Heb. 7:25). Since Jesus is alive for ever and ever, those who persecute his people should be afraid. Since Jesus holds "the keys of death and Hades," he is adored in heaven and feared in hell. Even the Devil can do nothing except under the permission of Christ. He is a chained enemy. Christ has him on a leash, and when he permits Satan to wander, he makes even the wrath of demons to praise him. Do you tremble at death? Then remember that Christ holds the keys of death. You are immortal until your Lord says, "Come home." You will not die until he unlocks the door of death. And then when he returns, Christ will unlock the door of your grave and call your body to himself.

"Write, therefore, what you have seen, what is now and what will take place later. The mystery of the seven stars that you saw in my right hand and of the seven golden lampstands is this: The seven stars are the angels of the seven churches, and the seven lampstands are the seven churches." (19–20)

The word *angels* literally means "messengers" in the Greek text. This is a good description of the churches' pastors, for they speak God's message. The identification of "the angels of the seven churches" as pastors is confirmed by the linking of them to "the seven stars," for we remarked in verse 16 that those stars are the pastors of the seven churches.

In Heaven Forever with Christ

THERE WILL BE THREE wonders in heaven. The first is that we will see so many people there whom we did not expect to see. The second is that we will miss so many we did expect to see. And the third wonder of heaven is the greatest of all—that we will find ourselves there!

Revelation 22 shows us the bliss of heaven. Yet some people could not be happy if they were allowed to enter heaven, for it is a land of the spirit, and they have neglected their spirits. Some even deny that they have spirits.

I breathe heaven. I drink heaven. I feel heaven. I think heaven. Everything is heaven. If there were no hell, the loss of heaven would be hell. To be in heaven is to be with Christ. Heaven without Christ is existence without life, feasting without food, sight without light. It is a contradiction in terms. There cannot be a heaven without Christ. He is the sum total of bliss, the fountain from which heaven flows, the element of which heaven is composed. Christ is heaven, and heaven is Christ. The true Christian life, when we live near Christ, is the rough draft of our heavenly intimacy with him.

Someone said to a Christian man, "What is your age?" and he replied, "I am on the right side of seventy."

He found out the old man was seventy-five and said, "You told me you were on the right side of seventy."

"So I am," he answered, "for that is the right side, for it is the side nearest heaven, my home." O that all Christians would be heavenly minded!

Then the angel showed me the river of the water of life, as clear as crystal, flowing from the throne of God and of the Lamb down the middle of the great street of the city. On each side of the river stood the tree of life, bearing twelve crops of fruit, yielding its fruit every month. And the leaves of the tree are for the healing of the nations. No longer will there be any curse. The throne of God and of the Lamb will be in the city, and his servants will serve him. They will see his face, and his name will be on their foreheads. There will be no more night. They will not need the light of a lamp or the light of the sun, for the Lord God will give them light. And they will reign for ever and ever. (1-5)

Here God and the Lamb unite in giving "the water of life." There is no other water of life except that which flows down to us by God's grace through the substitutionary sacrifice of Jesus, "the Lamb of God" (John 1:29). The river that flows "from the throne of God and of the Lamb" is well described as "the river of the water of life, as clear as crystal." What else but good and perfect gifts can come down from the throne of God? Because rivers take on the character of the source from which they come, we are not surprised that pure streams of mercy flow from the throne of the Lamb.

The fruit of this "tree of life" is for all who have drunk "the water of life" in verse 1. When Adam ate the forbidden fruit, he was cast out of Eden, lest he should also eat from the tree of life (Gen. 3:22-24). But our new tree of life gives us both medicine and food. Blessed are those who eat from it. They will find a great variety of good things: "twelve crops of fruit." They will also find a constant succession of blessings: "yielding its fruit every month." So this tree bears twelve different fruits—one every month! We will never be satiated with that heavenly fruit.

We understand this tree and its leaves to be symbolic. We believe our Lord Jesus Christ to be none other than that tree of life. As Adam lived only on the fruit of the Garden of Eden, so Jesus Christ is the food of his people. Manna was angels' food (Ps. 78:25), but what can I say of Christ? He is the satisfying, plentiful, and sweet food, the food that suits all the needs of our souls. Faith is the hand that plucks these golden apples. If at first you don't seem to get this fruit, shake the tree by prayer. Christ loves to hear our fervent cries.

What a happy place heaven will be, where even the leaves on the tree have such virtue in them! The end of verse 2 implies that the nations are sick and that there is an abundance of healing power in Jesus Christ. The text does not say that the leaves of the tree heal this or that malady. The medicine is universal in its cure. These leaves heal whole nations. The gospel has never been carried to a people whom it did not suit.

The curse shall be taken from the soil on which it fell obliquely when God said to Adam, "Cursed is the ground because of you" (Gen. 3:17). There will be no curse of sin, sorrow, or death. There will be nothing but blessing. Blessing will swallow up the curse, and God will be seen everywhere.

Happy servants, to be permitted to serve the Lamb! We try to serve God now, but we are hindered in our service. We are distracted, worried, carried away from holy service by a multitude of cares. But it will be heaven enough for us to be allowed to serve the Lord forever in glory.

Oh, to keep up fellowship with the Lord while you work for him, to serve him and to see his face! This is a double joy. This is to be like Martha and Mary in one person. We will not only "serve him" (v. 3) but also "see his face" (v. 4). What a happy blending—the hands busy but the eyes ravished with the wondrous sight of the face of God. There is no fellowship better than that which serves and no service sweeter than that of those who continue to see the face of their Master while they serve him.

In this life our vision of God is "a poor reflection as in a mirror," but then we will see him "face to face" (1 Cor. 13:12). That will be our heaven of heaven. When one of the greatest saints read this, he said, "Then let me see God's face and die." If we saw God's face on earth, no doubt we would die. But this sight would also make us live again!

Moses was allowed to see only the Lord's back (Ex. 33:23), but in heaven we will see far more than the hem of Christ's robe. Nor will we sit at his feet where we can see only his sandals. No, we "will see his face." I take this to mean we will be able to look into the very heart, soul, and character of Christ. We will finally understand him—his saving work, his eternal love, his all in all—as we have never understood him before. We will see Christ's face clearly, because all the clouds of worry and sorrow will be lifted from our eyes. When we see Christ's face, "we shall be like him, for we shall see him as he is" (1 John 3:2).

During our Lord's ministry, some Greeks said, "We would like to see Jesus" (John 12:21). I hope you have that same desire in a spiritual sense, for he himself has said, "Look unto me, and be ye saved, all the ends of the earth" (Isa. 45:22 KJV).

They will acknowledge him, and he will acknowledge them. They are glad to wear his name on their foreheads, but who wrote it there? He himself engraved it as the seal and token that they were his. They are truly happy whom God acknowledges as his special people while they acknowledge him as their only Lord. There will be no mistaking them. They will bear on their foreheads the glorious name of God, just as the high priest in the Old Testament had "HOLY TO THE LORD" written on his brow (Ex. 39:30-31).

Here on earth there are nights of ignorance, sorrow, sin, and fear. But there will be no night in heaven.

God puts aside the use of means. While we are here, we need lamps and suns. Doesn't it seem curious to put a lamp and the sun in the same sentence? Compared to God, lamps and suns are the same thing. Great and little lights are all limited and less than nothing compared to the infinite God, who is light and the source of all light that exists in heaven or on earth.

It must be a wonderful city in which every resident is a king—and not a dethroned king either, for "they will reign." Every redeemed person in heaven has also an eternal kingdom. "They will reign for ever and ever." This is the climax of the saints' blessedness. They will be like their Lord, for "he will reign for ever and ever" (Rev. 11:15). As they shared his reproach, they will also share his glory.

I hope our friends who always cut down the meaning of the word *eternal* will be good enough at least to let us have an eternal heaven. They have whittled "eternal punishment" (Matt. 25:46) down to next to nothing. Why don't they try to reduce the duration of heavenly bliss in the same way? Whether or not they do, we believe that the saints will reign "for ever and ever."

The angel said to me, "These words are trustworthy and true. The Lord, the God of the spirits of the prophets, sent his angel to show his servants the things that must soon take place."

"Behold, I am coming soon! Blessed is he who keeps the words of the prophecy in this book." (6–7)

Our Lord is on the road. He may arrive tonight while we are sitting here. Happy would be our communion service if he would come while we, for the last time, were doing as he commanded us in remembrance of his sacrificial death and expectation of his glorious return!

I, John, am the one who heard and saw these things. And when I had heard and seen them, I fell down to worship at the feet of the angel who had been showing them to me. But he said to me, "Do not do it! I am a fellow servant with you and with your brothers the prophets and of all who keep the words of this book. Worship God!" (8–9)

The Roman Catholic Church says John was right to worship an angel, but the Word of God says he was wrong. He mistook the messenger for the Master. I am not surprised that he did so, for the heavenly beings become like their Lord when they see him as he is (1 John 3:2). John was quickly set right, and his error was soon corrected. He was told to give no worship to one who, however bright and holy, was only his fellow servant. We must tolerate no worship of angels or departed people. "Worship God!" is the command to us as well as John.

Then he told me, "Do not seal up the words of the prophecy of this book, because the time is near. Let him who does wrong continue to do wrong; let him who is vile continue to be vile; let him who does right continue to do right; and let him who is holy continue to be holy." (10–11)

This is what will be said when Christ comes to judge in the future state. Today the voice of Jesus says, "Repent!" But once we cross the narrow stream of death, we pass out of the realm of mercy and our characters are fixed forever. If your character is not what it ought to be, do not delay your appeal to him who alone can change it, "because the time is near" when your character and state will be fixed forever.

As when there is a sharp frost and the water in the brook is soon solidified, so there are influences at work that stiffen character. Beware lest Christ's coming or the summons through death should find you unprepared and so cause you to remain forever just as you now are. If we believe the Word of God, we must banish from our minds the error that says all human beings will eventually be saved.

"Behold, I am coming soon! My reward is with me, and I will give to everyone according to what he has done. I am the Alpha and the Omega, the First and the Last, the Beginning and the End." (12–13)

The letter alpha is the first in the Greek alphabet, and it was frequently used to signify the best, just as we use the letter A. We say of a ship, for instance, that it is A-1. So Jesus may be said to be the Alpha in this sense.

Is he a prophet? Then all the prophets follow at a humble distance, bearing witness to him. Is he a priest? Then he is our "great high priest" (Heb. 4:14). He fulfills everything the Old Testament priests set forth symbolically. If Christ is a King and Lord, he is "the King of kings and Lord of lords" (Rev. 19:16). If he is a shepherd, he is our "Chief Shepherd" (1 Peter 5:4). If he is a cornerstone, he is the "chosen and precious cornerstone" (1 Peter 2:6).

Let Jesus be the Alpha and the Omega—the beginning and the end—of your trust, your love, and your witness. Is there anything else worth telling lost people besides Jesus Christ? If we leave Christ out of our witness, we leave the sun out of the day, the moon out of the night, the waters out of the sea, the soul out of the body, and joy out of heaven. There is no gospel worth thinking, much less worth proclaiming, if Jesus be forgotten.

"Blessed are those who wash their robes, that they may have the right to the tree of life and may go through the gates into the city. Outside are the dogs, those who practice magic arts, the sexually immoral, the murderers, the idolaters and everyone who loves and practices falsehood." (14–15)

We thank God that these people are shut out of heaven. Though we wish all people could be there, we wish no one to be there whose character is as these verses describe, unless she or he becomes washed and cleansed. Heaven would be no heaven if such people could be admitted there. They will not be. They must, by infallible justice, be excluded from the realms of bliss.

"I, Jesus, have sent my angel to give you this testimony for the churches. I am the Root and the Offspring of David, and the bright Morning Star."
The Spirit and the bride say, "Come!" And let him who hears say, "Come!" Whoever is thirsty, let him come; and whoever wishes, let him take the free gift of the water of life. (16–17)

This invitation to come is given both to the sinner and to Christ. It does not say, "The Spirit says, 'Come,' and the bride says, 'Come,'" but "The Spirit and the bride say, 'Come!'" So the Spirit speaks by the church when he cries, "Come!" and the church cries, "Come!" when she is moved by the Holy Spirit. True prayer is always a joint work. "The Spirit himself intercedes for us with groans that words cannot express" (Rom. 8:26). But if words could express the Spirit's groans within us, they would say, "Come, Lord Jesus!" We are sure Christ will come, if for no other reason than that the Spirit cries, "Come!" The Spirit cannot plead in vain.

This is the last invitation to sinners in the Word of God. It was placed there because it is the sum of the whole Bible. It is like the point of an arrow, and all the rest of the Bible is like the shaft with the feathers on either side of it. May all who have not yet accepted this invitation do so now, lest it should never again be uttered in their hearing.

You may say, "Shouldn't I pray?" It does not say so. It merely tells you to "take the free gift of the water of life."

"But shouldn't I go home and get better first?" No, just take the water of life. "But I must wash my glass." No. Just drink. God will never sell Christ. Judas did that, but the Father never will. The text does not say, "whoever understands, let him take the free gift of the water of life," but "whoever wishes." Are you willing to be saved? Then come with Christ's welcome!

Some will say, "But my heart is so hard, I cannot bring a tear to my eye. I cannot feel my sins as I think I should." But this text has nothing to do with your heart. It concerns your will. Are you willing to receive new life? It is "whoever wishes," not whoever feels. Others may say, "I cannot come to Christ. I wish I could, but I am unable." But this verse does not say, whoever is able may come, but "whoever wishes." Do you want salvation? Then take it!

"Yes," someone says, "God knows I want it, but I'm not worthy." But the invitation is given not to whoever is worthy but to "whoever wishes." All you must do is act on your desire, and Christ will save you.

I warn everyone who hears the words of the prophecy of this book: If anyone adds anything to them, God will add to him the plagues described in this book. And if anyone takes words away from this book of prophecy, God will take away from him his share in the tree of life and in the holy city, which are described in this book. (18–19)

God's revelation is perfect. To add to it or take from it would equally mar it. The terrible threats given here to those who add to this book ought to prevent this great crime against high heaven, yet many have dared and still dare to commit it. God will add to them every plague of which this book speaks.

You cannot take a line from this book without spoiling it. If you were to cut from it a solitary text, it would be missed, and the book would be marred. You would do this at your peril, for God threatens to deny the person a place in the holy city who takes words away from this book of prophecy.

He who testifies to these things says, "Yes, I am coming soon."
Amen. Come, Lord Jesus.
The grace of the Lord Jesus be with God's people. Amen. (20–21)

The Old Testament ends with a curse (Mal. 4:6). The New Testament ends with a benediction of grace. When we come to the end of our lives, all we will want is grace. It is God's grace that

> All the work shall crown
>   Through everlasting days;
> It lays in heaven the topmost stone,
>   And well deserves the praise.
> Oh, that you might have a share in this grace!

Scripture Index